MINIATURES *in* *The Wallace Collection*

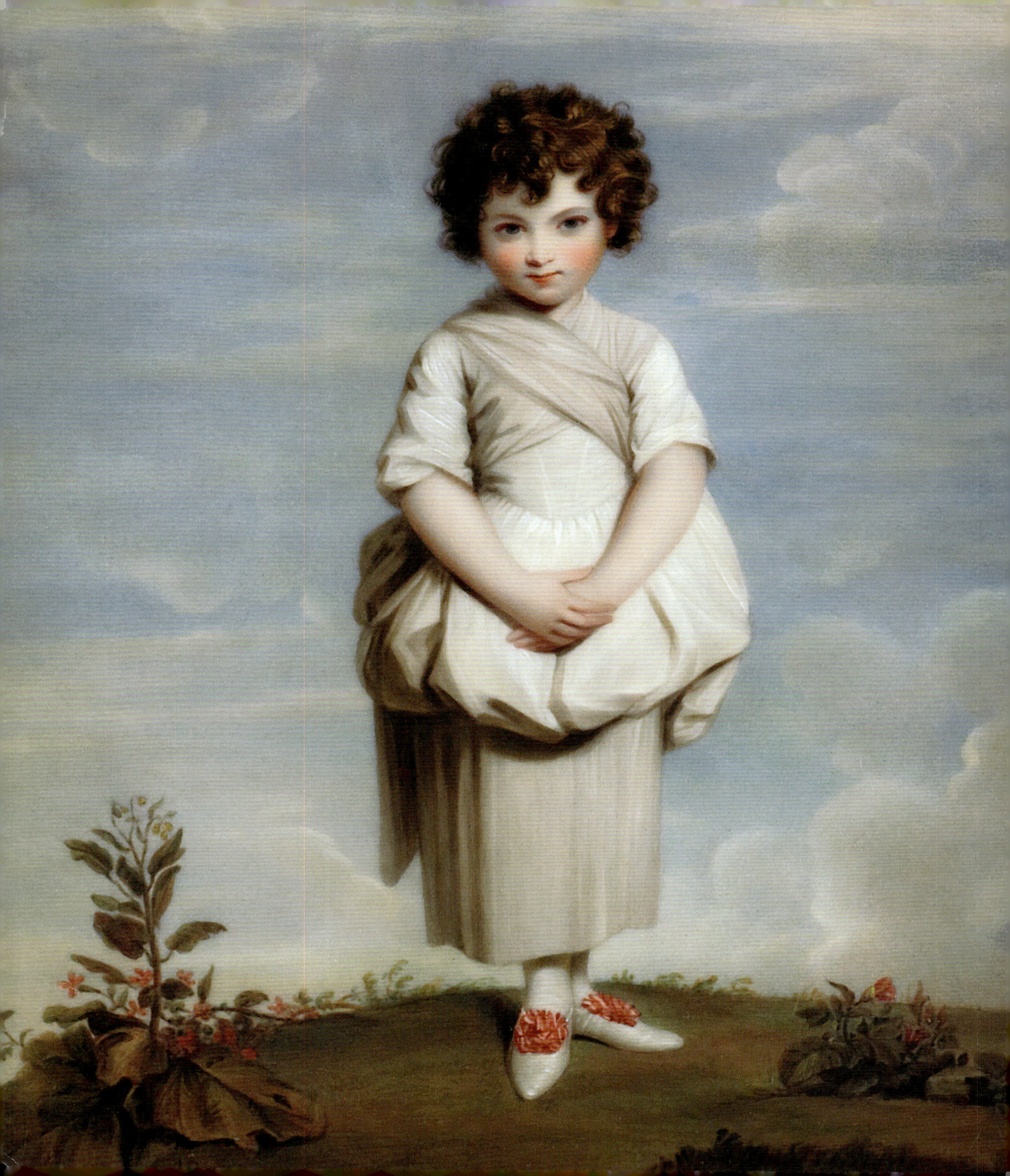

MINIATURES *in The Wallace Collection*

STEPHEN DUFFY *and*
CHRISTOPH MARTIN VOGTHERR

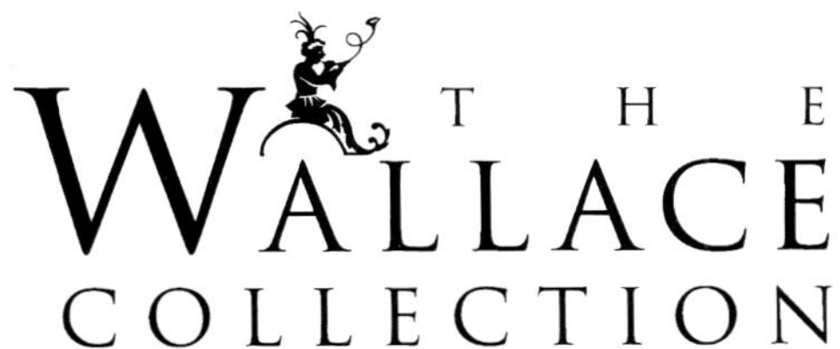

ISBN 978 0 900785 83 2

British Library Cataloguing in Publication Data
A catalogue record of this book is available from the British Library

Produced by Paul Holberton publishing
89 Borough High Street, London, SE1 1NL
www.paul-holberton.net

Deisgn by Laura Parker

Printed by E-Graphic in Verona, Italy

JACKET: Louis-Nicolas van Blarenberghe, *The Fair of St-Germain*, 1763 (no.16), detail on front cover and whole on back cover

FRONTISPIECE: Henry Bone, after Reynolds, *Lady Gertrude Fitzpatrick ('Collina')*, 1810 (no.53), detail

PAGE 21: Peter Adolf Hall, *Adélaïde-Victorine Hall, The Artist's Daughter*, *c.*1785 (no.22), detail

EXPLANATION

This book takes a close look at seventy of the miniatures in the Wallace Collection. Like other monographs on aspects of the Collection, such as Peter Hughes's *French Eighteenth-Century Clocks and Barometers* (1994) and Robert Wenley's *French Bronzes in the Wallace Collection* (2002), it is intended to give readers an insight into some of the museum's most fascinating objects, but it is not a full catalogue. Interested readers are still advised to consult Graham Reynolds's catalogue of all the miniatures in the Wallace Collection which was published in 1980, although the present book makes use of much research subsequent to its publication and takes the opportunity to discuss its objects more expansively than was possible for Reynolds.

The miniatures are considered in broadly chronological order, but this method has not been followed rigidly where it seemed more appropriate to group certain works by artist or nationality. The initials of the author appear at the end of each entry. All the entries have been written by either Stephen Duffy or Christoph Martin Vogtherr, except no.18, which was written by Mia Jackson. All seventy catalogued miniatures are shown actual size unless otherwise indicated.

CONTENTS

Director's Foreword

The Wallace Collection has a wonderful group of over three hundred miniatures. They range from portraits to genre scenes to landscapes, on vellum or ivory or enamel on copper and gold, and each is individually framed or mounted in a gold box.

The portrait miniatures represent in microcosm the human side of all the other works of art displayed at Hertford House. They are intimate, personal recollections of men, women and children, some famous, some unidentified, but cherished enough by family and friends to be recorded for posterity in miniature form. These are the people who would have viewed our paintings when the paint was still fresh, or sat in the chairs at our writing desks, or drunk coffee from our cups and saucers, or taken a pinch of snuff from our gold snuff boxes. Some are formal and very respectable, others coquettish and witty, and each reveals the fads and fashions of their age, from their costumes to their hairstyles, and from their complexions to their accessories. Here they can be seen today, brought alive in brilliant tiny brushstrokes, thanks to some of the most able and least recognized painters of the sixteenth to the nineteenth centuries.

While the nineteenth-century miniatures are shown in the Nineteenth-Century Gallery, the earlier examples have recently been redisplayed in the small Cabinet off Lady Wallace's former Boudoir at Hertford House. Here each is hung from small square brass hooks, echoing the way Sir Richard Wallace showed them in the Oval Drawing Room towards the end of the nineteenth century. The new display has led to a reassessment of the whole collection of miniatures, from curatorial research on both sitters and artists to careful conservation of all their myriad different frames and new photography, and this detailed work has led to this new publication.

One of the great miniatures experts of our day is David Lavender, and he has supported our recent work in his special field with gentle guidance and wisdom. But, best of all, he has also made a generous donation to the Wallace Collection for the publication of this book, so that its appearance can celebrate the new emphasis on our miniatures collection this year. Such individual philanthropy is always a delight, and especially so in this case, as David Lavender's affection for these miniatures has given them new life. Not only the sitters, but also the landscapes and other scenes are vibrant and vital once more in the pages of this beautiful book.

ROSALIND SAVILL
Director of the Wallace Collection

Foreword

I am delighted to have been given the opportunity to be involved in this new book about seventy of the best miniatures in the Wallace Collection. It has been a great pleasure working with the curators Stephen Duffy and Christoph Martin Vogtherr on this project.

I have always been deeply impressed by the miniatures in the Wallace Collection, and now that many of them have been redisplayed in new cases together with the stunning collection of gold boxes, every visitor will have the opportunity to see them at their very best. This book makes the perfect accompaniment to the new display, but will also have lasting value for all those who love these fascinating and beautiful treasures of the Wallace Collection.

DAVID LAVENDER

Acknowledgements

For their invaluable assistance we would like to thank Joseph Baillio, Eugene Barilo von Reisberg, Carole Blumenfeld, Sophie Bostock, Christopher Cavey, René Chartrand, Alan Donnithorne, Danielle Dufort, Udo Felbiger, Bodo Hofstetter, Ieuan Hopkins, Nigel Israel, Susan Jenkins, Bénédicte Lafarge, Merit Laine, Matthieu Lelièvre, Lars Ljungström, Magnus Olausson, Bernd Pappe, Catherine Purcell, Vanessa Remington, Janice Sacher, Desmond Shawe-Taylor, Erika Speel, Charles Truman, Simon Vinogradoff, Olivia Voisin, Rebecca Wallis, Jeremy Warren, Paul Wood, Sarah Wood, Stephen Wood and Fiona Woolley. Special thanks are due to Aileen Ribeiro and Diana Scarisbrick for their advice on the costume and jewellery in some of the miniatures. David Lavender has been not only the sponsor of this book, but a constant source of friendly advice and encouragement, and we have also benefited enormously from the excellent research and editorial skills of our colleague Mia Jackson (who has written catalogue no. 18). Any errors of fact or omission are our own.

STEPHEN DUFFY
CHRISTOPH MARTIN VOGTHERR

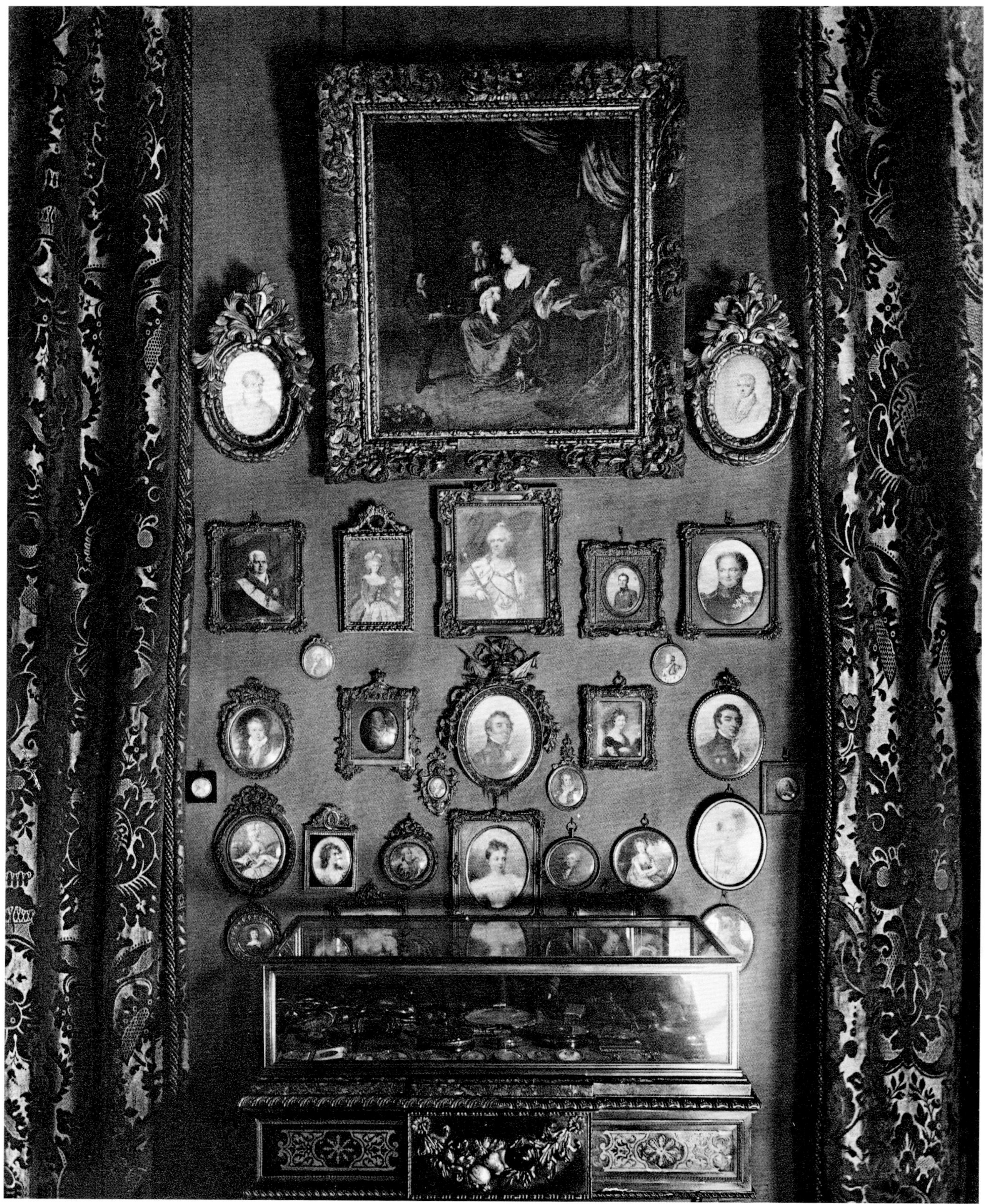

The Wallace Collection's Miniatures

STEPHEN DUFFY

OPPOSITE
Fig.1 The Oval Drawing Room, Hertford House, *c.*1897 (detail)

There are 334 miniatures in the Wallace Collection, plus three more acquired for the Library of Hertford House (now Hertford House Historic Collection) after Lady Wallace bequeathed the Collection to the nation in 1897. They are less celebrated than the paintings, but they seldom fail to attract the attention of visitors, who are often enthralled by the charm and beauty of these exquisite objects.

The Wallace Collection is a family collection in origin: it was acquired by the first four Marquesses of Hertford and the illegitimate son of the 4th Marquess, Sir Richard Wallace, between the mid eighteenth century and the 1880s.[1] Unfortunately it is not possible to trace the early provenance of most of the miniatures, beyond identifying when they first appear in Hertford/Wallace inventories or in an exhibition of Sir Richard Wallace's collection at Bethnal Green in 1872–5. It is far more difficult to find them in sale catalogues than it is to identify the Collection's paintings in similar records, and some were not even recorded until after the Wallace Collection opened as a museum in 1900. It is evident, however, that, as with the other major elements of the Collection, a very large proportion of them (well over 80 per cent) were bought by the 4th Marquess and Sir Richard Wallace, who spent most of their lives in Paris, between the 1840s and the 1870s. The miniatures collection was not acquired with the aim of comprehensiveness – almost invariably the Founders bought simply what they liked, and all their works of art reflect their tastes and prejudices as well as what was available to them at the time, either on the art market or direct from the artists themselves. The result in the case of the miniatures is an idiosyncratic collection, deeply marked by its predominantly Anglo-French origins. Although there are fine and important examples by artists of other schools, particularly the English, Swiss and Italian, it is (like the Wallace Collection's furniture and porcelain) the French works of the eighteenth and early nineteenth centuries that are most distinctive. Whereas there are only twenty-four miniatures of all schools painted before 1700, the eighteenth-century French works number well over one hundred, and the nineteenth-century French over 130. This emphasis is particularly unusual in a British context, in which, as with the paintings, the Collection is unique in scale and quality. It cannot compare in importance with the national collection of miniatures at the Victoria and Albert Museum, the Royal Collection, or in certain respects with other collections with aristocratic origins, such as (for early English miniatures) the Buccleuch collection or (for miniatures on gold boxes) the Rothschild collection, which was sadly stolen from Waddesdon Manor in 2003.[2] But, as with every other element of the Wallace Collection, the miniatures include works of the highest quality, and they occupy a worthy place among the other collections now at Hertford House.

Another parallel with the paintings is that some of the miniatures are family portraits which were no doubt handed down the family line. The first two Marquesses of Hertford were not collectors, but it is almost certainly to them that the Collection owes some of its early miniatures, such as Zincke's portraits of General Conway (no.8) and Lord Augustus Fitzroy (M316), younger brothers of, respectively, the 1st Marquess and the 1st Marchioness of Hertford. Some others, such as a sixteenth-century portrait of an unknown man (M30) and portraits by Bourdin and Hoskins (M29 and M204), probably have family origins.

The first member of the family to show a real interest in collecting was the 3rd Marquess of Hertford (1777–1842). A friend of the Prince Regent, later George IV, he shared the Prince's enthusiasm for Dutch paintings, French furniture and Sèvres porcelain. As a collector of miniatures the Prince particularly favoured the contemporary artists Richard Cosway and Henry Bone – he displayed enamels by Bone after Sir Joshua Reynolds in his bedroom and dressing room at Carlton House[3] – and, although it is not known if the 3rd Marquess bought any of the Cosways now in the Wallace Collection, he did acquire at least three of the Henry Bones, including two after Reynolds (see no.53) and a portrait of Mrs Paddon after W.J. Newton painted for the Marquess as a commission in 1817 (no.57). Nothing is now known of Mrs Paddon or of her relationship with the notoriously libidinous 3rd Marquess, but it is possible that she was one of his many mistresses and it is certainly tempting to conjecture that her miniature was among those seen by the courtesan Harriette Wilson when he gave her a tour of his private apartments at Dorchester House near Hyde Park. "After dinner," she recalled in her *Memoirs*, "he showed us miniatures, by the most celebrated artists, of at least half a hundred lovely women, black, brown, fair, and even carrotty, for the amateur's sympathetic *bonne bouche*. These were all beautifully executed; and no-one, with any knowledge of painting, could hear him expatiate on their various merits, without feeling that he was qualified to preside at the Royal Academy itself!"[4]

Surprisingly, most of these "half a hundred" miniatures are not listed in the posthumous inventory of the Marquess's property at Dorchester House in 1842, but the Bones after Newton and Reynolds are recorded in the library and in the Marquess's bedroom.[5] No miniatures were included in the 1842 inventory of his other London residence, St Dunstan's in Regent's Park. The Marquess's widowed mother lived at Hertford House (now the home of the Wallace Collection) until her death in 1834. The posthumous inventory of her property listed fifteen miniatures in the south-east drawing room; of these only the set of six artists' portraits by Giuseppe Macpherson (no.29) can be identified today.

The 3rd Marquess's son, the 4th Marquess of Hertford (1800–1870; fig.2), was probably the greatest collector of the miniatures, as he certainly was of the paintings, in the Wallace Collection. Brought up in Paris by his mother after she separated from the 3rd Marquess, he began collecting under her guidance in his twenties but became a passionate, even obsessive, collector shortly after he had succeeded his father in 1842 and

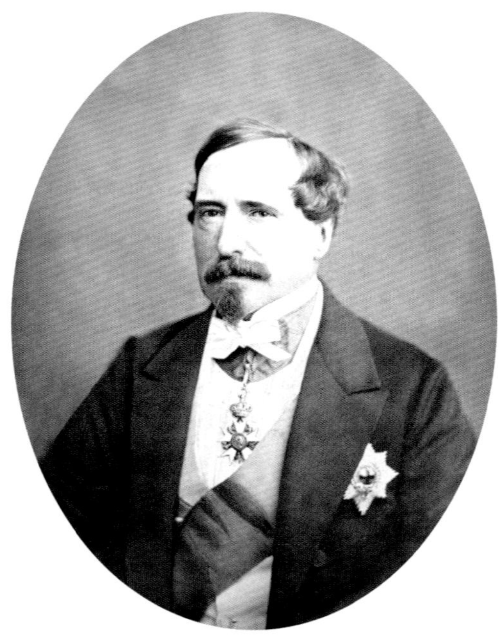

Fig.2 Richard Seymour-Conway, 4th Marquess of Hertford (1800–1870). Photograph by Étienne Carjat, *c.*1860

remained so until his death in 1870. It was also he who acquired the great majority of the other works of art which complement the miniatures in the Collection today – not just the French paintings but the furniture, porcelain and gold boxes. When the 4th Marquess began collecting in earnest in the 1840s, works of art associated with the *ancien régime*, including miniatures, were already recovering in France from the nadir of their fortunes after the Revolution, but by the time of his death they had become the expensive objects they have remained ever since. The Marquess was only exceptional among the plutocratic collectors of his time in being a member of the old British aristocracy rather than of the middle class or one of those whose titles were of more recent creation.

As with his forebears, his inventories tell us very little about his acquisition of miniatures, but there can be no doubt that he acquired the great majority of the outstanding array of works in the Collection by French masters of the eighteenth century, particularly Charlier and Hall, as well as the superb group of early nineteenth-century French miniatures centred on Augustin and Isabey. The Charliers and Halls accord perfectly with his paintings by Boucher, Fragonard and Greuze, and his purchase of many miniatures of Napoleon and his family, particularly by Isabey, was just one aspect of a sustained interest in the Napoleonic legend that extended also to paintings and books with Napoleonic themes. In his letters to his London agent Samuel Mawson the 4th Marquess sometimes reminded Mawson that he only liked "pleasing pictures": his miniatures were ideally suited to this taste, which essentially prized grace, sophistication and sensuality above intellectual challenge or the acknowledgement of life's more troubling aspects.[6] We get the briefest glimpse of how the Marquess kept his miniatures from the critic Théophile Thoré, who in 1867 was granted the very rare privilege of seeing Lord Hertford's collections at his main Paris residence, no.2 rue Laffitte. There Thoré noticed in the bedroom "a collection of more than two hundred miniatures and gouaches; little portraits from the époque of the Valois [presumably no.1 and its companion] up to Isabey …".[7]

Some of the people represented in his miniatures were known to the Marquess personally, but his collection, unlike that of his father, was little influenced by private considerations: nearly all his miniatures must have been acquired first and foremost as works of art. A rare exception was the portrait of his beloved mother by Cosway (see no.32), which he kept under his pillow when he slept. Among the other sitters represented in his miniatures, there is documentary evidence that he knew the Duke of Wellington and Mme Récamier (see nos.54–5), and no doubt he was also acquainted with others, but in nearly every case no evidence is available to prove it. He clearly, for example, was a devotee of the contemporary theatre, as is demonstrated by his ownership of portraits of leading actresses and singers, such as Mme Dugazon and Mlles Mars, Rachel and Sontag (no.47, M158, M224, M256 and no.68). In part these were modern

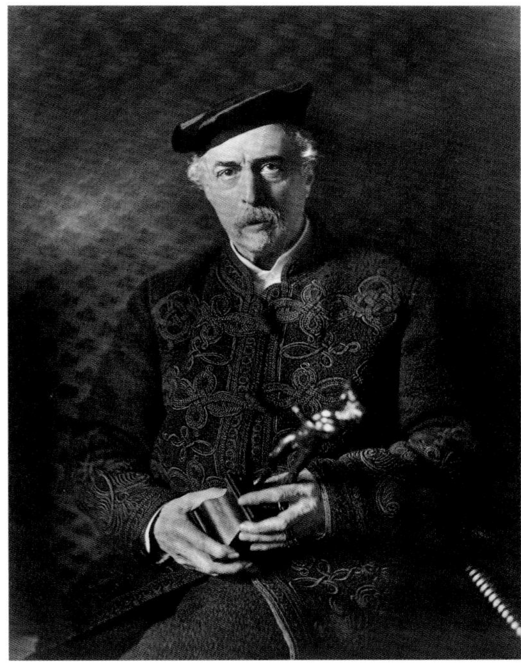

Fig.3 Sir Richard Wallace (1818–1890). Photograph by J.J. Thomson, 1888

equivalents of his earlier paintings and miniatures of theatrical figures – which usually of course were also attractive images of women – such as his eighteenth-century portraits of the dancers Mlle Camargo (no.7) and her unknown colleague painted by Pierre Chasselet (M82), but it is by no means impossible that he had also met some of these performers, who were the great celebrities of their age. He nevertheless always kept his social distance. It is not surprising that the theatrical world is unrepresented in an address book kept by the Marquess in the 1860s which is now in the Wallace Collection's archives, but it is interesting to note that artists are also almost entirely absent. The only entry relevant to his miniatures collection is "Mad^e Isabey 32 R de Verneuil".[8]

The 4th Marquess never married, but he had an illegitimate son, Richard Wallace (1818–1890; fig.3), who was brought up in Paris by his father and grandmother, and in time became his father's agent and secretary. When the Marquess died in 1870 he bequeathed to Wallace his unentailed property, which included the thousands of works of art he had collected and a large though indeterminate number inherited from the earlier Marquesses. Wallace himself had formed a notable collection which he had been forced to sell in 1857 to pay off his debts. It had included forty-one miniatures, including eleven attributed to Charlier, six to Fragonard and two to Hall, and so was very much in the taste of his father. It probably also, however, owed much to the 4th Marquess's younger half-brother, Lord Henry Seymour, who was a considerable collector, particularly of contemporary paintings. He almost certainly influenced the 4th Marquess's collecting, and was close to Richard Wallace. On his death in 1859 he bequeathed to Wallace his portrait of Hans Holbein (no.2), which he no doubt considered one of the key works of his collection.

It was Wallace who in large measure determined the eventual English domicile of what became the Wallace Collection when he brought over much of his collection from Paris to London shortly after his father's death. While Hertford House was being made ready to accommodate his family and works of art Wallace exhibited much of his collection at the Bethnal Green Museum in the East End of London as a philanthropic act. During the three years it was displayed there, between 1872 and 1875, it attracted huge numbers of visitors, drawn by the fame and quality of Wallace's celebrated but little known collection. No doubt the miniatures were not among the prime attractions – and it is worth noting that the 4th Marquess had seen the precipitous decline of the miniature from its heyday as a major European art form to its near irrelevance after the invention of photography – but the exhibition offered the first occasion on which they were shown publicly as a group. Presumably because of their reduced status in the artistic hierarchy by the 1850s and 1860s, the 4th Marquess's miniatures were never lent by him to exhibitions, though he did lend some of his finest paintings and decorative works of art for public display in 1857, 1860 and 1865.[9] The first edition of

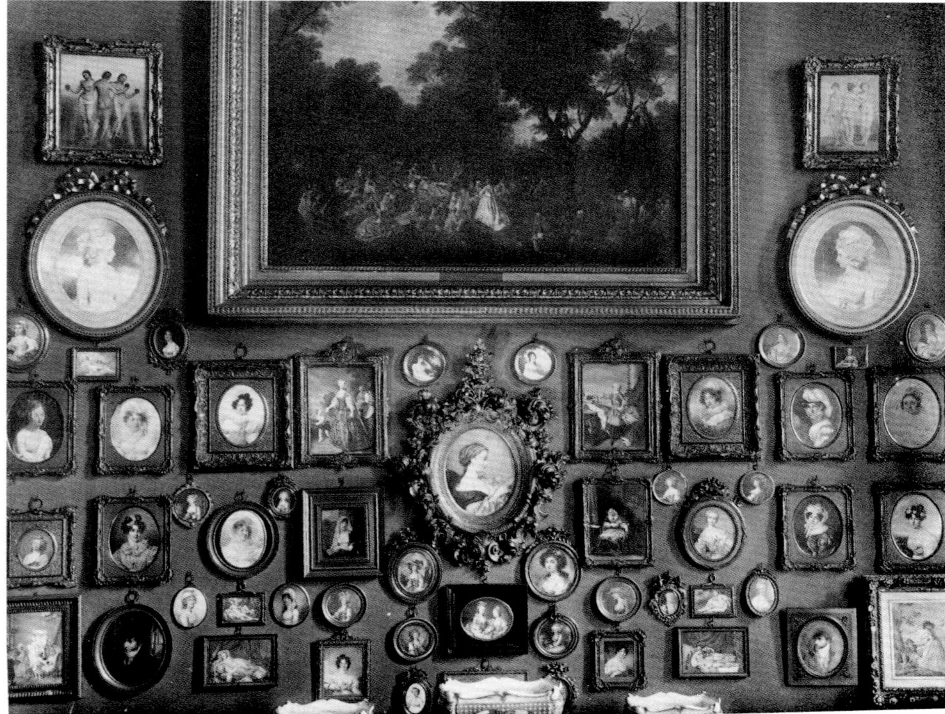

Fig.4 The Oval Drawing Room, Hertford House, *c.*1897 (detail)

the Bethnal Green catalogue listed 179 miniatures, a figure which had increased to 227 as early as the seventh edition published the following year. The museum's van book reveals that it was Wallace himself who delivered miniatures to the museum on 11 June 1872, with a further delivery, again by Wallace himself, on 1 July the same year.[10] The catalogues of the exhibition are exceptionally valuable because they provide the first irrefutable reference to many of the miniatures in the Collection today.

Wallace added some important miniatures to the collection he had inherited from his father, particularly Van Blarenberghe's *The Fair of St-Germain*, Hall's *The Painter's Family* and Dumont's *Louis-Charles, Dauphin of France* (nos.16, 21 and 27). The Dumont was one of the miniatures he had been forced to sell in 1857. All three were acquired at the Allègre sale in 1872: Wallace's collecting, not just of miniatures but of other works of art, was almost entirely confined to the first half of the 1870s, perhaps because he soon ran out of space at Hertford House. On his death in 1890 the inventory of Hertford House listed several hundred miniatures, mostly in the Oval Drawing Room on the first floor, and we are fortunate that two photographs survive of the miniatures in this room, showing how they were displayed in Wallace's time (see figs. 1 and 4).[11] They reveal that, as with the hang of the paintings, symmetry was apparently more important than juxtapositions based either on quality or on the appropriateness of the subjects. Thus, for example, the portraits of the Duke of Wellington and (?) Mrs Thistlethwayte (nos.55 and 57) in the centre of each hang were presumably placed there because of the ornateness of their frames, while the questionable suitability of hanging a poor imitation of Isabey's *Duke of Wellington* (M238) only two miniatures away from a superb original, or Mrs Thistlethwayte between Louis XV and his Queen, Marie Leszczynska (M284–5), was ignored.

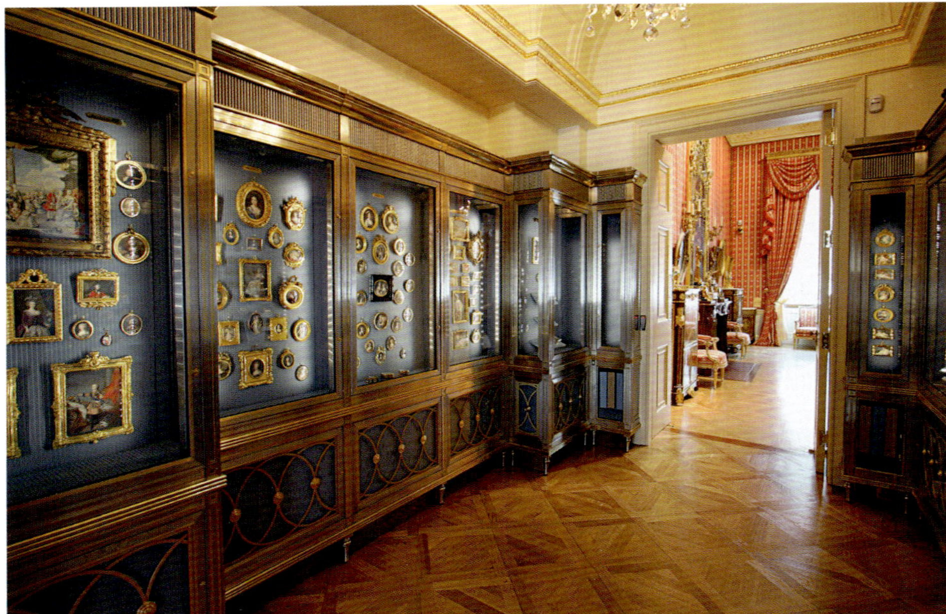

Fig.5 The Boudoir Cabinet, 2010

On Wallace's death in 1890 his possessions passed to his widow, Lady Wallace, who bequeathed the contents of the ground and first floors of Hertford House to the nation as the Wallace Collection on her own death in 1897. Although the first catalogue of objects other than paintings and arms and armour was produced two years after the opening of the Collection as a museum in 1900, the miniatures were not included, and it was another two years later before they were incorporated into a second edition. The first catalogue devoted solely to the miniatures, by W.P. Gibson, was published in 1935, superseded by a more thorough and better illustrated version written by Graham Reynolds and published in 1980, which is still the authoritative volume.[12]

With the opening of the museum the miniatures were transferred to the Dining Room on the ground floor and displayed in new upright cases. Although these provided adequate security, they did little to alleviate the problem of their continued exposure to light. *The Times* commented: "The miniatures used to be shown in the round drawing-room, crowded together on the walls; now they are admirably seen in upright cases near the window in a downstairs room – perhaps too near for perfect safety, if it is intended to keep them there always, exposed to the light. It would be better if the trustees were to tell the public that miniatures are delicate things which perish by exposure, and that these would only be shown in detachments for a month or two at a time."[13]

It is not recorded if some were subsequently taken off display, but leather covers for the cases were soon supplied. From that time all the miniatures were shown in similar flat and upright cases with covers, but in 2010 a new display combining the miniatures painted before 1800 with the gold boxes has been created in the space on the first floor now called the Boudoir Cabinet, between the Boudoir and the Study. Now provided with all the most modern facilities relating to climate, lighting and security, it is doubtful if the miniatures in the Wallace Collection have ever been shown to better advantage.

NOTES

1 On the history of the Wallace Collection and its Founders see Hughes.
2 See Lloyd 1996 and Grandjean. The Buccleuch collection was largely formed by the 5th Duke of Buccleuch (1806–1874), a near contemporary of the 4th Marquess of Hertford; the Waddesdon collection by Ferdinand de Rothschild (1839–1898) who was on friendly terms with Sir Richard Wallace.
3 Lloyd and Remington, p.22.
4 Quoted Hughes, p.20.
5 A list of Hertford/Wallace inventories in the archives of the Wallace Collection appears in Ingamells 1985, pp.13–14.
6 See Ingamells 1981.
7 *Paris Guide*, I, p.538.
8 The 4th Marquess of Hertford's address book, Wallace Collection archives.
9 The 4th Marquess was a major lender to the Manchester 'Art Treasures of Great Britain' exhibition of 1857, two exhibitions of French paintings at the Martinet gallery in Paris in 1860 and to the 'Musée Rétrospectif' in Paris in 1865.
10 Bethnal Green Museum van book 1872 (London, V&A Museum of Childhood archives).
11 A third photograph shows five enamel miniatures (M19-21 and M268-69) on one of the walls of Lady Wallace's Boudoir.
12 Wallace 1902; Gibson; Reynolds.
13 *The Times*, 1 August 1900.

Some Aspects of French Eighteenth-Century Miniature Painting

CHRISTOPH MARTIN VOGTHERR

Miniatures often lead a hidden life in museums. Many great collections are not exhibited permanently because the objects are usually fragile, light-sensitive and too small to be seen by more than one person at a time. In Hertford House, the miniatures were for a long time shown in cases with protective leather covers which could be lifted by visitors. In the spring of 2010 the Boudoir Cabinet opened, presenting the collection of eighteenth-century miniatures in a new and much improved way. This room was specifically created to exhibit the collection of late seventeenth- and eighteenth-century miniatures and gold boxes – a combination which reflects the similar precious and intricate qualities of the objects and their comparable environmental requirements within a modern museum context – and also highlights the fact that many gold boxes are actually adorned with miniatures. Both kinds of objects were originally meant to be seen in a very similar way – individually, from close to and held in the hand of the person enjoying them. Although this is no longer possible today if we want to preserve these exceptional objects for future generations, the Boudoir Cabinet was designed to heighten the intimacy and impact of these objects and to provide ideal environmental conditions.

The new room brings together many of the most important miniatures in the Collection. While there are other internationally important collections of miniatures in the United Kingdom – above all, in the Victoria and Albert Museum and the Royal Collection – the Wallace Collection is unequalled in this country in its holdings of eighteenth-century French miniatures. This essay examines some of the contexts of miniature production in eighteenth-century France.[1]

Miniatures are widely associated with portrait painting. These images were of a crucial importance before the invention of photography. The majority of miniatures were likenesses of friends, family, loved ones, celebrities or royalty, or reflected other types of relationships. Louis XIV used to give out so-called *boîtes à portrait*, which contained an enamel portrait of himself (see no.5), as an official sign of royal favour. The enamel portrait was a small but crucial element of a highly elaborate and expensive piece of jewellery. James Stuart, the 'Old Pretender', was painted in his French exile by the Swiss-born painter Jacques-Antoine Arlaud (see fig.1, a later version), probably for a Stuart supporter. François Dumont's likeness of the young Dauphin Louis (XVII) (no.27) was probably painted posthumously as a symbol of the Royalist cause after the boy had fallen victim to the French Revolution. Other royal portraits such as Peter Adolf Hall's portrait of Hedvig Elisabeth Charlotte of Holstein-Gottorp, Queen of Sweden (no.23), apparently served much more informal purposes within the royal family.

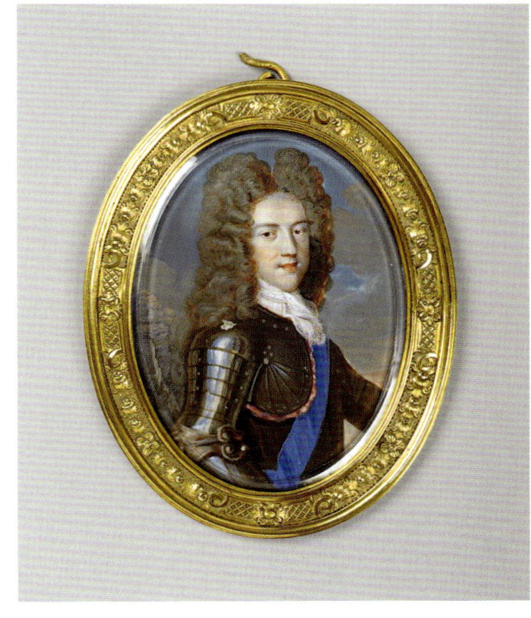

Fig.1 Style of Jacques-Antoine Arlaud, *James Stuart, the 'Old Pretender'*, early 18th century, ivory, 82 × 61 mm, London, The Wallace Collection (M2)

Many miniatures tell the stories, often lost, of families and friendship, courtship and love. Hall's portrait of his wife, sister-in-law and daughter (no.21) successfully evokes a more serene family life than the painter actually led. Jean-Urbain Guérin painted a double portrait of Georgiana, Duchess of Devonshire, and Lady Elizabeth Foster (no.28) as a particularly touching token of female solidarity, friendship and possibly even love. It was commissioned at one of the most dramatic moments in their lives, when Lady Elizabeth had chosen to accompany the Duchess into her Parisian exile after she had been banished by her husband.

These more sentimental and personal portraits achieved such popularity because miniatures had a particularly emotional appeal owing to their small size and the fact that they could be handled. They could also be hidden – an important advantage for tokens of love and symbols of certain political allegiances – and they could travel easily. Early portrait miniatures were often sent when weddings were being negotiated between royal houses, to give a first impression of a future bride or bridegroom who lived far away. They were taken on journeys as tokens of the beloved who had been left behind, or as reminders of friends and family. Hall probably based his depiction of the future Swedish Queen on a miniature which Gustavus III would have brought to Paris. She had stayed in Sweden and the artist was not able to see her in the flesh, but could base his portrait on a miniature painted *ad vivum* in Sweden. Another genre of miniatures at first seems unrelated, but in fact originated in a similar context – the Van Blarenberghes' portraits of important noble properties, such as Henri-Joseph van Blarenberghe's box with views of the château of Romainville (no.18). They served as souvenirs of a cherished place and could easily be taken along and shown to others. As portrait miniatures sometimes stood in for the presence of the person depicted, these miniature *vedute* (view paintings) refreshed the memory and served as a souvenir. Landscapes are otherwise rare in miniature painting, usually appearing in the context of genre scenes and *fêtes galantes*.

Miniature portraits could also serve as tokens of admiration of the celebrities of the day, and a means to disseminate their images. Female dancers were particularly popular subjects, since their celebrity status was enhanced by their beauty and, almost inevitably, a slightly tarnished moral reputation. This combination was obviously irresistible to the 4th Marquess of Hertford, who amassed large numbers of their portraits (see p.11). The portrait of Marie-Anne de Cupis de Camargo (no.7) and Jacques Thouron's portrait of Elisabeth Vigée-Le Brun after the artist's self-portrait (fig.2) are both brilliant examples of the celebrity portrait.

In France, genres other than portraiture played a much more important role than in Britain. This fact is directly mirrored in the Wallace Collection's holdings, where the majority of French eighteenth-century miniatures are genre scenes and mythologies, with also a few landscapes. This number is even larger if one includes heads disguised as portraits (nos.22, 25 and 29), which reflect a tradition of study heads or *têtes d'expression* (expressive heads). These heads drew some of their attraction from the fact that they could be perceived as immediately and intimately as portrait miniatures but revealed even more of the person – usually an anonymous young woman – and the

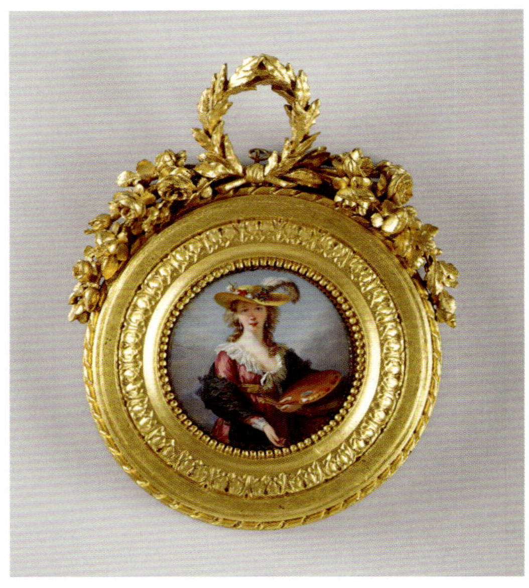

Fig.2 Jacques Thouron, after Vigée-Le Brun, *Elisabeth-Louise Vigée-Le Brun*, signed, late 18th century, enamel, 67 mm diameter, London, The Wallace Collection (M311)

body than a portrait might have done. The most important influence on this sub-genre was Jean-Baptiste Greuze (see no.22, fig.1), the rising star of French painting in the late 1750s and 1760s. He had originally painted similar heads as studies for his larger paintings and he then gradually began to produce finished works specifically for a market eager to buy emotionally and erotically charged images. The small scale and exquisite detailing of miniatures made them particularly appropriate vehicles for Greuze's innovation, translating it into another medium and creating a new type of up-market collectible. Even more than easel paintings, miniatures blurred the lines between portraits and study heads, as the medium of the miniature helped to add the implied reliability of portraiture to fictitious renderings of young women.

The distinctions between these acceptable images and pornography were hazy and are hard to determine from a distance of more than two centuries. Miniatures could easily be hidden and their small format encouraged private viewing. Together with books and prints they constituted a major medium for indecent or arousing art. Several miniatures in the Wallace Collection may have been judged indecorous in the eighteenth century, and evidently would have been categorized as such in the following century when they were acquired by the Hertford family. Jacques Charlier's boudoir scene (fig.3) is a case in point, as it reveals parts of the woman's body which could not have been shown in a painting on public view. Many of the entirely pornographic images were of a lower artistic quality. Like Charlier (or his workshop), however, Niclas Lafrensen was a skilled artist who could work on either side of the dividing line. *The Morning Conversation* and *The Morning Toilet Interrupted* (see no.19) were definitely risqué but not shocking, whereas his *Mysterious Swing* seems more obvious (see fig.4, a later copy).

Miniatures usually lagged considerably behind easel painting as an indication of artistic trends. In some cultures, however, they could be at the forefront of artistic developments, for example in England in the late sixteenth and early seventeenth centuries. But this usually happened in cultures with a distrust of images and a strong preference for portraiture. Neither was the case in eighteenth-century France. Only in very rare instances were French miniatures innovative in the strict sense. The Van Blarenberghes' portraits of properties – country houses and hôtels – are a rare example. Much more typical is the example of Peter Adolf Hall – one of the outstanding artists in the medium – who often followed templates which had been developed a decade earlier. His variation on Greuze's *têtes d'expression* (no.22) is a case in point: Greuze's models were painted in the 1770s, Hall's miniature in around 1785. Often the gap could be much more substantial. Marie-Anne Fragonard's expressive heads were based on works by her husband Jean-Honoré, which were, however, probably painted many years earlier, although the documentation is too imprecise for us to be certain of the chronology.

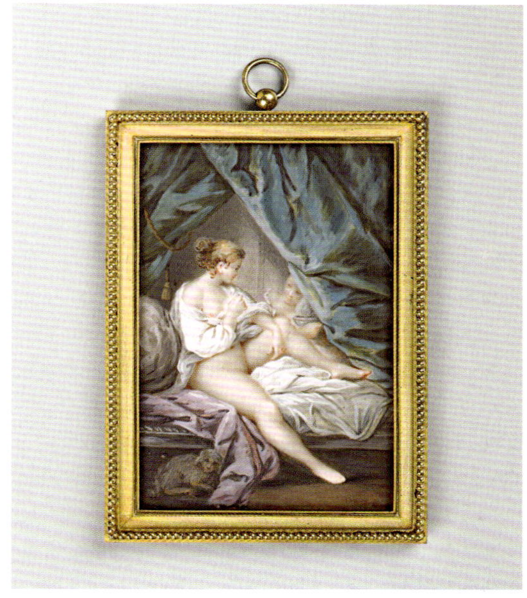

Fig.3 Jacques Charlier, *A Nude Woman on her Bed*, mid 18th century, vellum, 113 × 77 mm, London, The Wallace Collection (M81)

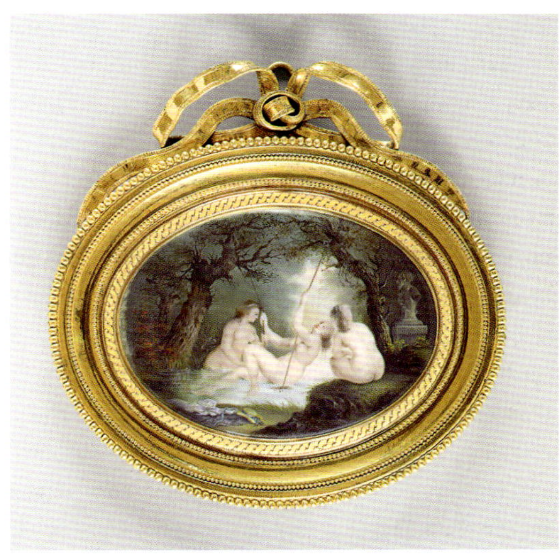

Fig.4 After Lafrensen, *The Mysterious Swing*, early 19th century, ivory, 70 × 94 mm, London, The Wallace Collection (M144)

The character of miniatures is often reproductive, which was also, more broadly, the conventional theoretical stance on portraiture in contemporary art theory. According to academic theory, portraiture was meant to depict an unidealized or only fractionally improved reality, and therefore did not require the genius necessary for history painting or ideal landscape. Miniature painting as a whole was considered similarly derivative. Many works in miniature are reproductions of easel paintings or prints, including portraits: the anonymous portrait of Mme du Châtelet (no.30) is after Marianne Loir's portrait – probably via a print – and Hall, more surprisingly, used a painting by Sir Joshua Reynolds as a source for one of his miniatures (fig.5). As a general rule, however, portrait painting on any scale has always been liable to make heavy use of existing prototypes, in order to guarantee the likeness of the sitter.

The reproductive character of miniature painting could also embrace history scenes. The Wallace Collection includes a large group of miniatures, in particular by Jacques Charlier, which either copy masterpieces by established painters or produce variants of their work, recycling successful details of existing paintings. These miniatures were more expensive but comparable in character to engravings, being also intended as reproductions and adaptations of famous works, assisting their diffusion into different contexts, such as room decoration or porcelain. Charlier's miniatures reproduced works by some of the most celebrated living painters, for example François Boucher (no.11) and Jean-Baptiste-Marie Pierre (no.13), but many miniatures would refer to or directly reproduce Old Masters. Charlier reproduced works primarily by Boucher with such frequency that one has to assume some relationship between the two artists. Apparently, these affiliations between miniature painters and the larger workshops of easel painters were not uncommon.

The margins could easily get blurred: an anonymous late eighteenth-century miniature based on a reproductive print after Watteau's *Harlequin and Columbine* replaced the woman with a more up-to-date female figure (fig.6). It is unclear in a case such as this whether a reproduction of a masterpiece was intended or whether a successful template was simply being reused by an unimaginative artist. As miniature artists were not primarily judged on their originality but on their technical finesse, they could openly copy or adapt easel paintings.

Many of the protagonists of miniature painting in France were foreigners, a tradition which goes back to the very beginnings of the art. Jean Clouet was born in Flanders (see no.1 for two works associated with his son François Clouet). Jean Petitot (no.5) came from Switzerland, and was preceded by another Swiss, Joseph Werner, the principal miniature painter to Louis XIV. Niclas Lafrensen (nos.19, 20) and Peter Adolf Hall (nos.21, 22) were members of a large and hugely important colony of Swedish artists in Paris. The Venetian Rosalba Carriera (no.6) only spent a year or so in

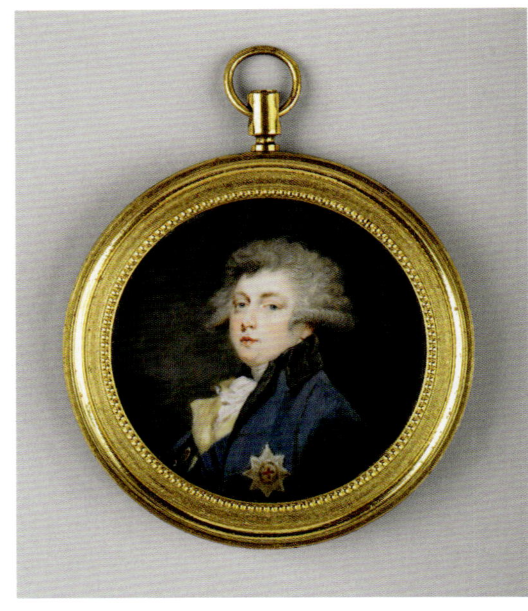

Fig.5 Peter Adolf Hall, after Reynolds, *George IV when Prince of Wales*, signed, *c.*1785–93, ivory, 73 mm diameter, London, The Wallace Collection (M39)

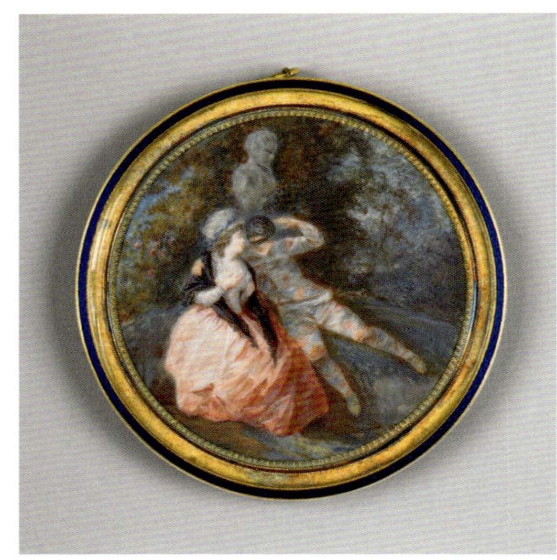

Fig.6 After Watteau, *Harlequin and Columbine*, *c.*1790, ivory, 66 mm diameter, London, The Wallace Collection (M142)

the French capital in 1720–1, but was so influential on the further development of French art that she might also be called part of the history of French painting. The Van Blarenberghes (nos.15–18) were brought up in a still largely Flemish tradition in Lille, a city that had only become French in 1668, and they used their specific cultural background to their advantage in Paris. Jacques Charlier (nos.11–14) is probably the most important eighteenth-century miniature painter to have Parisian roots, which may help account for the fact that he seems to have had some manner of official working arrangement with François Boucher, another native Parisian.

Eighteenth-century miniatures remained marginal in the overall context of French painting. Miniature painters were barely represented in the Academy in Paris. Throughout the entire century, only seven painters are known to have been received as full members and to have presented a miniature as their reception piece, most of them in the second half of the century:[2] Charles Boît (*c.*1663–1727), who became a member in 1717 with an enamel of *Roman Charity,* was an early, isolated case. Nicolas Vénevault (1697–1775) became a member in 1752 with two biblical histories on unknown supports. Shortly thereafter, André Rouquet (1701–1759) became a candidate in 1753 and a full member in 1754 with an enamel portrait of the marquis de Marigny. Pierre-Antoine Baudoin (1723–1769) became a candidate in 1761 and was received as a full member in 1763 with a particularly lavish miniature on ivory of *Phryne before the Judges* (fig.7). Pierre Pasquier (1731–1806) became a candidate in 1768 and a member in the following year with enamel portraits of Louis XV and Christian VII of Denmark. Jean-Baptiste Weyler (1747–1791) followed in 1779 with an enamel portrait of the comte d'Argenviller. Finally, François Dumont (see nos.26 and 27) became a candidate and one of the last pre-Revolutionary full members in 1788 with a miniature portrait of the painter Jean-Baptiste-Marie Pierre, probably painted on ivory (lost). Several other painters whose reception pieces were easel paintings also produced miniatures. Still, given the overall number of painters in the Academy, their number was small. As only candidates and members of the Academy could show their works at the Salon, miniatures as a result were only rarely seen in public in pre-Revolutionary France. Although there were other art exhibitions in eighteenth-century Paris, the Salon was by far the most important stage on which to be seen and discussed by a large audience. This is clearly reflected in contemporary exhibition reviews. Once the Salon became open to all artists in 1791, the presence of miniature painting increased dramatically.

The rare appearance of miniature painters was at least partly due to prevailing opinion within the institution itself. Miniature paintings were not seen as fulfilling the same intellectual standards as easel paintings. Hence miniature painters had both a lower reputation and received less advanced training. Drawing in particular was a skill with many academic connotations and drawing after the nude was a specific academic

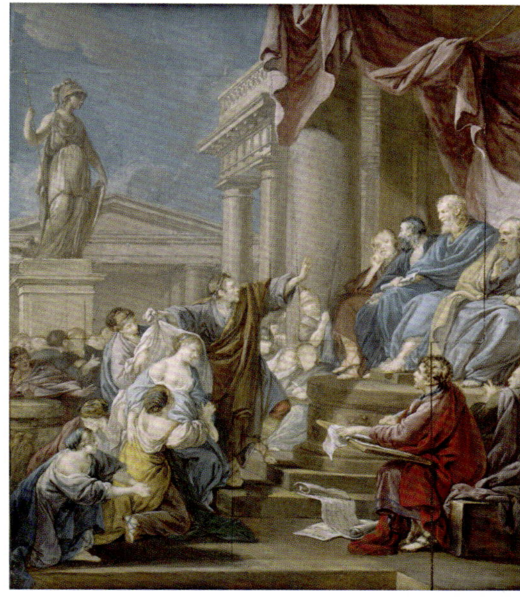

Fig.7 Pierre-Antoine Baudouin, *Phryne before the Judges*, 1763, ivory and paper glued on wood, 464 × 382 mm, Paris, Musée du Louvre (inv.23700)

privilege. Miniatures do not necessarily require preparatory drawings. Only in rare cases are drawings by miniature painters known. Occasionally miniature artists also produced larger drawings, usually as independent works. Rosalba Carriera's fame was increasingly based on her works in pastels. Whilst she was admitted as a member of the Accademia di San Luca in Rome with a miniature as her reception piece in 1705, she was accepted by the Academy in Paris in 1720 with a pastel, which she presented in 1722. Louis-Nicolas van Blarenberghe painted large-scale gouaches of battle scenes for Louis XV, thus venturing into the territory of proper history painting, a genre often inaccessible to miniature artists. Niclas Lafrensen produced large numbers of highly finished drawings for collectors, which explored the same subjects as his miniatures.

Miniature painters were thus usually not part of the central art establishment of their day. Peter Adolf Hall is probably the most notable exception to this general rule, as he was friends with major artists like Alexander Roslin and Jean-Baptiste Greuze, had become a candidate of the Academy in Paris and as such had obtained the right to exhibit at the Salon. Reactions by Salon critics show that his works were still regarded as inferior to easel painting and sculpture, but at the same time Hall enjoyed a visibility which few other miniature painters could boast. The patchy documentation is one of the main reasons why miniatures, which are relatively rarely signed, still pose exceptional problems of attribution. Very few comprehensive monographs on French eighteenth-century miniature painters have been written. Portraiture in general is a genre of painting where problems of attribution abound, and the private character of miniatures adds further difficulties. Personal presents of portraits, genre scenes and erotica for private enjoyment are more likely than other works to lose their history when they are passed on. Miniature portraits of unknown sitters are therefore a common phenomenon.

The most innovative and successful miniature paintings of the eighteenth century in France were painted on ivory, a material that was introduced by Rosalba Carriera into the mainstream of European miniature painting (see no.6). France was much slower in adapting to the new medium than Britain or the German lands. Peter Adolf Hall (see nos.21–4), born in Sweden, was the first to realise the full artistic potential of the new medium. In his work miniatures achieve a freedom of touch, a brilliance of brushwork and a translucent quality never before achieved in France. This was the moment when the medium reached its artistic zenith because, in his work, the most advanced trends in French painting were translated into an idiom adaptable to the size and materials of miniature painting (see detail opposite). The full painterly quality of eighteenth-century French painting was thus incorporated into the medium of miniature painting with considerable delay, but with outstanding results. The Wallace Collection is fortunate to own some of his exceptional miniatures which became great works of art in their own right.

NOTES

1 For references see the individual entries of the miniatures noted.

2 *Les peintres du roi* 2000.

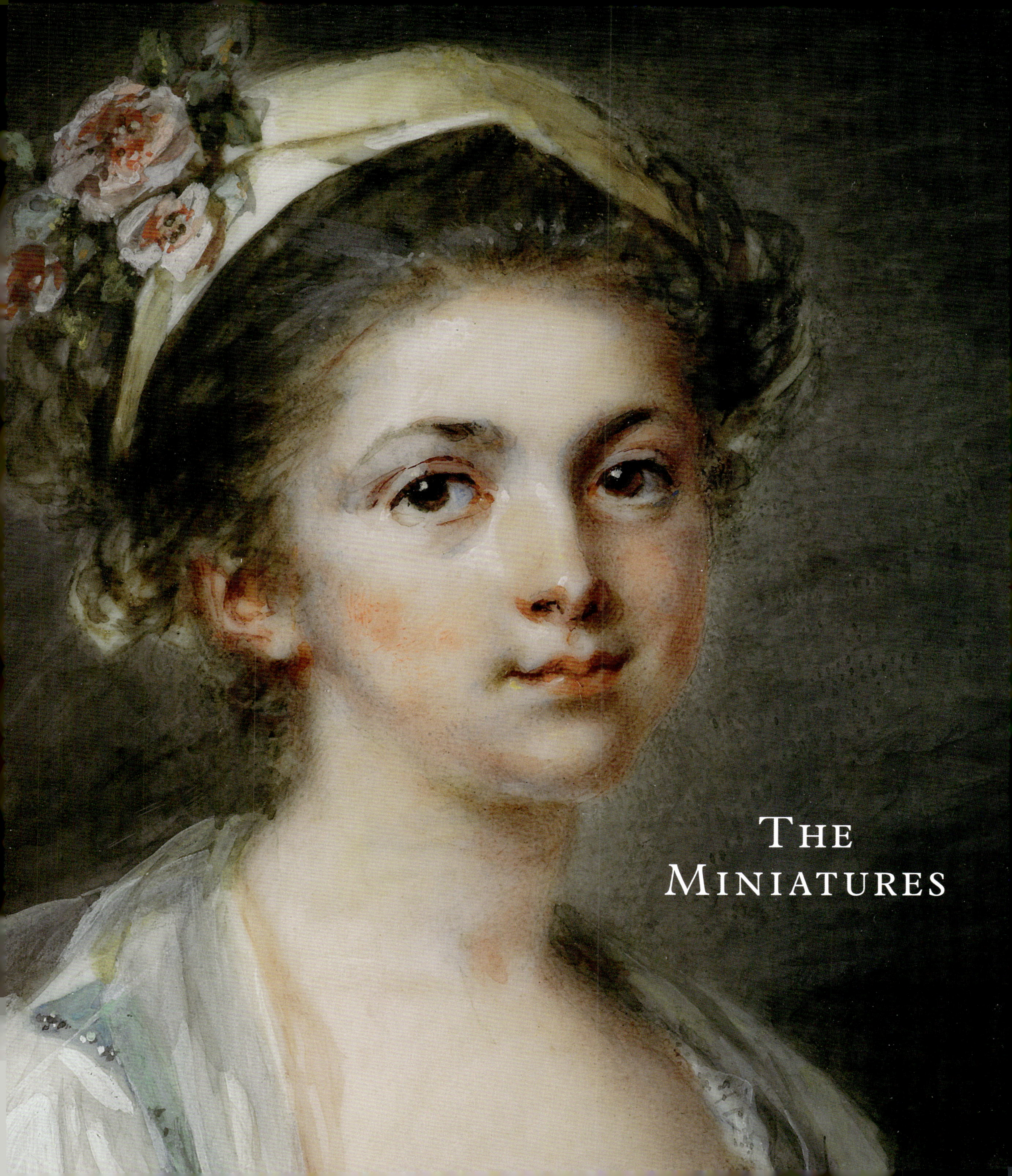

The Miniatures

1 Circle of François Clouet (*c*.1510–1572)
Jean de Thou, mid 1570s or later
Oil on card, 125 × 95 mm

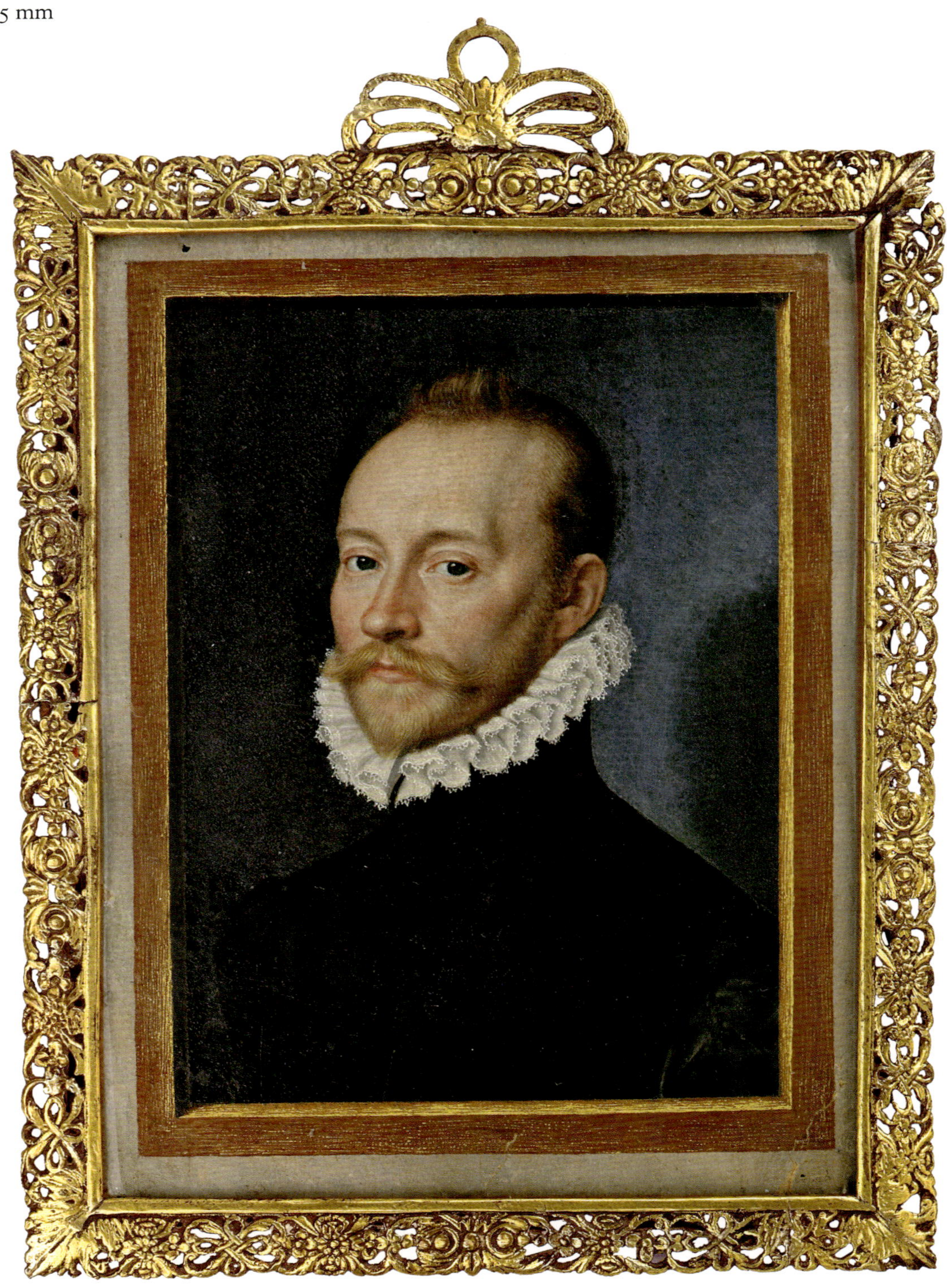

Inscriptions on the back of this miniature and its pendant (fig.1) identify the sitters as Jean de Thou and his wife Renée Baillet.[1] The inscriptions may be regarded as trustworthy since Jean de Thou was a lesser-known member of a noble family from the region of Orléans whose name would not have been used later to provide an interesting identity for an anonymous portrait.

Jean de Thou is not specifically mentioned in biographical accounts of the de Thou family. Information on him can, however, be found in a collection of poems which was published immediately after his death and in later annotated versions of the autobiography of his youngest brother, the famous historian Jacques-Auguste de Thou (1553–1617).[2] Jean and Jacques-Auguste were sons of Christophe de Thou (1508–1582) and Jacqueline de Tuleu. Christophe de Thou held many important offices and became Premier Président du Parlement in Paris, a title to which the inscription on the back of the male portrait makes allusion. Jean de Thou held the offices of Conseiller au Parlement and Maître des requêtes and died in 1579 at the age of forty-one. Accordingly, he must have been born in 1537–8. His son, René de Thou, became Introducteur des Ambassadeurs under Louis XIII. A later addition to the inscription on the back of the male portrait links the sitter himself to Louis XIII, which is impossible, given the style of the dress and of the portrait, but which might have arisen by confusion with his son. Jean's younger brother by two years, Christophe de Thou, Grand-maître des Eaux et Forêts de Normandie and Bailli de Melun, was assassinated with his son by the Catholic League during the Wars of Religion. After his two eldest sons had died, Christophe de Thou forced his youngest son, Jacques-Auguste, to marry in order to continue the family line.

While the identification of the sitter can be considered reliable, the attribution of the two miniatures is more difficult. They have traditionally been associated with the style of the Clouets. Jean Clouet and his son François are today credited with many masterworks of French sixteenth-century portraiture. Very little, however, is known about these two painters. Their dates and places of birth are still unknown and very few signed works survive. Jean Clouet (*c.*1475/85–1540) came to France from the Netherlands, possibly from Brussels. He is mentioned in the French royal accounts between 1516 and 1536. François took over the position of Valet de chambre et peintre ordinaire du roi of King François I upon his father's death in 1541. In his new contract François was described as an experienced painter, which makes it likely that he was born long before the date of *c.*1520 that is sometimes assumed. After François I's death, he worked for Henri II, François II and Charles IX of France and died in 1572. As part of his royal office he was charged with designing court ceremonies, such as kings' burials. A prolific portrait draughtsman, he painted portraits in oil and probably miniatures.[3] Although most of the portraits which are today attributed to him are of the royal family and household, he

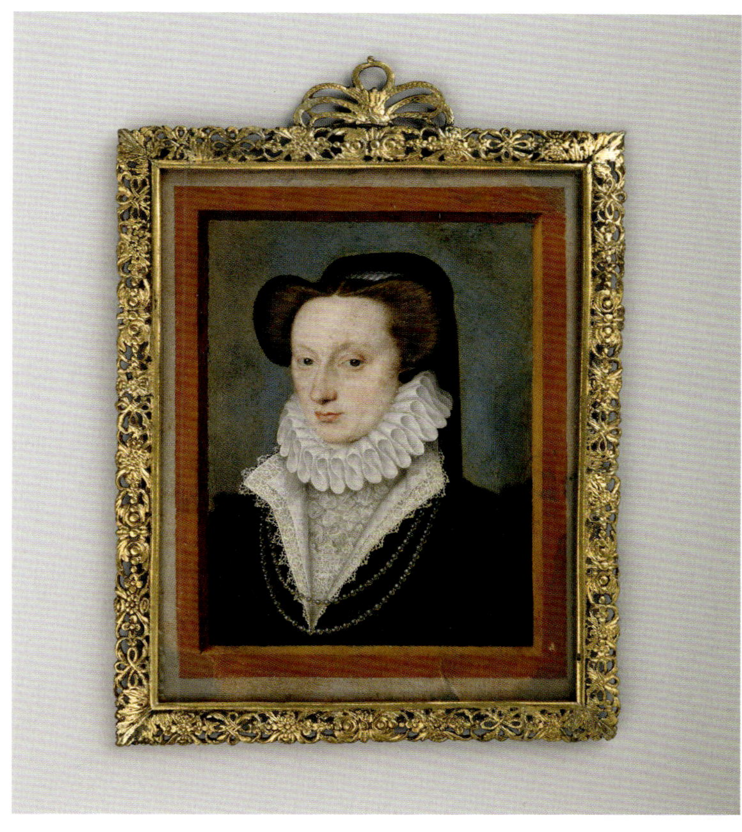

Fig.1 François Clouet, *Renée Baillet,* mid 1570s or later, oil on card, 125 × 95 mm, London, The Wallace Collection (M262)

also produced portraits of other sitters. The attribution of works to him is still widely debated. Only a few of his works are signed. In reality, the name Clouet describes not primarily a personal style of one or two individuals but rather a very large group of stylistically homogenous works by a workshop or even different painters who were active at that time.

Father and son Clouet developed a clearly recognizable type of portraiture which became immensely successful – bust-length portraits which show the sitters in a three-quarter profile in front of a strongly coloured, plain background. They were prepared by drawings which usually focus on the sitter's face, whereas most of the paintings also include the hands of the sitters. An equally strong emphasis is put on individual features and on the luxury dress of the time. Jean Clouet is credited with a crucial role in the development of the early European portrait miniature and some miniatures might also be attributed to his son François. The portraits of Jean de Thou and his wife Renée Baillet are not strictly speaking miniature paintings but small-scale oil paintings.

The portrait of Jean de Thou is based on a drawing in the so-called Album Lécurieux, a collection of fifty-six French sixteenth-century portrait drawings in the Bibliothèque nationale in Paris, acquired by the library in 1825. It contains drawings by different hands, and the portrait of Jean de Thou has been attributed to an anonymous painter from the immediate circle of François Clouet, the so-called Anonyme Lécurieux.[4] The painting follows the drawing literally but the dress is simplified into a black jacket. No drawing for the female portrait is known.

Jean de Thou's portrait must have been painted before his death in 1579. His wife's dress is dated by Aileen Ribeiro to the mid 1570s (personal communication), and Jean de Thou is probably shown in his thirties. Both these indications make it difficult to date the portrait to François Clouet's lifetime. Both portraits are conceived according to the Clouets' usual formula but the wife's one is possibly of a slightly inferior quality, although this difference may be due to the poorer state of preservation. Like the drawing in Paris, they are close in style to the few signed works by François Clouet but not close enough to justify an attribution to him. In the present state of knowledge it seems best to attribute both miniatures to the Clouet circle. CMV

PROVENANCE: Probably first recorded in the collection of the 4th Marquess of Hertford, 1867 (see p.11)

M263

2 Unknown Artist, England, after Holbein the Younger

Hans Holbein the Younger, *c.*1550–1600

Vellum laid on playing card, 36 mm diameter
Inscribed: *H H | · AN · 1543 · ETATIS SVÆ 45*

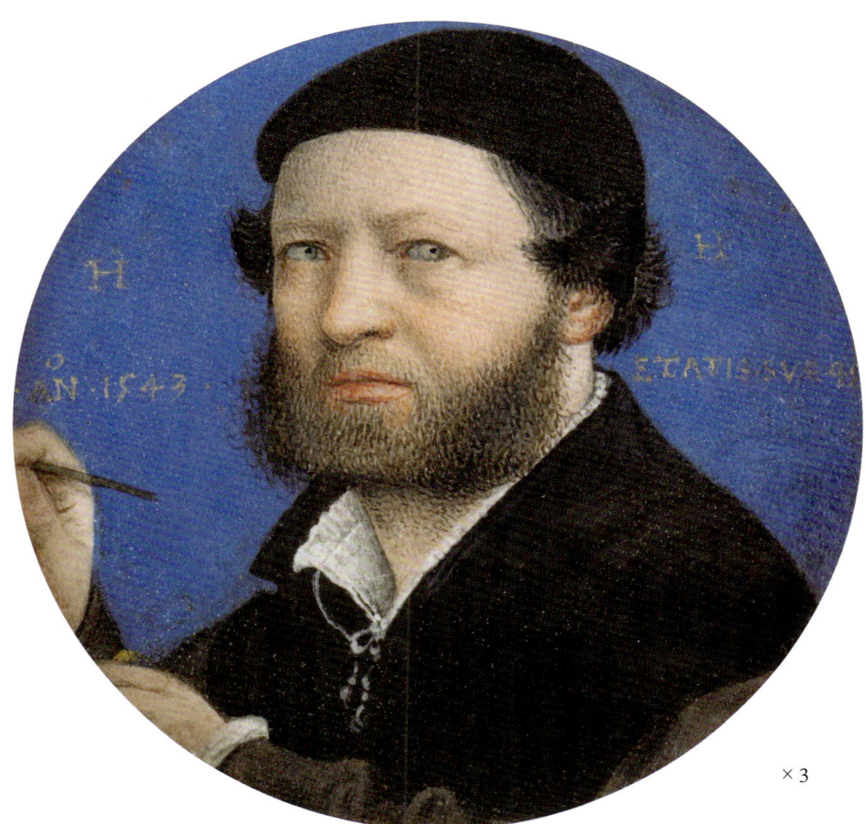

× 3

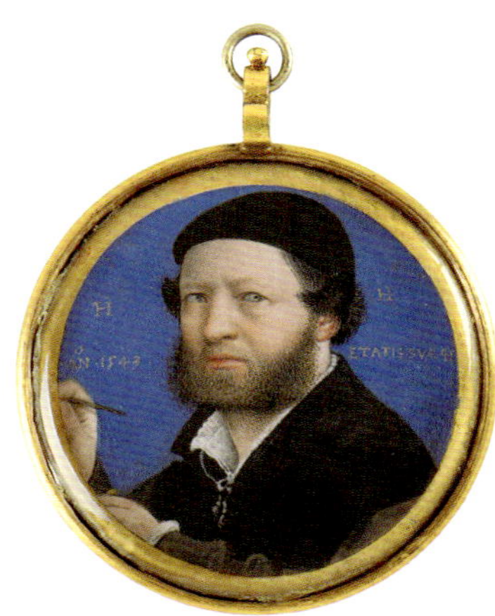

This miniature shows the German-born painter Hans Holbein the Younger (1497/8–1543) in a black doublet and cap, holding a brush or pen and intently gazing at the beholder. The artist's bust is shown against a strong blue background, while Holbein's monogram, the year 1543 and the painter's age in that year – the year of his death – are inscribed in gold capital letters on the blue background. The identification can be proven by the comparison with Holbein's self-portrait drawing in the Uffizi in Florence, which also shows Holbein at the age of forty-five, just before his death. Holbein stayed in England twice, the first time from 1526/7 for about two years, then again from 1532. His main patrons were the German merchant community and the court of Henry VIII. Both the Uffizi drawing and this miniature show him at the very end of his life, during his second stay in England.

The miniature passed through several important British collections, where it was long regarded as a self-portrait of the artist. Its quality and its provenance make it an outstanding example of an antiquarian and artistic interest in Holbein, who was venerated as the founding figure of painting in Britain. It has, however, proved difficult to determine the author of this famous work and to assign it its proper place in the early development of the portrait miniature in England. The miniature is considerably different in style from Holbein's accepted miniatures and of somewhat inferior quality, and since the 1950s the attribution to Holbein has gradually and correctly been abandoned. The artist is known to have been left-handed. In the miniature, he is shown holding the brush in his right hand, as would be the case for a self-portrait produced with the help of a mirror. If the miniature is not by Holbein it may be presumed to be based on an autograph self-portrait by the artist.

The most obvious model is Holbein's self-portrait drawing in the Uffizi in Florence. Although not dated, its inscription specifies the artist's age as forty-five. It shows Holbein in identical pose and expression, but with some minor differences: in the drawing, the artist wears a different cap, and details of his shirt and cloak have been changed. Most importantly, the drawing does not show the artist's hands. While the Uffizi drawing seems to be closely related to the miniature, it is far from obvious that it supplied the direct model for it. The situation is further complicated by the fact that the drawing may have been reworked at a later time.

Two further versions of the miniature exist, one in the collection of the Duke of Buccleuch and Queensberry (fig. 1), another one formerly in the Museum Mayer van den Bergh in Antwerp. All three show the artists' hands and are very similar in the details of the dress. The miniature in the Wallace Collection is of superior quality and can be regarded as the prime version. The closeness in composition of all three miniatures suggests that the Buccleuch and Antwerp versions might in fact derive from the Wallace Collection miniature rather than directly from the drawing in Florence. The Buccleuch miniature is now regarded on stylistic grounds as a seventeenth-century work, while the version formerly in Antwerp has been stolen and can no longer be examined. Although the portrait in the Wallace Collection might also be a much later work, its style strongly suggests that it was painted in the sixteenth century. There is also a group of small-scale portraits in oil of

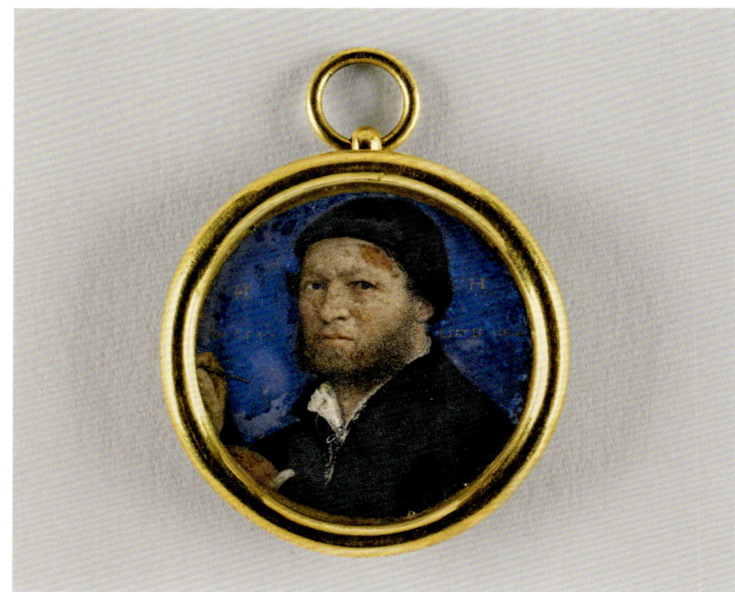

Fig. 1 English, 17th century (?), oil on card, 45 mm diameter, inscribed on the background: *H H / AN · 1543 · ETATIS SVÆ 45*, Dumfries, Collection of the Duke of Buccleuch and Queensberry

Holbein which are based on the same model. The prime version of these in Indianapolis has also been rejected as a genuine Holbein on the grounds of its weak quality.[1] Other versions in oils have even weaker claims to Holbein's authorship. It is likely that they all form one family and are derived from a Holbein self-portrait.[2]

It remains likely, especially because its inscription also gives the artist's age, that the drawing in Florence was the model from which all these works ultimately derived. This presumption, however, leaves one question unresolved. Why do all the miniatures show Holbein holding his brush or pen in his right hand – as it would have appeared only in a mirror and thus in a self-portrait – yet the drawing in Florence does not show the artist's hands? Either another self-portrait by Holbein existed which was related to the Florentine drawing or the first Holbein portrait of our series included the artist's hands in order to fabricate a convincing image. This image – by Holbein or a follower – must have provided the model for the entire group. The miniature in the Wallace Collection is among the early works within the group and is of high quality. It may well have been the starting point for an entire group of fictitious Holbein self-portraits, if these were not after all based on a lost work by Holbein himself.

This does not resolve the question of the identity of the artist, who perhaps also adapted the composition of Holbein's drawing to a round format. A close relationship between this painter and Holbein has always been assumed. Stylistically this view appears reasonable, but knowledge of Holbein's drawing and other known works by him might also have provided sufficient stylistic models for the work.

Until recently, the miniature in the Wallace Collection was attributed to the Flemish-born Lucas Horenbout, who came to England with his father, the book illuminator Gerard Horenbout, and his sister Susanna in the mid 1520s.[3] Lucas Horenbout is first mentioned in Henry VIII's chamber accounts in September 1525 and he died in 1544. The artist is only known from these sources and no documented works by him exist.[4] Attributing portrait miniatures to Lucas Horenbout thus remains highly conjectural.[5]

Leaving questions of attribution aside, the miniature is a fascinating example of early interest in the person of Hans Holbein. The style of the miniature supports a dating to the sixteenth century. The reliance on Holbein's own work, however, does not necessarily mean that the painter of the miniature had a direct relationship with the artist. Instead, it seems to be an early fabrication of a 'self-portrait' for an English clientele, amongst whom Holbein enjoyed considerable fame.

The miniature can first be identified with certainty in the collection of William, 3rd Earl of Stafford, where it is described in detail by George Vertue. At that time it still had a turned ivory cover, probably the original one. It is likely that it is identical with a version that had been in the collection of Thomas Howard, 2nd Earl of Arundel. An inscription on the back of the present frame states that the miniature was given as a present by Frederick, 2nd Viscount Bolingbroke in 1757. The recipient was George Augustus Selwyn, one of the two men who regarded Maria Fagnani, later 3rd Marchioness of Hertford, as his daughter. In his collection it formed part of a group of portraits of historically important figures in British history. Through Selwyn, it must have passed into the Hertford family. It is next recorded in the collection of Lord Henry Seymour, the half-brother of the 4th Marquess of Hertford, who bequeathed it to Richard Wallace in 1859. CMV

PROVENANCE: Probably Thomas Howard, 2nd Earl of Arundel; William Howard, 1st Viscount Stafford; Henry, 1st Earl of Stafford; William, 2nd Earl of Stafford; certainly William, 3rd Earl of Stafford; given to George Augustus Selwyn, 1757; probably Maria, 3rd Marchioness of Hertford; certainly Lord Henry Seymour; bequeathed to Richard Wallace, 1859

M203

3 Isaac Oliver (*c.*1560/5–1617)

Sir Richard Leveson, *c.*1597–1600

Vellum laid on plain card, 51 × 40 mm

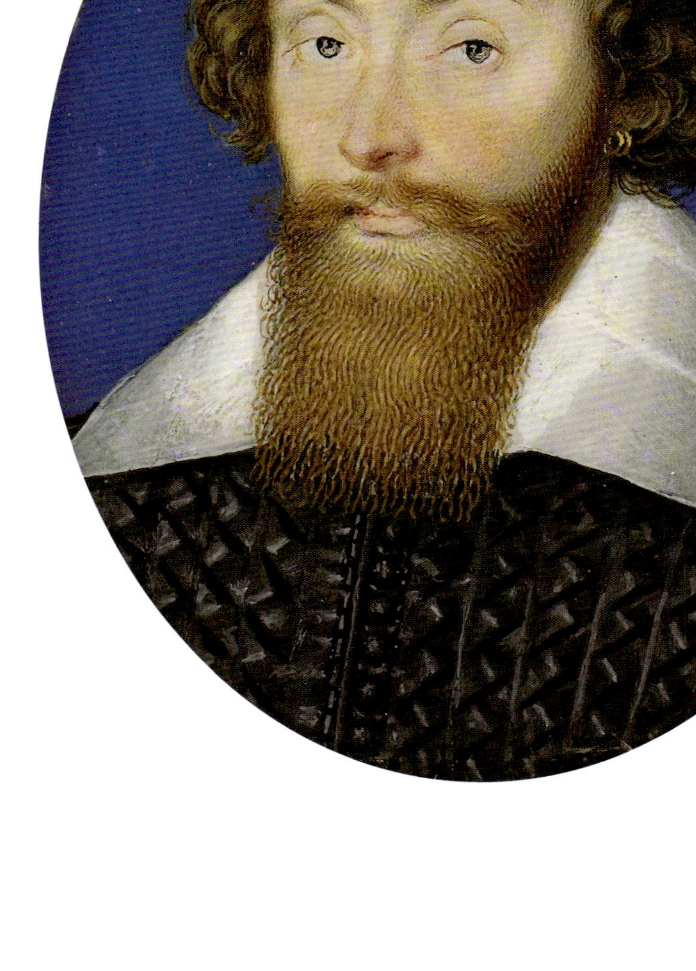

× 3

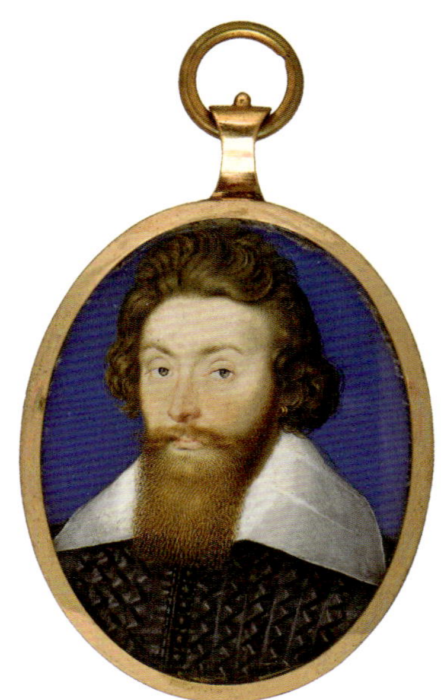

Isaac Oliver was the son of Huguenot parents from Rouen.[1] His father, the goldsmith Pierre Olivier, had settled in England with his family by 1568. Isaac learned miniature painting with Nicholas Hilliard, a choice which reflected the close ties that still existed between goldsmiths and miniature painters at the time. It is possible that he may have received initial training in Tournai, where he was recorded in 1586. His first known work is dated 1587. Hilliard and Oliver became the two eminent miniature painters of their period. Oliver's career was in the ascendant throughout and he became official limner (miniature painter) to Queen Anne of Denmark in 1605 and a member of the household of Henry Frederick, Prince of Wales, of whom he painted several brilliant portraits. Isaac's son, Peter Oliver (*c.*1594–1647), was trained in his father's workshop. Isaac Oliver worked mainly as a painter of portrait miniatures but several historical scenes by him are known and some of his drawings, in a strong Mannerist style, have survived.

Although Oliver was the younger artist, he died two years before Hilliard. Although they were contemporaries, their styles are easily distinguishable. Hilliard's miniatures were strongly and consciously stylized, two-dimensional in their depiction of people, and of an extreme and almost abstract elegance. Oliver's figures are much more convincing in their spatial rendering and have a stronger individuality. The disparities between the two artists would have been heightened by their age difference, but Oliver also remained closer to a European tradition of portraiture. Possible models for his art can be found in his native France, in the Netherlands (his second wife was a daughter of Marcus Gheeraerts) and also in Italy, where he travelled in 1596. His more modern style was well suited to a new generation of English clients who followed developments on the Continent more closely.

The present miniature is typical of Isaac Oliver's style. The sitter, Sir Richard Leveson (*c.*1570–1605), a naval officer during the Anglo-Spanish war (1585–1604), was knighted for his successes during the Cadiz expedition in 1596 – one of the crucial English successes against Spain – and played an important role in 1601 fending off the Spanish attempt to land in Ireland. In 1604 Leveson was appointed Vice-Admiral of England by James I and died the following year. Around the time that Oliver painted the portrait, Leveson's private life had changed dramatically. After his wife had become insane in 1602, he took up with a new partner, Mary Fitton, with whom he had a child in 1603.[2]

Oliver's portrait of Sir Richard Leveson exists in three versions, all of which seem to be autograph. The example in a private collection (fig.1) can be considered to be the prime example, surpassing the other two in quality.[3] It is identical in size to the version in the Wallace Collection but differs in some details, in particular in the rendering of Leveson's dress. Leveson died in 1605, which provides a *terminus ante quem* for the prime version of the portrait. According to Aileen Ribeiro (personal communication) the dress in the Wallace miniature points to a date very late in Leveson's life, around 1600, and Finsten dates it on stylistic grounds to 1597–8. It will therefore have been very close in date to the first version. CMV

PROVENANCE: First catalogued in the Wallace Collection 1904

M287

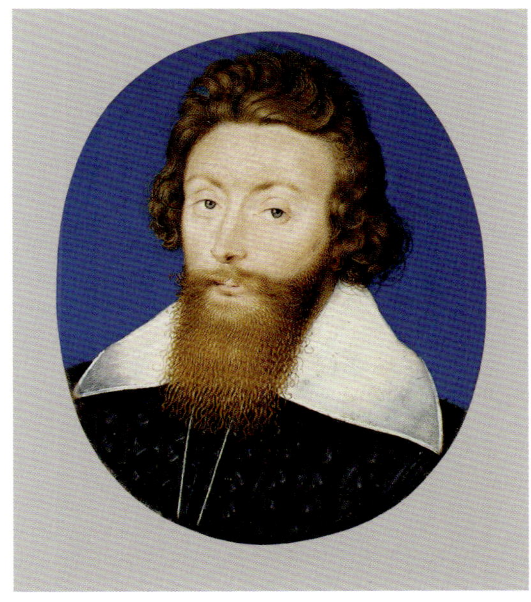

Fig.1 Isaac Oliver, *Sir Richard Leveson*, *c.*1597/1600, vellum, 52 × 43 mm, private collection

4 Samuel Cooper (1607/8–1672)

An Unknown Man, *c.*1660–5

Vellum, 47 × 38 mm

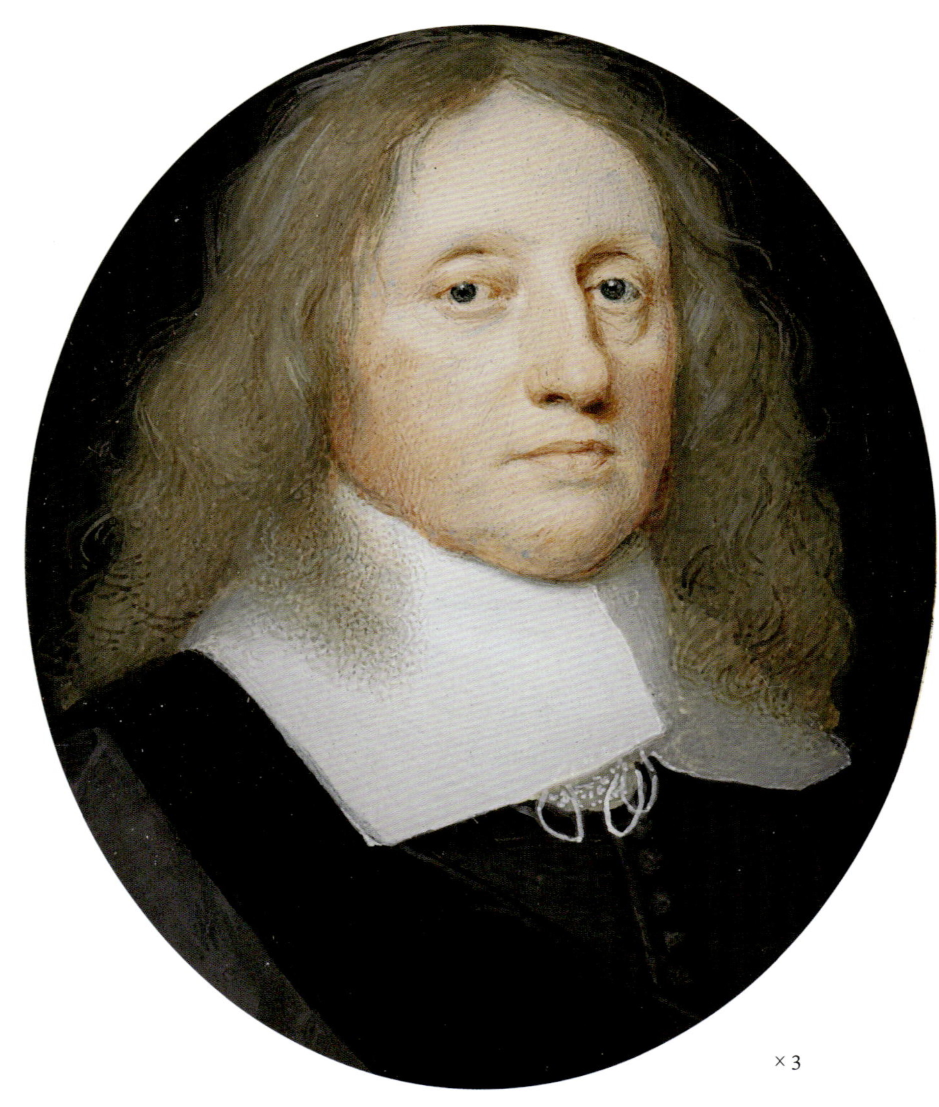

× 3

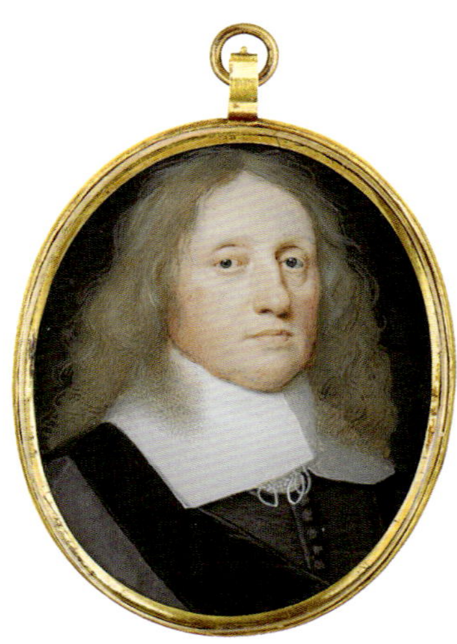

Samuel Cooper, the foremost miniature painter of his generation, learned his art with his uncle, the London miniature painter John Hoskins (*c.*1590–1664/5; see fig.1).[1] His brother Alexander was trained by Peter Oliver and also became an important miniature painter, although not of the same European fame as his brother. Samuel Cooper's earliest signed miniature is of Van Dyck's mistress, Margaret Lemon (Paris, Fondation Custodia), and indeed Van Dyck's influence on Cooper's work is obvious and was commented upon by contemporaries. The young Cooper could have known the Flemish painter personally.

Cooper set up an independent studio in *c.*1641–2, right at the beginning of the Civil War, and by 1650 was a financially successful artist. His career survived all régime changes during these years without problems. During the Commonwealth, he painted official miniature portraits of Cromwell. An early eighteenth-century copy by Christian Richter after his Cromwell portrait is also in the Wallace Collection (fig.2). In 1663 Cooper was appointed King's Limner (miniature painter) to Charles II. It is possible that Cooper converted to Catholicism later in his life. By the end of his career he was wealthy, famous and well-connected and regarded as the most important European portrait miniature painter.

While Cooper's earlier works directly follow Van Dyck's model in their combination of psychological understanding and easy elegance, his later miniatures seem to focus even more on the individuality of the sitters. Some of them are among the masterworks of European portraiture painting of the period. The present miniature is a good example of Cooper's outstanding ability to capture the character of his sitter through an unflattering, but sympathetic rendering of the features. The man's alertness is balanced by his courtier's poise.

The sitter of the miniature is unknown. According to Aileen Ribeiro (personal communication), the dress of the man dates to around 1660. The style of the miniature is closer to Cooper's work of the mid to late 1660s.[2] A date of *c.*1660–5 seems most likely. CMV

PROVENANCE: First catalogued in the Wallace Collection 1904

M205

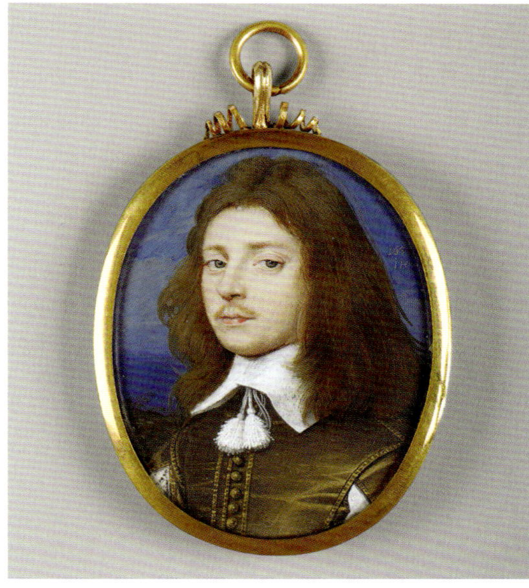

Fig.1 John Hoskins, *Edward, 1st Earl of Cosway*, 1653, vellum, laid on prepared card, 70 × 56 mm, London, The Wallace Collection (M204)

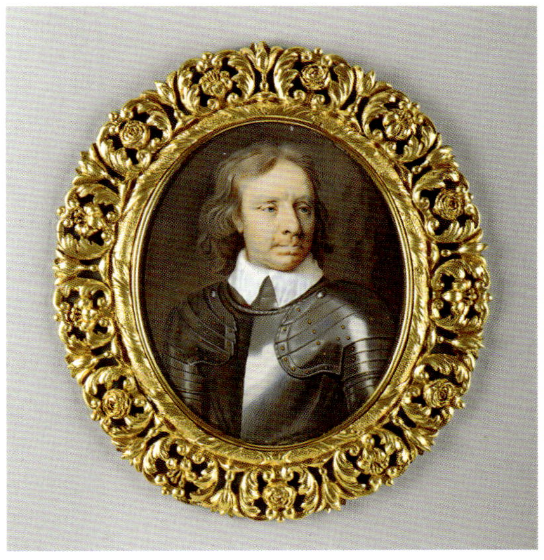

Fig.2 Christian Richter after Samuel Cooper, *Oliver Cromwell*, 1708, vellum, 105 × 85 mm, London, The Wallace Collection (M85)

5 # Jean Petitot (1607–1691)

Louis XIV, mid 1660s

Enamel on metal, 22 × 18 mm
The gold box (gold and enamel, 29 × 90 × 90 mm) by Nicolas Huguet, *c.*1814–19

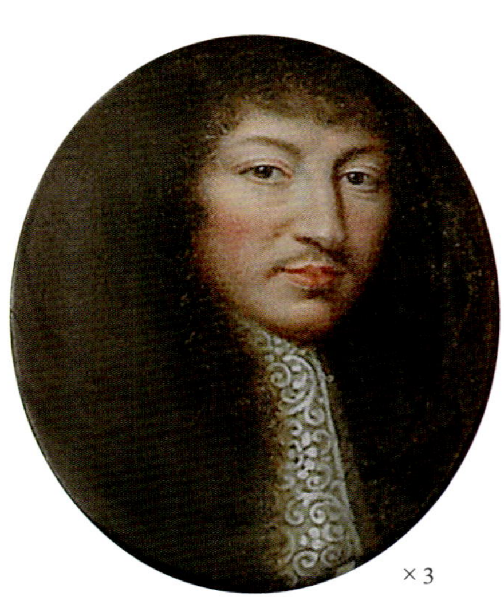

× 3

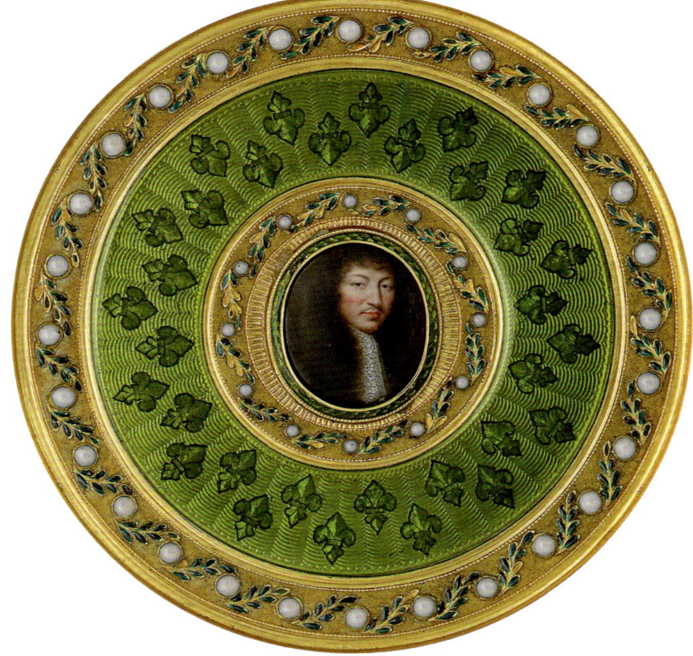

Fig. 1 Base of the gold box by Nicolas Huguet

Jean Petitot was the best-known and most successful painter of enamel portraits in seventeenth-century Europe.[1] In the mid eighteenth century, Dézallier d'Argenville called him "*le Raphaël de la Peinture en émail*". Born in Geneva, he settled in England after an initial short stay in Paris. According to tradition, Charles I was impressed by his talent and arranged for him to be trained by Van Dyck. After the outbreak of the Civil War, Petitot went to France in either 1643 or 1644. He could thus combine his experience of the well-developed tradition of enamel painting in Geneva with his first-hand knowledge of portraiture by Van Dyck and his followers at the English court, resulting in a winning formula that met with great success at the French court during the age of Louis XIV. He executed hundreds of enamel portraits for Louis XIV and the French court. A confirmed Reformist, he had to leave France after the revocation of the Edict of Nantes in 1685, returning to Geneva, where he lived and worked for the remaining years of his long career. It is obvious from the sheer volume of Petitot's production that he must have had significant studio assistance. Petitot's brother-in-law Jacques Bordier is known to have worked on miniatures with him. Jean Petitot the Younger, his son, was also an enamel painter and must have started his career in his father's workshop. While some of Petitot's English miniatures are signed, his French works are not, and it is thus hard to establish firm dates and a clear sense of his own share in the enormous output of the studio. It is safest to understand Petitot's French production as a collaborative studio enterprise. The largest collections of his work are in the Louvre, in the Musée Condé in Chantilly and in the British Royal Collection.

This miniature portrait of Louis XIV is one of a large group of several hundred royal portraits surviving in collections throughout the world. As individual enamels from Petitot's French period are neither documented nor dated, they can only be arranged according to the age of the sitter, assuming that Petitot was required to produce up-to-date portraits of the King. According to Dézallier d'Argenville, Petitot began with existing portraits of the King, modifying them during the sittings which he was granted with the monarch. This seems likely, as it is usually impossible to identify direct models for his portraits of Louis XIV. In this case, a possible starting point for Petitot might have been the portrait print of 1662 by Robert Nanteuil,

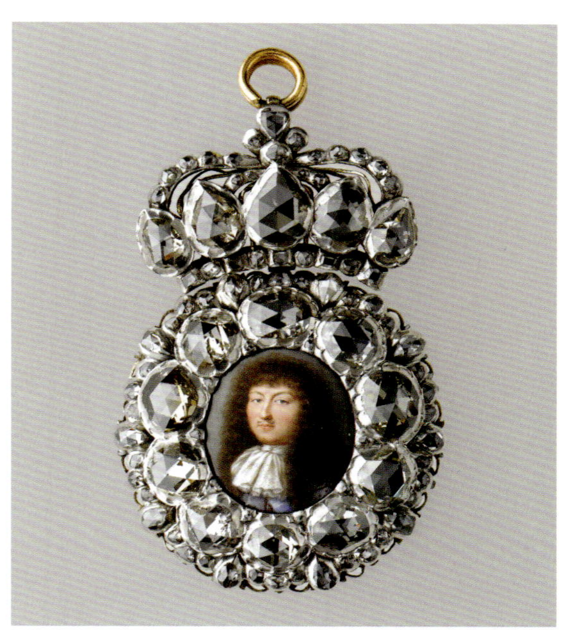

Fig.2 Jean I Petitot and Pierre or Laurent Le Tessier de Montarsy, *Louis XIV*, *c.*1670, enamel miniature framed with diamonds, 72 × 46 mm, Paris, Musée du Louvre, Département des objets d'art (OA12280)

which is comparable even as far as details of the hair. Particularly close to the Wallace Collection miniature are versions in the Royal Collection[2] and a miniature on vellum in the Musée Cognacq-Jay in Paris, which was also reused on a nineteenth-century snuff box.[3]

Enamel portraits of the King were usually part of so-called *boîtes à portrait*, pieces of jewellery featuring on one side the portrait of the King surrounded by diamonds or other precious stones.[4] In spite of their name, these objects were not boxes but rather took the usual shape of orders. They were passed out by the King as special signs of favour to ambassadors, artists and other individuals but not to other sovereigns (as they symbolized allegiance to the ruler). Three other complete examples survive in the Louvre (fig.2),[5] in Bologna[6] and in The Hague.[7] Petitot is documented as a provider of royal enamel portraits. His works were usually bought by goldsmiths and then sold to the royal administration as part of the *boîte à portrait*. Their value as part of a *boîte à portrait* was minimal compared to that of the precious stones and the goldsmith's work.

Around 410 *boîtes* are documented as having been presented by Louis XIV. The portraits of the King were usually taken off their *boîte à portrait* at a later time, usually to sell or to re-use the diamonds and precious metals. A large proportion of the accompanying portraits survive. Today, these enamels are usually found as isolated, framed miniatures, but it was not uncommon for them to be set into gold boxes later. This is what happened also to the enamel in the Wallace Collection, which was used in the early nineteenth century to decorate the base of a box by Nicolas Huguet, together with another, slightly later portrait of the French King on the lid, also by Petitot (fig.3). Huguet's box entered the collection of George IV and was sold in 1834, when it was given to the future 4th Marquess of Hertford by his father, the 3rd Marquess. CMV

PROVENANCE: King George IV; King William IV; Francis, 3rd Marquess of Hertford; given to the 4th Marquess of Hertford, 1834

G67

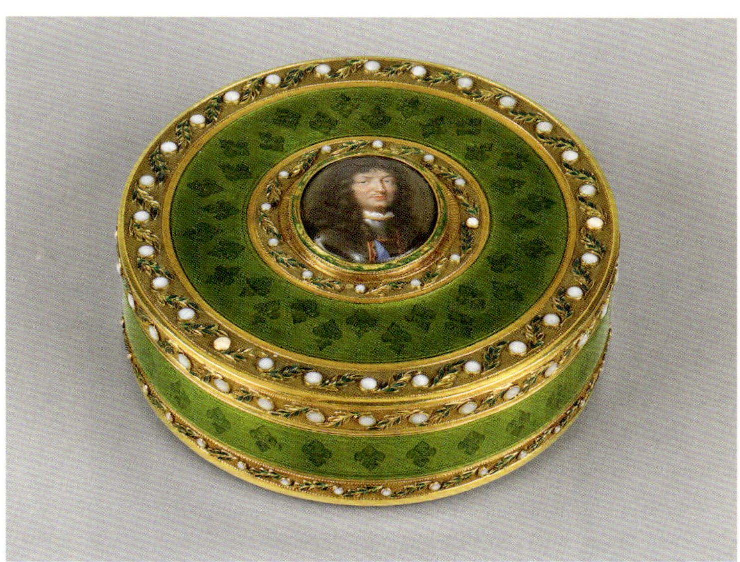

Fig.3 The gold box by Nicolas Huguet, seen from above, with miniature by Jean Petitot, *Louis XIV*, mid 1670s, on the lid, enamel on metal, 29 × 25 mm, London, The Wallace Collection (G67)

6 Rosalba Carriera (1673–1757)

Portrait of a Woman in an Italian Dress, c.1710–20

Ivory, 98 × 75 mm

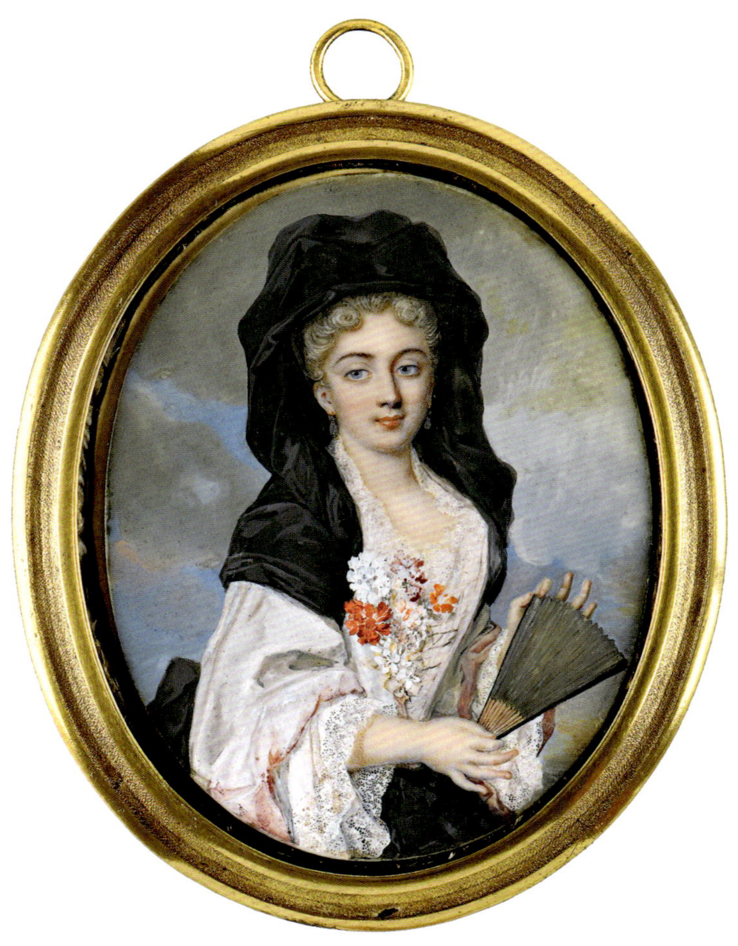

The Venetian painter Rosalba Carriera was one of the crucial figures in early eighteenth-century painting, both for the quality of her works and for her introduction of pastel painting and miniature painting on ivory into the mainstream of European art.[1] She is recorded as a pastellist from 1704 onwards but in the first decade of the eighteenth century was mainly active as a miniature painter. In 1705 she gave a miniature to the Accademia di San Luca in Rome as her reception piece. Later in her career, miniatures seem to have become less frequent; after her stay in Paris, pastels predominated. New miniatures are mentioned in her diary in 1726 and 1727 but seem to have become exceedingly rare afterwards.

Although pastel painting had been known since at least the sixteenth century, Carriera explored its full artistic potential in the context of the new eighteenth-century preference for the immediacy of the sketch. She paved the way for major artists working in the medium, such as Maurice Quentin de la Tour and Jean-Etienne Liotard. Her importance for the development of miniature painting was in every way comparable. Since the sixteenth century miniatures had almost exclusively been painted on vellum or in enamels on copper. Carriera's great innovation was to introduce ivory as a support into the mainstream of miniature painting. The new support material was significant because, once again, Rosalba had identified a medium that was particularly apt for the new artistic sensibilities of her period. Like no other material, ivory could render the special quality of pale skin which was so admired in the early eighteenth century, and it provided an ideal support for the exquisite pale colour schemes of early eighteenth-century art. In order to achieve this effect the ivory surface had to be left partially visible.

Carriera's interest in ivory was linked to her early beginnings as an artist by two of her eighteenth-century biographers. Both traced her use of the material to Venetian snuff boxes, which were often made of ivory.[2] Pierre-Jean Mariette, one of the foremost collectors of drawings of the century, claimed that Carriera had first worked as a designer of lace and later, for financial reasons, become a painter of ivory boxes. This influenced her choice of ivory as a support for miniatures. The unidentified author of an anonymous biography of Carriera, written in 1755, gave a slightly different account. According to him, Carriera started as a painter in oils, moved on to miniatures, and then to ivory boxes. She would therefore have started to use ivory as a support for miniatures before moving on to boxes. Although the two accounts differ slightly, both versions imply that Carriera discovered ivory as a material on which to paint miniatures through her experience in the decoration of ivory boxes. As portraits were not a common feature of these ivory boxes, Carriera also used the material in a new genre, where it could reach its full aesthetic potential.

Close to eighty miniatures by Carriera are known, and almost five times as many pastels. Carriera worked for a large clientele in Venice and soon became famous abroad. From 1700 onwards she painted for the Parisian collector Louis Vatin, who promoted her work in Paris. A stay in the French capital in 1720–1 brought her into contact with major French artists like Antoine Watteau and an influential group of private collectors. Her brother-in-law, the painter Antonio Pellegrini, together with Consul (Joseph) Smith, was instrumental in making her name in England. She was equally successful with clients from Germany and Scandinavia.

This female portrait is a good example of Carriera's work as a miniature painter. It shows her outstanding ability to endow her sitters with a fashionable elegance using a harmony of pale colours and an unequalled lightness of touch (see detail). Doubts about the attribution and the state of preservation of the miniature have been voiced, without obvious reason. The sitter of the miniature is unknown. While the work has been linked to an engraving from 1778 by Francesco Bartolozzi after a self-portrait, that print reproduces a different female portrait and cannot be used to support the claim that the Wallace miniature depicts the artist.[3] A comparison of the sitter with documented self-portraits shows no particular resemblance. The sitter of the miniature must thus remain anonymous.

Her dress is North Italian in style and can be dated to the second decade of the eighteenth century. As it was not unusual for tourists to sit for portraits in local clothing, we cannot be certain that the sitter was Italian.[4] CMV

PROVENANCE: First catalogued in the Wallace Collection 1904

M310

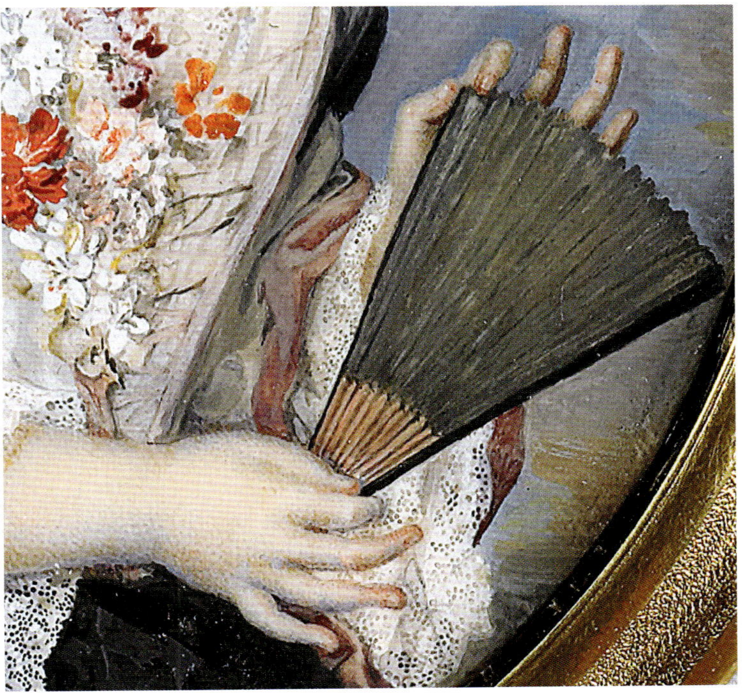

Detail of hands and fan

7 Unknown French Artist

Marie-Anne de Cupis de Camargo, 1730s

Vellum, 58 × 47 mm

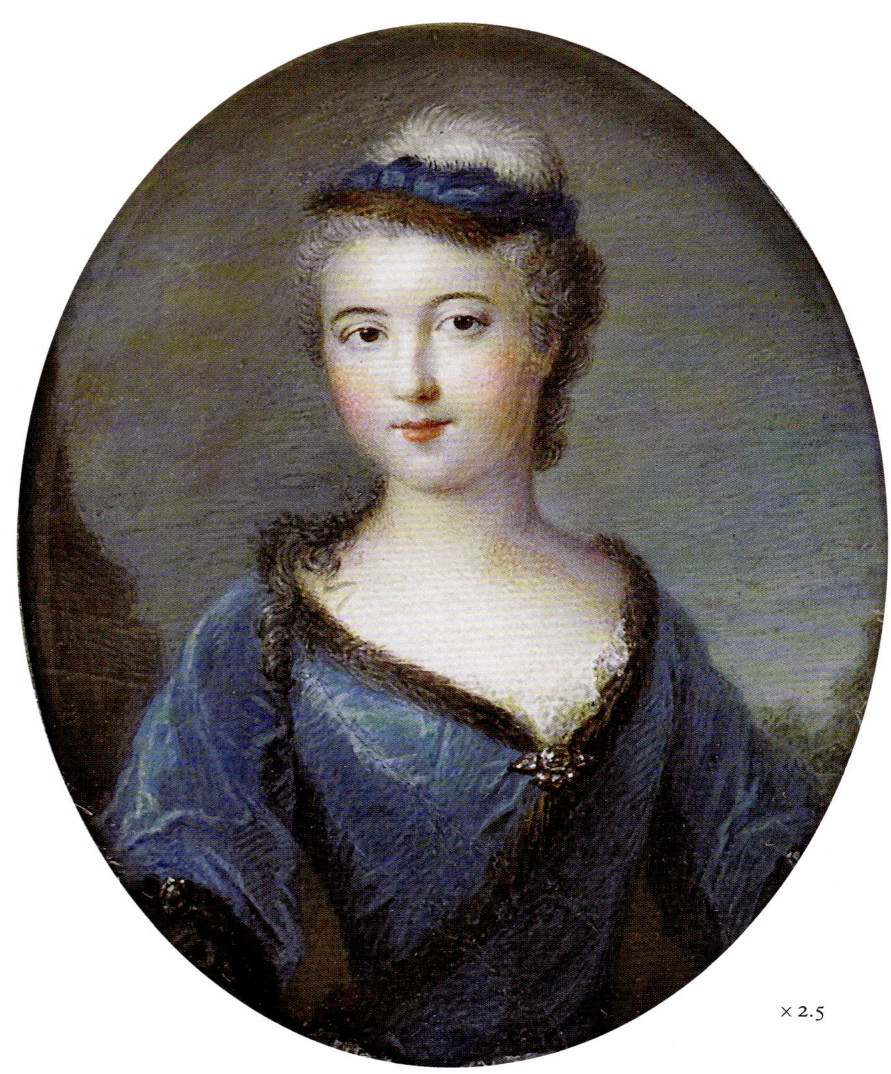

× 2.5

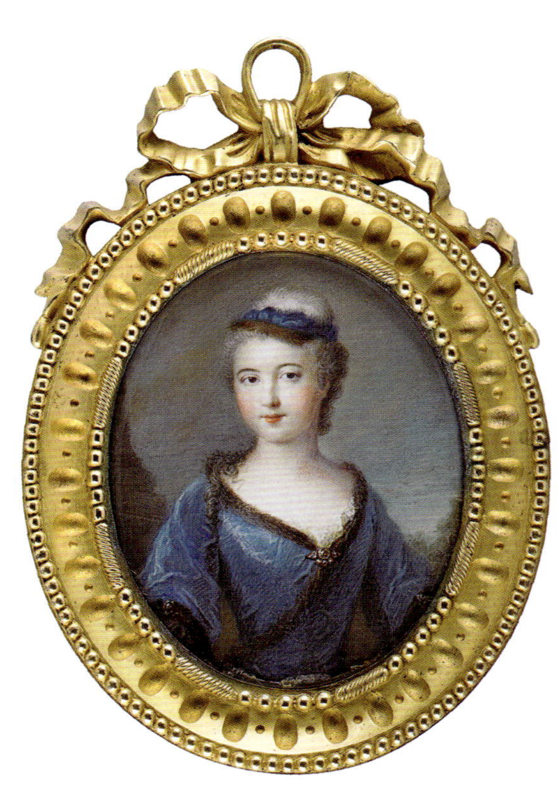

Marie-Anne de Cupis de Camargo (1710–1770) was one of the most famous dancers of the early eighteenth century in Europe, a truly international star. She belonged to a revolutionary group of female stage dancers at a time when ballet had just ceased to be a primarily male domain. Together with her rival Maria Sallé she initiated dramatic changes of style in movement and stage dress for dancers. While Sallé was known for her gracious movements, Camargo became known for a more athletic type of dance, which Lancret attempted to capture in his famous portraits of the dancing ballerina (fig.1).[1] Camargo's celebrity status led to the production of a large number of images and texts which were avidly collected across Europe.

This portrait miniature resembles documented portraits of Camargo closely enough to support the traditional identification of the sitter. Some of the woman's features, such as her wide jaw and small chin, are characteristic of Camargo. Her dress *à la polonaise* and the heavy make-up also support the identification with an actress or dancer. However, no known painted portrait of her has thus far been identified as a model for the miniature, nor does it resemble any of the numerous existing portrait engravings.

In its style, the portrait consciously echoes that of Jean-Marc Nattier (1685–1766), a particularly fashionable and trend-setting portrait painter of the period, who developed a new formula for the female portrait. Closest in style are Nattier's portraits of the 1730s, such as his portrait of Mlle de Chartres of 1731 (private collection). The 1730s were also the period of Camargo's greatest fame. The portrait is thus likely to be a contemporary rendering of the famous dancer painted in the 1730s. A comparable portrait miniature of Camargo, attributed to Jacques Charlier, is in the Louvre (fig.2).

Nothing is known about the provenance of the miniature or its acquisition by the Hertford family, although a visiting card used as part of the back of the miniature mentions the name Siegfried Lowenthal and an address in Frankfurt am Main, Germany. CMV

PROVENANCE: First catalogued in the Wallace Collection 1904

M130

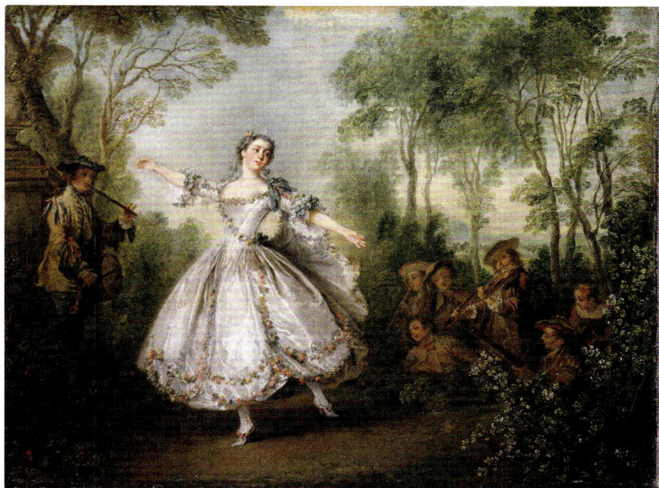

Fig.1 Nicolas Lancret, *Marie-Anne de Cupis de Camargo Dancing*, oil on canvas, 43.2 × 55 cm, London, The Wallace Collection (P393)

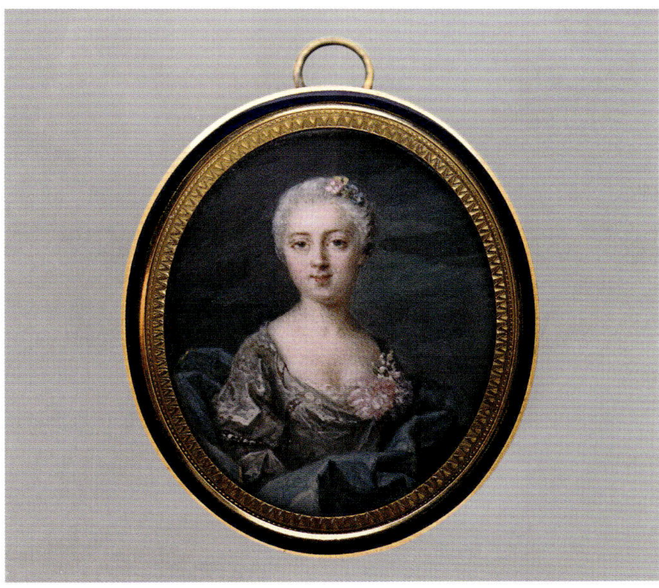

Fig.2 Jacques Charlier, *Marie-Anne de Cupis de Camargo*, ivory, 47 × 39 mm, Paris, Musée du Louvre, Département des arts graphiques (RF4269)

8 Christian Frederick Zincke (1683/4–1767)

General Henry Seymour Conway, *c.*1740–6

Enamel, 48 × 40 mm

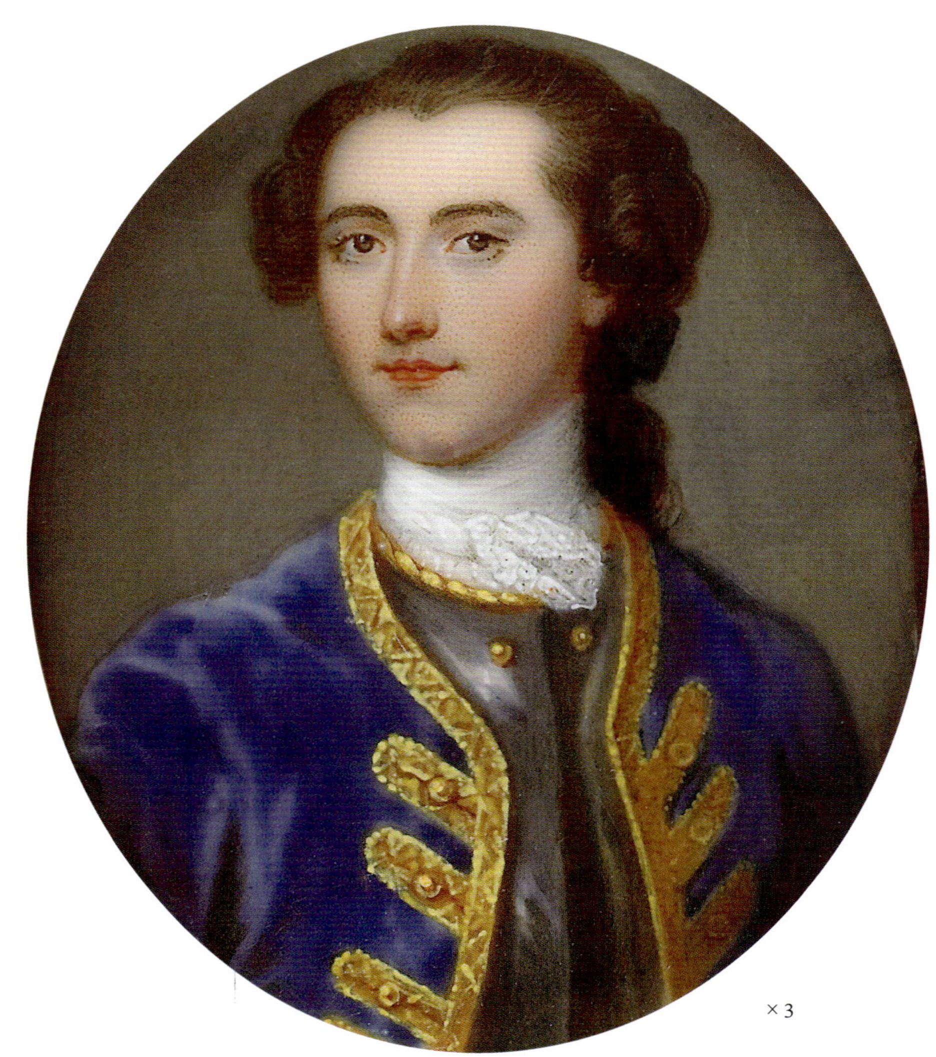

× 3

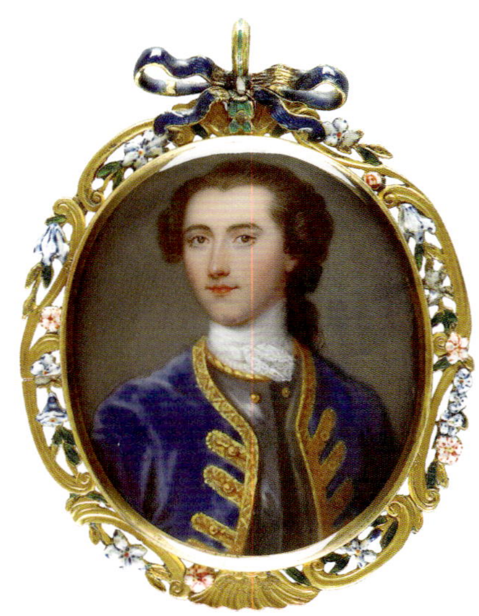

Christian Frederick Zincke was born in Dresden and came to London in 1706. He trained with Charles Boît (1662–1727), a leading enamel painter, born in Sweden from a Huguenot family, who was active in many European cities.[1] Zincke soon became very successful as a painter of enamel portrait miniatures. His German origins probably helped him to become one of the favourite artists of the British royal house. From 1729 he worked for Frederick, Prince of Wales, and three years later became "Cabinet Painter to his Royal Highness". A large number of portraits of the Prince by the artist are known. Zincke's portrait miniatures are celebrated for their high finish and exquisite colours, yet are repetitive in their poses and show little individuality in the sitters.

Henry Seymour Conway (1719–1795), an army officer and politician, was the younger brother of the 1st Marquess of Hertford.[2] When the miniature was painted he was in his early twenties and at the beginning of a long career which made him the most prominent member of the family in the eighteenth century. His military career began in 1737 and in 1741 he was first elected Member of Parliament. As an officer he took part in the War of the Austrian Succession, in the battle of Culloden and the Seven Years War. In 1755 he became Chief Secretary for Ireland, beginning the high-profile political career which he was to pursue in tandem with his service in the army until 1784. Its pinnacle was in 1765 when he was nominated Secretary of State in the Rockingham administration. He was instrumental in the repeal of the Stamp Act and opposed the war against the American colonies in 1775. Seymour Conway travelled extensively in Europe on his military missions and privately. Two towns in New Hampshire and Massachusetts are named after him.

Seymour Conway was a close friend of his cousin Horace Walpole, with whom he had an intimate, life-long correspondence. A large-scale portrait by John Giles Eccardt (active 1740–79) of 1746 in Horace Walpole's collection in Strawberry Hill was apparently painted after the miniature and can help to date Zincke's portrait.[3] Between 1737 and 1744 Seymour Conway was pursuing a relationship with Lady Caroline Fitzroy, but considered his income insufficient to propose. She could have been the intended recipient of the miniature, which was painted around that time. It could also have been intended for his future wife, Caroline Bruce, Countess of Ailesbury, whom he married in 1747. Both theories would explain why the miniature remained within the Seymour Conway family. The expensive frame, set with diamonds, rubies and emeralds, suggests an important recipient. A female portrait by Zincke, probably of Margaret, 2nd Duchess of Portland, has a very similar contemporary frame.[4] Henry Seymour Conway was later painted by both Reynolds (location unknown) and Gainsborough (Inverary Castle, Duke of Argyll). CMV

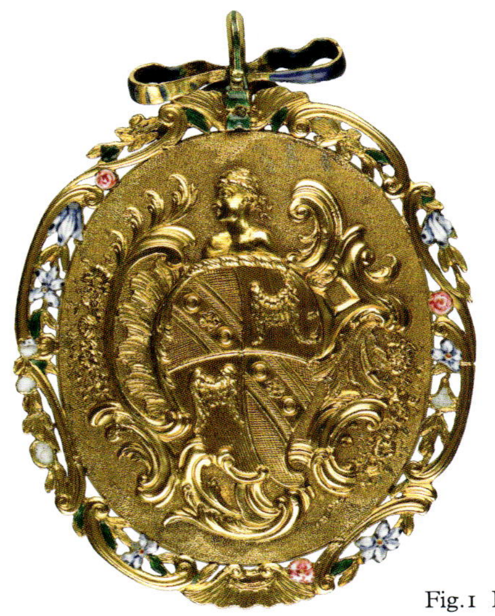

Fig.1 Reverse of no.8

PROVENANCE: Presumably Henry Seymour Conway; the 1st or 2nd Marquess of Hertford, and then by family descent

M314

9 Antonio Bencini (*c.*1710–after 1780?), after Van Meytens the Younger

The German Emperor Franz I Stephan, Maria Theresia and their Children, 1760

Vellum, 252 × 234 mm (277 × 255 mm including rim)

Inscribed (on the back of Franz Stephan's throne): *F I* [imperial eagle] *IMP/ LO GER/ 1760*; (on the back of Maria Theresia's throne): *M.* [imperial eagle] *T/ A.H B.G/ MORIAMUR/ PRO REGE/ NOSTRA*

The miniature is a portrait of the German Emperor Franz I Stephan (1708–1765; Emperor from 1745), his wife Maria Theresia, Queen of Hungary and Bohemia (1717–1780), and thirteen of their children, with the main entrance to Schönbrunn Palace in Vienna in the background.

The Emperor is shown on the left with the crown, sceptre and orb of the Holy Roman Empire on a table. The embroidered inscription on his throne refers to his titles of German Emperor and Duke of Lorraine and dates the miniature to 1760. Right next to him stand their two eldest surviving daughters, Maria Anna (born 1738) and Marie Christine (born in 1742; married Prince Albert of Saxony-Teschen). Maria Elisabeth, born in 1737, and Maria Karoline, born in 1740, had died in 1740 and 1741 respectively. On the right sits Maria Theresia with the crowns of Bohemia and Hungary by her side. These titles, which she held in her own right and not through her husband, are referred to in the inscription on the back of her throne. She is accompanied by her three eldest sons and a daughter – Joseph (born in 1741; later Emperor Joseph II), Karl Joseph (born in 1745; he died soon afterwards in 1761), Peter Leopold (born in 1747; the future Leopold II) as well as Maria Elisabeth (born in 1743, with the same name as her elder sister who died in infancy).

The miniature is based on a group portrait of the imperial family which the Swedish painter Martin van Meytens painted in several variations between 1752 and 1756.[1] Four versions of Meytens's portrait are known, all of which are based on the same design. The groups of the Emperor, the Empress and their eldest children on both sides are identical, whereas the group of the younger children was changed and adapted according to the actual number of children of the imperial family at the respective times. The first version, in the Hofburg, Innsbruck, shows the couple with nine children in 1752, one in Schloss Schönbrunn has eleven children in 1754 (both on long-term loan from the Kunsthistorisches Museum, Vienna), one in Versailles twelve in 1755 and one in the Palazzo Pitti in Florence thirteen in 1756. As the children of the imperial couple were born with only short intervals in between, the paintings can thus easily be dated.

The rendering of the parents and their first six children stayed the same (as in the version of 1752) in all four versions, whereas the position and age of the younger children was subject to change. As a consequence, the relative age of the sitters cannot be accurate in relation to any one specific time in the later three versions of the portrait, nor in the miniature. The version in Innsbruck shows Maria Amalia (born 1746; the future Duchess of Parma), Maria Johanna (born 1750; died in 1762) and Maria Josepha (born 1751; died in 1767) in the background. The painting in Vienna shows these three daughters at a slightly older age and adds Maria Caroline (born 1752; the future Queen of Naples and Sicily) and the infant Ferdinand Karl (born 1754). The group of the youngest five children was slightly changed in the version in Versailles (for example, Ferdinand is now wearing a white cap) and the young Maria Antonia (born 1755; the future French Queen Marie-Antoinette) was added, sitting on a miniature armchair next to her eldest sisters. The last version in Florence then combined elements of the versions in Vienna and Versailles, and rearranged the group of children in the background, where the youngest, Maximilian Franz (born 1756; the future Elector of Cologne), was added.

Although the miniature features thirteen children, as does the painting in Florence, it clearly took the version in Versailles as its starting point. The Versailles painting has the five children shown in the background, grouped in the same way and with Ferdinand wearing a white cap, although his cradle has been changed into a chair, reflecting his slightly more advanced age. Only the versions in Versailles and Florence show the small armchair in front of the emperor where Maria Antonia is seated. In contrast to the oil versions, in the miniature the youngest child, Maximilian Franz, is shown on the chair and the future Queen of France has taken centre stage. The date of the miniature, given on the back of the

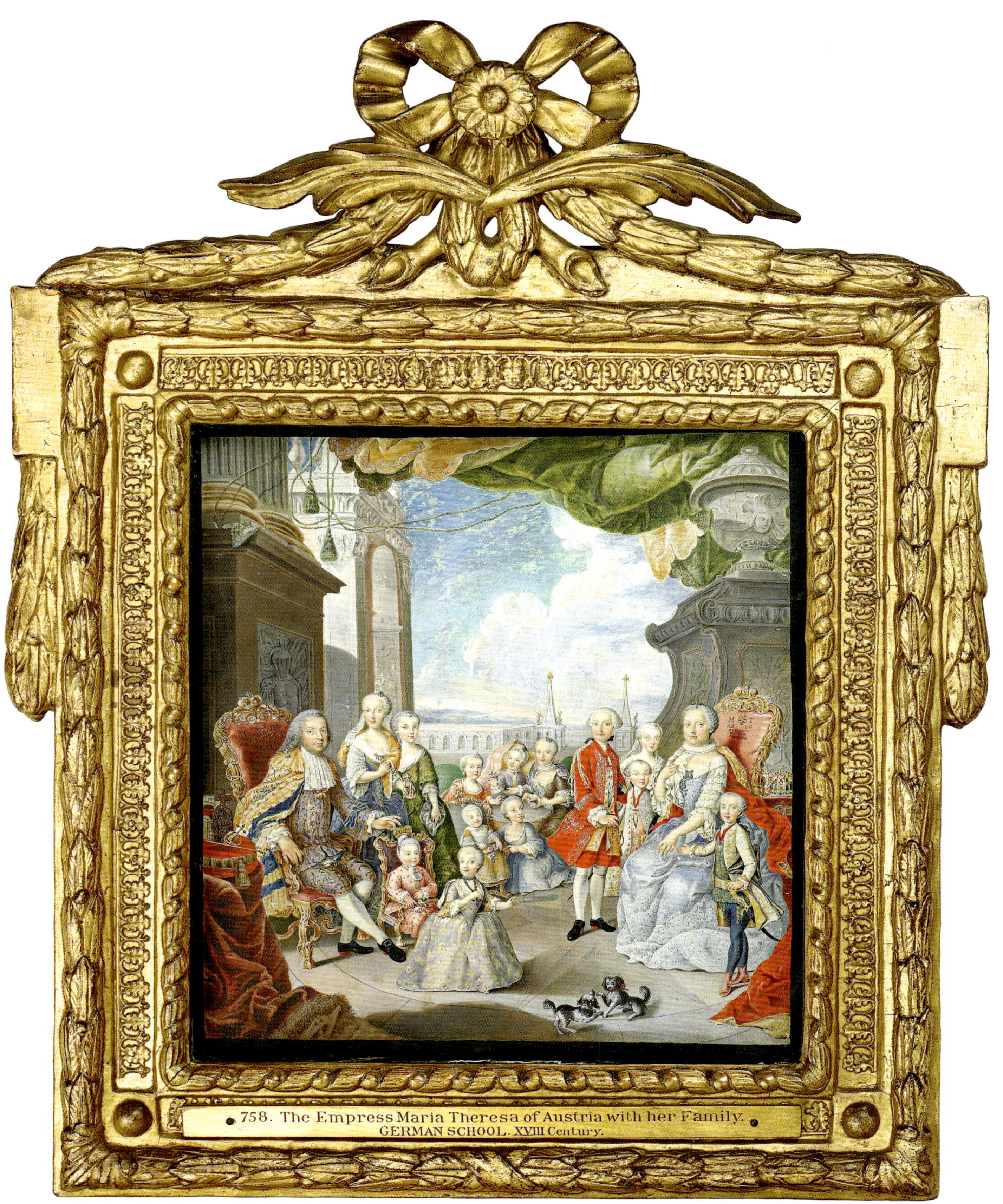
758. The Empress Maria Theresa of Austria with her Family.
GERMAN SCHOOL. XVIII Century.

× 0.5

Emperor's throne, accords with the number of children who were alive at the time but not necessarily with their ages. The last child, Maximilian Franz, had been born on 8 December 1756; Karl Joseph died in 1761, Maria Johanna in 1762. The youngest children would have been visibly older by 1760, which indicates that the miniature was based on already existing material. An engraving by Christoph Winkler after Meytens shows exactly the same composition as the miniature and is the most likely model for it (fig. 1).[2]

Another version of the composition in the Hessische Hausstiftung, Schloss Fasanerie, Eichenzell, is a signed work by Antonio Bencini. Little is known about this painter (not even his birth and death dates), who produced a large number of miniature portraits of members of the Habsburg family. While this miniature is not signed, it is close in style to the Eichenzell version and to a group of small miniature portraits in Vienna which are attributed to Bencini.[3]

Nothing is known about the provenance of the miniature. A long inscription on the back, written on a page of a heraldic book, probably in the hand of Sir Richard Wallace, identifies the sitters and (wrongly) identifies the painter as "F.P. Mignarde", probably because of Pierre Mignard's much earlier multi-figured portraits of the French royal family. The miniature must have been acquired primarily for its historical importance as one of the early portraits of the future Marie-Antoinette. CMV

PROVENANCE: First catalogued in the Wallace Collection 1900

P758

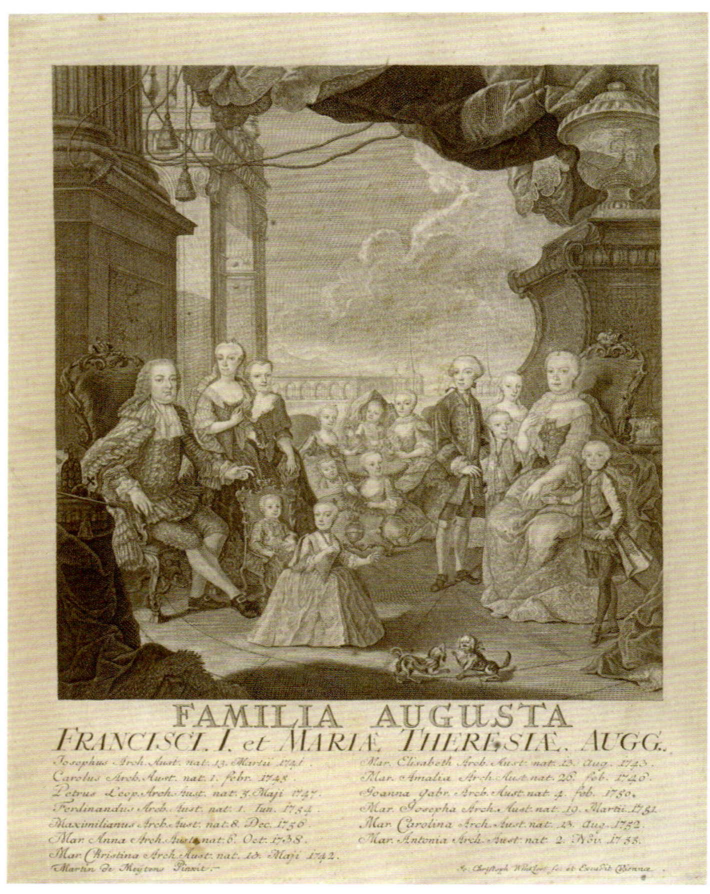

Fig. 1 Johann Christoph Winkler after Martin van Meytens, *The German Emperor Franz I Stephan, Queen Maria Theresia and their Children*, engraving, 35.5 × 28 cm

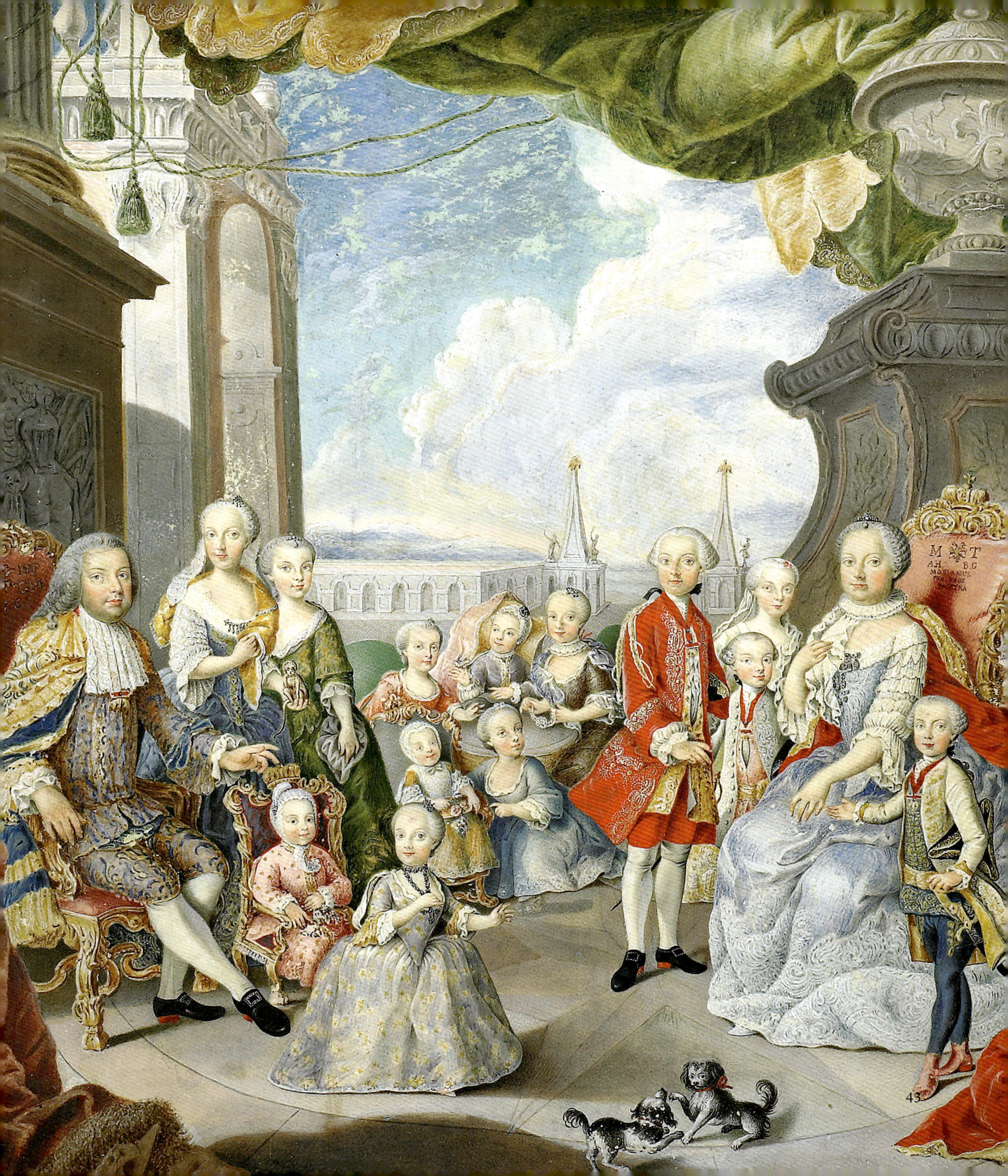

10 Unknown Austrian Artist

Two Men and Two Women in a Park, *c.*1740–50

Ivory, 57 × 80 mm

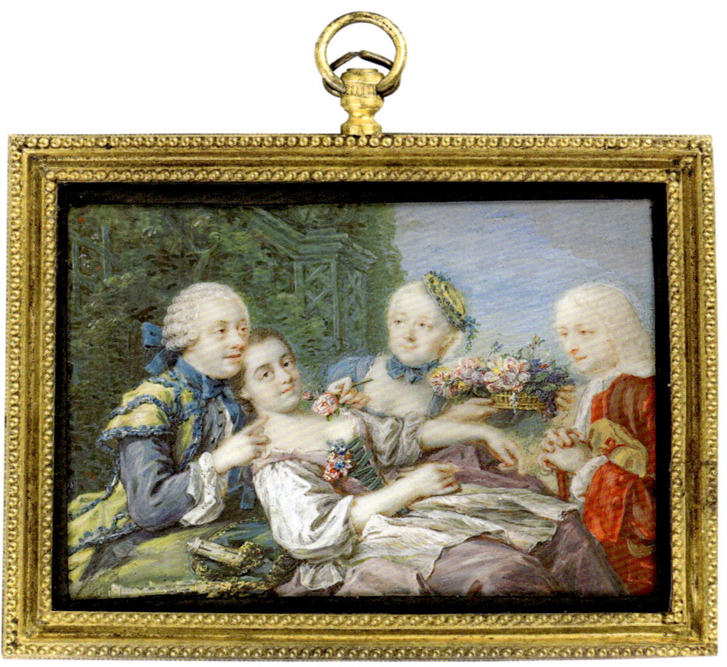

The miniature depicts a group of four people – two men and two women – in the open air. A trellis pavilion in the left background indicates that the scene is set in a garden. The main characters are dressed in pastoral but elegant costume. The man on the left, in a striking, blue and yellow stage version of a shepherd's dress, has put his *musette* aside. The *musette* (a variant of the bagpipe) had become a court instrument in late seventeenth-century France and was a stock instrument for the pastoral genre. As such it was also depicted regularly in portraits with pastoral overtones and in *fêtes galantes*.

The miniature is in fact a combination of these two genres. The woman in the centre who is leaning against the *musette* player is wearing a seemingly simple country-style dress. The small straw hat worn by the woman in the background and her lavish flower basket are also references to an idealized country life. The man on the right has put his ribboned hat under his left arm and is watching the scene, his hands resting on a cane. The elements of this scene derive from *fêtes galantes* by Antoine Watteau (1684–1721) and, even more directly, Nicolas Lancret (1690–1743). Lancret's *Midday* in the National Gallery, London, is just one of a number of works by the painter which could have served as a model for several elements used in the miniature. The genre of the *fête galante* originates in the work of Antoine Watteau. Knee-length compositions have no parallel in Lancret's work but often appear in Watteau's. Watteau's paintings *Pour nous prouver que cette belle* (fig. 1) and *Sous un habit de Mezetin* in the Wallace Collection are examples, and many such were widely known through engravings.[1] The combination of a formula taken from Watteau with additional elements derived from Lancret can probably be explained by the artist's desire to modernize the Watteau blueprint with additions from the more modern Lancret.

Whereas the *fête galante* elements in the miniature are undeniable, the individual faces of the four characters suggest that it was intended as a group portrait in pastoral guise. While the man and the woman on the left definitely form a couple, the same can also be assumed for the older figures on the right. The scene probably depicts two successive generations of a family or circle of two couples. Portraits using the formula of the *fête galante* showing the characters dressed in pastoral style were common in the second and third quarters of the eighteenth century. They conveyed friendship and a sense of carefree sociability, more usual in more private types of portraiture. Miniature portraits often had a very similar purpose.

The very characteristic shape of the figures' faces and the general composition of the miniature suggest that it is based on a lost model by Martin van Meytens the Younger (see no.9). His group portrait of the Tessin family (fig.2), painted in 1730–1, is very similar in both the composition and the rendering of the distinctive faces with their full cheeks and wide cheekbones.[2] The central figure of Brita Kristina Sparre seems like a sister to the two women on the miniature. Meytens could have known Watteau's knee-length compositions from prints but also from his stay in Paris in 1717–19, which coincided with a particularly successful period in Watteau's career. Meytens's lost original for the miniature could have been painted during his stay in Stockholm in 1730–1, as was the Tessin portrait, but it is more likely that it was a work from his Viennese period, therefore after 1731. The style of the miniature could very well be Austrian. Meytens himself learned miniature painting on enamel from Charles Boît during his stay in Paris, but the few miniatures which have been definitely attributed to Meytens are in enamels and are not sufficiently close to support an attribution of the Wallace miniature to him. An old inscription on the back wrongly attributes the miniature to Jacques Charlier.
CMV

PROVENANCE: Possibly first recorded at Bethnal Green (1872–5), no.1708; first certainly catalogued in the Wallace Collection 1904

M69

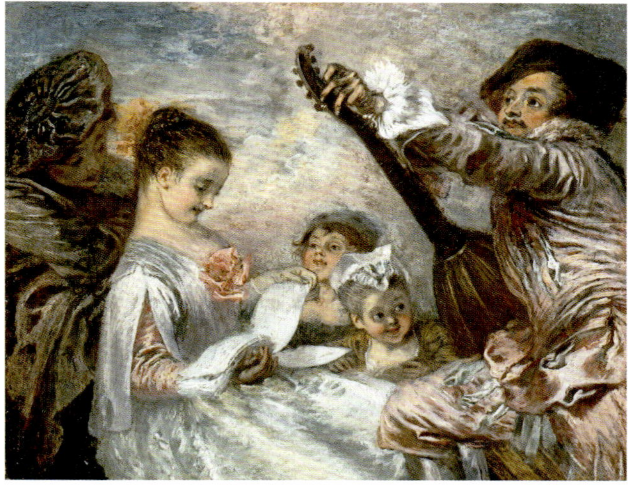

Fig.1 Antoine Watteau, *Pour nous prouver que cette belle*, *c.*1715–17, oil on panel, 18.6 x 23.7 cm, London, The Wallace Collection (P377)

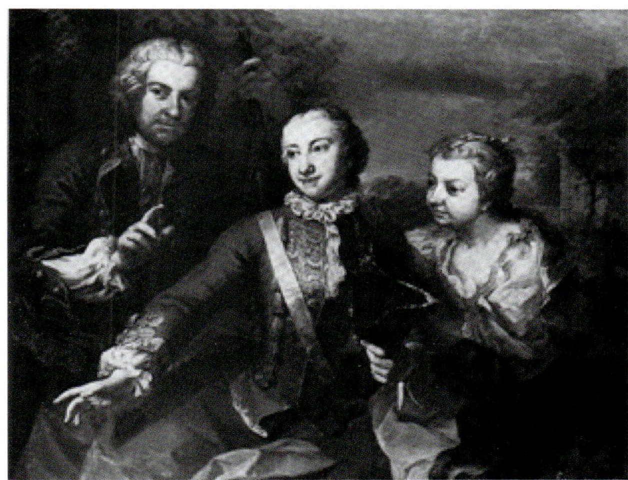

Fig.2 Martin van Meytens the Younger, *The Tessin Family*, *c.*1730–1, oil on canvas, Nynäs, private collection

11 Jacques Charlier (1706–1790), after Boucher

The Muse Clio, *c.*1756–70

Ivory, 53 × 79 mm

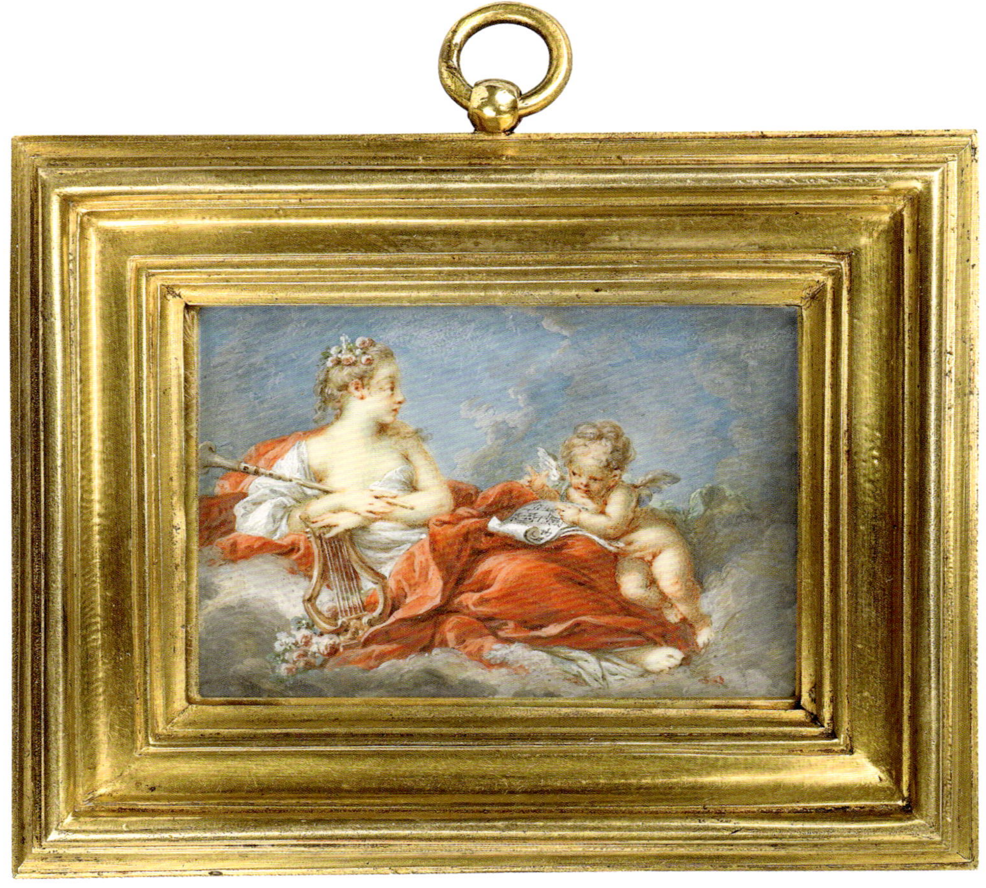

The French miniature painter Jacques Charlier is mainly known for his brilliant mythological and erotic scenes in the style of Boucher. He was avidly collected in the mid nineteenth century, at the same time when major collectors became interested in Boucher. The 4th Marquess of Hertford assembled the most important group of works by Boucher in the world and also by far the largest group of works attributed to Charlier.

Jacques Charlier's career as a miniature painter spans most of the eighteenth century. Although he worked for some of the most important patrons of his age, little is known about his life.[1] His exact birth date has only recently been proven to be 1706 (dates around 1705 and 1720 respectively had been proposed by earlier scholars) and nothing is known about his training. The sources mention him as a painter of portrait miniatures in the 1740s and 1750s but scarcely any examples have been identified. In 1748 Charlier executed miniature versions of the portrait of King Louis XV for the royal art administration. From that year on he worked for the Menus Plaisirs. In 1753 he became Peintre en miniature du Roi, but, like most miniature painters, he never became a member of the Academy in Paris. In 1754 he is documented as having produced four works for the royal household, one of them a copy after a portrait by Maurice-

Quentin de la Tour. The limited evidence we have for Charlier as an artist leaves many major questions unanswered. Charlier signed only very few of his works, and a stylistic chronology of his work has so far proven impossible to establish. It may be that our view of his oeuvre as we see it today is not a true reflection of his achievements.

The body of work associated with Charlier's name is heterogeneous in style. This might just be due to the involvement of different hands but may also reflect the length of Charlier's active career, which could well have spanned up to seven decades. [2] In the present state of knowledge, it seems best to regard the entire group as work by Charlier. Some works attributed to Charlier might have been painted by his workshop (if one existed) and pupils. He was described as an eager teacher in 1776. Another candidate for some of these works could be Boucher's wife Marie-Jeanne (1716–1796), who was a miniature painter herself, or Pierre-Antoine Baudoin (1723–1769), also known for having reproduced compositions by Boucher. Marie-Jeanne Boucher's work is described in a way very similar to Charlier's in the sources. So far little extant work has been definitively linked with her name.

There are few works by Charlier that are securely documented. Early catalogues (Caylus, 1773; Blondel de Gagny, 1776; duc d'Aumont, 1782) for sales within the artist's lifetime mention many of his works and indicate their subject-matter. They refer to portraits ("*Madame de Gonteau assise dans son laboratoire*" in the Blondel de Gagny sale, 1776), bust-length figures of women, pastoral landscapes and even still lifes. We can assume that the attributions in these early, prestigious sale catalogues were correct. However, we cannot securely identify them with extant works.

Most of the works traditionally connected with Charlier's name are mythological and erotic scenes, usually based on compositions by or in the style of François Boucher. Some also copy works by Jean-Baptiste-Marie Pierre and Old Master paintings. What today is known of Charlier's work refers to Boucher so often and so openly that some working arrangement between the two artists must be assumed. Charlier might have been charged with reproducing Boucher's work in miniature in the same way that several printmakers did for the print market. It is not necessary to assume that Charlier was trained by Boucher, as has often been proposed.

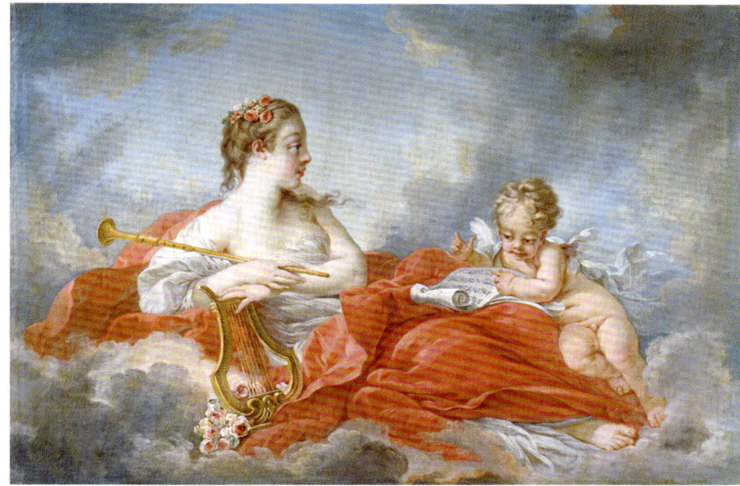

Fig. 1 François Boucher, workshop, *The Muse Clio*, oil on canvas, 101 × 147 cm, London, The Wallace Collection (P490)

Among the miniatures associated with Charlier's name this represents one of the most direct copies after a Boucher painting. Its model is a painting of *The Muse Clio* in the Wallace Collection (fig. 1), which was possibly painted as an overdoor for Mme de Pompadour. Another known version of Boucher's composition, sold in 2005, differs in certain details.[3] The miniature was obviously painted directly after the painting in the Wallace Collection as it follows the colours and composition closely – and it was evidently executed before the original canvas was enlarged. CMV

PROVENANCE: First catalogued in the Wallace Collection 1904

M67

12 Jacques Charlier (1706–1790)

Venus with Two Companions and Putti in the Clouds, c.1770

Vellum, 128 × 172 mm

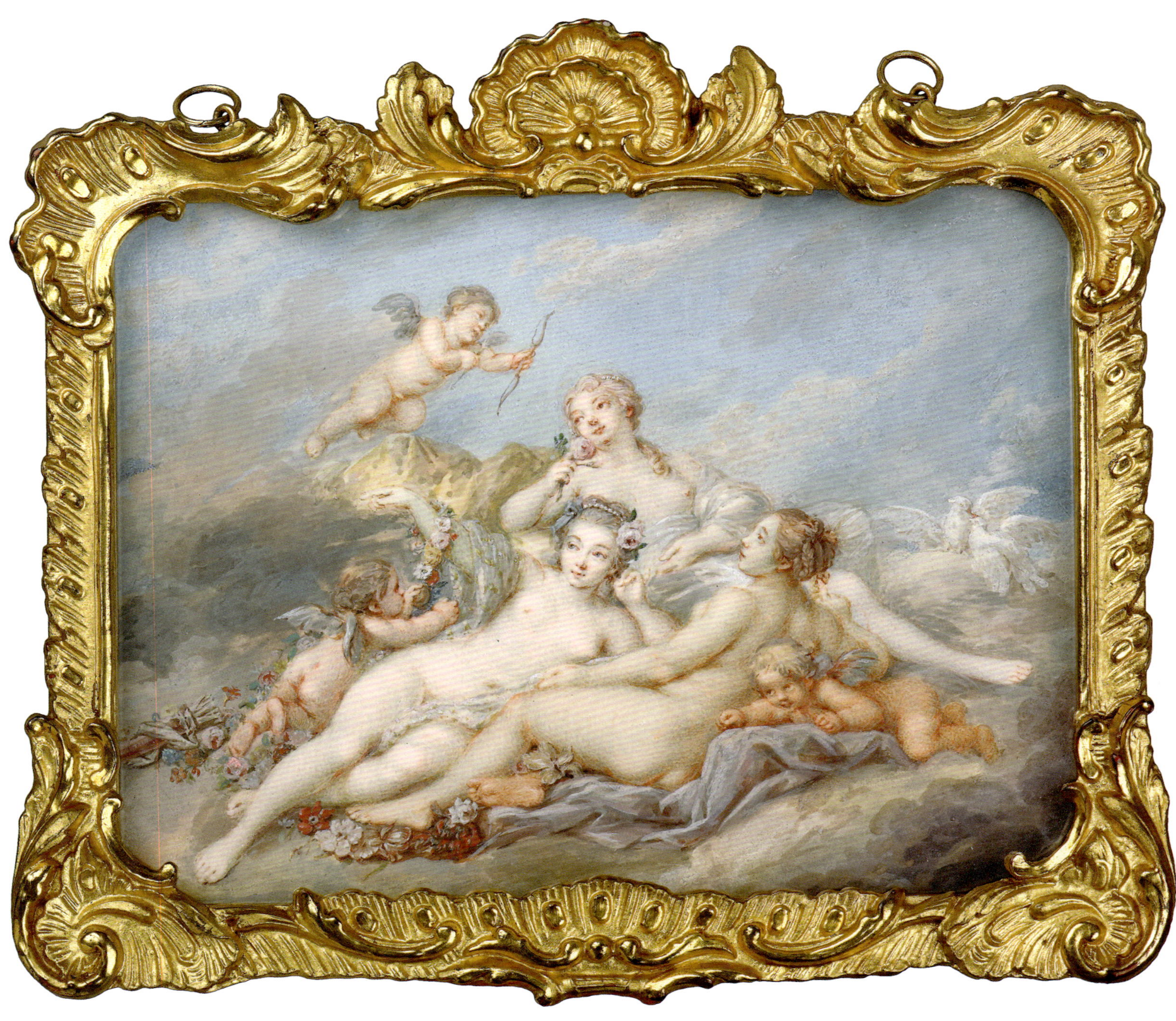

This miniature is one of a small number of larger miniatures on vellum by Charlier in the Wallace Collection. Its subject was formerly given as of nymphs and putti, but the doves in the background, the bow of the putto at the upper left and the flower garlands indicate that the main figure should be identified as Venus, accompanied by two members of her following.

While Charlier often copied the compositions of other painters literally (see no.11), he here combines in one miniature figures from several paintings by François Boucher. The starting point seems to have been Boucher's *Venus in the Forge of Vulcan* of 1757, now in the Louvre (fig.1). The reclining figure on the right and the woman in the background both appear, similarly spaced, in the background of the Paris painting, high up on the clouds. As in Charlier's miniature, the woman further to the left looks towards a putto (on the painting a small group of three winged children). In order to use this background group of Boucher's painting for the centre of his new composition, Charlier combined that group with two figures from Boucher's *Aurora and Cephalus*, in the J. Paul Getty Museum in Los Angeles. Charlier made the figure of Aurora the central feature, but reduced the drapery covering the lower body of the woman on Boucher's painting. The same figure appears in a miniature by Charlier formerly on the art market.[1] The putto immediately to the left of the woman in Charlier's miniature was also taken from Boucher's painting, although in reverse.

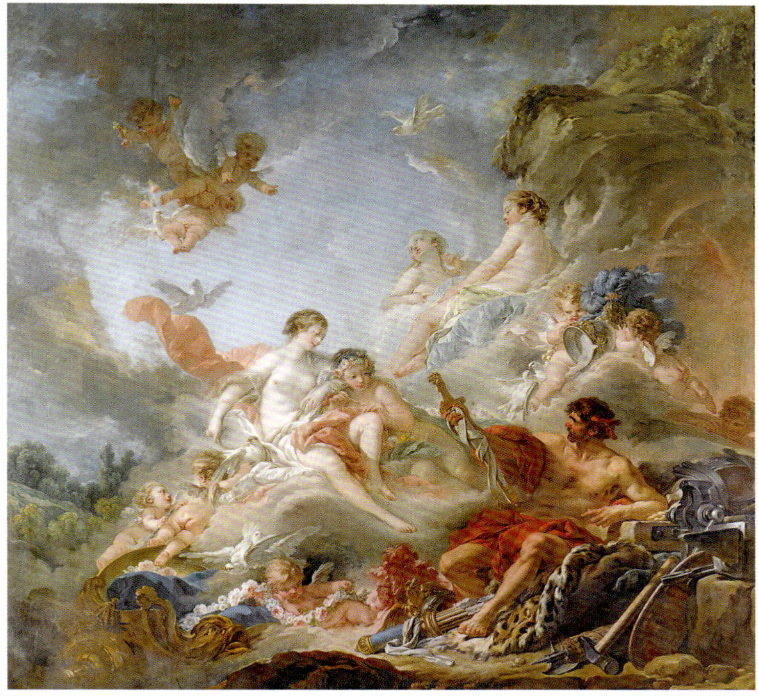

Fig.1 François Boucher, *Venus in the Forge of Vulcan*, 1757, oil on canvas, 320 x 320 cm, Paris, Musée du Louvre (inv.2707bis)

While Boucher's *Venus in the Forge of Vulcan* was painted in 1757 as a tapestry cartoon and afterwards kept at the Gobelins factory, *Aurora and Cephalus* was part of a series of six canvases painted in 1769 for the *financier* Jean-François Bergeret. As both paintings were used as models for the miniature, it must have been painted around 1769 or later. While *Venus in the Forge of Vulcan* was accessible in the reserves of the Gobelins, it might have been slightly more difficult for Charlier to have access to Bergeret's Parisian town house. It was probably easier for him to see it in Boucher's studio or use Boucher's own material, lending support to the idea that Charlier had some form of professional connection with Boucher. A date of around 1770 seems likely and fits with the restrained composition (which is much calmer than Boucher's paintings) and the reduced colour scheme of the miniature. CMV

PROVENANCE: First catalogued in the Wallace Collection 1904

M61

13 Jacques Charlier (1706–1790), after Pierre

Jupiter and Antiope, 1750s or 1760s

Ivory, 56 × 81 mm

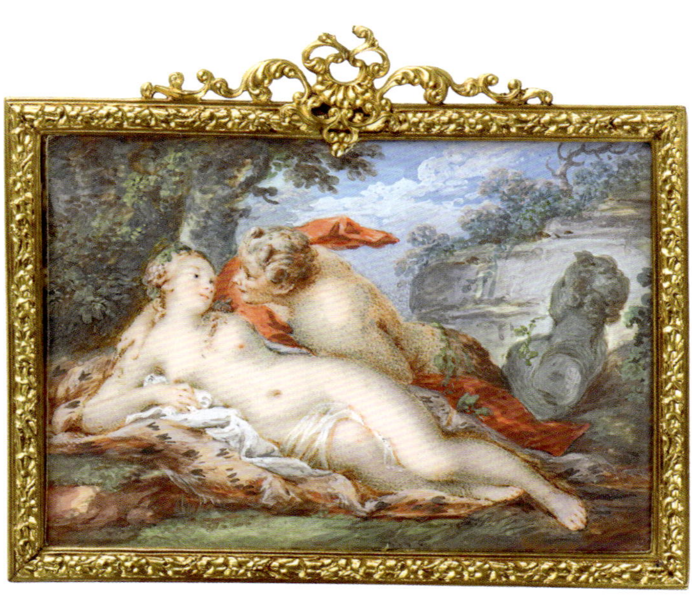

This miniature is copied from a painting by Jean-Baptiste-Marie Pierre (1714–1789) today in the Prado in Madrid (fig.1). Pierre's work, dated to the early 1750s on stylistic grounds, is paired with a painting of *Diana and Callisto*. Unfortunately, nothing is known about the provenance of the two paintings which could help to determine the date or earlier history of the miniature. The dimensions and composition of the two canvases in Madrid suggest that they were originally intended as overdoors – paintings which were hung above doorways, usually inserted into the decoration of the wall. The richly ornamented frames of Rococo overdoors often partly covered the corners of the canvases. Thus in Pierre's paintings the composition is concentrated in the centre of the canvas, leaving the corners empty. There is no doubt that Charlier worked from Pierre's original, because he followed its colours closely. He may, however, have seen the painting after it had been installed as part of a decorative scheme, since, while the central part with the two figures is copied literally from Pierre's model, the miniature differs considerably from the canvas in the upper corners, which may by then have been covered. The date of the model and the freer, sketchy style of the miniature both suggest a date in the 1750s or 1760s. A slightly embellished version, perhaps also by Charlier, was sold in 1975.[1] A miniature of *Danaë* by Charlier, also in the Wallace Collection (M139), is loosely based on Pierre's pendant painting in the Prado, *Diana and Callisto*, demonstrating that he must have had access to the pair.

Another miniature given to Charlier of a closely related subject (fig.2) is in turn based on Correggio's celebrated painting of *Venus, Cupid and a Satyr* in the Louvre, long regarded as depicting Jupiter and Antiope. Correggio's painting entered the French royal collections during the reign of Louis XIV and would thus have been accessible to the artist. Charlier took the figure of Venus and some elements of the composition from Correggio's painting, but reversed the figure. It is thus possible that in this case he based his miniature on an engraving. The two miniatures are close in style and might have been produced around the same time. In both cases serious doubts have been raised over their attribution and date. Given our limited knowledge of Charlier, it seems more cautious to also associate them with him and to explain stylistic differences by the difference in sources.

Together with Charlier's *Clio* (no.11) these two works exemplify a common function of miniatures – to reproduce well-known works by great painters, past or present, and translate them to a small scale. As this example shows, in eighteenth-century France there was a strong preference for works with an erotic character, to which the highly private, intimate character of miniatures is well suited. CMV

PROVENANCE: First catalogued in the Wallace Collection 1904

M62

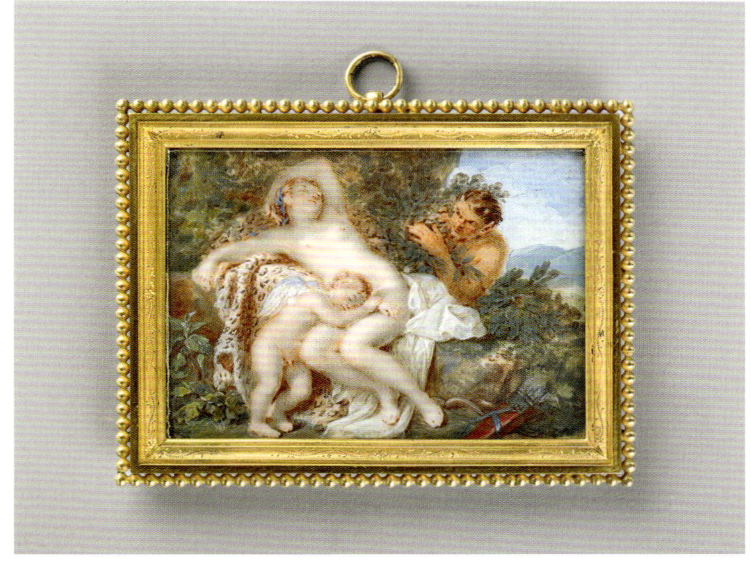

Fig.2 Jacques Charlier, *Venus, Cupid and a Satyr*, 1750s or 1760s, ivory, 59 × 83 mm (sight), London, The Wallace Collection (M77)

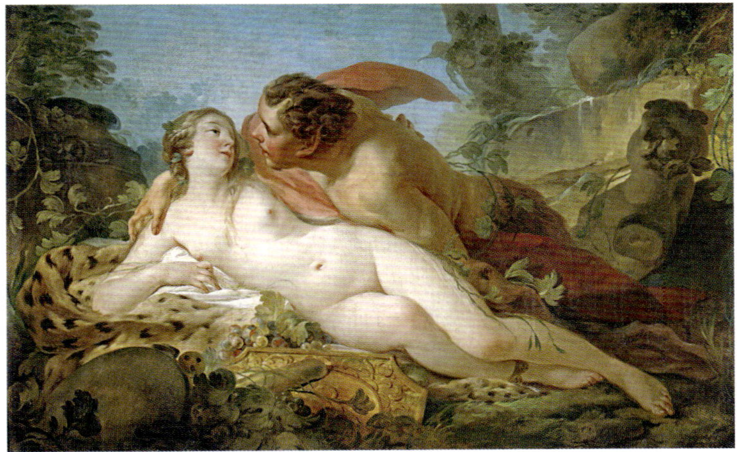

Fig.1 Jean-Baptiste-Marie Pierre, *Jupiter and Antiope*, c.1750–5, oil on canvas, 114 × 178 cm, Madrid, Museo Nacional del Prado (inv.3218)

14 Jacques Charlier (1706–1790)

Three Women Bathing, late 1770s or 1780s

Ivory, 59 × 83 mm

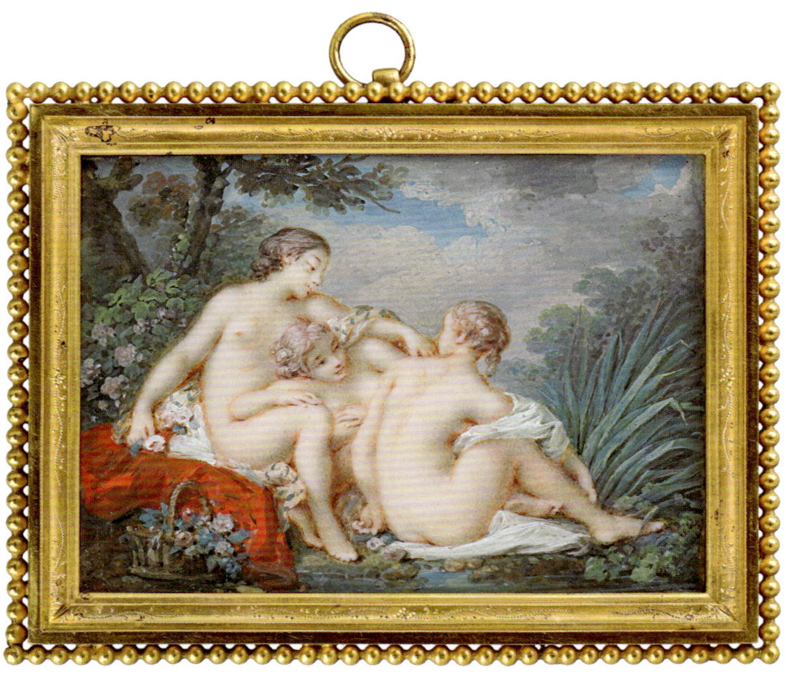

Among Charlier's earlier patrons were the households of King Louis XV and of Mme de Pompadour. Later in his career, during the early 1770s, he is recorded as having received important commissions from the leading Parisian collectors of the time. The prince de Conti commissioned twelve works from him to decorate a gold box in 1772. In 1773, Charlier worked on miniatures for a box in the dowry of the comtesse d'Arthois. The known addresses of Charlier were all in fashionable areas of Paris: in 1776, the artist was recorded as living in rue Richelieu; in 1777, in rue St-Honoré; in 1779, in rue Thérèse. When he died in 1790 he left a sizeable art collection.

However, the fact that on 20 October 1778 Charlier staged a sale of ninety of his own works indicates that he was experiencing financial difficulties at that time, probably due to changes in taste away from the Rococo. Another sale in the following year was a disaster. Charlier's output (as it has been traditionally understood) was so closely linked with the style of the mid century, and in particular with Boucher's work, that he was bound to meet difficulties as soon as the art of the Rococo began to fall out of favour. He died at the age of eighty-four, long after his model and major point of reference Boucher and in the first year of the French Revolution.

A productive career of more than sixty years leaves considerable space for stylistic development, and it remains to be determined how Charlier's output changed after Boucher had died and his influence had diminished. It is certainly possible that some of the stylistic variations in his oeuvre, usually interpreted as differences between the master and his followers, might instead reflect Charlier's stylistic development and the widening gap between the dominant style of the period and his own personal style.

This miniature is probably an example of Charlier's later work. The position of all three figures in a shallow front plane, the triangular composition and the very pale colour scheme all fit within the framework of developed Neoclassicism. While the figures are based on Boucher, they have lost his fluency of touch and Baroque force and seem closer to works by Louis-Jean-François Lagrénée (1724–1805). Charlier's *Diana and Nymphs Bathing* (fig.1) shares similar traits and must date from the same late period in the artist's career. CMV

PROVENANCE: First catalogued in the Wallace Collection 1904

M56

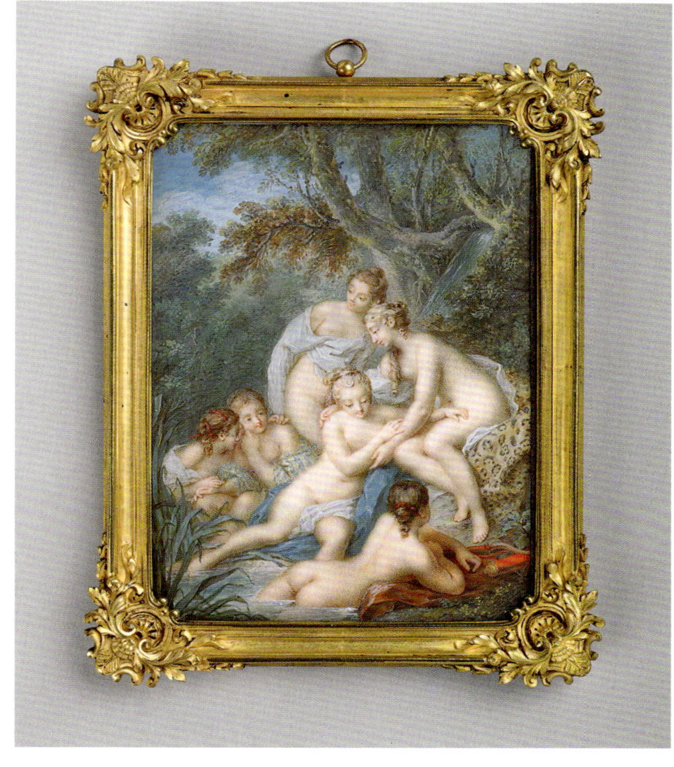

Fig.1 Jacques Charlier, *Diana and Nymphs Bathing*, late 1770s or 1780s, gouache on ivory, 14.9 × 11.1 cm (sight), London, The Wallace Collection (M51)

15 Louis-Nicolas van Blarenberghe (1716–1794)

Ten Scenes with Rural Amusements, c.1760

Vellum, 51 × 70 mm (top and bottom), 21 × 51 mm (front and back), 21 × 31 mm (left and right sides), 21 × 9 mm (four corner panels)

The box (gold and glass, 35 × 76 × 58 mm) probably Paris, 1765–8, re-used and added to by Jean Louis Leferre in 1819–38, probably before 1822

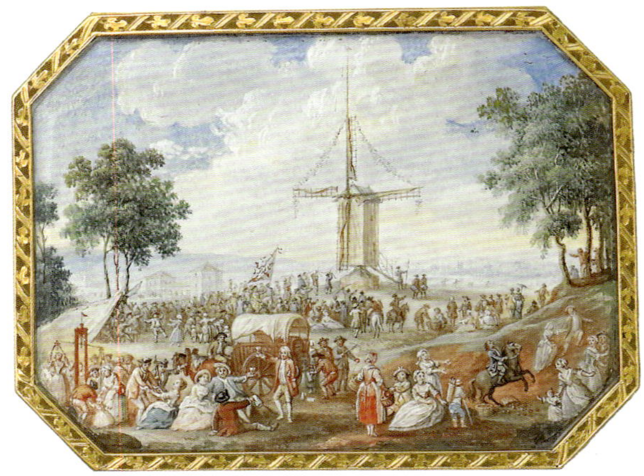

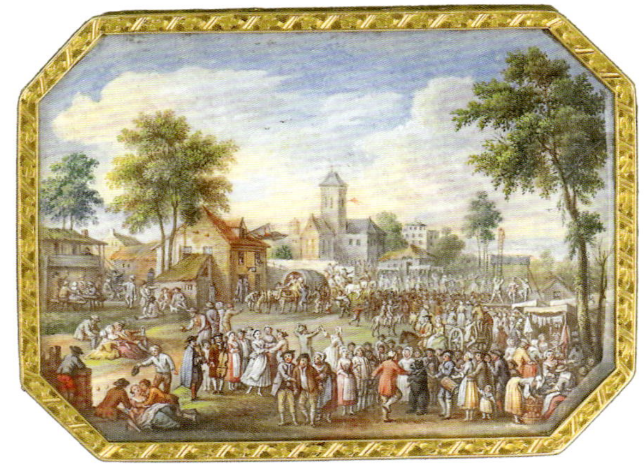

Eighteenth-century gold boxes were often decorated with miniatures on enamel or vellum. The most famous and refined French eighteenth-century artists producing gouache miniatures to be set into gold boxes were Louis-Nicolas and Henri-Joseph van Blarenberghe.[1] The Van Blarenberghe family originated in Lille, where the first known painter of that name, Hendrick, worked from around 1680. Lille had been conquered by Louis XIV only in 1668, and a strong Flemish tradition survived well into the eighteenth century. The Van Blarenberghes were members of the local guild of painters. In Paris during the eighteenth century there was a strong fashion for Netherlandish paintings and for works in a Netherlandish style, among both collectors and artists. When Louis-Nicolas moved to the capital in 1751, the first member of the family to do so, he was particularly well placed to build a career there because – like Antoine Watteau and Jean-Baptiste Pater before him – his family came from a largely Flemish tradition but were equally adapted to French mainstream culture. Louis-Nicolas and his son successfully turned their provincial background at the northern borders of France to their advantage, and their distinctive style led to success. Miniature painters in Paris were mostly foreign, principally Swiss or Swedish, or sometimes German, while the Italian Rosalba Carriera had been very well received during her visit to the city. Louis-Nicolas and Henri-Joseph van Blarenberghe joined the ranks of the most fashionable miniature painters of the period. Today, they are particularly famous for their miniatures incorporated into gold boxes, but it must be stressed that most of their output consisted of independent works.[2] The greatest nineteenth-century collectors of eighteenth-century art – such as the Rothschilds and the Hertfords – were particularly attracted by their intricate, exquisite works mounted in gold boxes, which often boasted impressive provenances.

It is difficult to make attributions to individual members of the Van Blarenberghe family. While Hendrick (1646–1712) and his

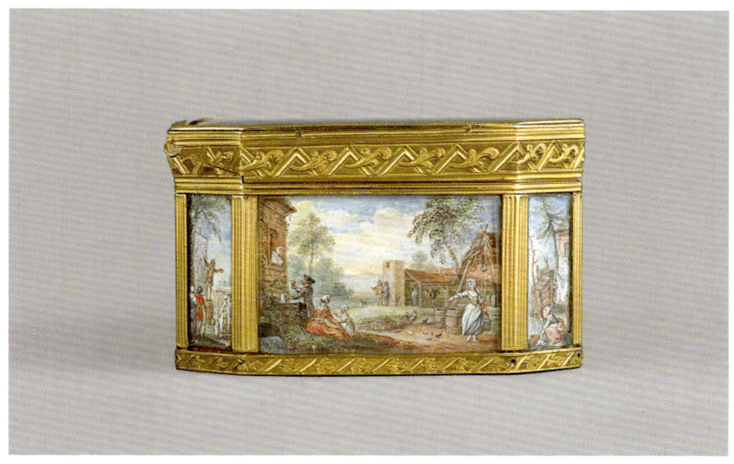

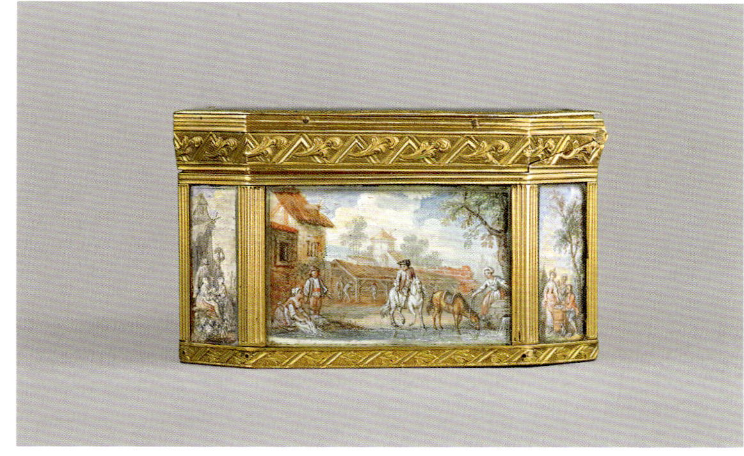

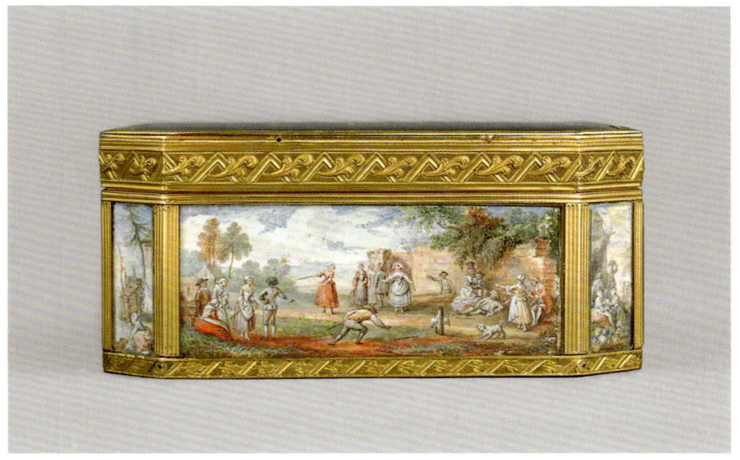

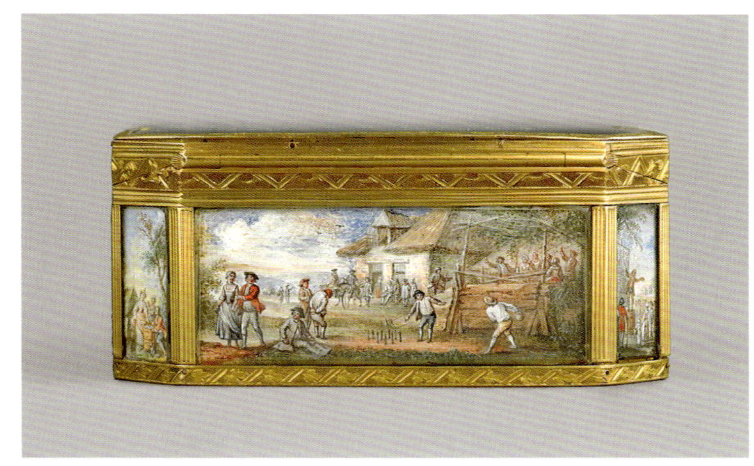

son Jacques-Guillaume (1661–1742) are distinctive in their styles (and artistically less important), it has always been particularly difficult to distinguish between the works of Louis-Nicolas and his son Henri-Joseph, who worked in similar styles and both signed works with their last name only. Recent research has, however, helped considerably in identifying their respective oeuvres. Further confusion had stemmed from the fact that Henri-Joseph repeatedly used the birth date of an older brother of the same name to further his career. Since it has now been established that he was born in 1750 and not in 1741, it is certain that signed and dated works by 'Van Blarenberghe' from before 1769 must be by Louis-Nicolas. In 1778 Louis-Nicolas was commissioned by Louis XVI to paint a series of battle scenes – which survive in Versailles – on which he worked until 1790. During that time he was officially not allowed to paint for other patrons. Whilst it is not clear whether he strictly obeyed this rule, his output beyond the series of battle paintings for the King can only have been minimal. From 1778 onwards, signed works by 'Van Blarenberghe' are thus likely to be by Henri-Joseph.[3]

Louis Nicolas's series of ten miniatures for this gold box features two large landscapes on its lid and base with eight smaller depictions of landscapes with scenes of soldiers and games. The miniatures on the lid and base feature detailed renderings of country fairs with a variety of attractions. The most obvious inspiration for the two larger miniatures are the landscapes of Jan Brueghel the Elder (1568–1625). Louis Nicolas might also have drawn inspiration from the earlier work of the Flemish artist Hans Bol (1534–1593), who specialized in detailed landscapes in watercolours on vellum. While Brueghel provided a stylistically more up-to-date source, Hans Bol might aptly have served as a reference point because he used the same medium, adopted a similar, powdery colour-scheme and produced exquisite small-scale works, created for more intimate contexts. Bol's *Village Fair with Church and Castle* of 1586 in Dresden (fig.1) might serve as an

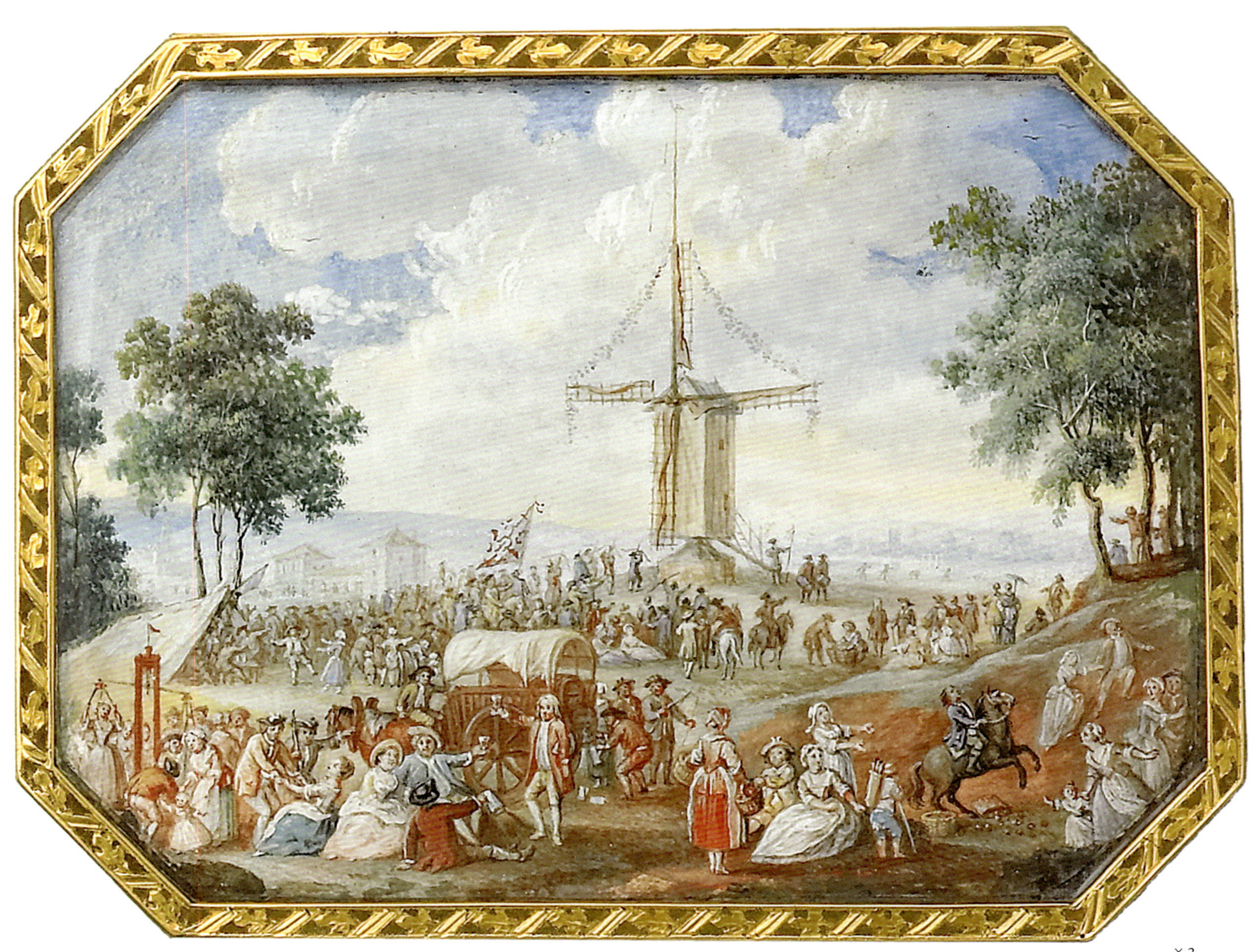

× 3

example of the type of work which was adapted and modernized by the Van Blarenberghes, using their knowledge of later Flemish and French landscape painting. The eight smaller miniatures around the body of the box, however, strike a very different note. They are much more French and contemporary in character, painted in the tradition of Pater and Lancret. Even the two large landscapes with fairs take many distinctive elements from depictions of country fairs by Watteau and his followers from the early 1710s.

The *Village Fair* on the bottom of the box is almost identical to a miniature in Paris (fig.2) which is signed and dated 1762. It provides the best available indication of a date for the ten miniatures in this gold box. Numerous similar scenes exist in Louis-Nicolas's oeuvre, but the Parisian miniature is the earliest dated example.[4] It seems likely that the ten miniatures of this box are also among the artist's earlier scenes of country fairs and amusements.

Van Blarenberghe's miniatures on vellum are mounted under glass in a gold octagonal snuff box *à cage* with vertical walls. The miniatures were either at one point removed or might not even have been originally mounted in this box. It is in fact possible that the box, which in its present shape dates from the early nineteenth century, might have been produced bespoke specifically for these miniatures. It might be the Van Blarenberghe gold box mentioned by the 4th Marquess as a possible purchase in 1822.[5] It is first securely recorded as part of the Wallace Collection when it was exhibited in Bethnal Green in 1872–5. CMV

PROVENANCE: Possibly 4th Marquess of Hertford; first certainly recorded at Bethnal Green (1872–5), no.1967

G36

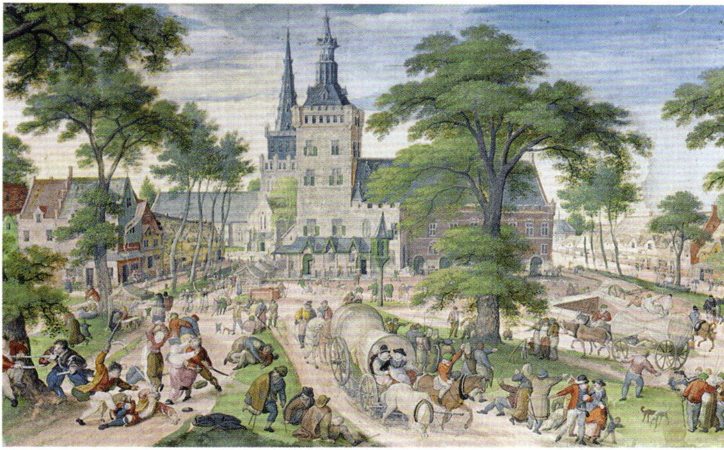

Fig.1 Hans Bol, *Village Fair with Church and Castle*, signed and dated 1586, vellum on oak, 14 x 21 cm, Dresden, Gemäldegalerie Alte Meister (inv.823)

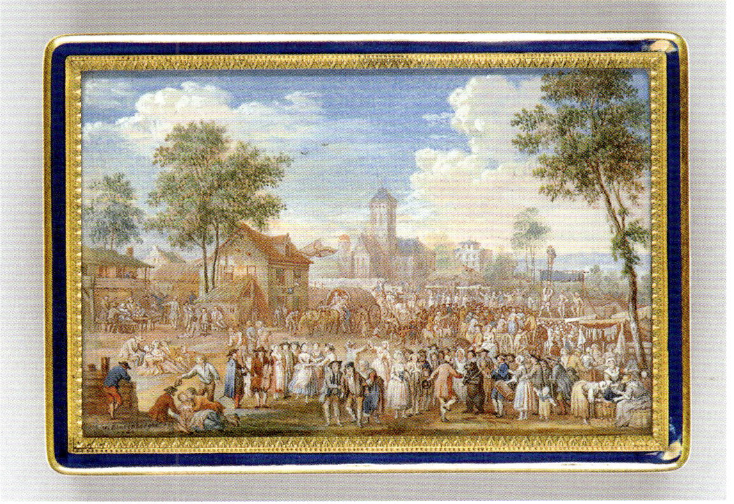

Fig.2 Louis Nicolas van Blarenberghe, *Village Fair with Performing Bear*, 1762, paper, 56 x 82 mm, on gold box by Adrien Vachette, *c.*1798–1809, Paris, Musée des Arts Décoratifs (inv.26619)

16 Louis-Nicolas van Blarenberghe (1716–1794)

The Fair of St-Germain, 1763

Vellum, 60 × 80 mm
Signed and dated (on beam on the left): *v. Blarenberghe/ 1763*

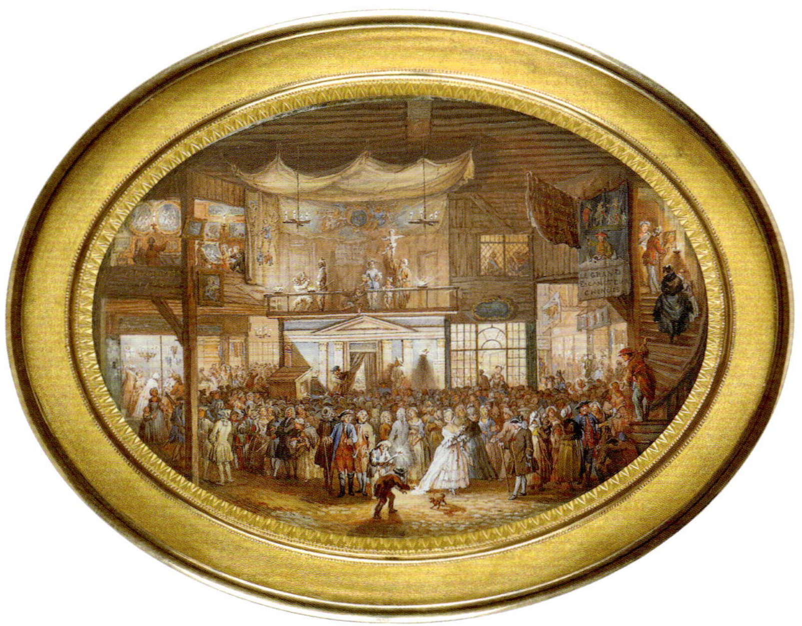

Louis-Nicolas van Blarenberghe's *Fair of St-Germain* is one of the painter's masterworks, and ranks amongst the most fascinating images of life in eighteenth-century Paris. Its shape and size suggest that it was originally mounted in the lid or bottom of an oval gold box. In 1858, it was recorded as set into a rectangular tortoiseshell box, but this was probably a subsequent rather than the original use of the miniature. In Van Blarenberghe's oeuvre oval miniatures are usually set into boxes of the same shape (see no.17). That the miniature was reused and later framed as an independent work testifies to its extraordinary quality, and its attractiveness to later collectors.

The fair of St-Germain, held annually in February and March, was one of the oldest and most popular fairs in Paris.[1] From the sixteenth century, it was situated between St-Sulpice and the Abbey of St-Germain-des-Prés in what is today the 6th *arrondissement.* A fair had taken place regularly in this area since the twelfth century. The annual fair was housed in semi-permanent buildings on a designated site where textiles, paintings and other fashionable and luxury goods were among the items on sale. It developed into a centre for the theatre and was crucial in the development of the Commedia dell'arte and other forms of popular theatre. In his miniature, Van Blarenberghe shows different stalls and structures within one large interior. Italian actors on the central balcony promote the performance which is about to begin in the theatre on the ground floor. The theatre is surrounded by all kinds of stalls. On the upper level on the left, several customers visit a picture dealer. Street signs advertise shops and theatre performances. Artificial lighting fuses the scene into one magical image of entertainment.

A great fire destroyed the fair's installations during the night of 16 March 1762, the year before Van Blarenberghe painted the miniature. Rebuilding started in late 1762, and by 3 February 1763 a first theatre performance was given. Work was carried out quickly enough not to cause a hiatus in the annual rhythm of the fairs held in early spring. It has in the past been suggested that Van Blarenberghe's miniature commemorates the old fair architecture but it is much more likely that it celebrates the opening of the fair in its new buildings in February 1763. It is impossible to establish the exact location of the scene using plans of the fair, and it is doubtful whether a precise location was actually intended. The miniature seems to be an idealized, condensed depiction of a fair very much in keeping with Louis-Nicolas's village fairs and *fêtes galantes*.

The miniature can today be securely attributed to Louis-Nicolas van Blarenberghe. His son Henri-Joseph, who worked in a similar style, was born only in 1750 and was thus too young to be the author of this miniature in 1763. Very few miniatures of theatre scenes and public entertainment can be securely attributed to Louis-Nicolas. Several more were painted when he apparently worked with his son between 1769 and 1778, but they constitute a small fraction of their overall output and are remarkably rare.[2] *The Fair of Saint-Germain* is the masterpiece of the genre. CMV

PROVENANCE: Possibly Daugny sale, Paris, 10 March 1858, lot 204; certainly Sampayo; Allègre sale, Paris, 16 May 1872, lot 254, bought Mannheim for Sir Richard Wallace, 30,100 fr.

M17

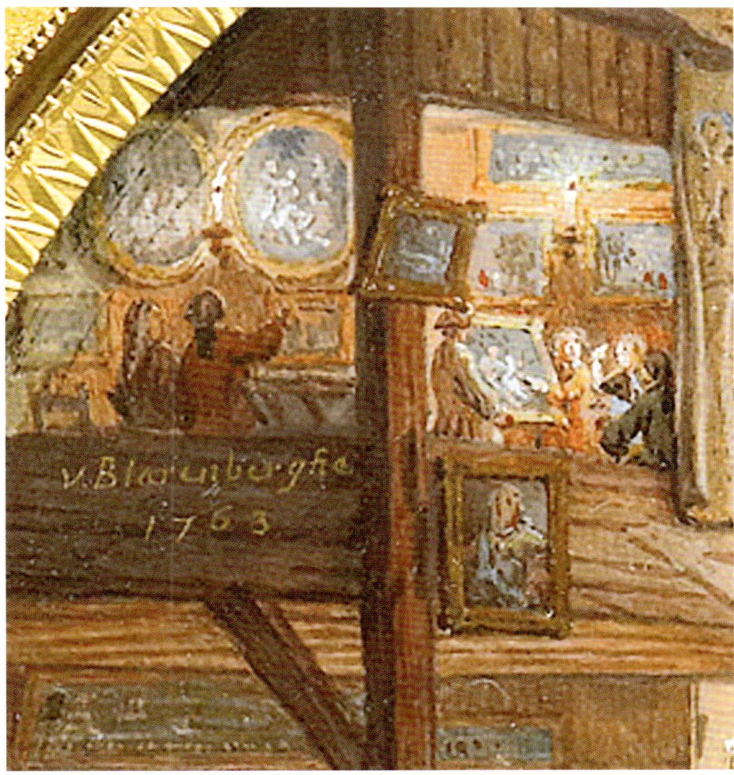

Detail of picture dealer's gallery and artist's signature

17 Louis-Nicolas van Blarenberghe (1716–1794)

Six Genre Scenes, 1767

Vellum, 44 × 64 mm (top), 42 × 62 mm (bottom), 18 × 32 mm (back), 16 × 32 mm (front), 16 × 30 mm (left and right)

The snuff box (gold and glass, 37 × 80 × 58 mm) by Henri Bodson, Paris, 1765–7

Signed and dated on lid: *v. Blarenberghe 1767*

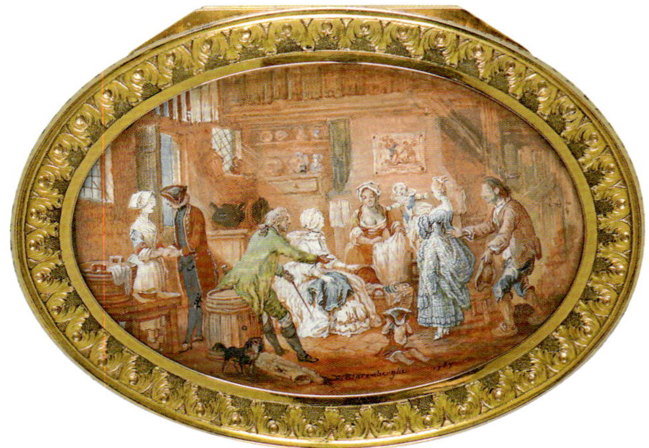

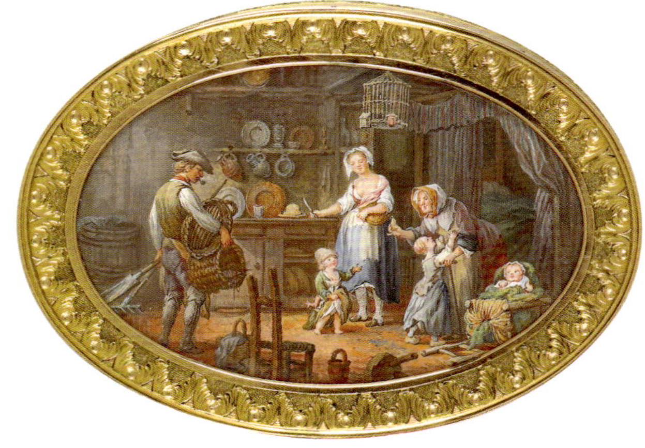

This oval gold box features six miniatures by Louis-Nicolas van Blarenberghe – two large ovals on the lid and bottom and four smaller miniatures around the body of the box. In contrast to many others, this box has not been altered and the miniature on the lid is signed and dated. The series of miniatures provides an idealized image of life in the countryside. The scene on the bottom shows a family in a humble but orderly interior, the father returning home from work, the mother cutting bread, and the grandmother giving a slice of bread to one of the three children. The room is depicted with an obvious delight in still-life elements taken from Netherlandish seventeenth-century works. Four scenes on the sides of the box show equally romanticized pleasures of country life: a young gallant brings flowers to a woman whose reputation is carefully guarded by a friend and an older woman, a man watches a woman ironing, children look into a peep-show presented by a Savoyard, and a man rests outside next to a woman spinning. These five scenes quite literally provide the basis for the most elaborate miniature on the lid of the box, in which an affluent family of city dwellers visit a family of peasants with a young child. This scene depicts the custom of farming out children to wetnurses in the countryside, a practice which had begun to arouse criticism around the time these miniatures were painted but remained relatively common for many years to come. Van Blarenberghe's miniature gives an entirely positive image of wetnursing. The happy and healthy environment of the farm benefits the baby from the wealthy family.

The genre scenes on the box do not seem to have exact models. They form part of a wider trend in French painting for moralizing rustic subjects, but, even in comparison with easel paintings, the subjects and style of Van Blarenberghe's scenes are very early

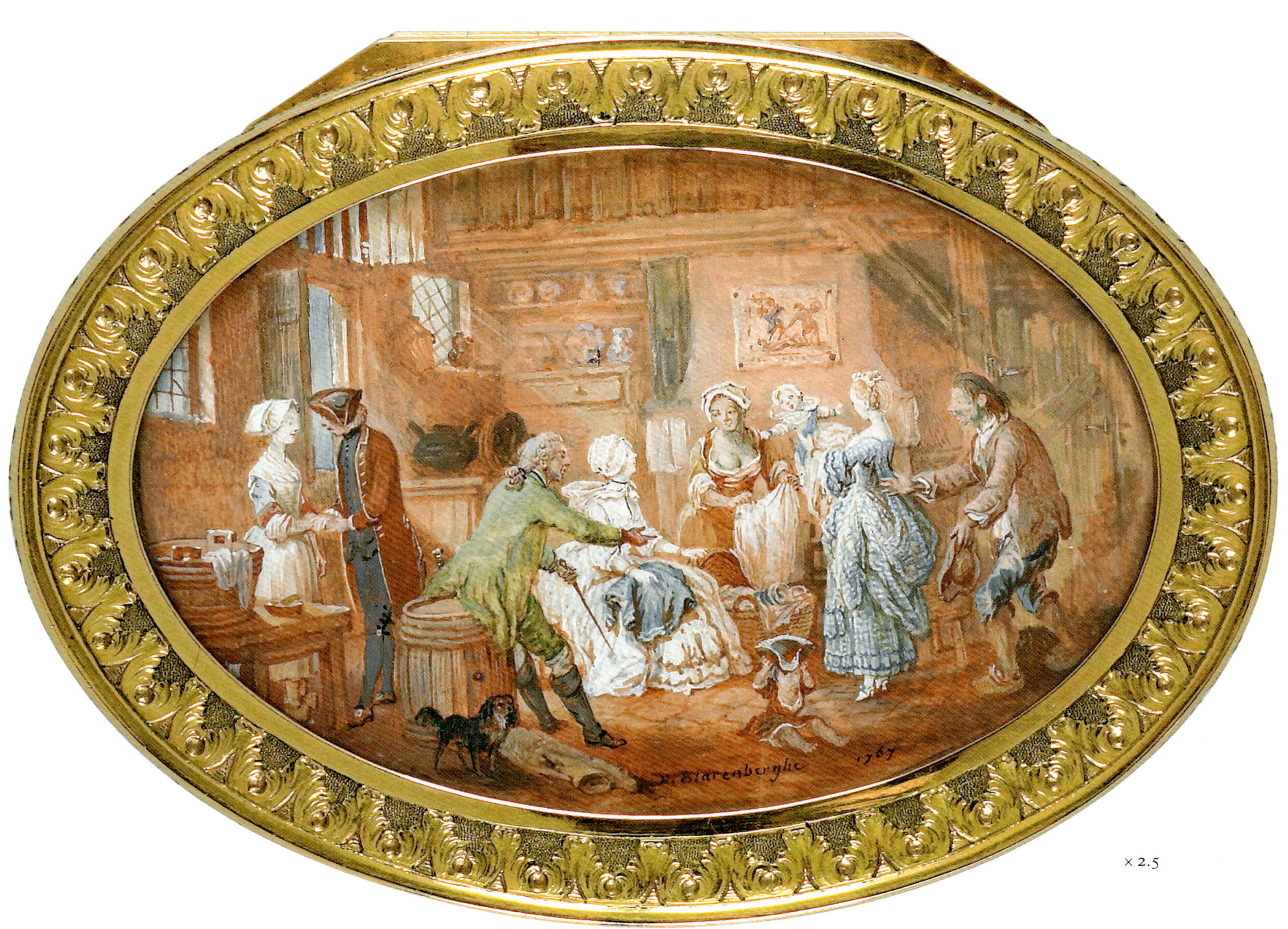

× 2.5

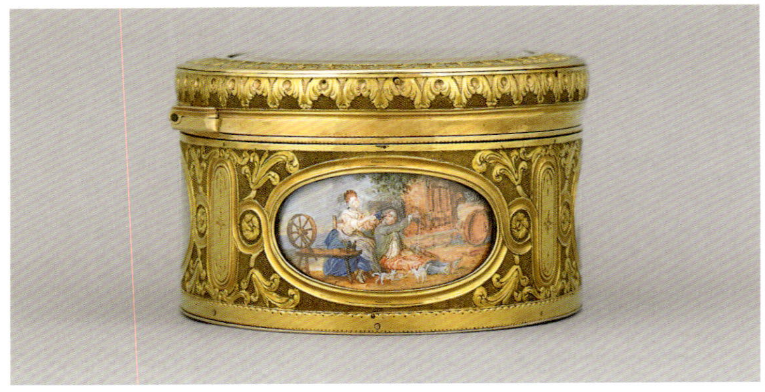

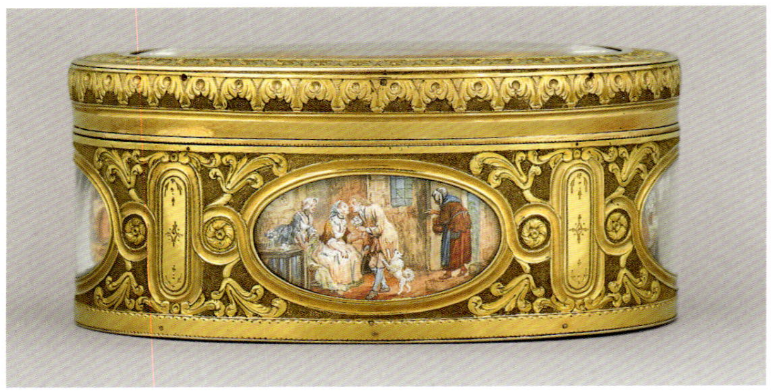

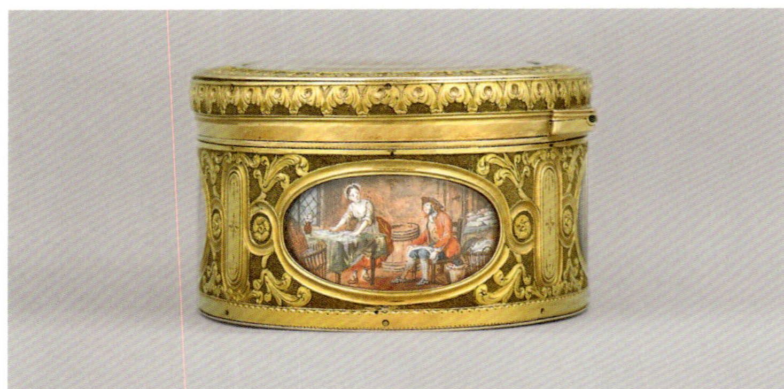

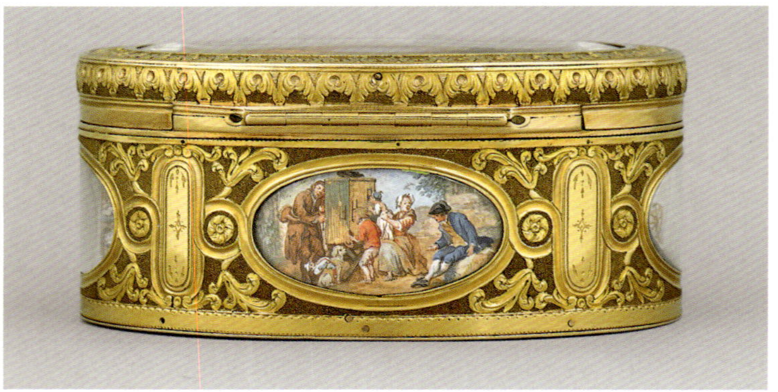

examples of the trend. He obviously refers to the early genre scenes of Jean-Baptiste Greuze, whose *L'Enfant gâté* (St Petersburg, Hermitage) and *Silence* (British Royal Collection) could have furnished many details of the two main miniatures and also the general style of the female figures. Both were exhibited at the Salon, *Silence* in 1759, *L'Enfant gâté* in 1765, where they enjoyed enormous popularity. Another source could have been Noël Hallé's *Education of the Poor* and *Education of the Rich* (private collection), both exhibited at the Salon of 1765, where several figures and the general setting of the humble interior are close to Van Blarenberghe's scenes. It seems most likely that Van Blarenberghe took the paintings at the Salon of 1765 as the starting point for his exploration of this relatively new subject. He is known to have produced a small number of similar genre scenes from at least 1762 – which makes his contribution to the rustic genre remarkably early[1] – but these earlier miniatures are more comic in character. Only with the gold box in the Wallace Collection does he seem to have incorporated the elevated moral tone pioneered by Greuze. No similar scenes by his son Henri-Joseph are known.

The recent attribution of these miniatures to Louis-Nicolas can be regarded as certain. Henri-Joseph, Louis-Nicolas's son (see no.18) worked in a very similar style, but he was born in 1750 and still an apprentice when the miniatures for this box were produced.
CMV

PROVENANCE: Daugny sale, Paris, 10 March 1858, probably lot 216; Allègre sale, Paris, 15 May 1872, lot 2, bought Mannheim for Sir Richard Wallace, 27,200 fr.

G42

18 Henri-Joseph van Blarenberghe (1750–1826)

Six Scenes of the Château de Romainville, 1782

Vellum, 53 × 74 mm (top and bottom), 20 × 49 mm (front and back), 20 × 45 mm (left and right)

The snuff box (gold and glass, 32 × 81 × 64 mm) by Pierre-François Drais, Paris, 1781–3

Signed and dated along bottom edge of lid: *van Blarenberghe/ 1782*

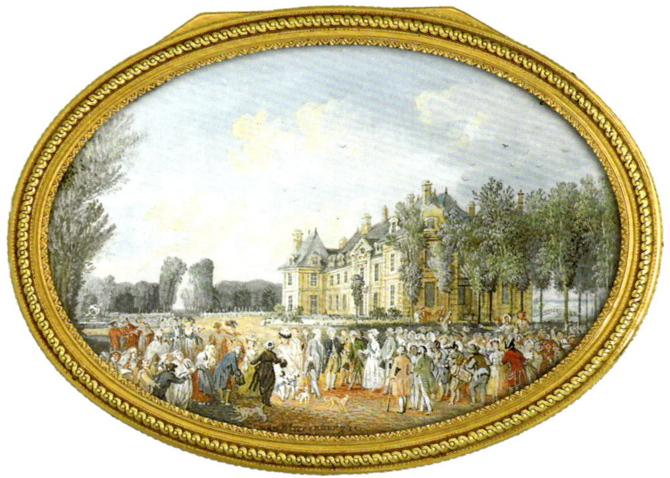

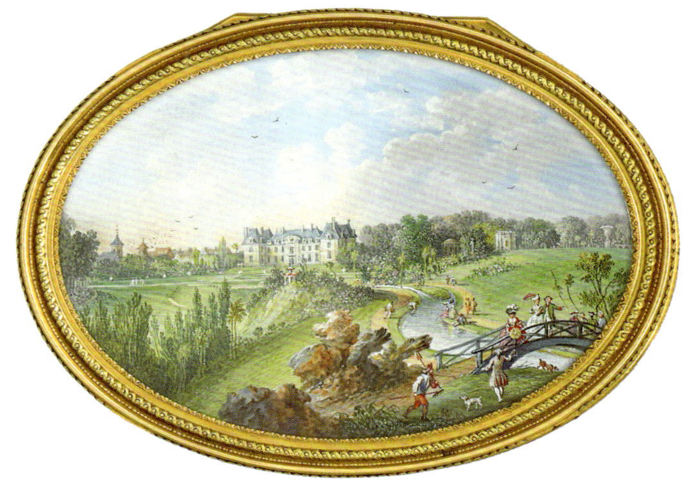

This gold box, of a type known as a *tabatière à cage*, encases under bevelled glass six miniatures painted by Henri-Joseph van Blarenberghe, son of Louis-Nicolas (see nos.15–17). Born in 1750, Henri-Joseph moved with his father to Paris in *c.*1755 and was presumably trained in his father's studio. He worked in tandem with his father until 1778, when Louis-Nicolas was commissioned by Louis XVI to paint a series of battle scenes and was forbidden to accept other commissions. Thus any miniature securely dated after 1778 (this set bears the date *1782*) can be attributed to Henri-Joseph.[1] When young he worked with his father, accompanying him during his travels as Peintre des ports et des côtes (painter of ports and coastlines). The Van Blarenberghes' *entrée* at court came with Henri-Joseph's appointment as drawing master to the Enfants de France in 1779. He also taught Mme Elisabeth and another of the King's sisters, Mme Clothilde. Henri-Joseph was in an ideal position to accept commissions from the court and the nobility.

The panels of miniature paintings depict the Château de Romainville and its gardens. The box and its miniatures must have been commissioned by the château's owner, the marquis de Ségur, who became Minister of War to Louis XVI in 1780. Romainville's gardens were redesigned in 1780 in the latest fashion. The 'Anglo-Chinese' type of landscaped garden, an alternative to formal gardens with their lines of topiary, became especially popular in France in the 1770s and 1780s. It was a studied imitation of nature in an English style, with carefully placed Roman temples, artificial lakes, Chinese pagodas and gently rolling hills. Indeed, it was through the depiction of the gardens that the château on the box could be finally identified in 1950, from Georges-Louis Le Rouge's *Les Jardins Anglo-Chinois* (Paris, 1774–89), a compendium of gardens in this new style with large illustrations and plans drawn by Le Rouge. Elements depicted in the miniatures have identifiable counterparts in the prints. Fashionable architectural features such as the Egyptian Statue, the Medici Vase, the Roman Temple, the Chinese Pagoda and the Octagonal Pavilion are depicted with such accuracy in the miniatures that their correspondence with the images in the published prints is unmistakeable.

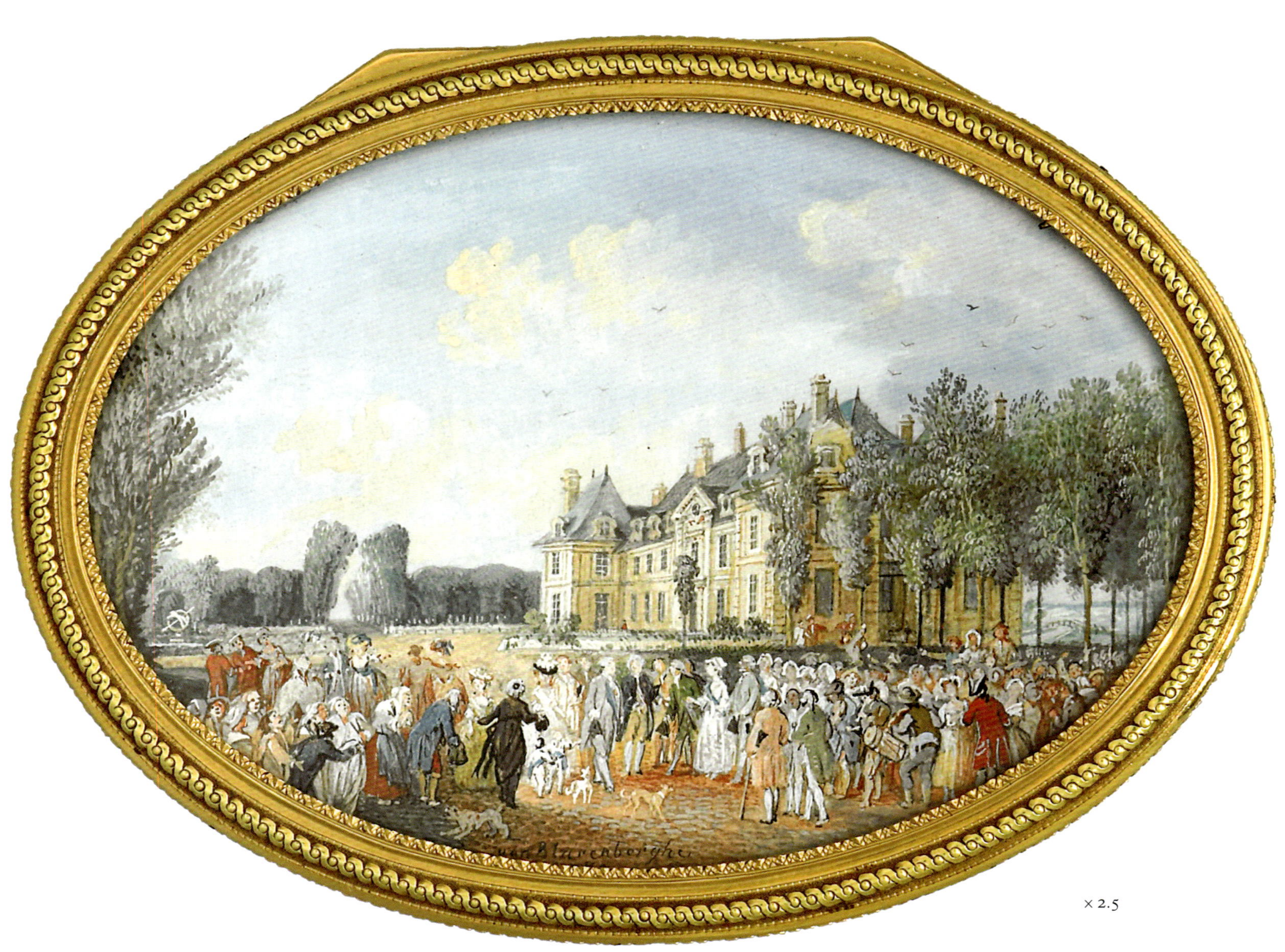

× 2.5

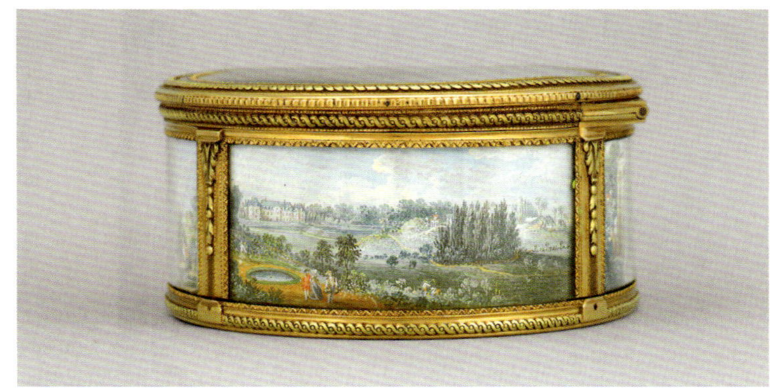

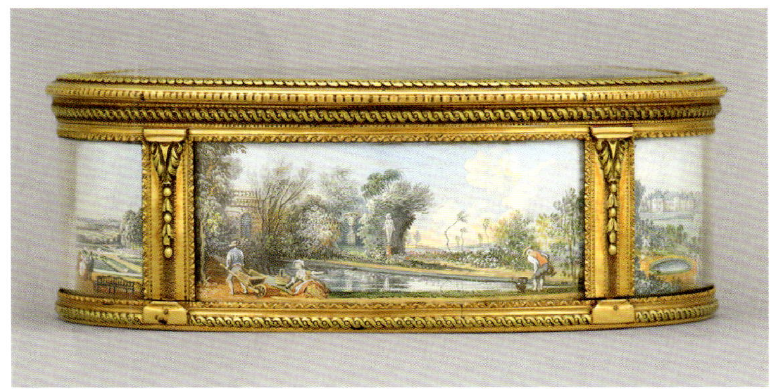

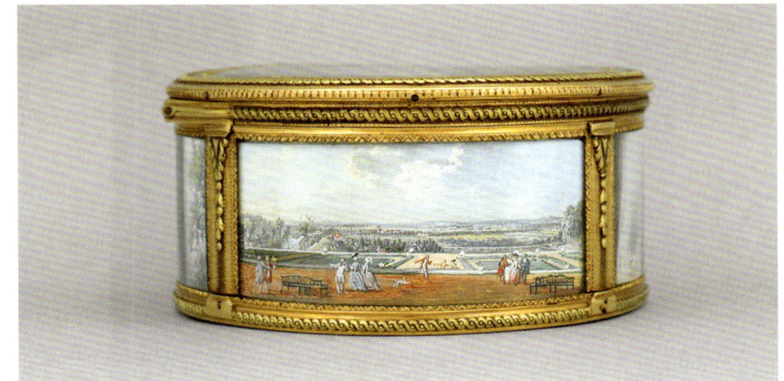

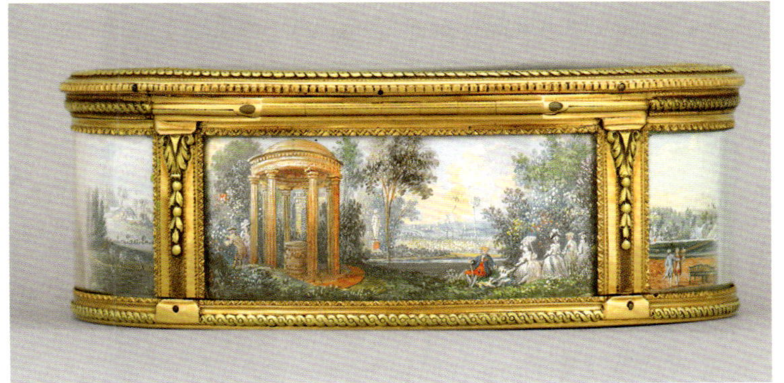

The marquis de Ségur himself appears on the lid, where we see the château behind a village festival known as the *rosière*. This ceremony, which came to epitomize certain eighteenth-century ideas of natural virtue and pastoral idylls, first became popular in 1766, when the author Mme de Genlis visited the village of Salency, Picardy, and 'discovered' its traditional festival, during which a village girl, her virtue determined by the village priest and the *seigneur*, would be crowned with a wreath of roses and presented with her dowry. Through pamphlets, plays and poetry, the idea became popular, imitation *rosières* being set up by nobles in their country estates.[2] The *rosière* at Romainville was initiated in 1774, after a celebrated court case further popularized the ceremony and the ideals behind it. In 1773, the lord of Salency, Charles-Laurent-Antoine Danré, refused to do his traditional duty and certify and crown the winning girl from three chosen by the villagers at Salency. The villagers were so outraged that they took him to the local judiciary, and then to the Parlement in Paris. He lost the case and the villagers, represented by two of the most famous lawyers of the day, vindicated their right to have their ceremony according to the wishes of their community and church. Imitation ceremonies abounded in the wake of this scandalous case, as nobles wished to dissociate themselves from the philosophical ideas thought to be embodied by Danré, and instead ally themselves to Rosseauist ideas of natural virtue and its reward by society.

The box thus represents the marquis as not only a man of fashion, in his modern garden, but also as a benevolent philanthropist. It is the only box in the Wallace Collection whose original patron is personally identified. In a social setting the box would have been viewed by all those who wished to partake of snuff and was a perfect way for the marquis to be seen by his peers. MJ

PROVENANCE: Baron Roger; Prince Anatole Demidoff sale, Paris, 16 January 1863, lot 31, bought by the 4th Marquess of Hertford, 11,000 fr.

G62

19 Niclas Lafrensen (1737–1807)

The Morning Toilet Interrupted, *c.*1780

Gouache on ivory, 68 mm diameter

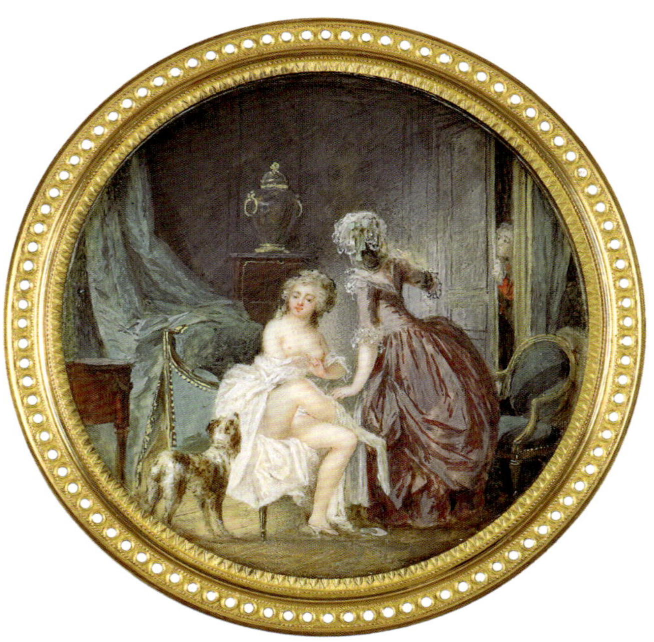

Niclas Lafrensen (fig.2) was one of numerous important Swedish artists who settled in Paris in the eighteenth century. He was born in 1737 in Stockholm, the son of a portrait and miniature painter of the same name. As a student he resided in the French capital from 1762, returning to Sweden in 1769. After five years he came back to Paris and stayed on until 1791, when the French Revolution forced him to go back to Stockholm. Lafrensen became successful as a painter of miniature portraits and of miniatures and larger gouaches of genre scenes, often openly erotic in character. The largest collections of his works are in the Nationalmuseum in Stockholm and in the Louvre. The Wallace Collection owns important genre scenes by the artist. Lafrensen followed a fashion set by Pierre-Antoine Baudouin (1723–1769) for stylish, erotic interior scenes, often in gouache. Lafrensen studied in Paris at the time when Baudouin had his greatest successes at the Salon, in particular with *Le Modèle honnête*, which was shown and widely commented upon at the Salon of 1769.[1]

Lafrensen's *Morning Toilet Interrupted* depicts an interior scene in a fashionable setting. An otherwise naked young woman wrapped in a towel after bathing is attended by a female servant. Both are interrupted by the lapdog which has just spotted a man peeping through the door. The servant has turned away from us to talk to the intruder and to cover her mistress from his view. The simple narrative can immediately be grasped and its titillating character is only slightly veiled. The miniature, meant to be held and seen from close up, plays with the voyeurism inferred in the story. While the young male intruder does not succeed in getting a glimpse of the woman's naked body, the observer of the miniature sees the entire scene.

The miniature forms a pair with another roundel with an erotic subject, *The Morning Conversation* (fig.1). Like its pendant it implies that we can see behind the scenes. While the intruder in *The Morning Toilet Interrupted* makes forbidden viewing part of the scene's storyline, we are here presented with a scene of female confidentiality, which is not meant to be seen yet is obviously arranged for the male viewer. This point is also made by the oval painting in the background, one of the many versions of Fragonard's *L'Amour en sentinelle,* in which Cupid is depicted as the guardian of secrets. Both miniatures are interesting for their rendering of luxurious Neoclassical Parisian interiors with up-to-date furniture in both the Transition and Louis XVI styles.

The two roundels take their erotic character, the obvious storyline, the picturesque disorder of the rooms and the Transition style from Baudoin, but the style of the objects and the coiffure suggest a date during Lafrensen's second stay in Paris, well into the period of Louis XVI, even though stylistically the chronology of Lafrensen's work is yet to be clearly established. His *La Soubrette confidente*, an etching of which by Gérard Vidal was published in 1782, is similar in style and has comparable objects depicted in an interior. Another work known through an etching published in 1779, *Le Curieux,* depicts a similar incident of male voyeurism: a man observes through a glass pane in a door a servant giving an enema to her mistress. These works might help to date the two Wallace Collection roundels to around 1780. Another version of *The Morning Toilet Interrupted* is in the Louvre.[2] Identical figures appear in an untraced gouache by Lafrensen, and with variants they reappear in several of his larger gouaches.[3] CMV

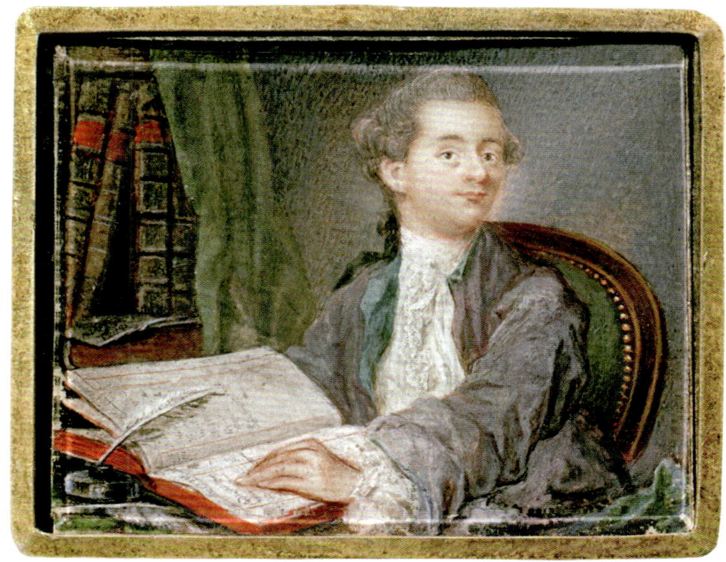

Fig.2 Niclas Lafrensen, *Self-portrait*, signed and dated 1768, watercolour and gouache on paper, Stockholm, Nationalmuseum (NMB 212)

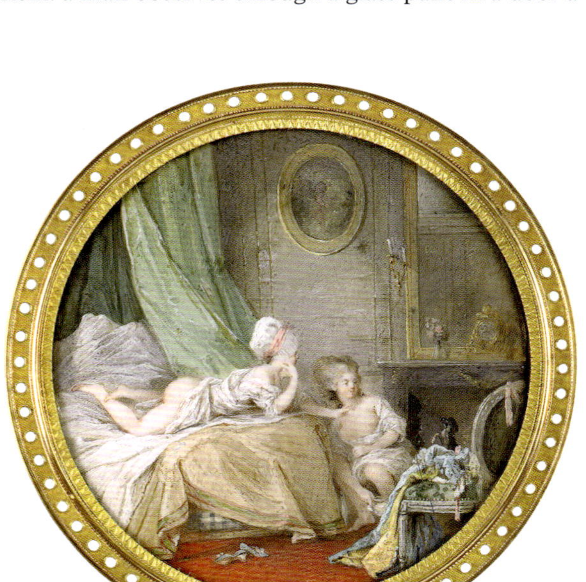

Fig.1 Niclas Lafrensen, *The Morning Conversation*, *c.*1780, gouache on ivory, 69 mm diameter, London, The Wallace Collection (M260)

PROVENANCE: First catalogued in the Wallace Collection 1904

M259

20 Niclas Lafrensen (1737–1807)

The Hunt Breakfast, late 1770s–early 1780s

Gouache on ivory, 69 mm diameter

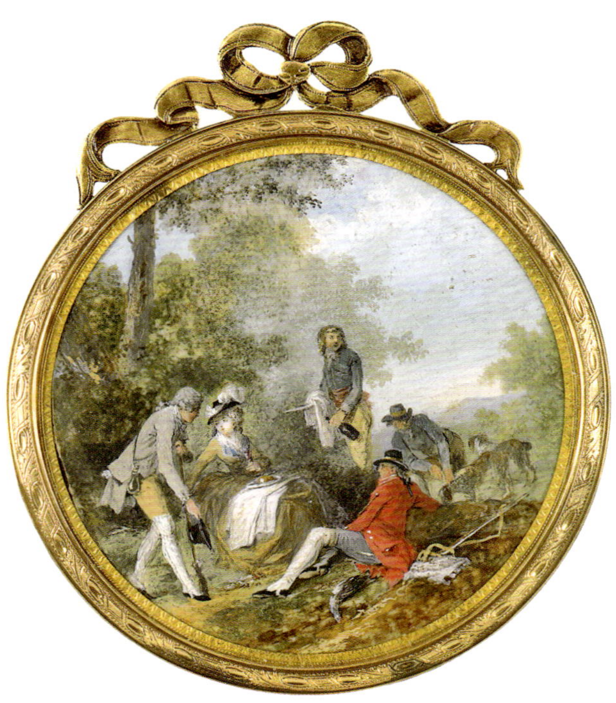

A fashionable hunting party is having a picnic in an extensive landscape, near a small clump of trees and bushes. A woman in a yellow dress forms the centre of the group. She is eating from a plate in her lap, a huntsman in a red jacket reclines on the floor next to her, another man with a rifle approaches her from the left. A servant and a keeper with a dog are visible in the background.

The topic of *The Hunt Breakfast* was introduced into the mainstream of French painting by Watteau with his painting in the Wallace Collection of *c.*1720–1 and by François Lemoyne's celebrated canvas in São Paulo of 1723.[1] Roughly twenty years earlier, the French artist Joseph Parrocel had painted a similar scene (today in the National Gallery, London).[2] Nicolas Lancret painted several examples of the subject (*c.*1736–8) which are particularly close to Lafrensen's miniature.[3] However, these paintings were already in the collection of the Prussian King Frederick II in Potsdam when Lafrensen's miniatures were painted. The link between Lafrensen and Lancret is Carle Van Loo's large-scale *Hunt Breakfast* which he painted as a young artist in 1737 for the Petits Apartements of Louis XV in Fontainebleau, under the strong influence of Lancret's renderings of the subject (fig.2).[4] Lafrensen took several elements directly from Van Loo – the central figure of a seated woman in yellow eating from a plate on her lap turning to a companion further on the left, the reclining huntsman in red, the standing servant, and also the overall spatial arrangement with a clump of trees behind the figures on the left, a wide view into the landscape sloping down on the right and a more distant group of figures further down that slope. Van Loo's painting was in Fontainebleau until 1793 and thus easily accessible during Lafrensen's Parisian years.

The Hunt Breakfast forms a pair with *The Walk in the Park* by the same artist (fig.1), which is marginally larger in diameter. The two roundels contrast the hunt with the more civilized nature of the park and also the two fashion styles associated with these different settings. In the centre of both scenes are figures of women flirting with their male companions. Lafrensen thus created variations on amorous pursuits in outdoor settings.

The Walk in the Park is directly based on much earlier paintings of *fêtes galantes* by Watteau and – again – Lancret. The seated woman covering her mouth with a fan is part of this tradition, as is the couple disappearing into the background on the left or the towering sculpture of a woman in antique dress. As in the *Hunt Breakfast*, Lafrensen has taken care to translate these traditional scenes into contemporary fashion and make them look and feel contemporary. A gouache by Lafrensen, also in the Wallace Collection, shows a standing woman in a fashionable long dress and a man sitting on the ground reaching out to her. It is similar both in its *fête galante* character and in the slim, angular style of the figures.

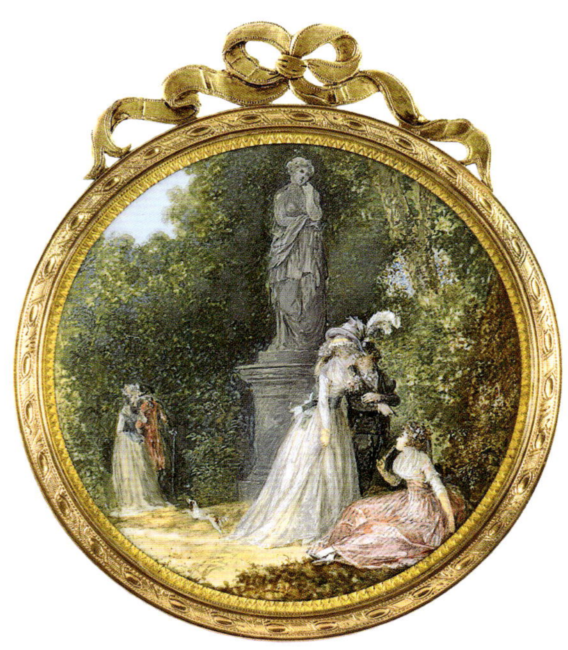

Fig. 1 Niclas Lafrensen, *The Walk in the Park*, late 1770s–early 1780s, ivory, 73 mm diameter, London, The Wallace Collection (M257)

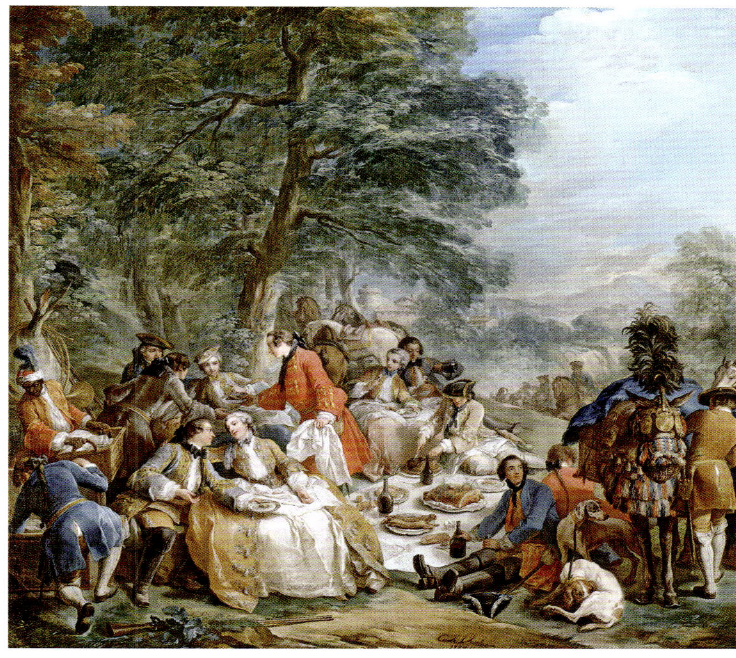

Fig. 2 Carle Van Loo, *The Hunting Breakfast*, oil on canvas, 220 x 250 cm, Paris, Musée du Louvre (inv.6279)

Both miniatures are inscribed on their backs with the name of the Parisian firm of Leferre Bijoutier in the rue St-Martin. The firm is documented in Paris between 1806 and 1860 and might have reframed the miniatures or even have sold the two works. CMV

PROVENANCE: Perhaps Vente X, Paris, 1860, 550 fr. (according to Bénézit); possibly recorded at Bethnal Green (1872–5), no.1693; first certainly catalogued in the Wallace Collection 1904

M258

21 Peter Adolf Hall (1739–1793)

The Painter's Family (Adelaïde Hall, the painter's wife, their daughter Lucie and Adelaïde's sister Victoire, Comtesse de la Serre), 1776

Gouache on ivory, 89 × 109 mm

Signed in the background, lower left: *hall 1776*

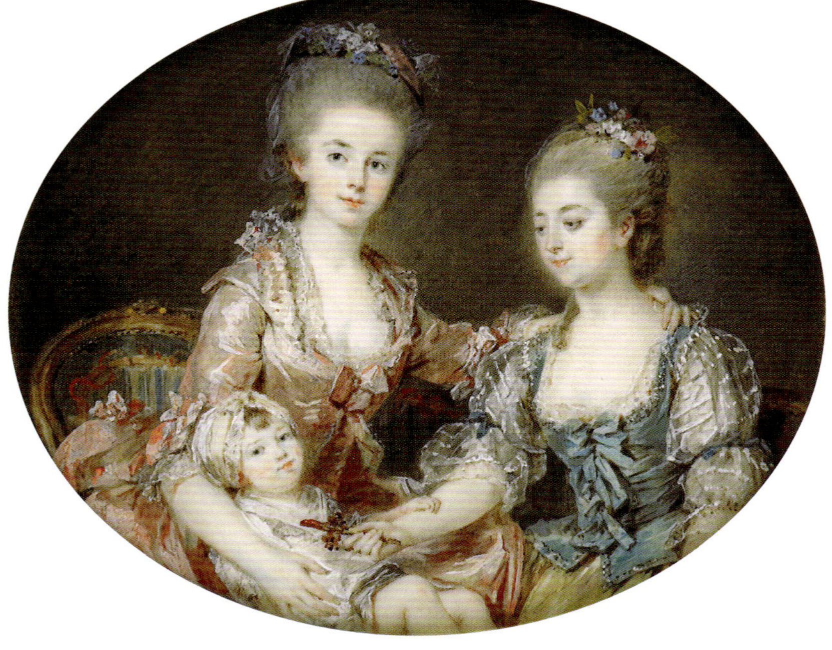

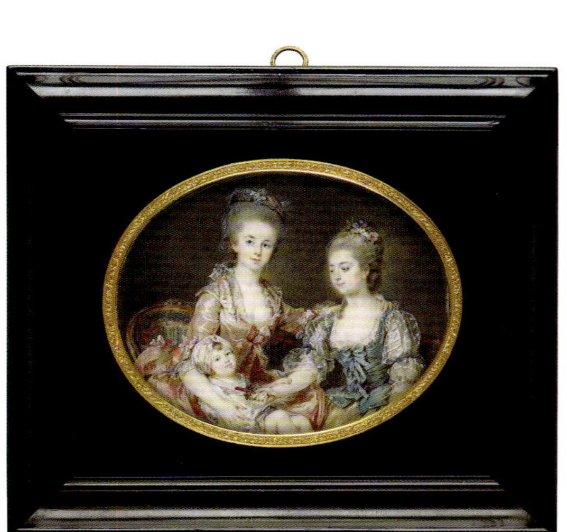

× 0.4

Peter Adolf Hall was born in Borås near Gothenburg in 1739. After studying in Uppsala he lived in Germany between 1755 and 1759, where he initially trained with the miniaturist Reichard in Hamburg and with Modestinus Eckardt the Elder (1684–1768), drawing teacher at the Academy of Fine Arts in Berlin. Hall then returned to Sweden and worked in the workshops of two of the leading artists in Stockholm, first with the French sculptor Pierre-Hubert Larchevêque, then with the pastel painter Gustav Lundberg. In 1766, he left Stockholm for Paris, joining an important group of Swedish artists in the French capital.

Immediately following his arrival in Paris, Hall began to paint portraits of the royal family. The first was a portrait of the Dauphin in 1767. This connection was probably established with the help of the Swedish-born painter Alexander Roslin, who became Hall's main mentor and supporter and also sometimes acted as an artistic model for Hall's miniatures. Hall was accepted as a candidate (*agréé*) for election to the Academy in 1769 but never tried to become a full member. As an *agréé* he could exhibit at the Salons, and almost immediately became the most celebrated Parisian miniature artist of his generation. A review of the Salon in the

Mémoires secretes of 1773, which singled him out among enamel painters (a sideline of his activities from 1771 onwards) for the close likeness of his portraits and his great skill in rendering skin and fabric, is a good illustration of Hall's critical success.

Hall also had a remarkably successful social career. In 1771 he married Adélaïde Gobin, with whom he had three daughters and a son. The family lived in the highly fashionable Place des Victoires in 1781. Because of his close ties with the French royal house Hall left Paris for Brussels in 1791, leaving behind his wife, from whom he had already been estranged for a while, and his family. He died in Liège in 1793. His daughter Adèle was also a painter and became a member of the Stockholm Academy in 1792.

Hall was one of the most important European miniature painters of the eighteenth century. He almost exclusively painted portraits, but also produced a small number of works in enamels, oils, pastels, large-scale gouaches and watercolours. Hall's fame was based on the animated and natural character of his portraits and on his brilliant, loose brushwork, using the more painterly qualities of contemporary easel paintings for traditionally more meticulous miniatures. Through this stylistic device, miniatures gained a new immediacy and a sketch-like character very much in keeping with the taste of the third quarter of the eighteenth century. The *Mercure de France* of 1769 described his work accordingly: "All his portraits are of a great beauty. They are treated in an entirely different manner from the one miniature painters usually employ … nothing restrained, nothing laborious; his brushstrokes are free and his style is as loose as that of a history painter."[1]

This portrait of the painter's wife, sister-in-law and daughter is often considered Hall's masterpiece. It shows his wife Adelaïde, née Gobin (1752–1832), holding probably their second daughter Lucie, born in 1774. Adelaïde's younger sister Marie-Victoire, the comtesse de la Serre, holds a rattle and teething stick for the child. Later portraits of Lucie in Stockholm (Nationalmuseum), Paris (fig.2) and in a private collection are known. The miniature in the Wallace Collection is one of the most brilliant examples of Hall's

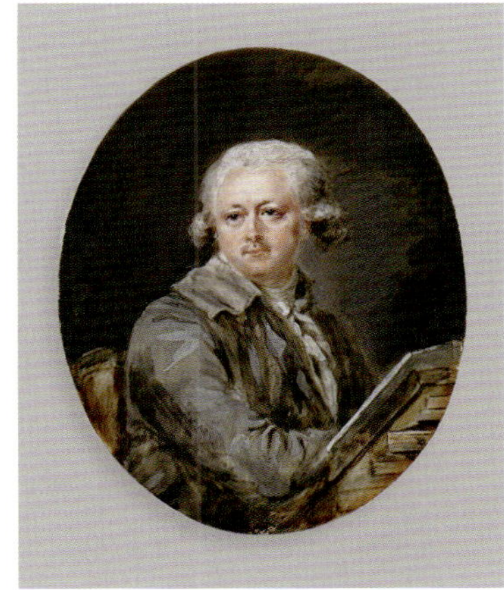

Fig.1 Peter Adolf Hall, *Self-portrait*, *c.*1778–9, 143 × 112 mm, Stockholm, Nationalmuseum (NMB123)

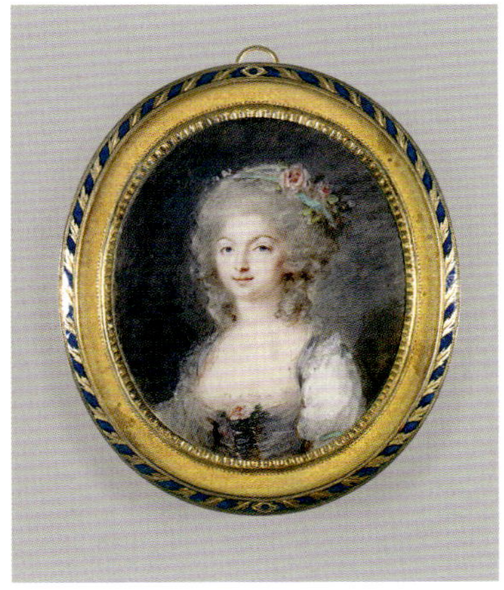

Fig.2 Peter Adolf Hall, *Lucie Hall*, *c.*1790, 55 × 46 mm, Paris, Musée Cognacq-Jay (V736)

portraiture, his most ambitious group portrait and an outstanding example of the free brushwork lauded by his contemporaries.

The importance of the piece is reflected in the high price of 19,000 francs that Richard Wallace paid for it when he bought the miniature in 1872.[2] Before then, it can be traced back through several Parisian nineteenth-century collections. In 1800, it was mentioned in the inventory of an unidentified collection in Paris containing twenty miniatures by Hall. A copy was with Phillips in 1987. The Wallace Collection preserves the most important group of Hall's works after the Nationalmuseum in Stockholm and the Louvre. CMV

PROVENANCE: Daniel Saint sale, Paris, 7 May 1846, lot 326; Daugny sale, Paris, 10 March 1858, lot 200; Allègre sale, Paris, 16 May 1872, lot 256), bought Mannheim for Sir Richard Wallace, 19,000 fr.

M186

22 Peter Adolf Hall (1739–1793)

*Adélaïde-Victorine Hall, The Artist's Daughter, c.*1785

Gouache on ivory, 107 × 91 mm

Signed in the background, lower right: *hall*

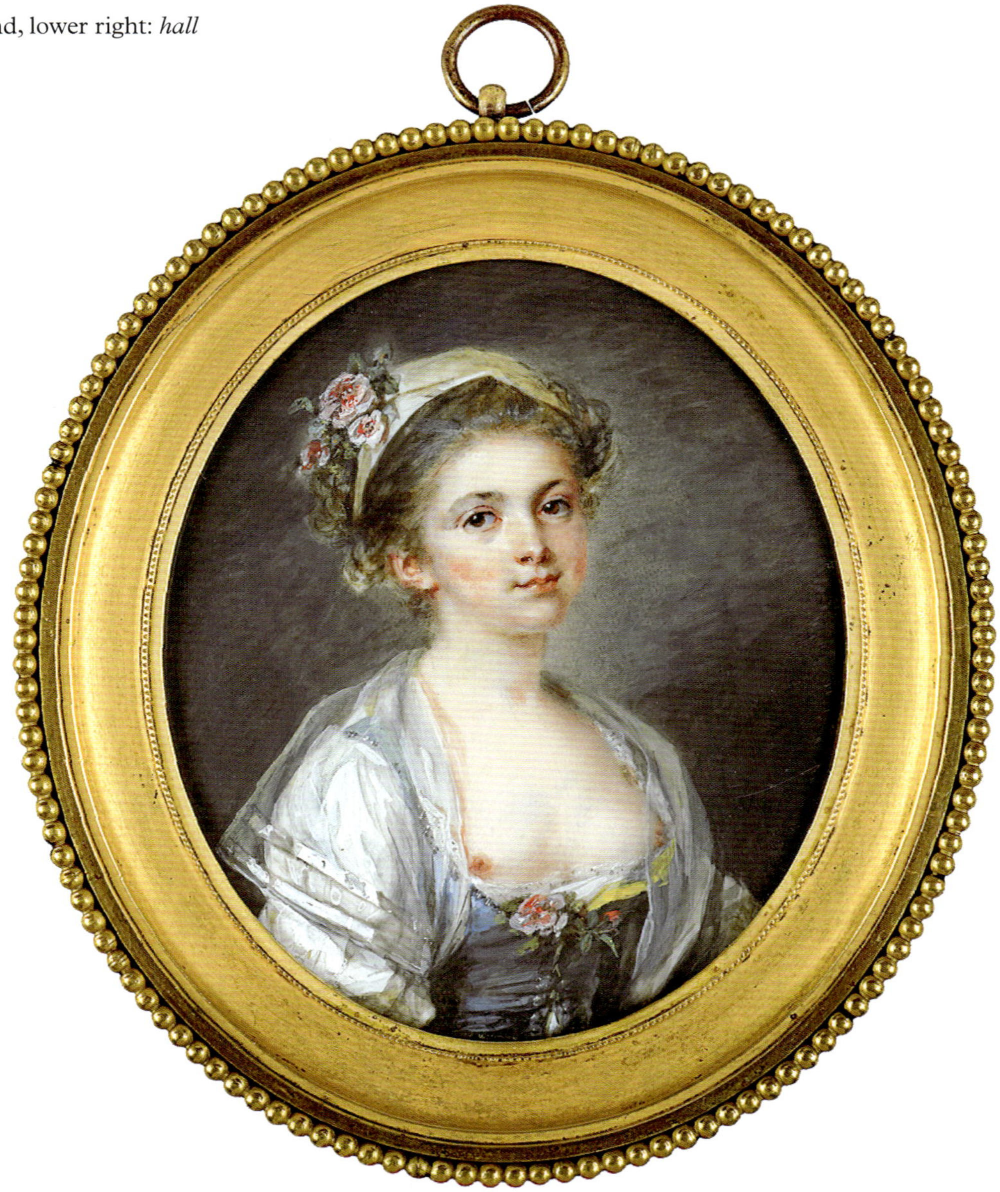

This miniature shows the artist's eldest child, Adélaïde-Victorine. A label on the back of the frame indicates that it was exhibited in the Paris Salon of 1785 (no.139). Hall was accepted by the Paris Academy as a candidate in 1769, giving him the right to exhibit at the annual Salons in the Louvre. The Salons were the main art exhibitions in Paris, indeed in Europe, in the eighteenth century and crucial for any artist to attract critical attention, public acclaim and potential patrons. Hall apparently considered it sufficient to have the right to exhibit at the Salons and did not aspire to full Academy membership. He never presented his reception piece, a work required to prove one's artistic skill in order to become a full member.

The submissions to the Salon were obviously important for artists and their future success. Very often, they tried to exhibit a careful selection of different works, demonstrating the entire spectrum of their abilities. The *livret* (exhibition catalogue) of 1785 includes two numbers with Hall's work. No.138 was a portrait of the Swedish King Gustavus III (two portraits of the King by Hall are preserved in the Nationalmuseum, Stockholm), singled out because of the famous sitter. No.139 described a group of several works as: "*Plusieurs Portraits & Têtes d'études sous le même numéro*" (Several portraits and study heads under the same number). Only the label on the back of the miniature in the Wallace Collection confirms that this miniature of Hall's daughter formed part of the group. Hall obviously considered this work important enough to represent a facet of his artistic output of that year.

Critical reactions to Hall's submissions were positive. The *Mémoires secretes*, one of the main literary and art journals of the day, mentioned Hall's miniatures in its review of the Salon: "Hall has the lightness of touch, the strength of colour, the firmness in his stippling, and he is well-adapted to different characters of heads and in particular to the variety and grace of approach." [1] This point is amply illustrated by the miniature of Hall's daughter which shows the artist's colouring and lively sketch-like style at its best.

The work could not have been intended as a portrait in the strict sense of the word. Adélaïde-Victorine was born in 1772. Assuming that the miniature was painted shortly before the Salon, she can only have been thirteen at the time. The revealed breast and the openly erotic character of the depiction seem particularly inappropriate for an adolescent, but it is worth noting that the miniature might have been shown as one of the 'study heads' mentioned in the catalogue without any reference to the identity of the sitter. Hall refers in this image to a well-known type of painting by his extremely successful contemporary, Jean-Baptiste Greuze (1725–1805), who was widely known for eroticized half-length paintings of anonymous girls and young women. Hall's miniature is directly based on two of Greuze's works, the *Girl with a Gauze Scarf* in the Wallace Collection (fig.1; probably painted in the 1770s) and *La Crûche cassée* (The broken pitcher) in the Louvre, painted in 1771 for Madame Dubarry. The dress and posture, the inclined head, the flowers in the hair and the exposed breasts are all extremely close to Greuze's model. Hall would have seen this work as a miniature version of Greuze's erotic

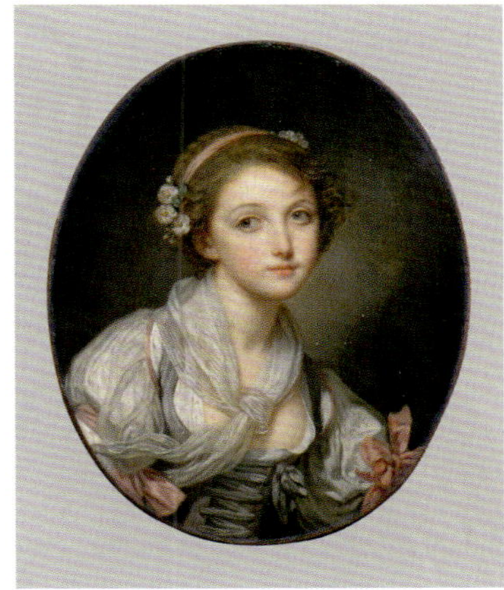

Fig.1 Jean-Baptiste Greuze, *Girl with a Gauze Scarf*, 1770s, oil on canvas, 56.3 × 45.4 cm, London, The Wallace Collection (P415)

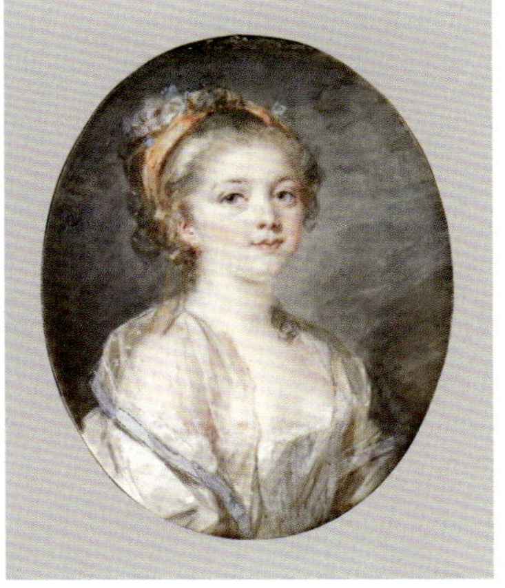

Fig.2 Peter Adolf Hall, *Adélaïde-Victorine Hall, The Artist's Daughter*, *c.*1783–5, ivory, 74 × 58 mm, Toronto, Royal Ontario Museum (977.219.2)

genre paintings rather than as a portrait. Like most contemporary artists, Hall was highly conscious of Greuze and his work. The relationship, however, must have been more than one of artistic influence as Hall himself painted a portrait of Greuze's daughter and used Greuze's *Boy with a Dog* (Wallace Collection) as a model for a portrait of his son Adolphe.

Another miniature by Hall, obviously of the same sitter, is in Toronto (fig.2). Adélaïde-Victorine is shown properly dressed and the miniature is much smaller in scale than the Wallace Collection version, suggesting that it was painted as a portrait, not as a genre scene. Hall's daughter seems slightly younger in the miniature in Toronto. As a standard portrait miniature, it might have served as the starting point for the larger and more unusual work. CMV

PROVENANCE: Probably V[illot] sale, Paris, 25 January 1864 (lot 67), probably bought by Richard Wallace for the 4th Marquess of Hertford; possibly recorded at Bethnal Green (1872–5), no.1634; first certainly catalogued in the Wallace Collection 1904

M189

23 Peter Adolf Hall (1739–1793)

Hedvig Elisabeth Charlotta of Holstein-Gottorp, Duchess of Södermanland, c.1784–7

Gouache on ivory, 72 mm diameter

Signed on stone ledge: *hall*

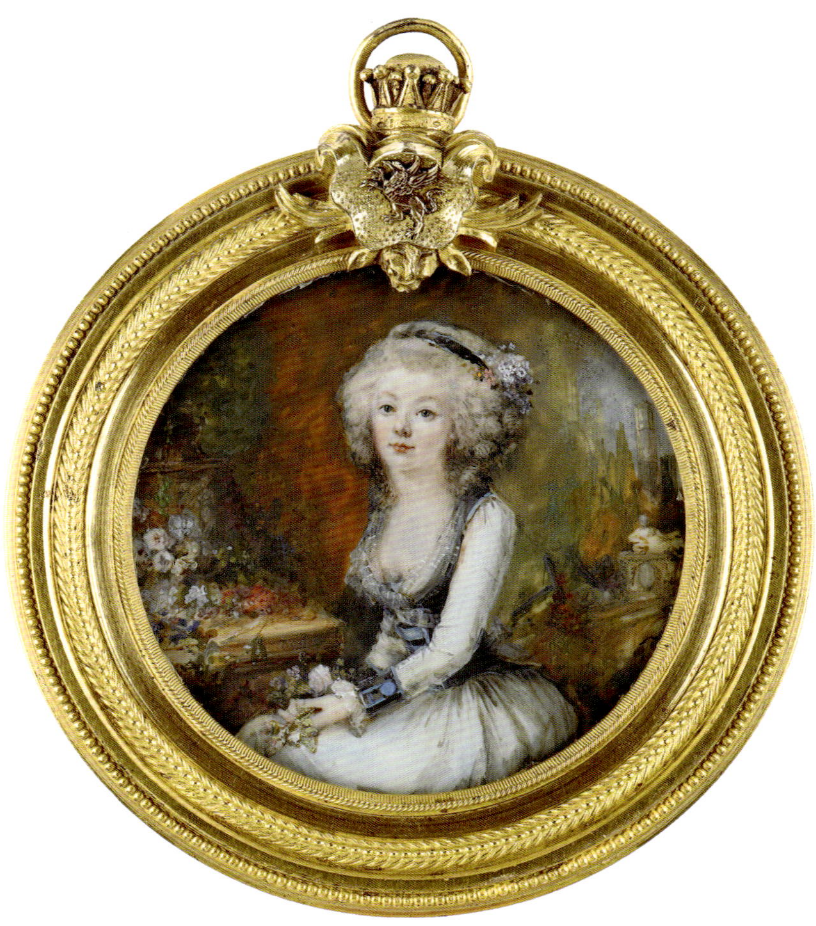

Hedvig Elisabeth Charlotta of Holstein-Gottorp was born in Eutin, Holstein (now in Germany), in 1759. In 1774 she married Karl, Duke of Södermanland (the official title of the eldest brother of the Swedish King), who became King of Sweden as Karl XIII in 1809, succeeding his nephew, Gustavus Adolfus IV. The griffin of Södermanland in the coat of arms and the crown refer to her title. It is thus likely that the frame was made before 1809 and might be contemporary with the miniature. Hall uses the visual language of sensibility for the portrait of the Duchess. She is dressed simply sitting outside at a table with a flower bouquet, the broken column and a sarcophagus in the background referring to a landscape garden setting.

Hall could have met Hedvig Elisabeth Charlotta in 1766 when he passed through Holstein before settling in Paris. At that time she was only seven years old, certainly younger than in the miniature. Hall never returned to Sweden. The Princess is known to have travelled abroad only once, in 1798–9, long after Hall had died. Hall thus almost certainly painted her portrait using another artist's work as a model.

The Swedish King, Gustavus III, brother-in-law of Hedvig Elisabeth, went to Paris in 1784 and even visited Hall, who was an important member of a small colony of Swedish artists in Paris. It is very likely that the portrait of the Princess was commissioned then, together with numerous portraits of the King, his family and entourage. The Princess would have been twenty-four at the time, and certainly seems around that age in the miniature. Fragments of a manuscript list written by Hall of his portrait miniatures are preserved. A copy of a portrait of the Princess is mentioned under 1787. Unfortunately no list for 1784 remains, but her name does not appear on the list for the two subsequent years, although other members of the Swedish Royal house and nobility are mentioned. Hall may have painted Hedvig Elisabeth's portrait in 1784 and then been commissioned to paint a copy in 1787, although by then his first portrait would have already been sent back to Sweden. The Wallace miniature could thus be either of the possible two versions. The entry in the list could also imply that the portrait was copied after another artist's model. A miniature portrait of the Princess was painted by the Danish artist Cornelius Höyern in 1783 and belonged to Gustavus III (gouache on ivory, 132 × 88 mm, oval, Stockholm, Nationalmuseum, NMGrh1790). This could have been brought to Paris by the King and served as a model for Hall's portrait. In 1787 Hall received 240 *livres* for Hedvig Elisabeth Charlotta's portrait, the amount the artist usually charged for a smaller portrait miniature.[1] The same price appears in his list under 1785 for a portrait of Count Fersen, Marie-Antoinette's Swedish lover, who had accompanied Gustavus III in 1784. CMV

PROVENANCE: Perhaps recorded at Bethnal Green (1872–5), no.1642; first certainly catalogued in the Wallace Collection 1904

M187

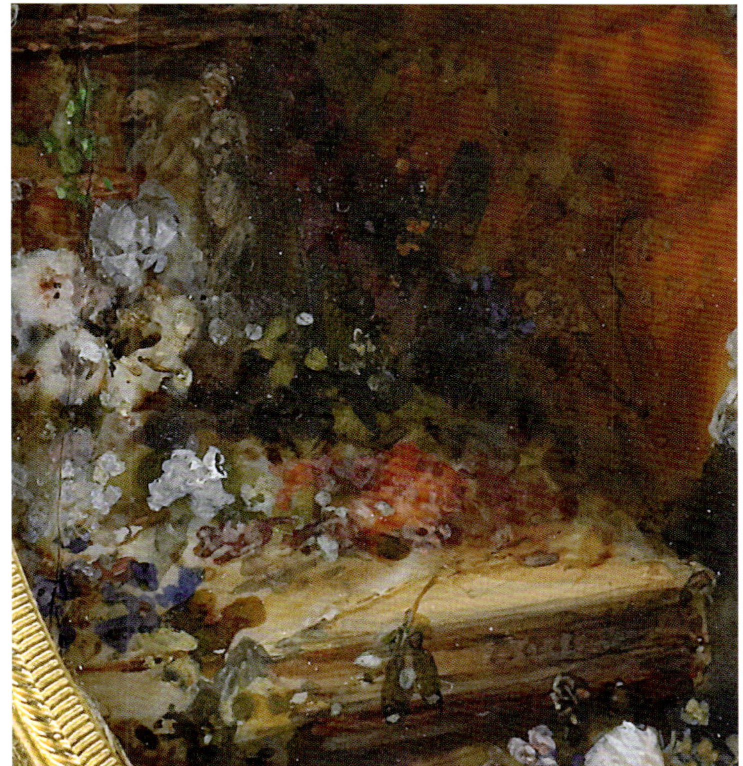

Detail of flowers on the table

24 Peter Adolf Hall (1739–1793)

Portrait of a Woman, c.1790

Gouache on paper, 79 × 65 mm oval

Signed on the left (on lower edge of painted portrait): *hall*

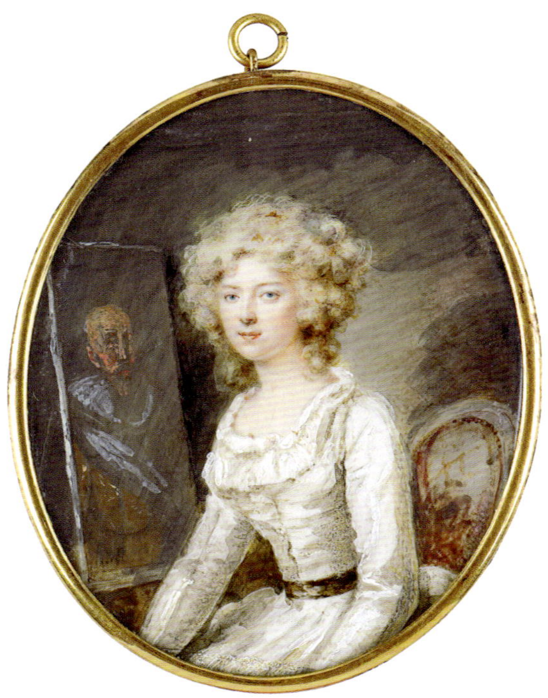

On the basis of a handwritten note on the back of the miniature, the woman has traditionally been identified as Jeanne-Philiberte Ledoux (1767–1840), painter, pupil of Jean-Baptiste Greuze and daughter of the architect Claude-Nicolas Ledoux. Unfortunately, this attractive theory cannot be sustained. Two documented portraits of Ledoux – her self-portrait in Paris (Musée des Arts Décoratifs) and her portrait by Jean-Baptiste Greuze (Durham, North Carolina, Semans Collection) – show a woman with quite different features and dark, brownish eyes, not the bright blue eyes of Hall's miniature.[1]

The painting on the easel in the background has been considered the work of the sitter but there is no indication that the woman in Hall's portrait is actually a painter. She is holding neither the pen or chalk nor the brush and palette that usually feature in the portrait of a painter (see nos.2 and 26). The painting on the easel is a seventeenth-century work, as the dress and hairstyle of the sitter and the style of the painting indicate. In the early nineteenth century it was identified as a portrait of Henri IV's minister, the duc de Sully, but the resemblance is not convincing. It bears a certain resemblance to portraits of the Swedish King Gustavus Adolphus, leader of the Protestants during the Thirty Years War and a Swedish national hero. If this assumption is correct, it could indicate that the woman is Swedish or it might be a reference to the King's name. Hall's first name was Adolf, his third daughter was called Adolphine (she does not resemble and is too young to be the sitter), his son and fourth child Adolphe. Hall's signature on the lower edge of the painting might suggest a specific reference. A portrait miniature of Gustavus Adolphus by Hall after a seventeenth-century model is known.

The style of the miniature and the woman's dress seem to indicate that the miniature was painted shortly before Hall left France in 1791. CMV

PROVENANCE: Daniel Saint sale, Paris, 7 May 1846, lot 328; Allègre sale, Paris, 16 May 1872, lot 258, bought Mannheim for Sir Richard Wallace, 3,000 fr.

M193

25 Marie-Anne Fragonard (1745–1823)

Head of a Girl, *c.*1770–90

Gouache on ivory, 65 × 48 mm

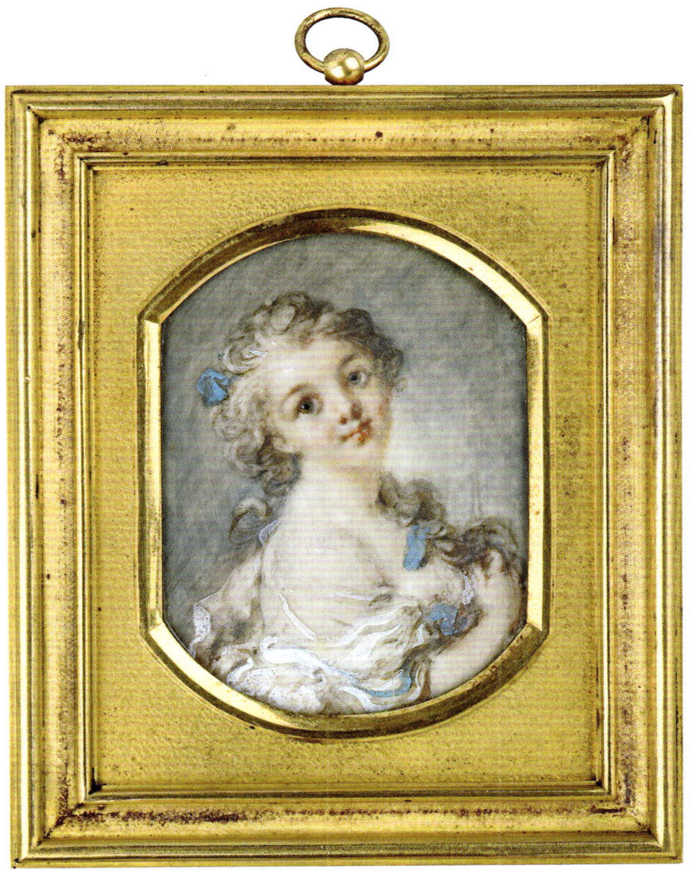

This *Head of a Girl* belongs to a group of miniatures which all have a close relationship with the work of Jean-Honoré Fragonard (1732–1806). They are similar in style and subject to his work and have traditionally been attributed to Fragonard. Occasionally, they have been regarded as works by his wife Marie-Anne, and for good reasons this theory has more recently gained support. Marie-Anne Fragonard is mentioned as a miniature painter in eighteenth-century sources. She exhibited at the Salon de la Correspondance, a regular independent art exhibition, in 1779 and 1782, and her name appears in several sale catalogues in the eighteenth century. While it is certain that Marie-Anne was working as a miniature painter, any evidence for Jean-Honoré's activity in this area is slim. Only in a few isolated cases is a miniature related to Jean-Honoré in the earlier sources. It would have been most unusual if he had practised miniature painting. While miniature painters ventured occasionally into making larger drawings and easel paintings, we know of no major easel painter of the period who was also active regularly as a painter of miniatures. A combination of pastel and miniature painting seems to have been more usual (see no.6, Rosalba Carriera). In the case of the *Head of a Girl*, the title of a slightly later engraving by an otherwise unknown artist, Delaneau, confirms that it was painted by Marie-Anne.

Jean-Honoré built up a successful workshop of family members who all worked in styles close to his own and helped to meet the substantial demand for his works. His sister-in-law, Marguerite Gérard (1761–1837; see no.26), became his pupil, and even today it is very hard to distinguish their respective styles from the 1780s onwards. Fragonard's son Alexandre-Evariste (1780–1850) was also a gifted painter who started out in a style close to his father's. It thus seems likely that Marie-Anne and Jean-Honoré's marriage was the starting point for the family workshop, which profited from the growing success Fragonard began to achieve with private collectors from the mid 1760s.

Marie-Anne and Jean-Honoré, both from Grasse in southern France, married in Paris in 1769, at an important moment in Jean-Honoré's artistic development. Although the evidence is somewhat weak, the entire group of Jean-Honoré's so-called *Têtes de fantaisie* (fantasy heads) – paintings of single male or female half-length figures in a brilliant, particularly sketch-like style – have been dated to this year. It is in this sketch-like quailty that their importance lies, as they are not obviously releated to any finished work but, instead, were created by Fragonard for sophisticated collectors who could appreciate works in the stylistic guise of preparatory sketches. Although some of them were portraits of known individuals (such as Diderot), they were all primarily painted as an exercise in a free style and as a demonstration of artistic genius. They were part of a rapidly growing interest in study heads in French painting of the 1760s, which, without placing the figure in a narrative context, focused on the expression and the often erotic qualities of an isolated face. Jean-Baptiste Greuze explored this idea at roughly the same time as Fragonard. Soon after, this successful genre was also translated into miniature painting (see no.22, an example by Peter Adolf Hall, inspired by Greuze's heads). What we know of Marie-Anne's artistic output (as typified by the miniature discussed here) belongs to this fashionable genre. While the general idea of her portraits seems to be based on her husband's work of the late 1760s, their style seems still closer to his paintings of the 1770s and 1780s (fig.1), which might also be when Marie-Anne painted most of her miniatures. None of Marie-Anne's miniatures is known to reproduce a work by her husband literally, but instead they are all essays in his style, free and personal translations of his ideas into another medium.

A closely related miniature, also by Marie-Anne, is in the Louvre in Paris (fig.2). A copy with variants in the same collection is much firmer in handling and of a lower quality (fig.3). Another *Head of a Girl* in the Wallace Collection might very well be another, less successful work by Marie-Anne.[1]

Marie-Anne's work in the style of Fragonard and the copies after her work must be distinguished both from numerous literal and often much later copies after Jean-Honoré's work and from a large number of miniatures in his style. They testify to several waves of fashion for Jean-Honoré Fragonard's painting. The Wallace Collection owns several examples of these later miniatures

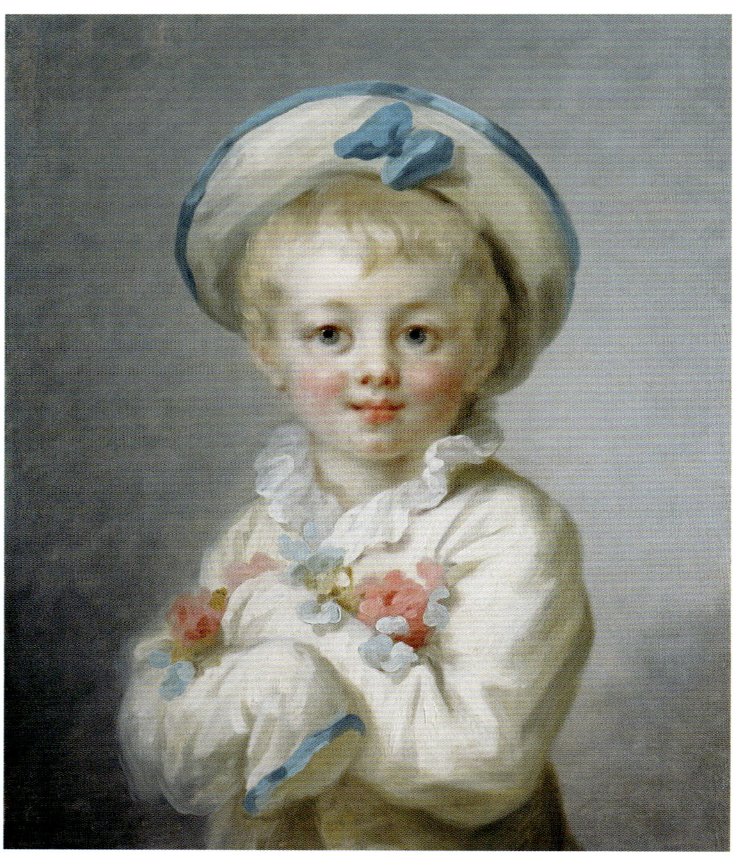

Fig.1 Jean-Honoré Fragonard, *A Boy as Pierrot*, 1770s or 1780s, oil on canvas, 59.8 × 49.7 cm, London, The Wallace Collection (P412)

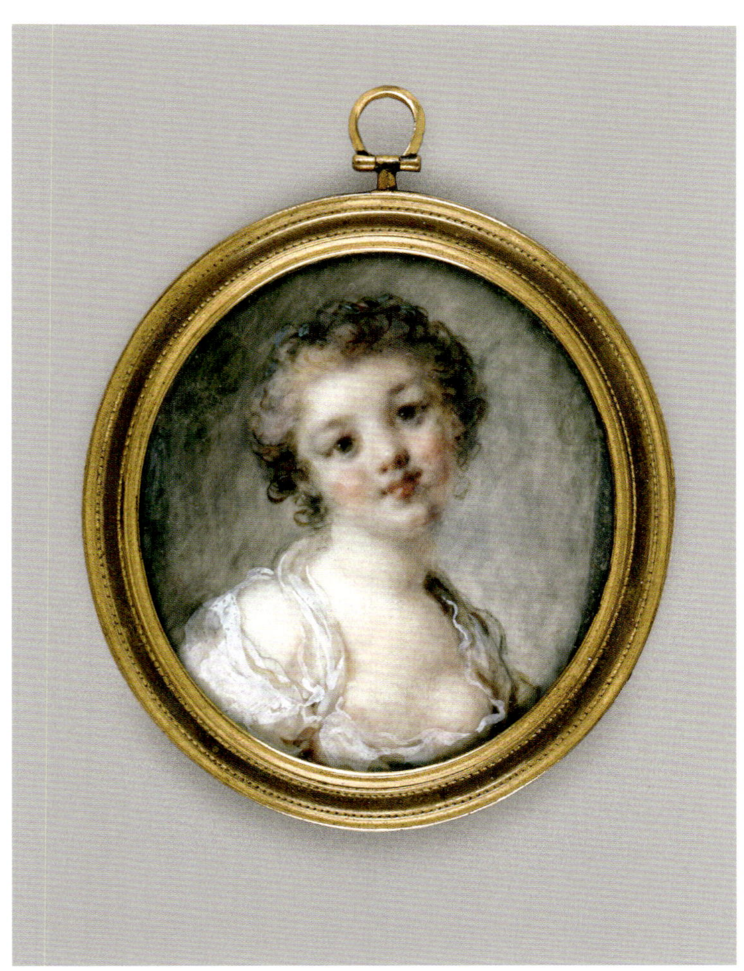

Fig.2 Marie-Anne Fragonard, *Head of a Girl, c.*1770–80, ivory, 68 × 56 mm, Paris, Musée du Louvre, Département des arts graphiques (RF4995)

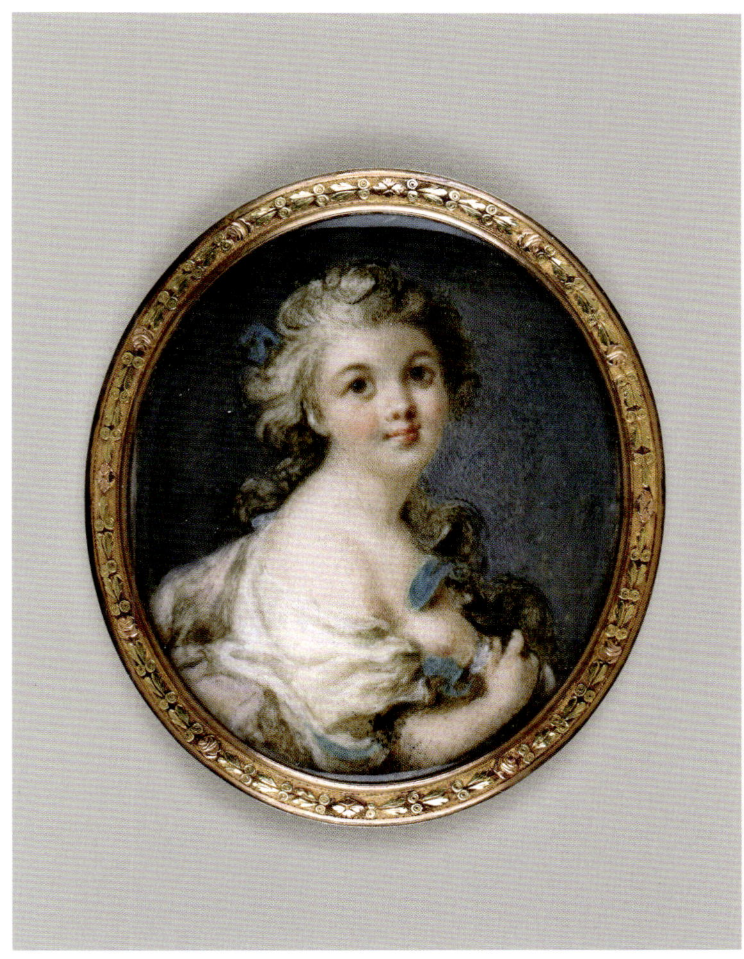

Fig.3 After Marie-Anne Fragonard, *Head of a Girl*, late 18th century, ivory, 66 × 54 mm, Paris, Musée du Louvre, Département des arts graphiques (RF4287)

in Fragonard's manner, which were highly fashionable in the mid nineteenth century when the Hertford family was building its collection of miniatures. CMV

PROVENANCE: First recorded at Bethnal Green (1872–5), no.1652

M110

26 François Dumont (1751–1831)

Marguerite Gérard, 1793

Ivory, 158 × 118 mm

Signed and dated on the left: *Dumont/ 1793*

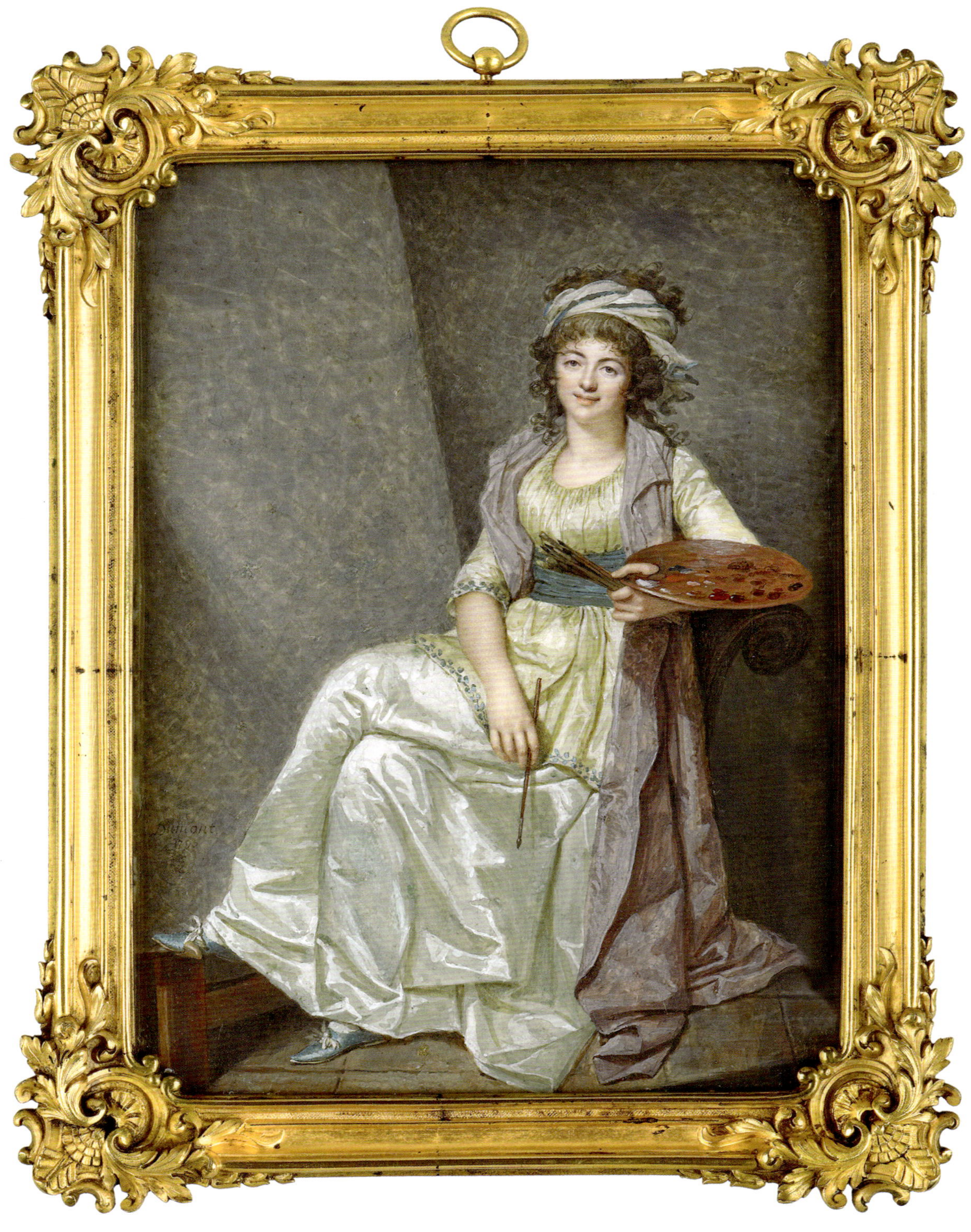

This full-length portrait of a female painter is one of the most beautiful miniatures by Francois Dumont.[1] He was born in Lunéville in the kingdom of Lorraine and moved to Paris in 1768 after his patron, King Stanislas, had died and the territory had been annexed by France. Soon after his arrival in the capital he was already painting for an important clientele, including the comte d'Artois. From 1777 onwards, he was painting portraits of the royal family, commissioned by Queen Marie-Antoinette. Together with Louis Marie Sicardi (*q.v.*) he became her favourite miniature painter. During the French Revolution and the Empire, Dumont was less in demand, probably because of his strong earlier ties to the royal family, but he became popular again during the Restoration, when he specialized in posthumous portraits of the pre-Revolutionary French court.

François Dumont's miniature shows a woman holding a palette and several brushes in her left hand, and another brush in her right, in front of a large, blank canvas. She is wearing a yellow silk tunic with sleeves and embroidery of green leaves, a white skirt and a sleeveless painting robe. A striped scarf is tied around her hair. The full-length miniature portrait was a format Dumont used from very early in his career, and a considerable number by him are known. They are among his finest works.

The sitter was formerly identified as Elisabeth-Louise Vigée-Le Brun (1755–1842), as inscribed on a label on the back of the miniature. The identification was probably made because Vigée-Le Brun was by far the best-known female painter of the period. There is, however, no real resemblance between her self-portraits and Dumont's miniature. It has also been suggested that the miniature might be of Dumont's wife, Marie-Nicole Vestier (1767–1846), who would have been twenty-six in 1793,[2] but evidence for this identification is inconclusive.

In 1981, Joseph Baillio and Sarah Wells-Robertson proposed to identify the miniature, instead, as a portrait of the painter Marguerite Gérard (1761–1837), who was thirty-two when it was painted.[3] The identification of the sitter as Gérard was based on two other miniatures by Dumont.[4] The sitter's identity in this miniature, signed and dated 1793, is supported by its provenance from the Fragonard family. A portrait of Marguerite Gérard is mentioned in Dumont's manuscript list of his own works. Since the re-identification of the Wallace Collection miniature, it has often been reproduced as a genuine contemporary portrait of Gérard, one of the foremost genre painters of the late eighteenth century and the first important female genre painter in France. She was not able to become a member of the Parisian Academy, which had limited the number of its female members to four. Only after the Revolution was she allowed to exhibit at the Salon, which by then was open to all artists. Works by her hand of the size of the blank canvas shown on the miniature, however, are not known. Gérard was famous for her highly finished small-scale genre paintings, which followed Dutch models. She was the sister of Marie-Anne Fragonard (see no.25) and lived with her and her brother-in-law Jean-Honoré Fragonard. CMV

PROVENANCE: Probably V[illot] sale, Paris, 25 January 1864 (lot 51), probably bought by Richard Wallace for the 4th Marquess of Hertford, 469 fr.; first certainly recorded at Bethnal Green (1872–5), no.1792

M101

27 François Dumont (1751–1831)

Louis-Charles, Dauphin of France (Louis XVII), late 1790s

Ivory, 52 mm diameter

Signed on the left: *Dumont*

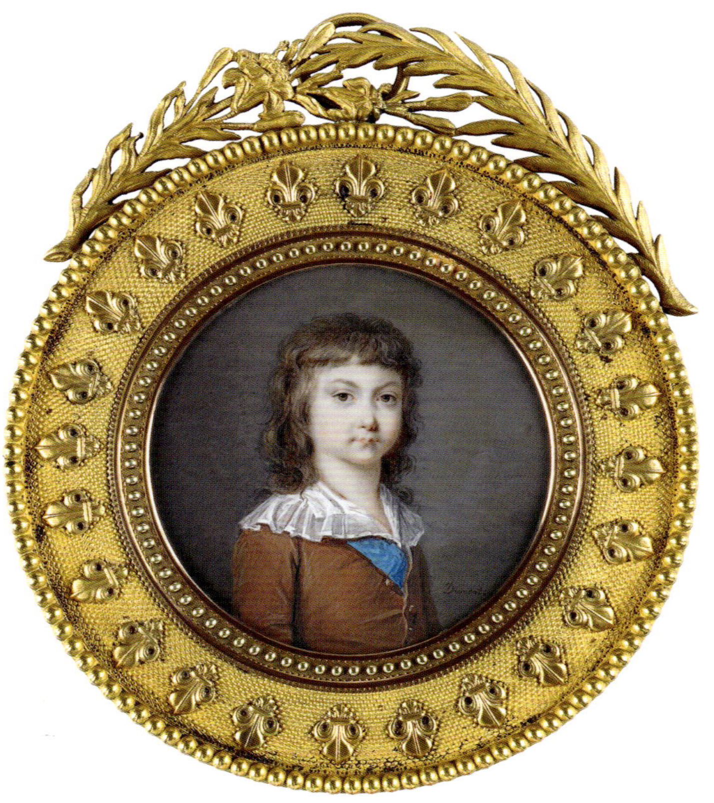

Louis-Charles, Duke of Normandy (1785–1795), was the third child and second son of Louis XVI and Marie-Antoinette. When his elder brother Louis-Joseph, born in 1781, died in June 1789, Louis-Charles became his successor as Dauphin. Together with the royal family he was imprisoned in the Temple in August 1792. He died in 1795, still imprisoned, as a result of the ill treatment he received.

The miniature is signed by Dumont. Although its attribution and signature have been doubted, the style is sufficiently close to other signed and documented works by the artist for it to be accepted as his work. François Dumont became Marie-Antoinette's favourite miniature painter after the death of the Italian artist Ignazio Pio Vittoriano Campana in 1786. He produced numerous portraits of the Queen and also painted the Dauphin several times.[1] In Dumont's manuscript list of his own miniatures, under 1790 the Dauphin features twice on his own and was also listed in portraits with his mother and elder sister Marie-Thérèse-Charlotte. The Dauphin appears younger in these miniatures, which survive.[2] While he does not appear in the list for the following years, a posthumous portrait of the Dauphin by Dumont was shown at the Salon of 1814.

In the Royalist view, Louis-Charles became King of France as Louis XVII when his father, Louis XVI, was executed on 21 January 1793. The *fleur-de-lis* ornament and two crowning lilies on the front of the frame as well as the inscription *LOUIS XVII* and an engraved broken lily on its back represent the Dauphin as a martyr for the French monarchy and the Royalist cause. On stylistic grounds, the frame should be dated to the early or mid nineteenth century.[3] It seems likely that the portrait is posthumous

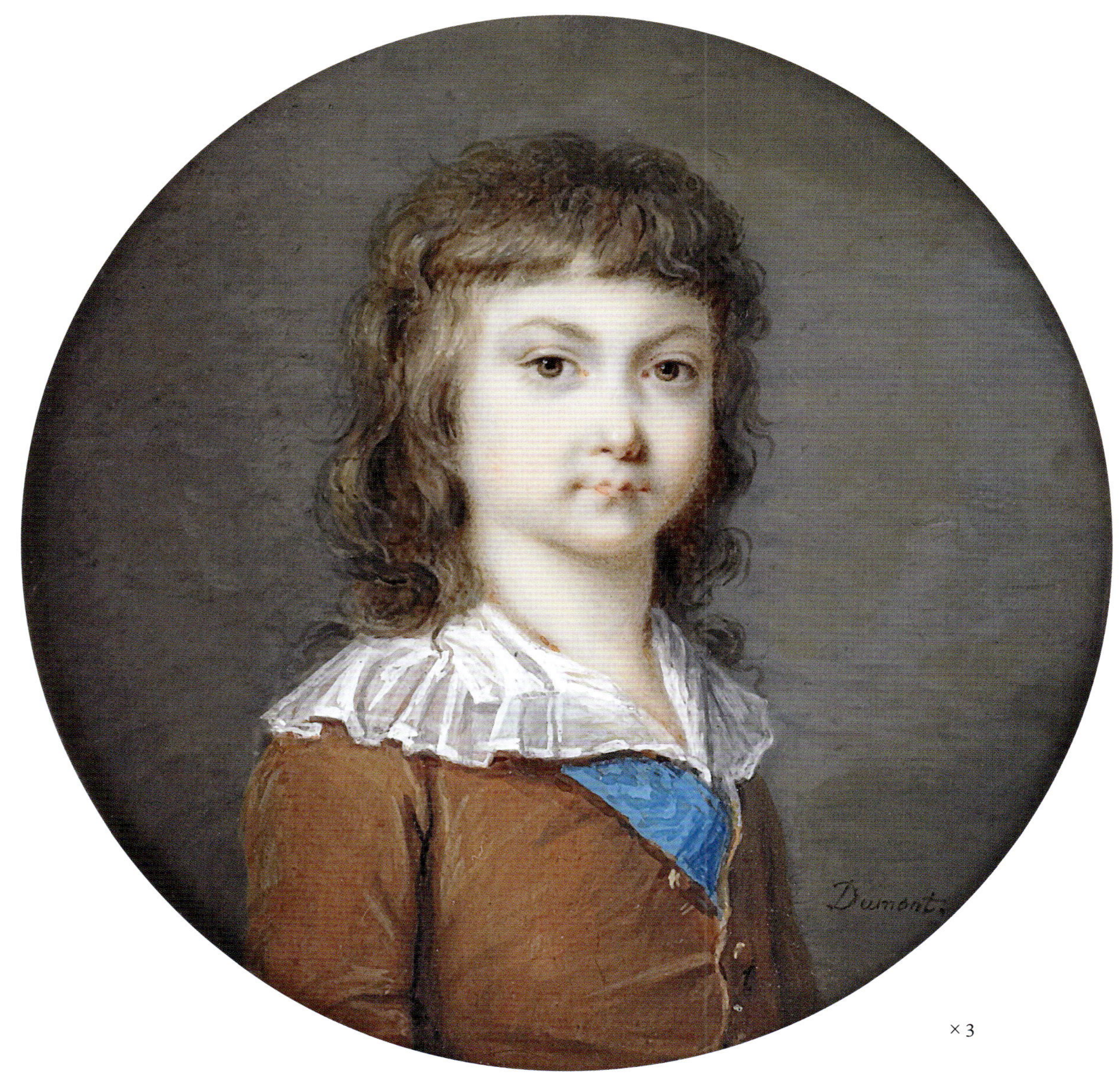

× 3

and was painted as a Royalist token after the death of the child. The later date might also explain why the blue sash of the Order of the Saint-Esprit is worn incorrectly.[4] The style of the miniature does not seem to tally with a date of 1814 but it is conceivable that Dumont was exhibiting then a work he had painted earlier, or that this miniature is another earlier posthumous portrait of the Dauphin. Portraits of his former patroness Marie-Antoinette and her family became a speciality of the artist during the Restoration.
CMV

PROVENANCE: Richard Wallace sale, Paris, 26–8 February 1857, lot 38, 132 fr.; Allègre sale, Paris, 16 May 1872, lot 269, bought Mannheim for Sir Richard Wallace, 1,450 fr.

M100

28 Jean-Urbain Guérin (1760/1–1835/6)

Georgiana Cavendish, Duchess of Devonshire and Lady Elizabeth Foster, 1791

Ivory, 94 × 68 mm

Signed, bottom left: *Guerin f.*

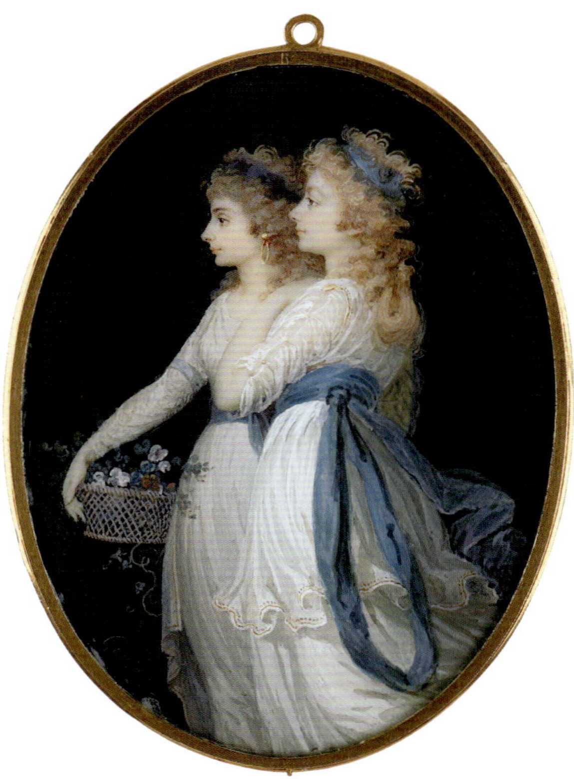

Jean-Urbain Guérin was born in Strasbourg but worked in Paris, where he became part of a circle of artists from his native Alsace.[1] Like many miniature painters he did not originally have official ties to the Academy and even dropped out of its school. As a member of the royal guard, he defended the royal family in the Tuileries on 20 June 1792 and avoided Paris during the following phases of the Revolution. He only returned in 1798, after then regularly exhibiting at the Salon. The output of his second Parisian phase was in a strict Empire style that was quite different from the more playful and elegant early Neoclassicism of the work produced during his first stay in the city. Guérin became very successful as a portraitist of leading officers of the French army and then also of the imperial family.

The double portrait of Georgiana Cavendish, Duchess of Devonshire (1757–1806) and Lady Elizabeth Christiana Foster, née Harvey (1757–1824), is one of the masterpieces of Guérin's first Parisian period. The identification of the sitters is based on another version of the miniature recorded in the collection of a Miss Clifford but today untraced. An inscription on the back of that version in Elizabeth Foster's handwriting identified the sitters. Miss Clifford is likely to have been a relative or descendant of Sir Augustus Clifford, half-brother of the 6th Duke of Devonshire and illegitimate child of the 5th Duke and Elizabeth Foster, which would explain the inscription in her hand.[2]

The two sitters were celebrities of their time and key *dramatis personae* in one of the most high-profile English society scandals of the period. Georgiana, née Spencer, married the Duke of Devonshire in 1774 and immediately became a fashion icon and celebrity. In 1780 she joined the campaign of the Whig politician Charles James Fox. In 1782 the Devonshires met Lady Elizabeth Foster, who soon became the Duke's, and possibly also the Duchess's, lover.[3] After Georgiana's death in 1806, Elizabeth became the Duke's second wife. The love lives of both women, which included further affairs and relationships, their public *ménage à trois* with the Duke, and the battles between the three protagonists were eagerly followed by a wide public.

The Duchess of Devonshire and Lady Elizabeth stayed together in Paris twice, first between May and August 1790 and then again in November and December of 1791. The second stay correlates with a note in Guérin's journal that he had made a drawing of the Duchess on 12 November 1791. The miniature can thus be dated to 1791, a time when Georgiana had just been sent into exile by her husband, the 5th Duke of Devonshire, after she had become pregnant with her daughter Eliza Courtney by the young Whig politician Charles Grey.[4] Foster decided to accompany the Duchess into exile. Guérin's miniature should be understood as a token of friendship, even love, between the two women, which is emphasized by the fact that two versions were painted, one for each sitter. Both women returned to England in 1793 to continue their previous living arrangement with the Duke.

Guérin's miniature is part of a group of portraits of female sitters in profile, single or in groups, before a black background, which are modelled after the isolated figures on dark grounds seen in Roman ('Pompeian') wall painting from after *c.*15 BC.[5] Guérin applied the attitudes of these Roman models to portraiture and created images of an extraordinary elegance at a time when the excavations in Pompeii and Herculaneum were being widely discussed and used as models for contemporary architecture and the applied arts, and even contemporary fashion. His miniatures were apparently based on portrait drawings in a much less idealized style which were then transformed into compositions in an antique 'Pompeian' manner.[6] A copy after another, closely related miniature from the same group is also in the Wallace Collection (fig.1).[7]

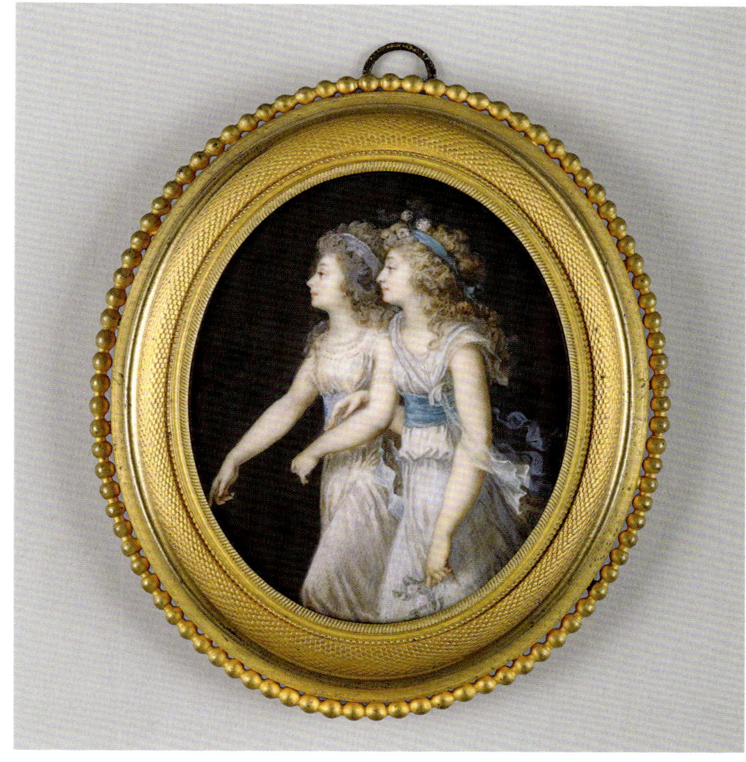

Fig.1 After Jean-Urbain Guérin, *Two Women*, ivory, 81 × 67 mm, London, The Wallace Collection (M179)

Only a year earlier, the English miniature painter Richard Cosway had painted a portrait miniature of Lady Elizabeth Foster following a much more traditional type of portrait painting.[8] A copy after Guérin of only the Duchess's face was made by Horace Hone in 1812.[9] CMV

PROVENANCE: First catalogued in the Wallace Collection 1904

M177

29 Louis Marie Sicardi (1743–1825)

Head of a Woman in a Chequered Shawl and Turban, 1799

Ivory, 64 × 51 mm

Signed and dated, lower right: *Sicardi 1799*

× 2.5

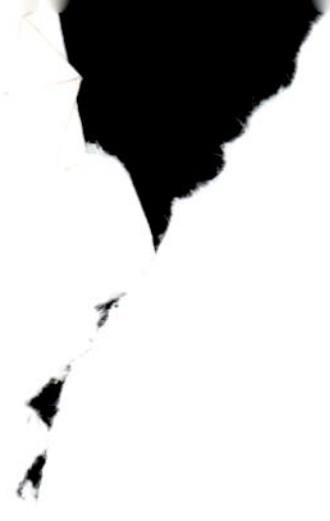

Louis Marie Sicard, known as Sicardi, was born in Avignon and first studied with his father, the painter Pierre-Antoine Sicard. He is first mentioned in Bordeaux in 1769 and came to Paris in 1774–5. In Bordeaux he became a member of the local Academy which was being established at that time. He also started, somewhat mysteriously, to use the title of Painter to the King of Portugal. Between 1780 and 1788, Sicardi worked for the Menus Plaisirs, the royal department responsible for entertainment, festivities and for objects handed out as state presents. In this function he painted numerous portraits of Louis XVI. As he was not a member of the Parisian Academy he was only allowed to exhibit at the Salon after the Revolution, from 1791 onwards. A short stay in England in 1789–90 might have been caused by the political situation around the outbreak of the Revolution, but his career seems to have survived the political changes in France without major problems. Sicardi's artistic output consists mainly of portraits and expressive heads, but he also painted some genre scenes, mythologies and landscapes.

Sicardi's *Head of a Woman* is a good example of the long-lasting fashion for female study heads, often with strongly emotional expressions and in different stages of erotic undress. The phenomenon originated in paintings by Jean-Baptiste Greuze in the 1760s and after a certain delay reached miniature painting, in works by Sicardi, Hall (for an example of 1785 see no.22) and others. An earlier example by Sicardi, signed and dated 1780, is also in the Wallace Collection (fig.1). Sicardi himself owned a painting by Greuze of "*Une jeune fille. le sein découvert* [A young woman with her breast exposed]". The *Head of a Woman in a Chequered Shawl and Turban* demonstrates that the fashion for Greuze's expressive heads continued without significant interruption during the Revolution and after.

The shawl and turban of the woman have long been assumed to be in a tartan pattern. Aileen Ribeiro, however, has recently pointed out that this type of chequer pattern was highly fashionable in Paris in the late 1790s and does not refer to Scottish dress. While the date of the signature could also be read as '1789', Ribeiro's observation confirms the traditional dating to 1799.

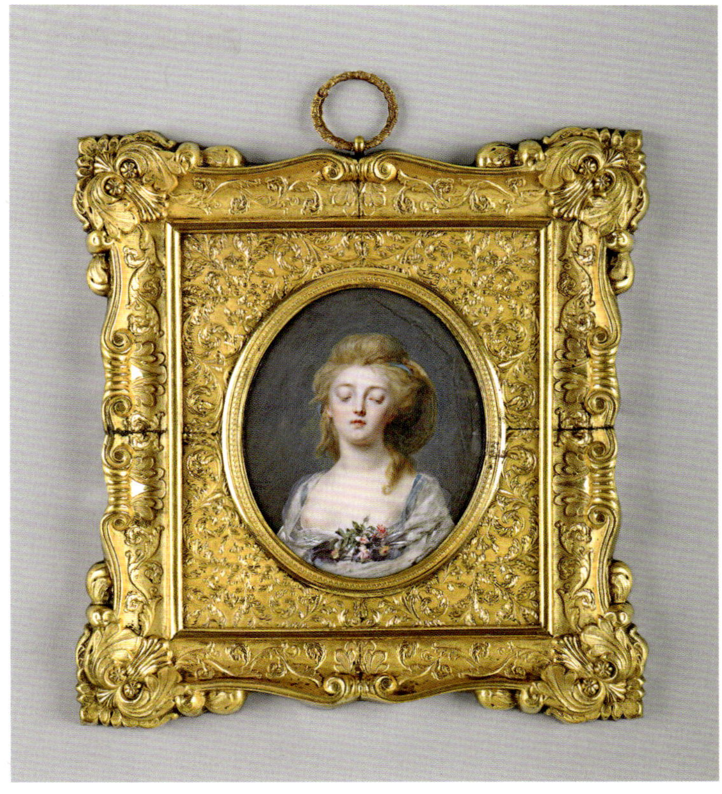

Fig.1 Louis Marie Sicardi, *Unknown Woman*, signed and dated 1780, ivory, 90 × 70 mm, London, The Wallace Collection (M301)

A reference to another version illustrated by Lespinasse in 1929 is based on an error. However, an unsigned version in a private collection might be autograph.[1] CMV

PROVENANCE: First catalogued in the Wallace Collection 1904

M303

30 Unknown Artist, France (?), late 18th or early 19th century

François-Marie Arouet de Voltaire and *Gabriel-Emilie Le Tonnelier de Breteuil, marquise du Châtelet*

Ivory, 44 × 34 mm

The two miniatures are mounted back to back in a secret slide of a snuff box. The box (carnelian, mounted in gold, 35 × 83 × 58 mm) by Johann Christian Neuber, Dresden, *c.*1775

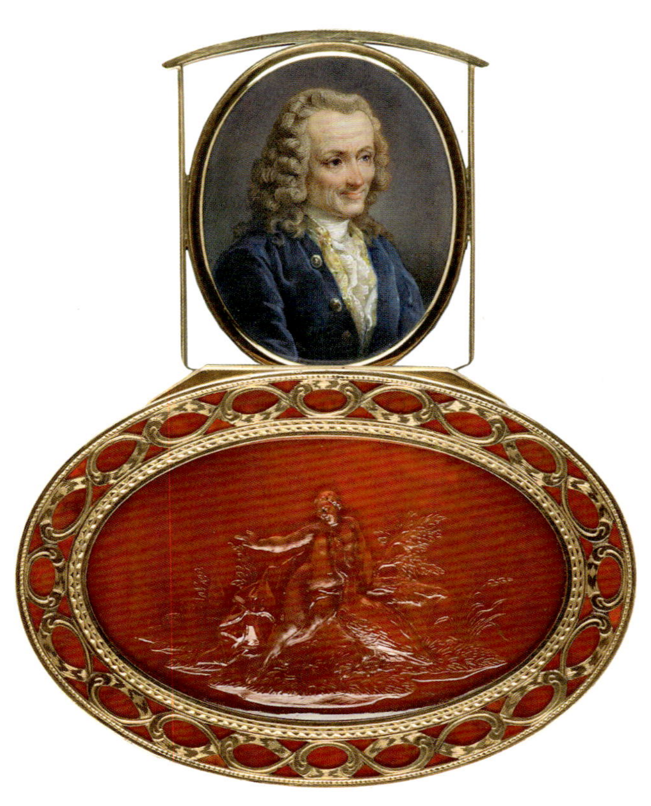

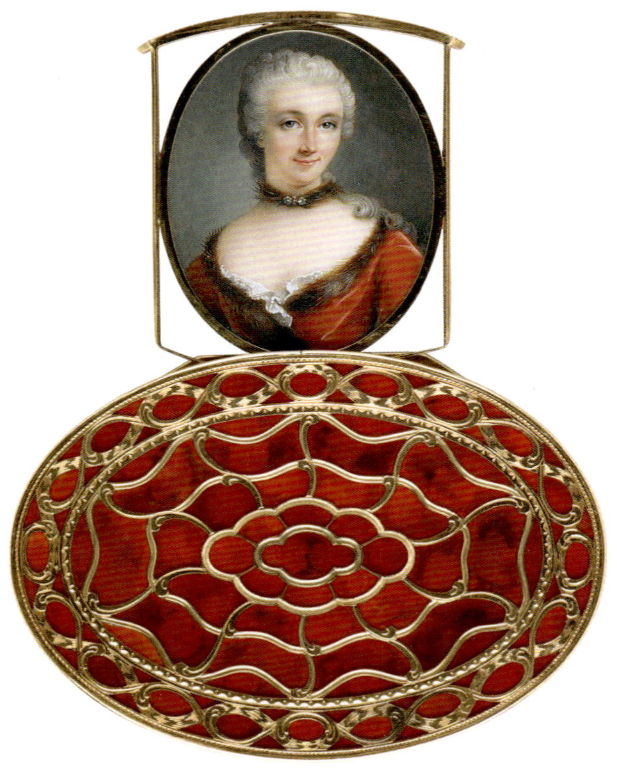

A secret slide in this outstanding Dresden snuff box frames two miniatures on ivory, mounted back to back, with portraits of Voltaire (1694–1778) and Mme du Châtelet (1706–1749). Both were among the outstanding intellectuals of their time in Paris, Voltaire being widely considered the leading playwright and one of the best authors of his time, Châtelet a celebrated mathematician and translator of scientific texts. They had a renowned affair – which the miniatures and the box celebrate – between 1733 and Châtelet's death in 1749. The mythological scene of Leda and the Swan on the lid of the box, however, is incongruous in the company of the two portraits. When the box was produced, Châtelet had been dead for about twenty-five years and Voltaire was much older than he appears in the portrait. The miniatures seem to be a product of historic interest in the famous couple.

An old attribution to Drouais goes back to the 1865 sale catalogue and has been interpreted as a reference to Hubert Drouais (1699–1767). Little is known about him as a miniature painter and his dates cannot easily be reconciled with the dates of the snuff box. His son François-Hubert (1727–1775) was one of the most prominent portrait painters of the *ancien régime* and closely associated with the royal house. His name was extremely well known in the art trade in the nineteenth and twentieth centuries. It is most likely that the reference was intended to indicate the younger and more famous Drouais, whose name added cachet to portraits from the later eighteenth century. He died rather too early to have supplied miniatures specifically for this box, although in theory it might just have been possible.

The portrait of Châtelet is ultimately derived from Marianne Loir's painting in Bordeaux which was painted shortly before the death of the marquise.[1] The miniature shows the sitter in reverse and dressed in red instead of the blue dress she is wearing in the painting. The basis for the miniature was an engraving by Pierre-Gabriel Langlois of 1786. A similar miniature in enamel showing Châtelet in a red dress but wearing a choker was painted by Nicolas André Courtois (1734–1806).[2] The portrait of Voltaire does not directly follow any known portrait of the writer. It seems to be a combination of different portraits of Voltaire as an older man by Jean Huber (1721–1786) and a drawing by Jean-Etienne Liotard of 1734, lost but known through an engraving, showing Voltaire at a much younger age.[3]

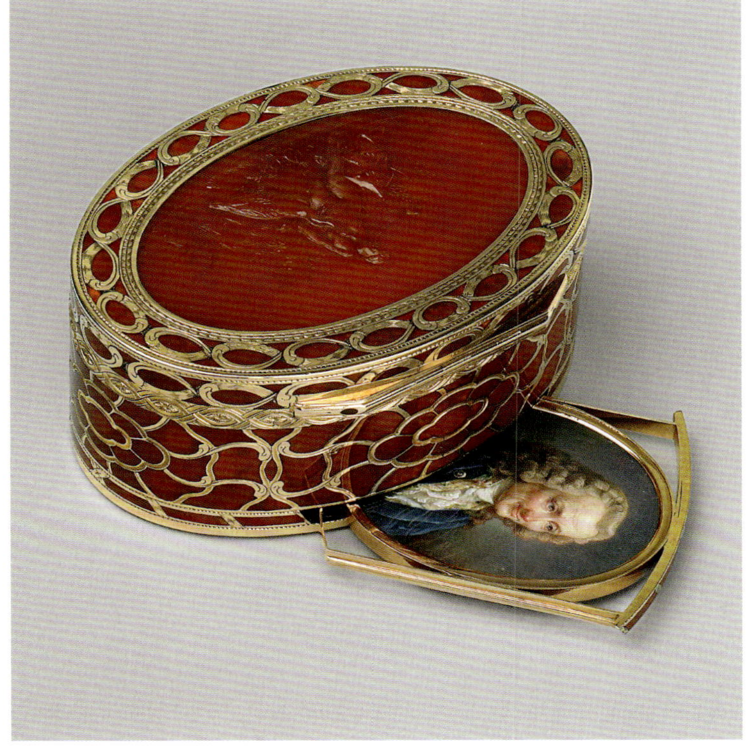

Fig. 1 The box by Johann Christian Neuber with the miniature portrait of Voltaire revealed

The miniatures were produced at some later date to replace others which were originally in the secret slide of the box but which were not of interest to a later owner, perhaps a dealer. They would have been chosen to embellish an object of outstanding artistic quality with reference to famous eighteenth-century figures. CMV

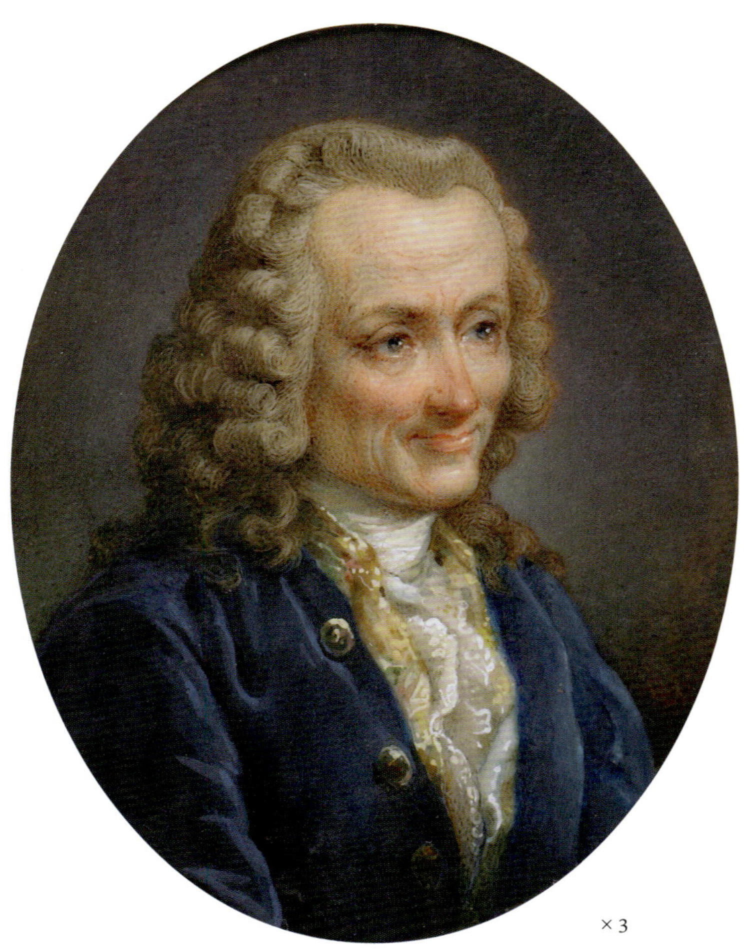

× 3

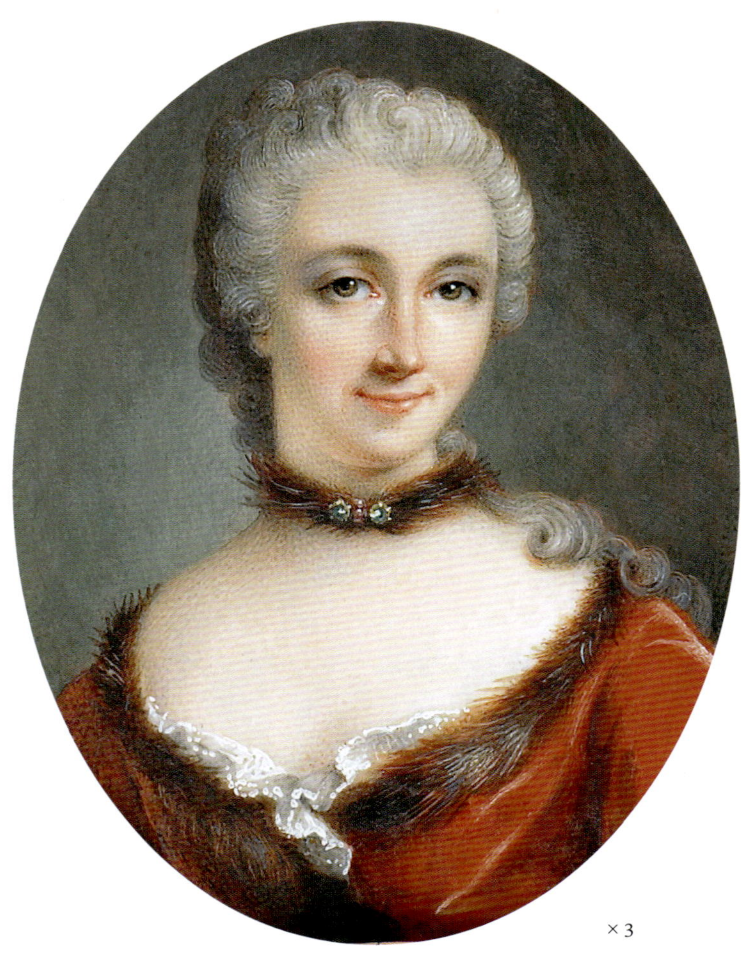

× 3

PROVENANCE: Soret sale, Paris, 5 May 1863, lot 62; duc de Morny sale, Paris, 31 May 1865, lot 382, 3,790 fr.; the Empress Eugénie; F. Davis (dealer); bought 22 February 1872 by Sir Richard Wallace. Their existence was subsequently forgotten and they were rediscovered only in 1976.

G80

31 Giuseppe Macpherson (1726–*c.*1780)

Six Portraits of Artists, *c.*1760–85

Six separate miniatures on ivory, mounted on a common frame, each miniature 66 × 52 mm

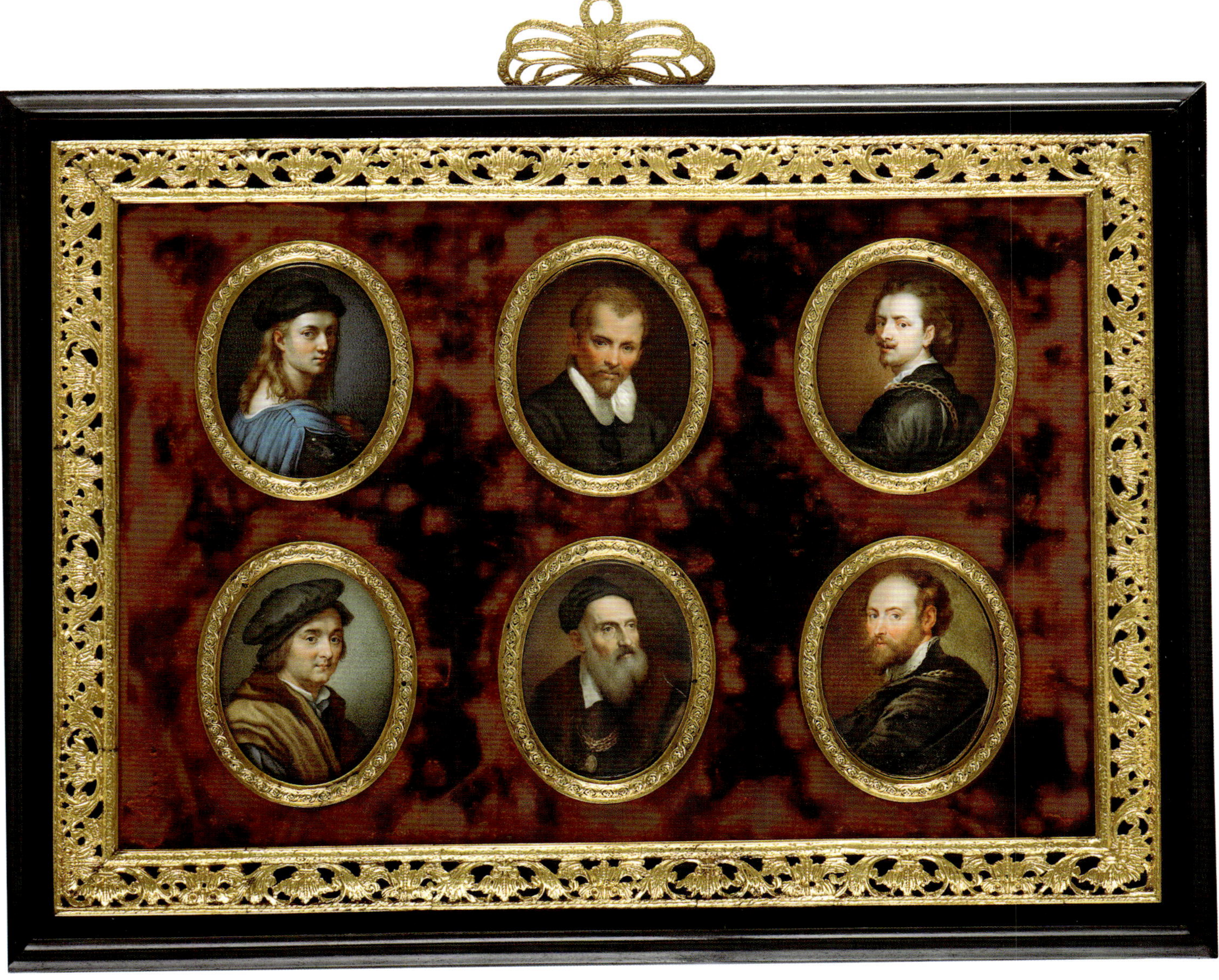

× 0.5

Six miniature copies after self-portraits of great Italian and Flemish artists are combined in one frame. When the copies were painted the originals were believed to represent Raphael, Andrea del Sarto, Titian, Annibale Carracci, Rubens and Van Dyck. Until recently, the miniatures were dated to the nineteenth century, a period with an almost obsessive interest in artists and their portraits. However, the miniatures are closely related to a series of 224 similar works documented as the work of Giuseppe Macpherson which entered the Royal Collection in 1773 and 1786 (see fig. 1). The six portrait miniatures in the Wallace Collection all have exact counterparts in the larger series in Windsor.

Giuseppe Macpherson was born in Florence in 1726 into a Scottish family and became a pupil of Pompeo Batoni. In the 1750s he worked in Milan, Germany, Paris and London, where he is mentioned in 1754. By 1764, he was back in Florence. Macpherson worked in the Uffizi over long periods of time, copying works from the grand ducal collection. An application in 1777 to copy works by Correggio and Guercino in the Uffizi galleries has, for example, been preserved.

Macpherson worked on ivory and in enamel on copper,[1] producing portrait miniatures and copies after Old Masters in miniature. By far the most important group of his works is the series of artists' portraits in the Royal Collection.[2] They were commissioned by George, 3rd Earl Cowper and presented to George III in 1773 and 1786. Cowper's commission is apparently first mentioned in 1764. In 1767, he lent a group of sixty of these miniatures to an exhibition at the Florentine Academy, and the series must have been well advanced by that time. All of them are based on self-portraits in the Florentine collection except Macpherson's own signed self-portrait, which proclaims him as the author of the series. Self-portraits of artists had already featured at the beginning of each artist's biography in the second edition of Giorgio Vasari's *Lives* of 1568. The then ruler, Cosimo I, Duke of Tuscany began a collection of artists' self-portraits which is still continued by the Uffizi today. It was an important attraction for visitors to Florence and was widely studied by artists. The Wallace Collection also owns a group of four wax reliefs from the same period after self-portraits by Lucas Cranach the Elder, Pontormo,

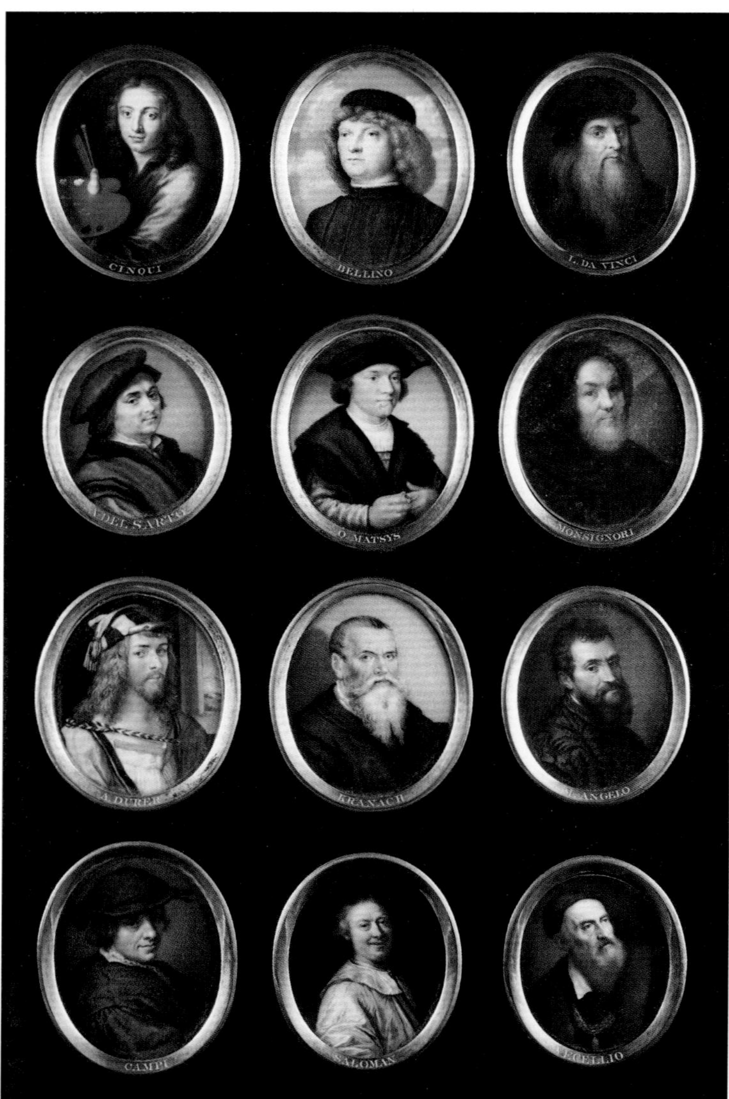

Fig. 1 Giuseppe Macpherson, *Twelve Portraits of Artists* (including Andrea del Sarto and Titian), c. 1760–86, ivory, c. 70 × 55 mm each, British Royal Collection (RCIN421171–82)

Francesco Salviati and Domenico Passignano in the Uffizi.[3]

A copy in enamel by Macpherson after a self-portrait of the painter Francesco Londonio is in the Gilbert Collection in the Victoria and Albert Museum, but the only other group of these copies is the set of six in the Wallace Collection. Self-portraits by Macpherson also are in the Uffizi and in the Kunsthalle in Hamburg, while another was on the Roman art market in 1988.

While the series in the Royal Collection is remarkable for its scope, covering artists from the late fifteenth to the eighteenth centuries, the group of six in the Wallace Collection closely reflects artistic ideals of the time. Raphael, Andrea del Sarto, Titian and Annibale Carracci were at the time seen as the highest embodiments of the classical ideal in Italian art, Rubens and Van Dyck as the pinnacle of Flemish art and as the greatest colourists of the seventeenth century.

The models for five of the miniatures are still in the Uffizi.[4] The so-called self-portrait of Annibale Carracci is today catalogued as a Venetian portrait of an anonymous man. The original of Titian's self-portrait is in the Gemäldegalerie in Berlin and Macpherson based his miniature on a seventeenth-century copy in Florence which, unlike the painting in Berlin, shows the artist dressed in a white shirt. Macpherson's portrait of 'Raphael' (fig.2) is today known to represent the banker Bindo Altoviti but was believed to be a self-portrait by the artist in the eighteenth century. The original is today in the National Gallery in Washington but was still in the Altoviti collection in Florence in Macpherson's time.

The series was perhaps acquired by the 3rd Marquess of Hertford and is first mentioned at Hertford House in 1834. Because of his close ties to the Prince of Wales, the future George IV, he was probably familiar with the series in the Royal Collection. The 3rd Marquess was too young, however, to have commissioned the miniatures himself from Macpherson. The combination of artists suggests that they might have been painted for an English patron. CMV

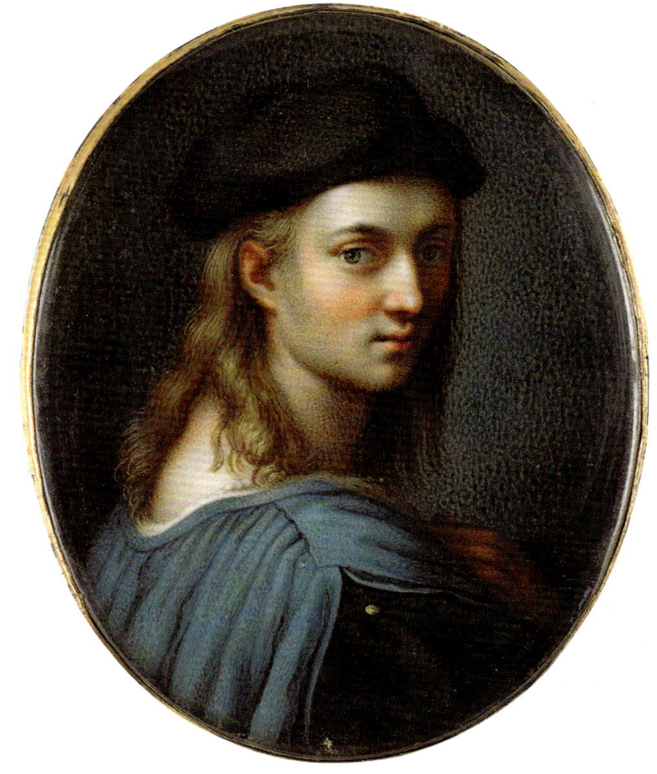

Fig.2 Giuseppe Macpherson, *Six Portraits of Artists* (detail): 'Raphael'

PROVENANCE: First recorded at Hertford House 1834

M251

32 Richard Cosway (1742–1821)

Maria Cosway, *c.*1785–90

Ivory, 71 × 58 mm

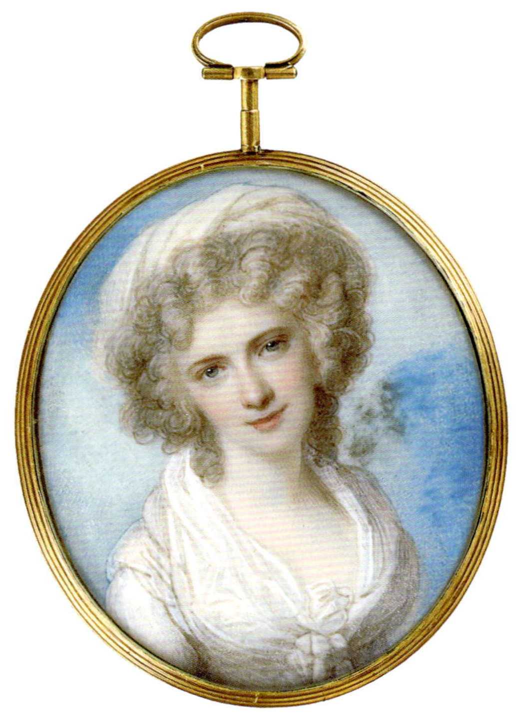

Richard Cosway was by far the most famous and successful English miniature painter of the later eighteenth century.[1] He was born in Oakford in Devon in 1742 and had a successful early career in London. By 1764 he had already received his first royal commission, a portrait of the infant George, Prince of Wales, later George IV. Cosway was active in the organizations that were the forerunners of the Royal Academy and became an associate of the newly founded Academy in 1770. In 1781 he married Maria Hadfield (1760–1838), who had moved to London in 1779 after growing up in an English expatriate family in Florence. She was an important painter in her own right, an accomplished musician and, together with her husband, the centre of a highly fashionable circle. Their marriage contributed to their carefully organized joint social and business success. The Cosways were celebrities of their day, famous both as artists and as social figures. Their stormy relationship and affairs added to the public interest in them. Richard became official painter to the Prince of Wales in 1785. His output was prolific: sittings with up to twelve sitters per day are recorded. The Cosways' only daughter Luisa was born in 1789, shortly before the couple's first separation in the following year, and died in 1796. Maria Cosway spent most of her life from 1790 in France and Italy and was in effect separated from her husband, although they still lived together at times and never lost touch. The Cosways' art collection was important and extensive.

This portrait miniature is regarded as one of Cosway's greatest masterpieces. The brilliant use of the ivory colour of the background, the translucent quality of the paint, its apparent lightness of touch and the contrast between finely painted areas and the sketchy, blue background all add to the strong appeal of the portrait.

An inscription on the back of the miniature identifies the sitter as Mrs Fitzherbert (Maria Smythe), mistress and illegal wife of the Prince of Wales. However, documented portraits prove that this identification is untenable. The features of the woman are entirely different from Fitzherbert's, whose eyes, in a miniature by Cosway that is genuinely of her, are brown.[2] Stephen Lloyd suggested in 2005 that the sitter might be Cosway's wife Maria, and comparisons with documented portraits of her strongly support the identification. Cosway's drawing of his wife with a bust of Leonardo in the collection of the Cosway Foundation in Lodi (fig. 1) apparently shows the same person. It and the Wallace Collection miniature also document Maria Cosway's particular preference for turbans, a fashion typical of the late 1780s.[3] The view slightly from above indicates a more personal relationship between artist and sitter: in more formal portraits, sitters are usually on or above the artist's eye level.

The previous identification of the sitter as Mrs Fitzherbert might have made the miniature of particular interest to the Hertford family. She was like a second mother to the 4th Marquess after he had been called back to England by his father in 1816 to receive an English education. It is not known at all when the miniature entered the collection.

A date of 1790 is scratched into the frame of the miniature. Maria's dress might date from the late 1780s.[4] Given that the Cosways were widely known for their sense of fashion it seems unlikely that Maria Cosway would have worn last season's dress. In any case, the miniature must have been painted in the second half of the 1780s. CMV

PROVENANCE: First recorded at Bethnal Green (1872–5), no. 1722

M87

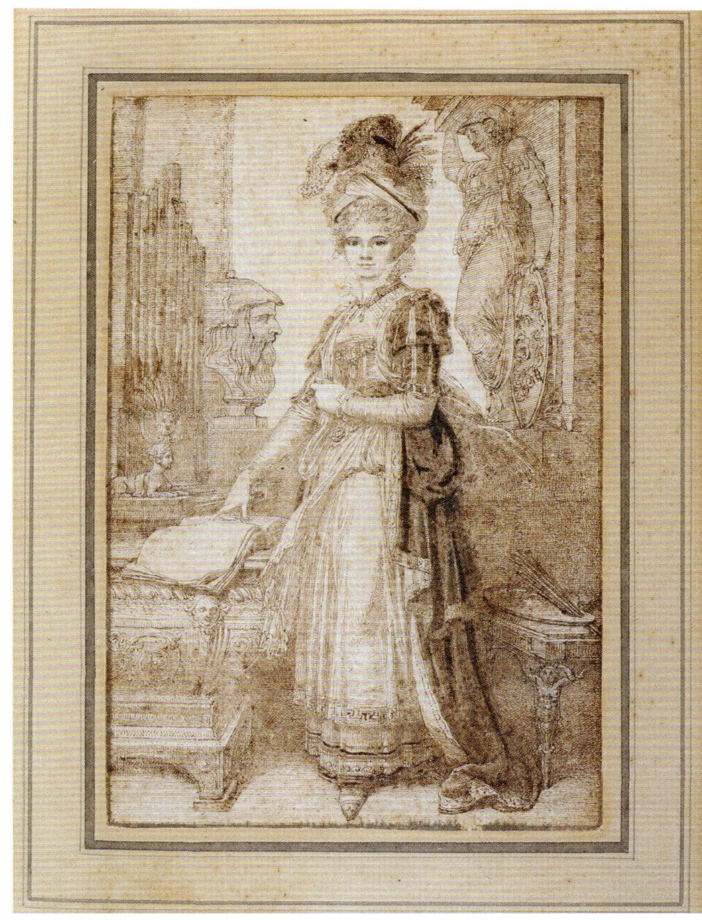

Fig. 1 Richard Cosway, *Maria Cosway with a Bust of Leonardo*, c. 1789, pen and brown ink, 23.7 × 15.4 cm, Lodi, Fondazione Cosway (I.2)

33 Richard Cosway (1742–1821)

Maria Fagnani, 3rd Marchioness of Hertford, 1791

Ivory, 76 × 63 mm

Signed and dated on the back of the mount in ink: *R^d. Cosway/ R.A./ Primarius Pictor/ Serenissimi Walliæ/ Principis/ Pinxit/ 1791*

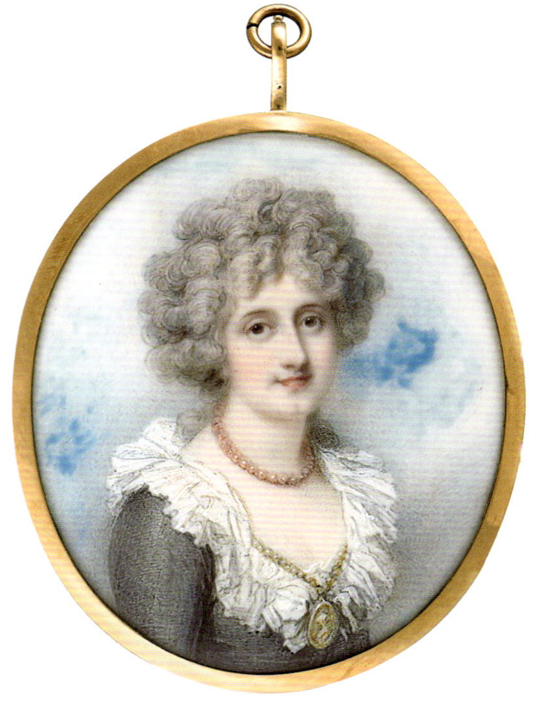

Maria Fagnani (1771–1856) was the illegitimate daughter of the Marchesa Fagnani, an Italian former dancer. In 1798 Maria married Francis Charles Seymour-Conway (1777–1842), from 1822 3rd Marquess of Hertford. The 3rd Marquess became the first great art collector of the family. He acquired outstanding Dutch paintings, French furniture and Sèvres porcelain. His ambitious collecting was partly made possible by the enormous fortune that his wife brought into the family. Both George Augustus Selwyn and the 4th Duke of Queensberry left Maria Fagnani, known as Mie-Mie, their considerable fortunes because each man regarded her as his daughter. Together with the Hertford family fortune, her money assured the family enormous wealth, a consideration which might have helped to smooth over the difficulties of her turbulent and socially unequal marriage to the future 3rd Marquess.

Richard Cosway painted this miniature of Fagnani in 1791, eight years before the wedding and at a time when her future husband was only fourteen. It was not commissioned by the much younger future 3rd Marquess, but entered the family collection during the lifetime of the 4th Marquess, Fagnani's son. He is known to have kept a miniature of her under the pillow of his bed. The portrait shows Fagnani wearing the portrait miniature of a woman on a chain around her neck, most likely a depiction of her mother, the Marchesa Fagnani. The miniature might have been painted for her mother and then been given to her after her mother's death, subsequently to be passed on by Mie-Mie.

This miniature is a typical work by Cosway. The blue background, the soft and pale colour-scheme based on the sophisticated use of the ivory colour of the ground and the slight stippling are typical of his work around 1790. In 1785, Cosway had been appointed Principal Painter to the Prince of Wales. In that function Cosway was producing drawings and numerous portrait miniatures for the Prince, but the painter was also involved in the decoration of his London residence, Carlton House. An autograph Latin inscription on the back of the mount proudly cites the title. Similar inscriptions appear on the backs of numerous Cosway miniatures from the same period. CMV

PROVENANCE: Probably Richard, 4th Marquess of Hertford; Sir Richard Wallace; Lady Wallace; Sir John Murray Scott sale, London, Christie's, 24–6 June 1913, lot 26; Arthur Tite, from whom bought, 1959, by the National Art-Collections Fund, £325, and presented to the Library of the Wallace Collection (now Hertford House Historic Collection).

HHHC2007.2

34 Richard Cosway (1742–1821)

Miss Crofton, *c.*1800

Ivory, 72 × 55 mm

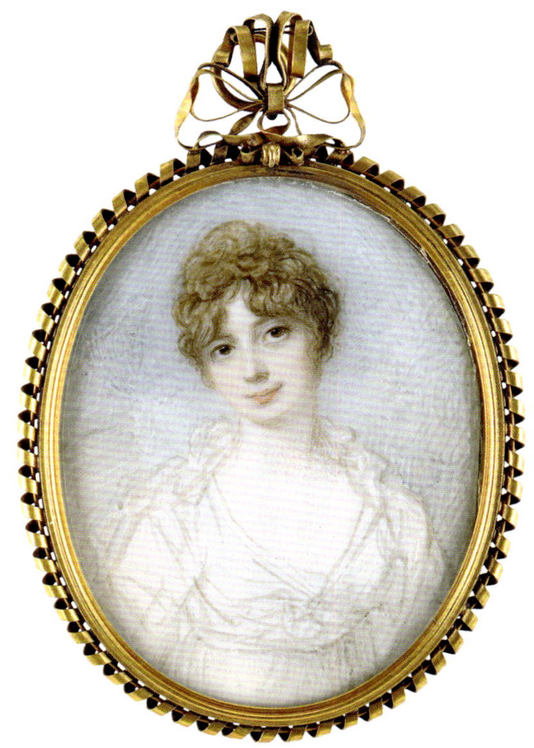

Richard Cosway became the most fashionable English miniature painter of the late eighteenth century, having developed a distinctive style of miniature painting. He had an unerring sense of style and chose attitudes for his sitters according to contemporary ideals of elegance and sensibility. His artistic hallmark became his brilliant way of using the surface of the ivory as part of the miniature's colour scheme, mainly for the fashionably pale skin of the sitters. Many of his works leave a considerable amount of the ivory surface visible and combine it with blues, blacks and greys to achieve a light and elegant colour scheme.

In Cosway's portrait of Miss Crofton this effect is pushed further than intended by the artist. As the comparison with other works (see nos.32 and 33) demonstrates, this miniature has not reached the same level of finish. While the head of the sitter and part of the background above her head might already have reached the final stage, the woman's upper body and her dress have only been roughly sketched out. In its half-finished state, the miniature gives a fascinating insight into Cosway's working method and his technique. A first outline in grey was used to determine the composition, before different parts of the miniature were then finished with finer brushstrokes in different colours. Cosway obviously did not work evenly across the surface but finished certain areas before he touched in the next part. Miss Crofton's face features delicate browns and reds. Cosway was an assiduous and efficient portrait painter, recorded to have had up to twelve sittings on a single day. The portrait of Miss Crofton gives us an impression of what a portrait miniature might have looked like after the first sitting.

The name of the sitter is indicated in an inscription on the back of the miniature. Nothing is known about her. The style of her hair and her dress suggest a date of *c.*1800. CMV

PROVENANCE: First recorded at Bethnal Green (1872–5), no.1711

M88

35 Louis-Ami Arlaud-Jurine (1751–1829)

An Unknown Lady, *c.*mid 1790s

Ivory, 108 × 85 mm

Signed, lower right: *Arlaud*

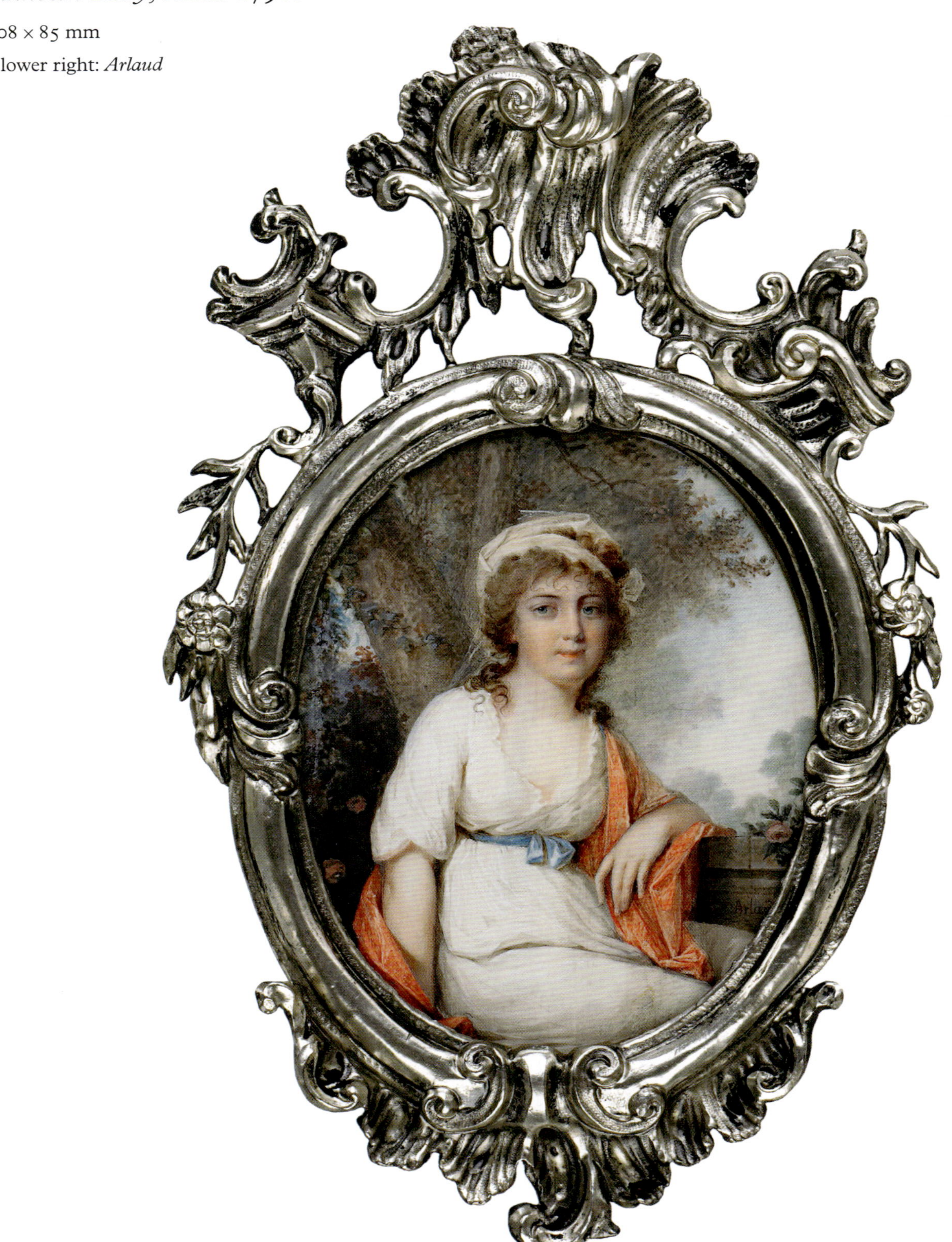

Born in Geneva, Arlaud-Jurine was a Swiss painter of miniatures and enamels who came from a family of artists, including the well-known miniature painter Benjamin Arlaud, who worked in London in the early years of the eighteenth century.[1] He was a pupil of the celebrated Swiss artist Jean-Etienne Liotard and of the history painter Joseph-Marie Vien in Paris. He returned to Geneva in 1778, according to the historian Leo Schidlof, and spent the rest of his career there, apart from a stay in London 1792–1802. There is some uncertainty about his exhibition history in London because the Royal Academy's lists do not always give an artist's Christian name and English writers often had problems with foreign names, but he may have shown more than forty miniatures at the Royal Academy's exhibitions between 1792 and 1800, and then a further work in 1825 (a portrait of a guide at Chamonix). He was also frequently represented at exhibitions in Geneva and on one occasion, in 1808, at the Paris Salon. According to his own account book, which he began in 1808, he painted 1,554 miniatures.[2]

This miniature, probably painted in London, shows a lady wearing a white muslin dress of a kind to be seen in many portraits of women from the 1790s by artists such as Romney, Hoppner and Opie. She has also wrapped a white muslin scarf round her head, perhaps in imitation of some Revolutionary French styles which had crossed the Channel by this time.[3] In England Arlaud-Jurine's sitters included Princess Sophia of Gloucester and Edward, Duke of Kent,[4] but the identity of the lady in this miniature, clearly of a lower social standing, is unknown. It is painted in a precise, carefully stippled manner, and Arlaud-Jurine has paid particular attention to the calligraphic swirls of the sitter's hair. The Rococo-style frame of poor quality silver does not fit the miniature properly. SD

PROVENANCE: First catalogued in the Wallace Collection 1904

M3

36 John Hazlitt (1767–1837), after Reynolds

Mrs Mary Robinson ('Perdita'), late 18th (after *c.*1790)–early 19th century

Ivory, 117 × 95 mm

John Hazlitt was an elder brother of the much better known writer and painter William Hazlitt (to whom he gave painting lessons). He exhibited portraits at the Royal Academy from 1788 to 1819, many of unnamed ladies and gentlemen, but also including Samuel Taylor Coleridge, Edward Jenner and the artist Henry Edridge. He spent the last five years of his life in Stockport, Cheshire. He is identified as the artist of this miniature of Mrs Robinson by comparison with a similar version in the Maidstone Museum and Bentlif Art Gallery, Kent, where there is a collection of his work.[1]

Mary Robinson, born Mary Darby (1758–1800), was an actress and author. She married Thomas Robinson, a clerk, in 1774, and made her debut on the stage in 1776 in the role of Juliet. Her most famous performances, however, were in 1779 as Perdita in *The Winter's Tale*, when she attracted the attention of the Prince of Wales, becoming the first of his many mistresses. After the affair ended in 1781 she sold the Prince's love letters to the Crown for £5,000 and was granted an annuity of £500, though it was not paid on a regular basis. She was soon to have other lovers, including Charles James Fox and the soldier and politician Banastre Tarleton, for whom she retained the deepest affection. Her voluminous writings, including poems, novels, plays and essays, kept her in the public eye in her later life, which was cruelly marred by paralysis of the legs and hands brought about by a miscarriage in 1783.[2]

The 2nd Marquess of Hertford and his wife were loyal friends of Mrs Robinson. They acquired portraits of her by Reynolds, Romney and Gainsborough – the last, a superb whole-length exhibited at the Royal Academy in 1781, being a gift to the Marquess by the Prince of Wales in 1818. A further portrait by Reynolds was acquired by the 4th Marquess much later, in 1859. All these are now in the Wallace Collection with the exception of the first by Reynolds, the model for this miniature, which is at Waddesdon Manor, Buckinghamshire (National Trust).[3] Painted in 1782, it was bought by the 2nd Marquess of Hertford at auction in 1796, and sold by the 6th Marquess to the dealer C.J. Wertheimer in 1894 or shortly afterwards.[4]

The provenance of this miniature is unknown, and it was first recorded after the Wallace Collection opened as a museum in 1900. There was a miniature inventoried in 1842 in the 3rd Marquess of Hertford's library at Dorchester House as an enamel by "Bone" of "Mrs Robinson" (see also no.57), but, although it cannot now be identified, it seems unlikely that this was an erroneous notice of Hazlitt's miniature, which is not in enamel. It is evident that Hazlitt did not have an outstandingly successful career and he is now little known, but this miniature demonstrates that he was an able artist. He has deftly captured Reynolds's manner, even on this much reduced scale, while Perdita's powdered hair, her lace and feathers – the composition owes much to a portrait by Rubens of his second wife, Hélène Fourment[5] – are convincingly defined with great delicacy. The miniature is framed in a nineteenth-century version on a reduced scale of an early eighteenth-century French frame for an oil painting. SD

PROVENANCE: First catalogued in the Wallace Collection 1904

M40

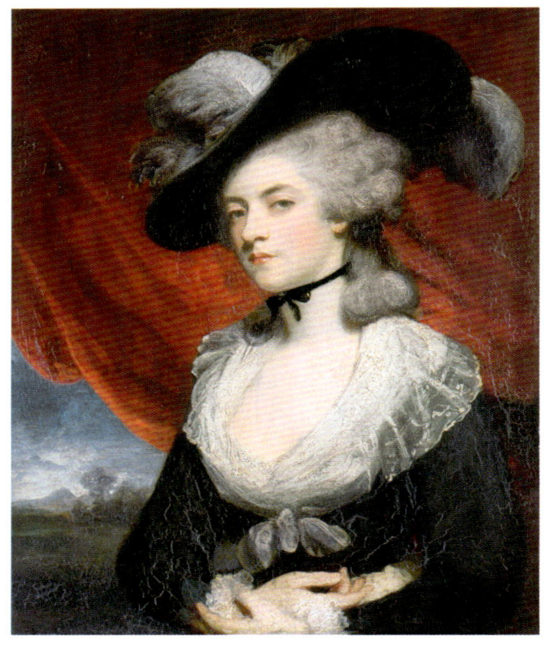

Fig.1 Joshua Reynolds, *Mrs Mary Robinson ('Perdita')*, 1782, oil on canvas, 73.7 × 63.5 cm, Waddesdon, The Rothschild Collection (The National Trust)

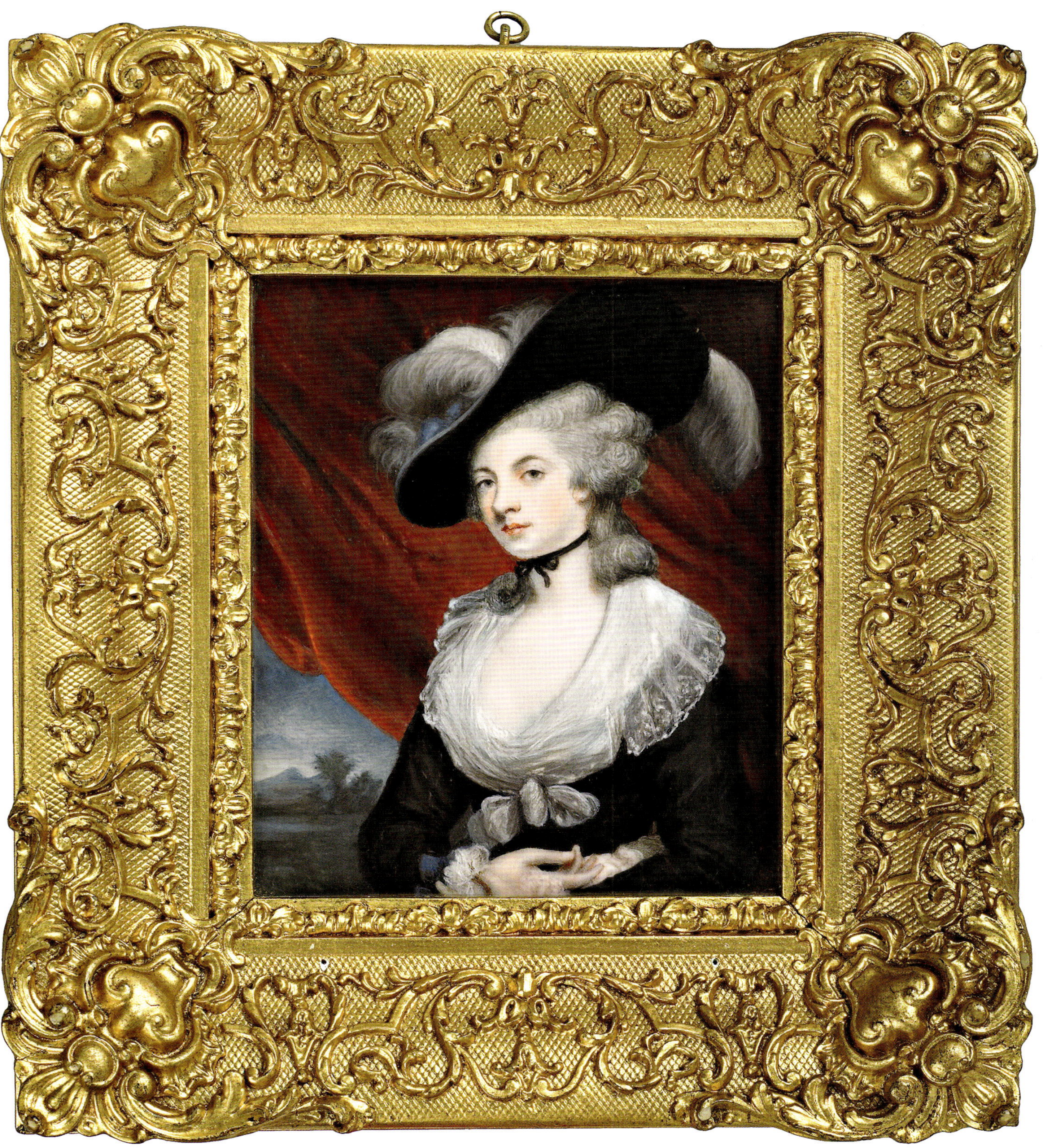

37 Jean-Baptiste Isabey (1767–1855)
Self-portrait, *c.*1795–1800

Ivory, 163 × 126 mm

Signed, lower left: *J. Isabey*

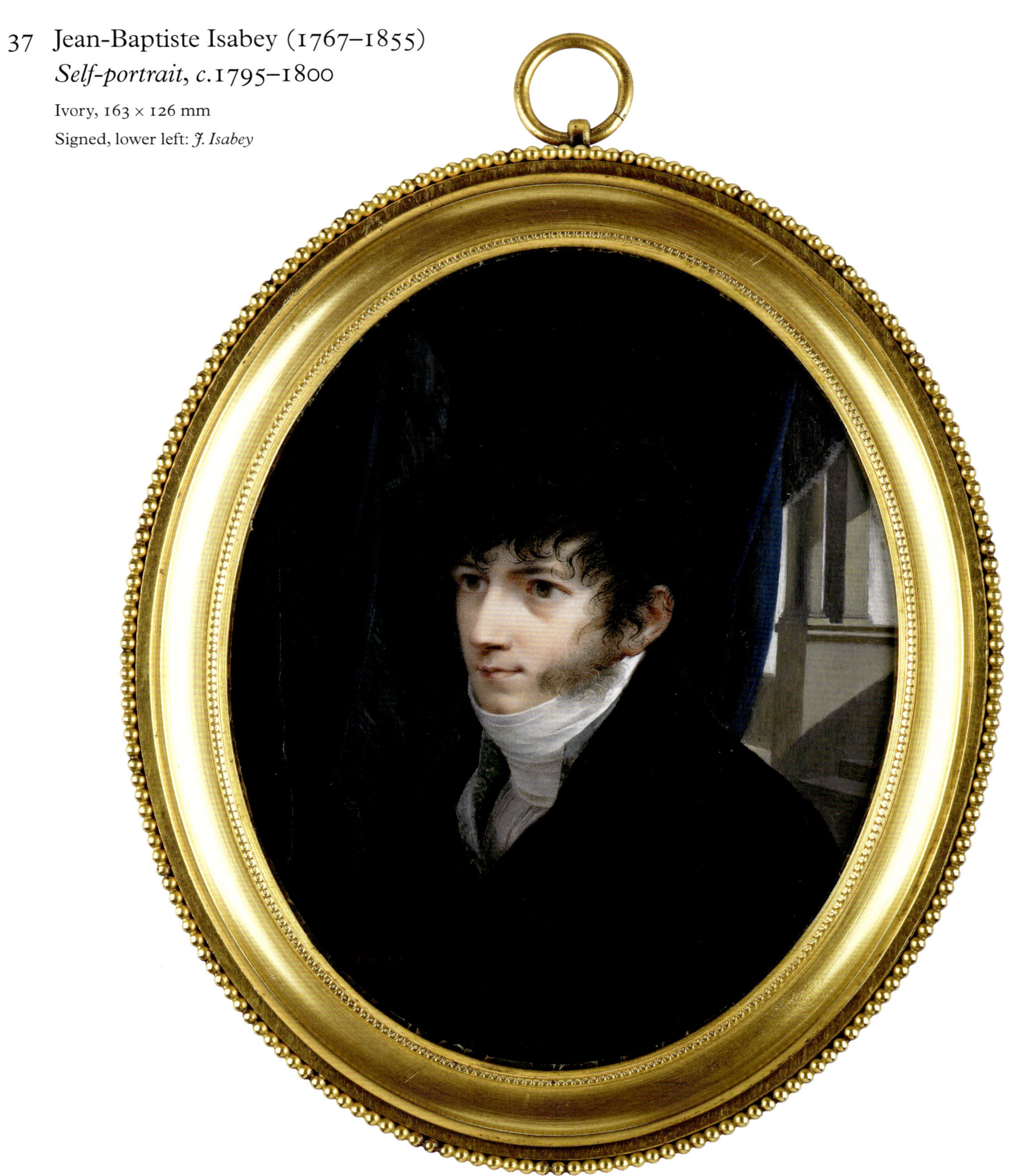

Jean-Baptiste Isabey was the most important figure in French miniature painting of the early nineteenth century. Born in Nancy, he studied first with two local artists, Girardet and Claudot, before moving to Paris in 1785, where he became a pupil of the great history painter Jacques-Louis David. Blessed with an attractive, socially astute personality as well as a broad range of artistic ability, he soon won the favour of the court at Versailles and later of the Bonapartes, painting with the aid of his large studio countless portraits of the Emperor and his family. Appointed Peintre dessinateur du cabinet de S.M. l'Empereur, des cérémonies et des relations extérieures in 1804, he was not only Napoleon's principal miniature painter but also played an important role in designing and organizing festivities for the imperial court. After the fall of the Empire he painted many of the representatives at the Congress of Vienna and continued to receive patronage, though on a much reduced scale, from Louis XVIII and his successors, Charles X and Louis-Philippe. When he died in 1855 at the age of eighty-eight he was in receipt of a pension from Napoleon III.[1]

Isabey produced self-portraits throughout his career. Like many of his rivals, including Augustin (nos.38, 42 and 56), he was well aware of their value for promoting an artist's career. With the opening of the Paris Salon to non-Academicians after 1791, this institution became a more competitive environment in which portraits, including self-portraits, played a much more significant role than they had done previously.[2] Isabey painted a self-portrait at least as early as 1786, exhibited one to much acclaim at the Salon of 1796, and two years later, also at the Salon, showed a large drawing in black chalk (a medium in which he also specialized) of himself and his family in a boat which became the basis for a famous engraving (*La Barque*) by François Aubertin.[3] As late as 1850, only five years before his death, an engraving of perhaps his last self-portrait was published.[4] In almost every image of Isabey, even works by other artists, he is shown looking towards his right – presumably because he regarded this as presenting his 'better side'.

On the basis of the costume, this work may be dated *c.*1795–1800. It is painted with broad brushstrokes in the costume and background and with minute stippling in the face. Isabey wears a black coat, white shirt and white stock – dress similar to that in his well-known portrait with his daughter by François Gérard exhibited at the Salon of 1796 (Paris, Louvre).[5] He is also shown similarly dressed (though on this occasion with a red coat) in Boilly's *A Reunion of Artists in Isabey's Studio* of 1798 (Paris, Louvre) – another painting conceived in part to advance Isabey's reputation.[6] The slightly dishevelled look and the "cravat of ferocious stiffness which made it difficult to move the head"[7] were fashionable with many well-to-do young men in Paris in the late 1790s. The mutton-chop whiskers were also clearly something of a trademark for the artist: on the evidence of his portraits it seems that he retained them for the rest of his life.

The Wallace Collection's miniature was copied in his studio by some of Isabey's numerous pupils, including Aubry and Singry (see nos. 44–5 and 59).[8] No doubt this was part of their training, but of course it was also in line with Isabey's practice of disseminating his portrait as widely as possible. SD

PROVENANCE: First recorded at Bethnal Green (1872–5), no.1822

M226

38 Jean-Baptiste-Jacques Augustin (1759–1832), after Greuze

A Bacchante, 1798–9

Ivory, 78 mm diameter

Signed and dated, right (by the left shoulder): *Augustin./ an.7.* (*i.e.* September 1798–September 1799)

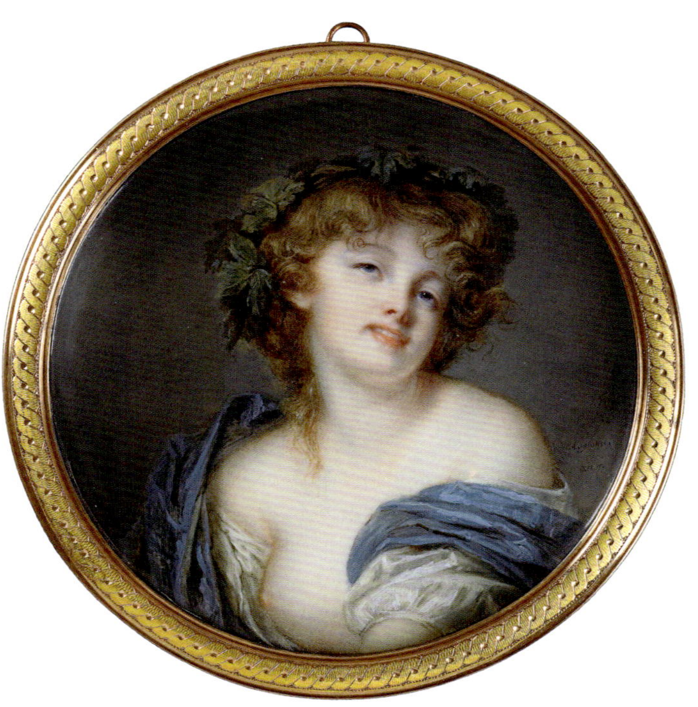

Augustin and Isabey (*q.v.*) were the two most successful and influential French miniature painters of the early nineteenth century. Born at Saint-Dié near Nancy, where he probably received his earliest training as an artist, Augustin moved in 1781 to Paris, where over the following decade he gradually secured a place for himself among the city's miniature painters. He exhibited regularly at the Paris Salon between 1791 and 1831, achieving a notable success with his *Self-portrait* (location unknown) shown at the Salon of 1796. Under the Empire he was, after Isabey, one of the principal painters supplying miniatures of Napoleon and his family (see no.42). Favoured by Louis XVIII, for whom he produced many miniatures in gouache and enamel, in 1819 he was named Premier peintre en miniature de la chambre et du cabinet du Roi, though in his final years his meticulous style became increasingly unfashionable. Among his many pupils – more than four hundred in all – were his wife, Pauline Du Cruet, Daniel Saint and Mlle de Mirbel (nos.50, 60).[1]

In Augustin's posthumous sale, 19–21 December 1839, there was a painting of a young bacchante by Greuze which was almost certainly the basis for this miniature. It is now untraced, but several versions of the composition are recorded, including a painting now in the Wallace Collection (fig.1).[2] Jean-Baptiste Greuze (1725–1805) produced many small-scale expressive heads of this kind – more than a dozen are owned by the Wallace Collection – which were popular with collectors well into the nineteenth century (see nos.22 and 25). Although the girl in this miniature does not wear a leopard's skin, one of the traditional attributes of bacchantes (the female followers of Bacchus, the god of wine), she is identifiable as a bacchante from her abandoned pose and the vine leaves in her hair (see also no.39).[3]

Augustin owned two paintings by Greuze, and the artists may well have been known to each other. In the late 1790s Greuze was still a fashionable and successful artist. At the 1795 Paris Salon Augustin exhibited a miniature of an unspecified subject after Greuze, and the Wallace Collection's miniature is dated no more than four years later. In his *Lettres sur la Miniature* of 1823 Mansion (see no.61) would recommend that students copy Greuze's works, and no doubt Augustin's two paintings by the artist were used as a model for copies by his pupils as well as himself.[4] This miniature is painted in the beautifully controlled manner for which Augustin was renowned. Although the drapery seems to have been brushed in with some vigour, the hair and flesh tones have all the extraordinary precision and delicacy which from the beginning of his career distinguished Augustin's works from those of Hall and his generation (*cf.* no.22). It was this attention to detail which would lead Mansion to call Augustin "the Gerard Dou of the miniature".[5]

The Louvre owns an undated enamel version by Augustin of the Wallace Collection's miniature.[6] SD

PROVENANCE: First recorded at Bethnal Green (1872–5), no.1756

M14

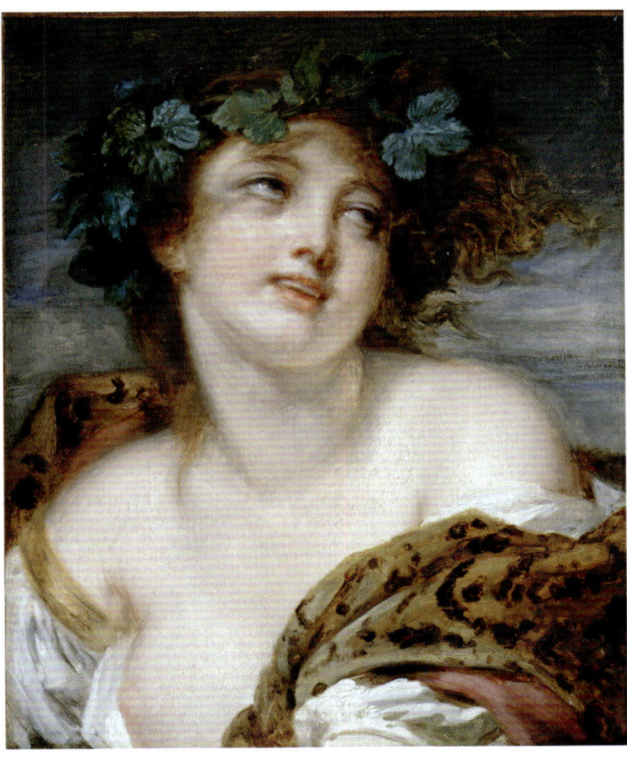

Fig.1 Jean-Baptiste Greuze, *Bacchante*, 1780s, oil on canvas, 45.7 × 37.3 cm, London, The Wallace Collection (M407)

39 Henry Bone (1755–1834), after Vigée Le Brun
Lady Hamilton as a Bacchante, 1803

Enamel on copper, 222 × 280 mm

Signed and dated, bottom left (along the side of the cymbal): *H Bone 1803* (the *HB* in monogram)

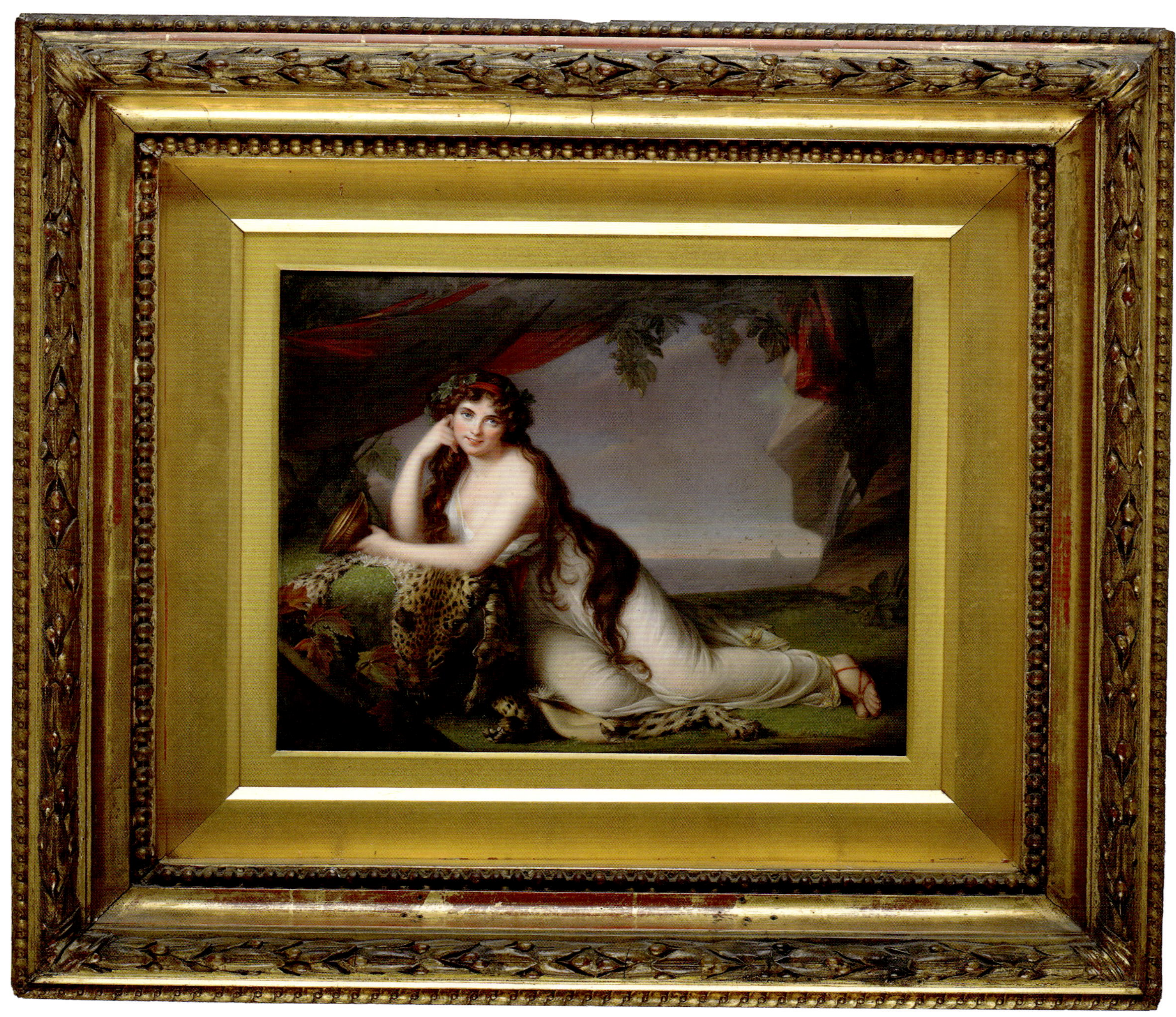

× 0.4

Not many works of art can be associated with the great naval hero Lord Nelson, but one of the few is this enamel miniature by Henry Bone of Nelson's famous mistress, Emma, Lady Hamilton. In fact, it was bequeathed to Nelson by Emma's husband, Sir William Hamilton, after he had sold to Nelson the oil painting by Vigée Le Brun on which Bone's miniature was based.

Emma Hart (1765–1815), born Amy Lyon, was a notorious courtesan who had been the mistress of Sir William Hamilton's nephew Charles Greville before marrying Hamilton in 1791. Her husband was the British envoy in Naples and an important collector of art, particularly classical antiquities. In Naples Emma came into contact with a cultured group of antiquarians, expatriates and visiting artists. Already in London she had acted as a model for several painters, including Reynolds and Romney, but it was in Naples that she became famous for her 'attitudes', a combination of poses and dance which allowed her to flaunt her beauty, sometimes in a frankly lascivious manner. It was after his brilliant victory at the Battle of the Nile in August 1798 that Nelson became her lover, a situation which was tolerated by Sir William Hamilton with apparent equanimity.

In 1790, shortly before their marriage, Hamilton ordered the portrait in oils on which Bone's miniature was based. Vigée Le Brun was one of the most successful French painters of her time, and a close friend of Queen Marie-Antoinette, whose portrait she painted on several occasions. She had arrived in Naples having fled France soon after the outbreak of the Revolution. Bone's enamel of Lady Hamilton, a faithful copy of Vigée Le Brun's original composition, is dated on the back *March 1803*. It, too, was painted for Sir William Hamilton, but bequeathed by him to Nelson almost immediately after completion. Nelson had bought Vigée Le Brun's original from Hamilton two years earlier to stop it from appearing in a public sale, and lent it back to Hamilton in order that Bone's miniature could be made. The painting is today in a private collection.[1]

Emma was frequently depicted in mythological guises. Here she is shown as a bacchante, a follower of Dionysus, the Greek god of wine, a guise in which she had earlier been painted by both Reynolds and Romney. Vigée Le Brun also painted another portrait of her as a bacchante, dancing with Mount Vesuvius in the background (now in the Lady Lever Art Gallery, Port Sunlight). Here the drinking bowl she holds in her left hand, the vine leaves and the panther skin all allude to Dionysus. However, in a letter of 1790 to Mme du Barry, Vigée Le Brun also referred to the painting as a representation of Ariadne, the daughter of the King of Crete who helped the Greek hero Theseus to escape from the Labyrinth after he had killed the Minotaur, but who was abandoned by him on the island of Naxos. (The ship on the horizon may therefore be carrying the departing Theseus.) According to some versions of the myth, Ariadne later married Dionysus – an interpretation particularly relevant to Emma, who was discarded by Greville before becoming the wife of another man and living in a foreign land. Her smiling face in this picture, inappropriate for such a poignant subject as Ariadne's desertion by Theseus, would be apt for her discovery by Dionysus.[2] Apparently, the performances of Emma herself could suggest such ambivalent interpretations. Vigée Le Brun noted that "... nothing was more curious than the facility that Lady Hamilton had acquired of suddenly making her features show sadness or joy, and of posing marvellously to portray different characters. With her animated eyes and her dishevelled hair, she could portray a delightful bacchante, then abruptly her face would express grief, and one saw an admirable repentant Magdalen."[3] Indeed, in a further twist to this complex image, Emma's long hair, recumbent pose and revealing dress also evoke many traditional representations of the Magdalen – perhaps an appropriate reference in view of her colourful early history.[4] Romney painted her as the Magdalen for the Prince of Wales in 1792, a picture which apparently passed later into the collection of the Prince's friend, the 3rd Marquess of Hertford.[5]

Henry Bone was a specialist painter of miniatures in enamel (see also nos.53, 57 and 63). Appointed Enamel Painter to George III, George IV and William IV, he became an Associate of the Royal Academy in 1801 and a Royal Academician in 1811. His copies after oil paintings earned him an enormous reputation in his lifetime, culminating in the extraordinary price of 2,200 guineas paid in 1811 for his copy (which for an enamel was on an unprecedented scale) after Titian's painting *Bacchus and Ariadne* which is now in the National Gallery.[6] SD

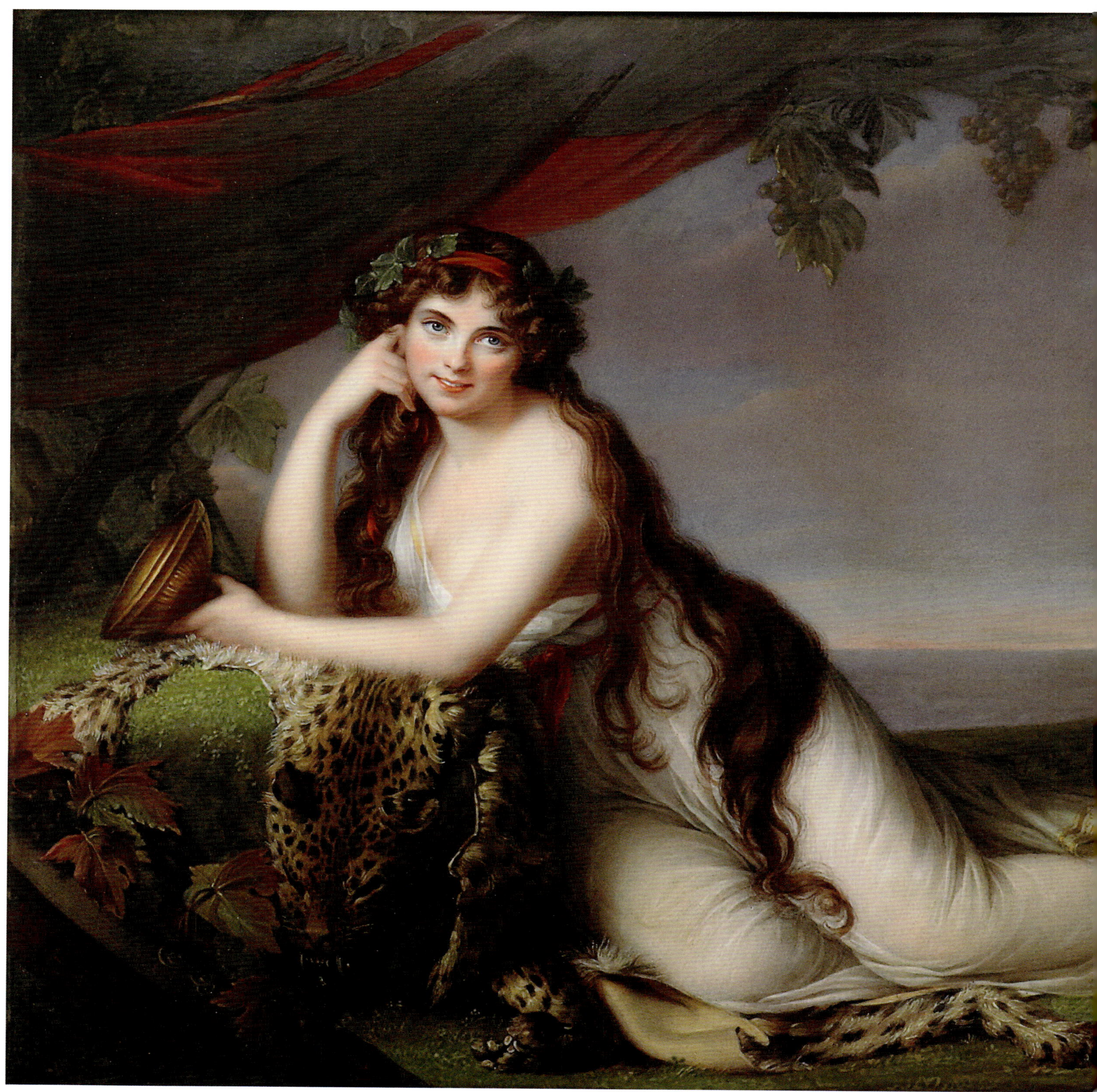

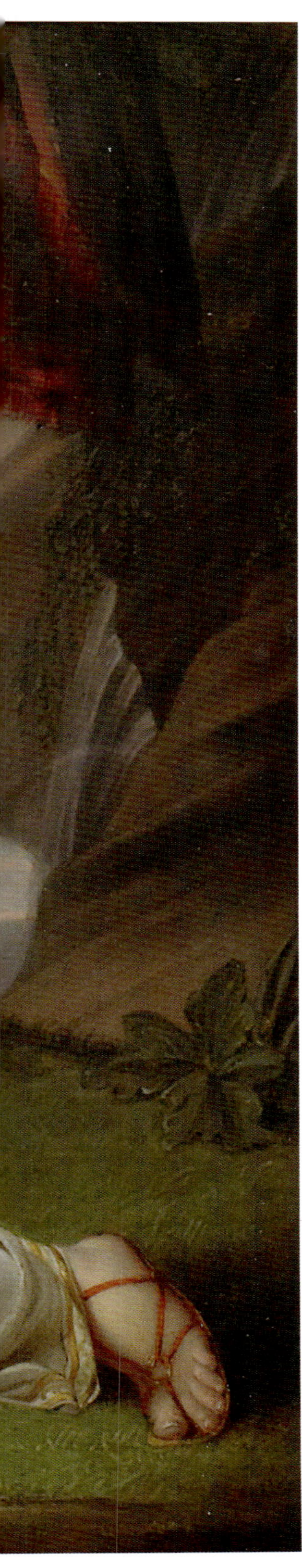

PROVENANCE: Sir William Hamilton; bequeathed to Horatio, Lord Nelson, 1803; Alexander Davison sale, Christie's, London, 21–8 April 1817, lot 818, bought in?; sold by Davison, 28 June 1823, for £147; bought by the 4th Marquess of Hertford, through his agent Samuel Mawson, at the Northwick sale, Christie's, London, 19 August 1859, lot 1620, for 700 guineas (£735)

M21

40 Louis-Ami Arlaud-Jurine (1751–1829)

Mme de Staël, c.1805

Ivory, 82 × 84 mm

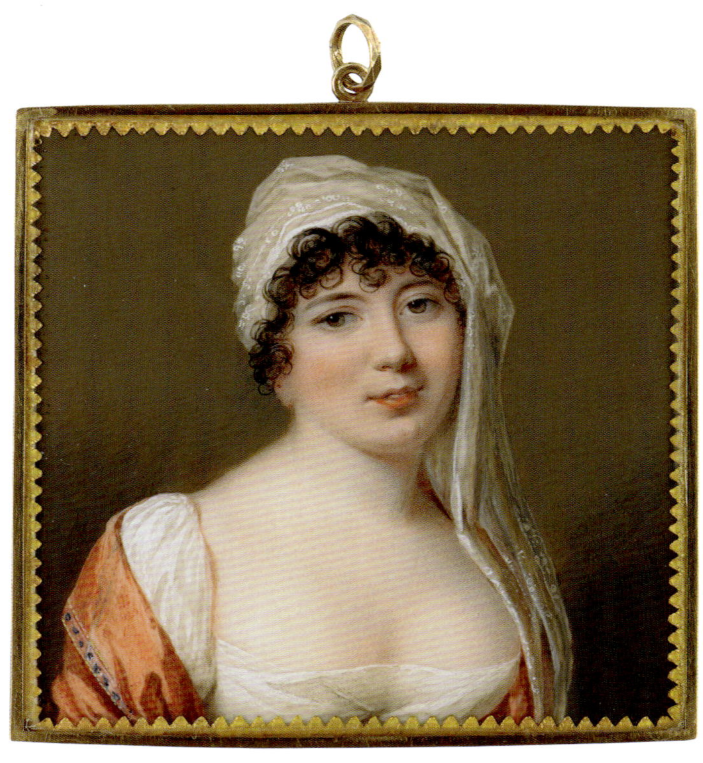

Many of Arlaud-Jurine's later miniatures were painted in a firmer, more richly coloured manner which may be associated with the Neoclassicism which had been pioneered by his Parisian master Vien (see no.35).

Anne Louise Germaine Necker, baronne de Staël-Holstein, usually known as Mme de Staël (1766–1817), daughter of Louis XVI's famous finance minister Jacques Necker, was a writer best known for her novel *Corinne* and for her opposition to Napoleon. Although she spent much of her life at her father's estate of Coppet on Lake Geneva, she also lived for extended periods in Paris and visited Germany, Austria, Russia, Sweden and Finland. It is not known for certain that she was acquainted with the Hertford family, but she visited England in 1793 and from 1812 to 1814, when she was lionized by London society, which makes it likely that at some time she became acquainted with the 2nd Marquess and Marchioness of Hertford, as well as their son, the future 3rd Marquess.[1]

This miniature relates closely to a portrait in oil of Mme de Staël and her daughter Albertine attributed to Marguérite Gérard which is now in the Musée de Coppet.[2] Both portraits show de Staël wearing vaguely classical costume and with an embroidered scarf on her head, though Arlaud-Jurine's bust-length miniature omits Albertine and the landscape setting. Miniatures based on oils frequently simplify the composition of the original work. The oil may be dated *c.*1804, and the miniature a little later, the period in which de Staël wrote and published *Corinne*. Another version of the Wallace Collection's miniature and a drawing of Mme de Staël by Arlaud-Jurine, but with the pose reversed, are also recorded.[3] SD

PROVENANCE: Possibly first recorded at Bethnal Green (1872–5), no.1765

M180

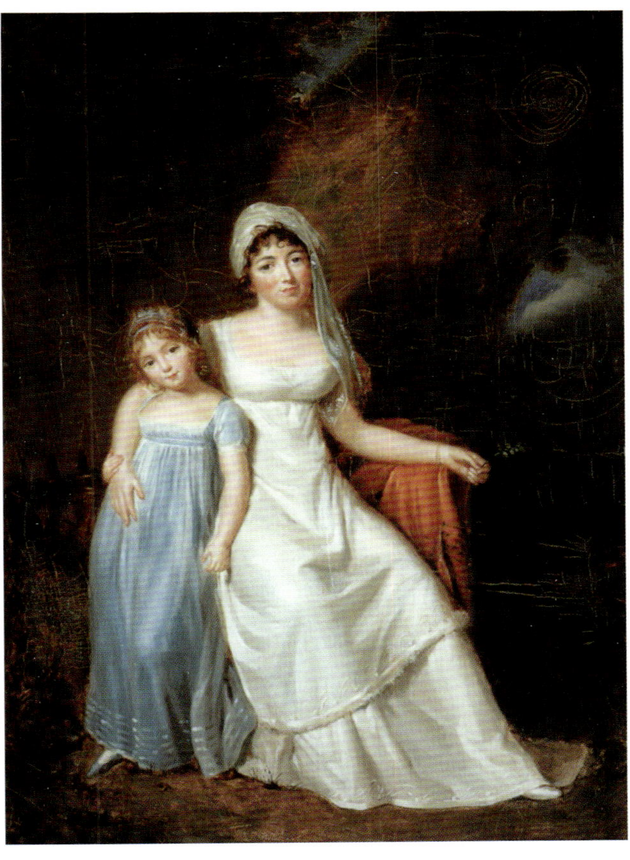

Fig.1 Attributed to Marguérite Gérard, *Mme de Staël, c.*1804, oil on canvas, Coppet, Musée de Coppet

41 Jean-Baptiste Isabey (1767–1855)

Napoleon I, *c.*1805–10

Ivory, 36 × 26 mm

Signed, vertically, along right-hand edge: *Isabey*

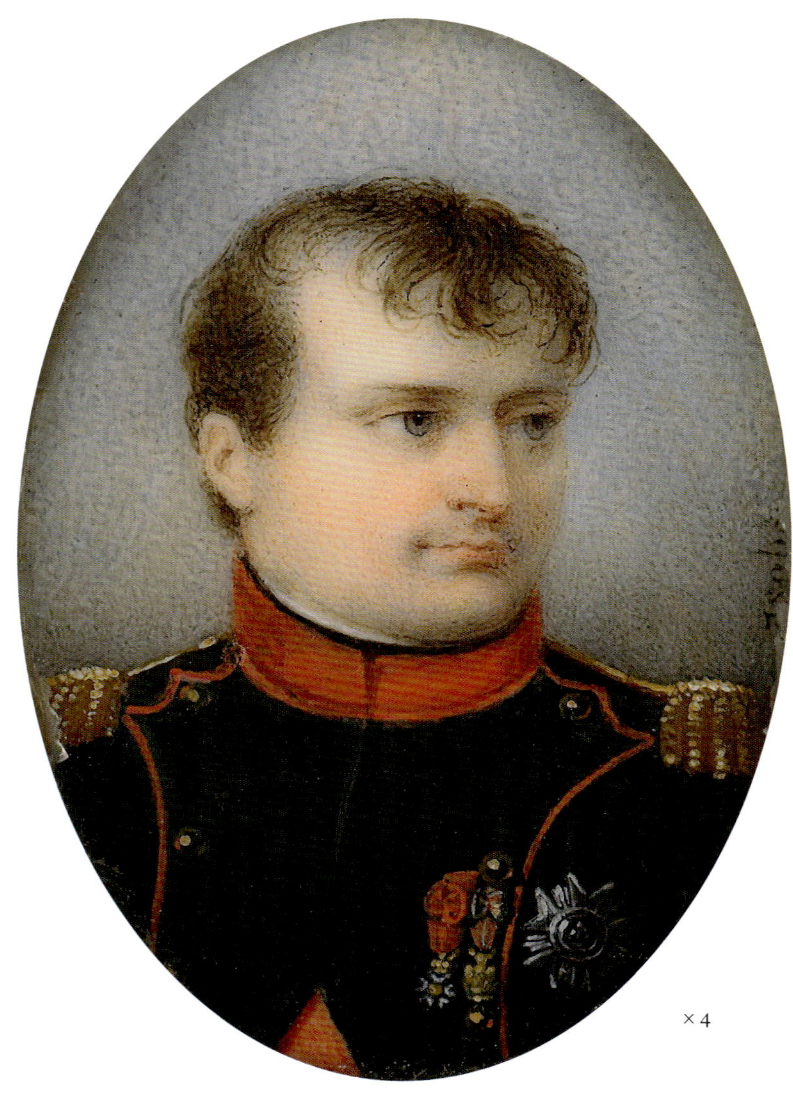

× 4

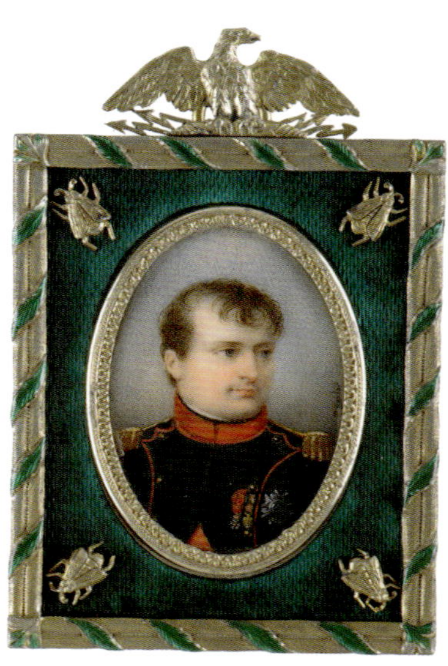

Napoleon set out to revive the arts, as he was well aware of their use as a support for his regime. One of the many ways in which he did this was to renew, and indeed far enhance, the patronage of miniature painters practised by the Bourbons of the *ancien régime*. In the year 1780, under Louis XVI, fewer than ten portraits destined to be diplomatic gifts were ordered from miniature painters; in 1808, under Napoleon, the corresponding figure was more than forty.[1]

This is one of innumerable small bust-length portraits of Napoleon looking to his left painted by Isabey and his studio. It is difficult to date precisely because they were produced to a similar pattern, the head being adjusted slightly to take account of changes in Napoleon's appearance as he grew older, while the uniform and orders might be altered according to individual circumstances. Here he is shown wearing the uniform of the Chasseurs à cheval, the ribbon and cross of the Legion of Honour, the star of the Iron Crown and the badge of the Grand Eagle of the Legion of Honour. The miniature has a frame of green enamel over silver with bees and an eagle (both Napoleonic symbols) at the corners and top.[2]

Isabey's first portrait of Napoleon, exhibited at the Paris Salon of 1802, was a drawing showing him walking in the grounds at Malmaison, the country house near Paris shared by him with Joséphine. The image became famous through an engraving by Lingée and Godefroy.[3] Napoleon refused to pose for this or any later portrait, but Isabey was more fortunate than his rivals in that he was a member of Napoleon's entourage and could therefore observe him at close hand. In part because of this, his miniatures became the models for those of many other artists (see no.42). Nevertheless, such was the demand for portraits of Napoleon, for use as diplomatic gifts but also occasionally as more private objects, that nearly all those provided by Isabey were produced in a mechanical manner without the stimulus that would have been provided by novelty. In reality, most were also painted in part or entirely by pupils or other artists working on his behalf.

In August 1807 eighty portraits of the Emperor were ordered from Isabey, with nearly fifty more the following month.[4] So great was the pressure on him that he is said to have had three or four studios in Paris where painters were employed to copy his originals.[5] Even the most able among his pupils, such as Muneret and Aubrey (see nos.44–5), produced miniatures which were signed by Isabey as his own work. It is therefore impossible to be sure if Isabey was directly involved in the painting of an accomplished miniature like this or it is entirely the work of one of his more talented pupils. Demand for his portraits enabled Isabey in 1807 to increase his price from five hundred to six hundred francs per miniature, though in that year he also received a severe rebuke from Géraud Duroc, Grand maréchal du palais, because "His Majesty [had recently] … been very dissatisfied with the portraits of M. Isabey, and he would like either that he does better, or that we employ another painter".[6] Duroc's assistant Daru proposed a division of tasks between several artists in order to establish "a sort of rivalry for improvement", and it is clear that by 1808 Isabey's privileged position as almost the sole officially acknowledged producer of miniature portraits of Napoleon was over.[7] Paradoxically, however, such was Isabey's renown that by 1810 he was allowed to fix his price per portrait at 1,200 francs, double the figure he had charged only five years earlier. Other artists with lesser reputations were charging the 600 francs that Isabey had demanded formerly. They owed this advance in the income and status of miniature painters, unthinkable under the *ancien régime*, not only to the needs of the Napoleonic state but to the skills, both artistic and promotional, of Isabey. SD

PROVENANCE: First recorded at Bethnal Green (1872–5), no.1619

M211

42 Jean-Baptiste-Jacques Augustin (1759–1832)
Napoleon I, *c.*1806-10

Ivory, 40 × 30 mm

Signed, left (above right shoulder): *Augustin*

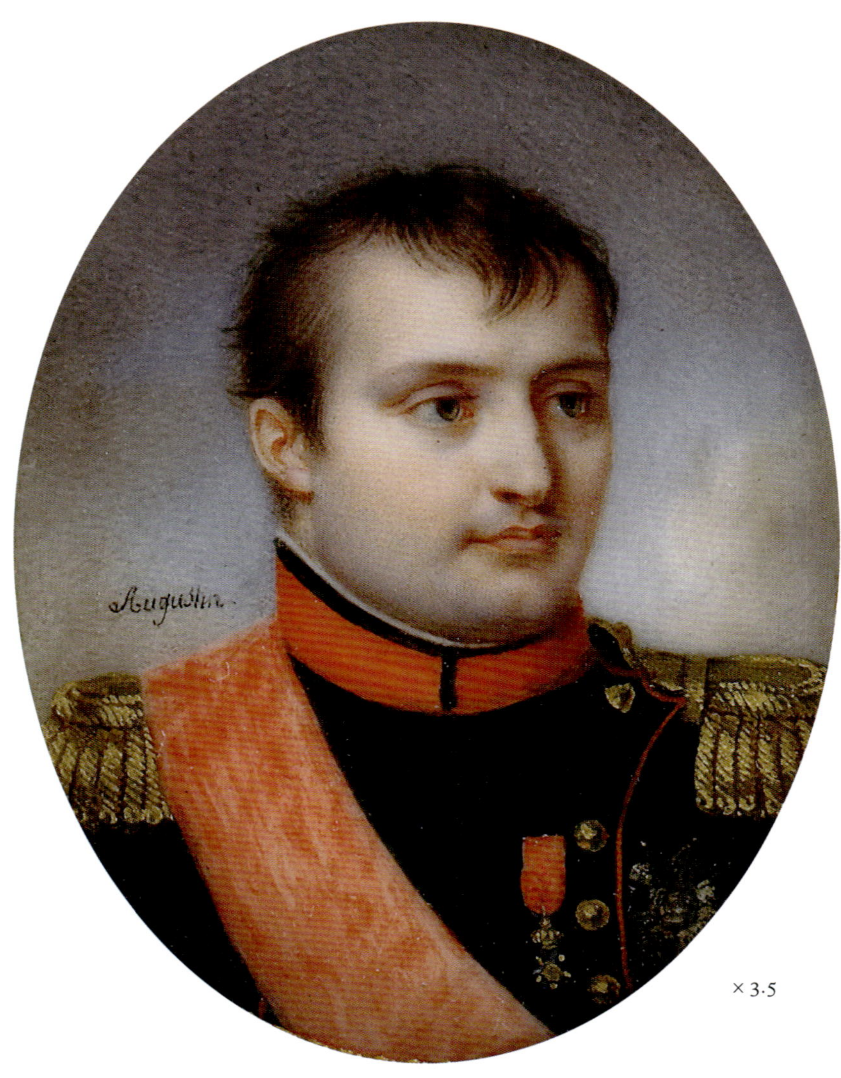

× 3.5

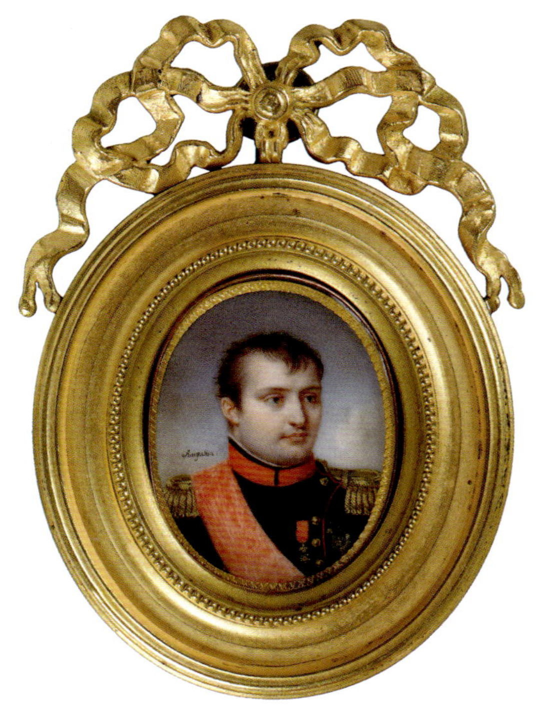

Augustin exhibited a portrait of Napoleon in enamel (now unlocated) at the 1806 Paris Salon, where he was awarded a gold medal. Although two years earlier Isabey had been appointed the official provider of portraits of Napoleon for diplomatic presents, in practice so great was the demand for images of the Emperor that between 1806 and 1814 many other artists, including Augustin, Aubry, Quaglia, Saint (see nos.46–52) and Muneret, were employed to produce diplomatic gifts and other images.[1] Like Isabey, these artists (some of whom had been Isabey's pupils) faced the problem of Napoleon's refusal to pose, but, unlike him, they also had the disadvantage of exclusion from his entourage. Given the demand from the court and others that they all were required to satisfy it was inevitable that their portraits (often painted entirely or in part with the aid of pupils) soon became formulaic. Faced with this problem, in 1807 Duroc, Grand maréchal du palais, who was responsible for diplomatic gifts, recommended artists to "devote themselves less to a perfect likeness than to presenting the idealized image [*le beau idéal*], while preserving certain distinctive traits".[2]

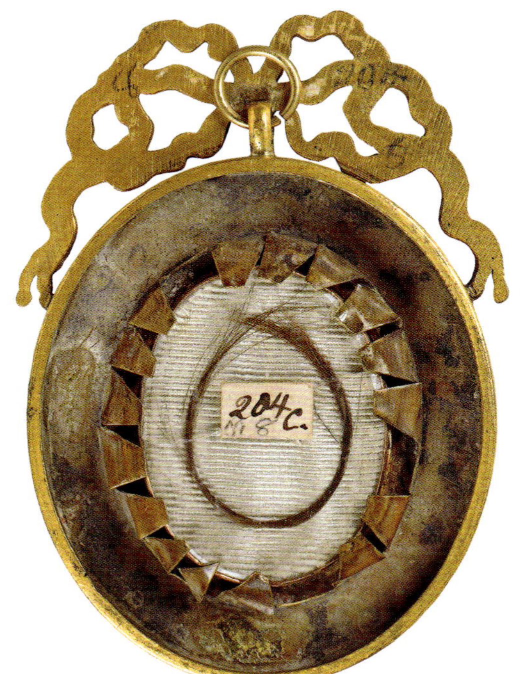

Fig.1 Reverse of no.42

This miniature by Augustin is characteristic of a type established by Isabey that was also produced in large numbers by other artists (see no.41). Here the head has been painted with considerable skill, but the shapeless body (which may be the work of a pupil) has been rendered in a rather dry, perfunctory manner. Napoleon is shown wearing the uniform of the Chasseurs à cheval and the ribbon, cross and Grand Eagle of the Legion of Honour with the star of the Iron Crown. Both these orders had been founded by Napoleon himself, the Legion of Honour in 1802 and the Iron Crown (named after the Iron Crown of Lombardy) in 1805. A lock of hair, presumably believed to be Napoleon's own, is set into the back of the miniature. Portrait miniatures of the Emperor intended as diplomatic gifts were usually set into snuff and other precious boxes. It was by no means unknown for the recipients of such gifts to return the boxes to the original maker in return for the value of the gold and jewels. However, whether this miniature (or the others in the Wallace Collection), was originally part of a diplomatic gift is impossible to say. The lock of hair suggests that it perhaps had a purpose more personal than a diplomatic gift. The commonplace frame probably dates from a few years after the miniature. SD

PROVENANCE: W. William Hope sale, Christie's, London, 15 June 1849, lot 1, £16; first recorded in Hertford/Wallace ownership at Bethnal Green (1872–5), no.1616

M8

43 Jean-Baptiste Isabey (1767–1855)

Napoleon I, 1810

Sepia heightened with white gouache on card, 215 × 170 mm

Signed and dated twice, to the left (on the column) and along the lower edge:

J. Isabey 1810

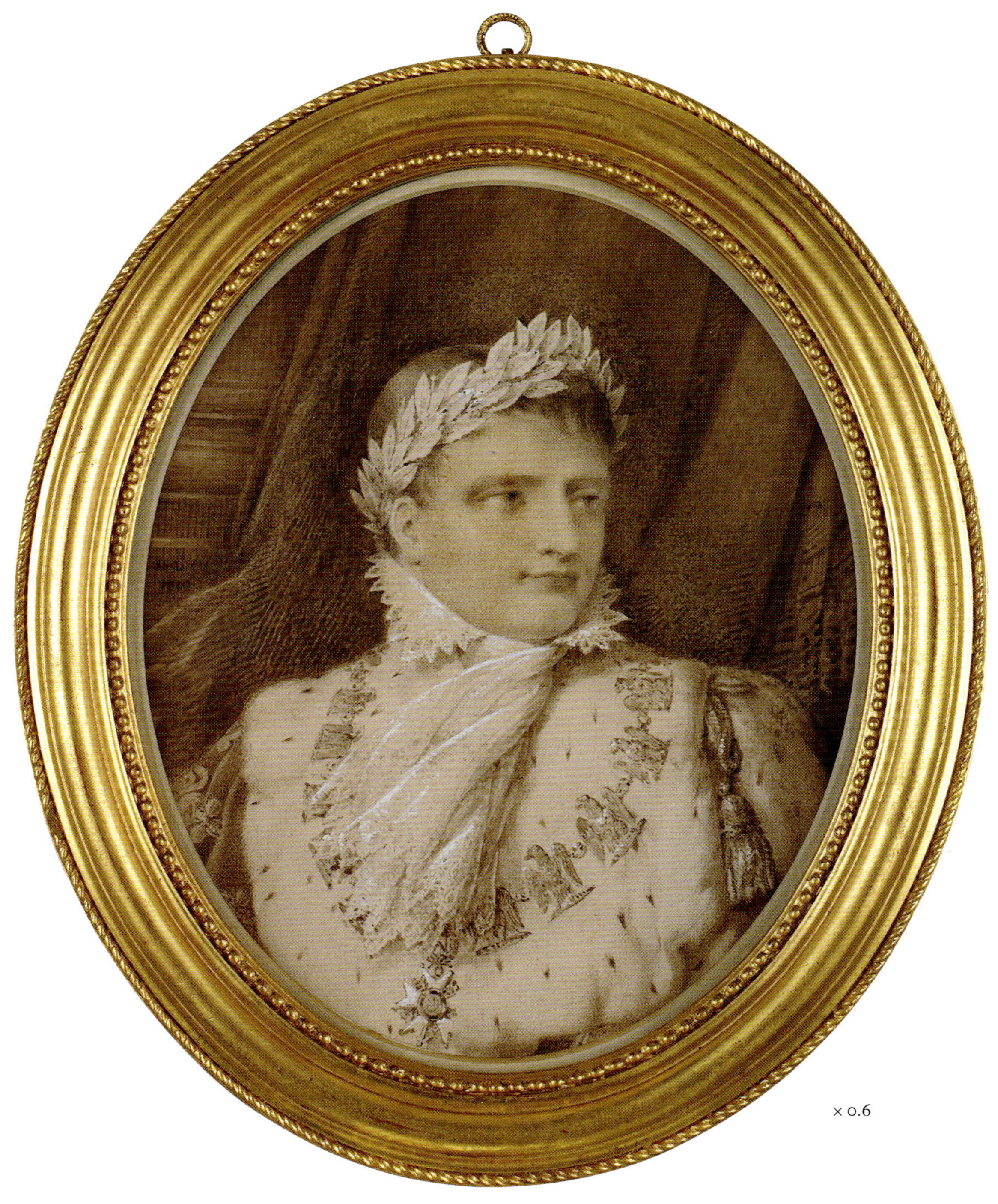

× 0.6

Although this should probably be classed as a drawing, it is included here because it has always been listed among the Wallace Collection's miniatures, and it is a fine work by the foremost miniature painter of his time.

Isabey was a highly skilled draughtsman who was as adept with watercolour, chalk and – as here – sepia as he was with watercolour and gouache. The original purpose of this portrait, which dates from the year of Napoleon's marriage to Marie-Louise, is unknown, but, with its large scale and unusual medium, it is clearly one of the more important of Isabey's images of the Emperor. Utilizing broad stippling in the face but smooth strokes in the costume and background, he shows Napoleon wearing his imperial robes, as did several other artists, including David, Ingres, Gérard and Robert Lefèvre, in full-length oil portraits painted between 1805 and 1811. With varying degrees of success, these paintings played a major role in establishing the iconography (original and yet clearly contrived from historical precedents) which was required by the newly established imperial state.[1] In this head and shoulders drawing Isabey was unable to include the orb and sceptre that played such important symbolic roles in the oil portraits, but he does include Napoleon's sumptuous velvet mantle and ermine cape, his laurel wreath and also his chain of the Legion of Honour. It is an almost disembodied image of the Emperor as national sovereign rather than as a soldier (*cf.* no.42), though it conforms to Isabey's standard formula of showing Napoleon head and shoulders, looking determinedly towards his left.

With the establishment of the Empire and Napoleon's coronation in 1804 an imperial iconography had to be devised in a matter of months, and in this process Isabey played a crucial role. A painter who was able to turn his hand with ease to theatrical design and the organization of balls and parties, he designed the costumes and jewellery for Napoleon's coronation and even helped the Emperor to dress for the occasion. After the event he also made drawings for a commemorative manuscript volume devoted to the subject of the coronation, which is now in the Louvre.[2] SD

PROVENANCE: First recorded at Bethnal Green (1872–5), no.1601

M232

44 Louis-François Aubry (1767–1851)

*The Empress Joséphine, c.*1805–10

Ivory, 65 × 44 mm

Signed, vertically, left centre: *Aubry*

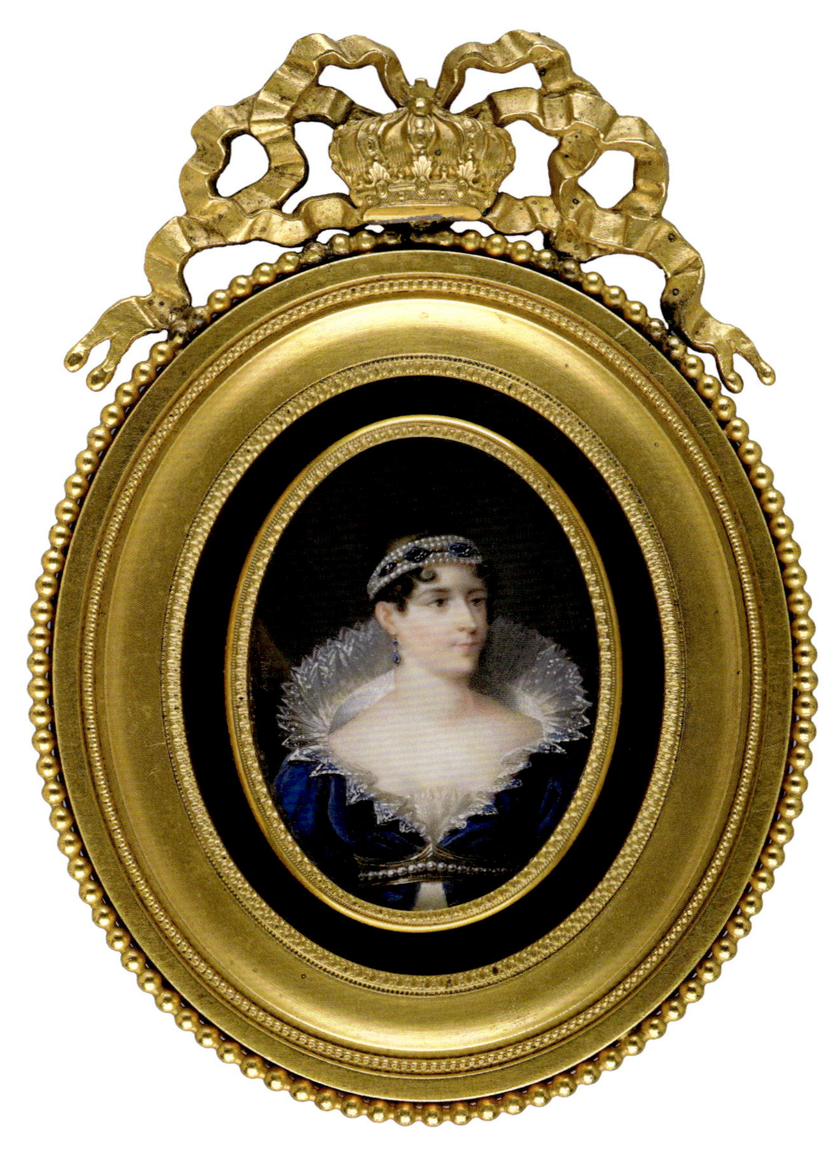

Marie-Rose-Joséphine Tascher de la Pagerie (1763–1814) married Napoleon, her second husband, in 1796. Her first husband, the vicomte de Beauharnais, had died two years earlier, leaving her with two children, Eugène (see no.50) and Hortense. On the establishment of the Empire in 1804 she became Empress, but the barrenness of her marriage to Napoleon led to their divorce in 1809. Nevertheless, Napoleon remained fond of her, and he was much affected by her death in 1814. Her reputation for generosity, charm and gentleness of manner was a valuable counterpart to the essentially military and legalistic tenor of his regime. Many contemporaries emphasized Joséphine's sensitivity and her genuine enthusiasm for the visual arts – often no doubt in part as a contrast to her husband's cultural interests, which were largely confined to philosophy and the theatre.[1]

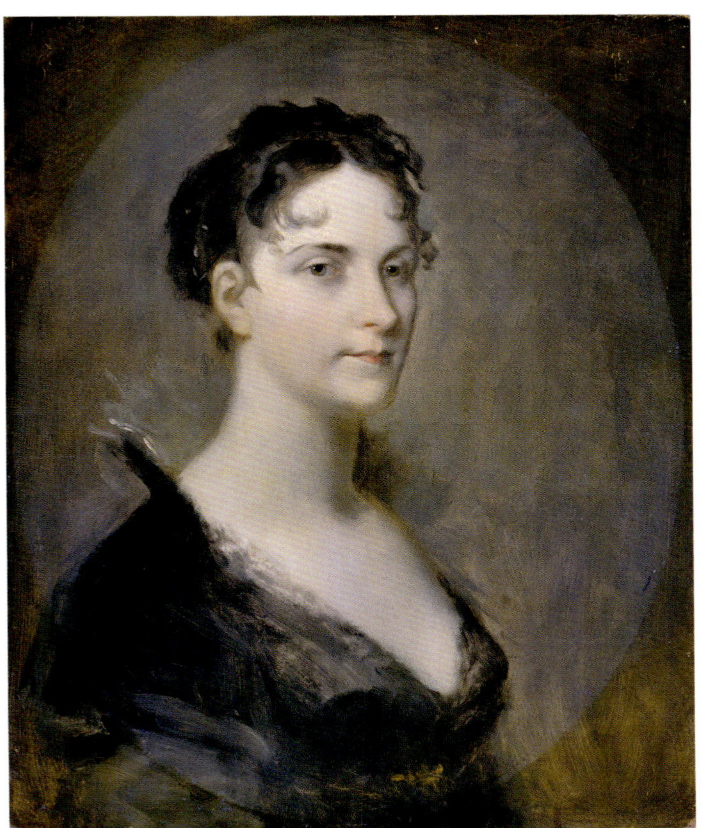

Joséphine is shown wearing a costume inspired by the *style troubadour*, of which she was probably the most significant patron. She collected paintings by leading artists of this style, which combined late medieval and Renaissance subject-matter with the meticulously detailed technique of the seventeenth-century Dutch *fijnschilders*, and she also had a fondness for at least one item of dress associated with the sixteenth century, the raised collar known as a *chérusque* which crowns the blue velvet dress she is wearing here (*cf.* also no.45). (At Napoleon's coronation Joséphine had worn a collar of this kind in silk lace embroidered in gold.)[2] Her jewellery comprises a double row of pearls bordering a sequence of huge cabochon sapphires; matching sapphire top and drop-style earrings; and a high-waisted belt, also with large pearls. As the sapphires would beautifully complement the dress, so the pearls would harmonize perfectly with the *chérusque*.[3] An unfinished portrait of Joséphine by Prud'hon now in the Wallace Collection (fig.1) shows her wearing a dress similar to that in Aubry's miniature. Both works are difficult to date precisely, but were surely painted no more than five years after Prud'hon's famous whole-length of the Empress, reclining supposedly in the grounds of Malmaison (Paris, Musée du Louvre), which was completed in 1805. Aubry's miniature has been painted in his characteristic soft stippling, but with sparkling highlights on the *chérusque* which have been touched in with great brio. SD

PROVENANCE: First recorded at Bethnal Green (1872–5), no.1602

M5

Fig.1 Pierre-Paul Prud'hon, *The Empress Joséphine*, c.1805–10, oil on canvas, 60 × 49.5 cm, London, The Wallace Collection (P315)

45 Louis-François Aubry (1767–1851)

Caroline Murat, Queen of Naples, *c.*1808–12

Ivory, 66 × 51 mm

Signed, vertically, centre right: *aubry*

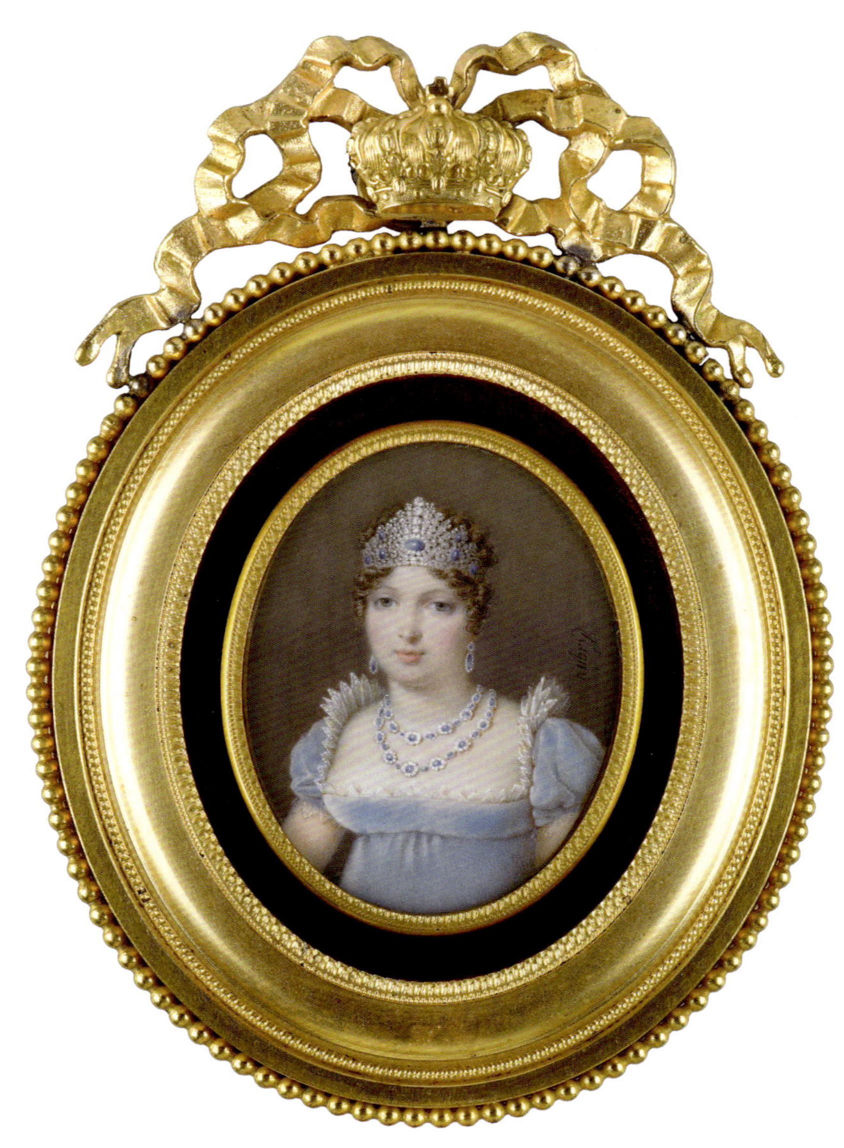

Louis-François Aubry studied under the oil painters Durameau and Vincent before becoming one of the many pupils of Jean-Baptiste Isabey (*q.v.*) and specializing in miniature painting. A regular exhibitor at the Paris Salon between 1798 and 1833, in 1810 Vivant Denon, the first director of the Louvre, informed Napoleon that Aubry was one of the most able miniature painters in Europe. He was a notable teacher, his many pupils including François Meuret, Simon-Jacques Rochard and perhaps Daniel Saint (nos.46, 52). Like Isabey, he was long-lived, but miniatures from the last years of his life are rare. He occupied a post of restorer at the Louvre from 1833 to 1848.

Aubry painted many portraits of members of the imperial family, including the Emperor himself. This miniature has always been catalogued at the Wallace Collection as a portrait of Pauline Bonaparte (1780–1825), Napoleon's second sister and his favourite sibling, but it is clear on comparison with other images that it is actually a portrait of her younger sister Caroline (1782–1839), who had a rounder face than the famously beautiful Pauline. Moreover, it is in fact a slightly simplified copy of a portrait of Caroline by Isabey which is now in the Louvre.[1] Many artists, including some who were not his pupils, copied Isabey's works. Isabey's miniature was probably painted *c.*1808, and Aubry's version presumably dates from shortly afterwards.

Caroline was the third surviving daughter of Carlo Buonaparte and Letizia Ramolino. In 1800 she married Joachim Murat, one of Napoleon's most flamboyant fellow army officers who had played a leading part in the coup of 18 Brumaire which had overthrown the Directoire and established Napoleon as the dominating political figure in France.[2] In 1806 the Murats became Grand Duke and Grand Duchess of Berg, and then in 1808 King and Queen of Naples. Caroline was intensely ambitious, and her relations with Napoleon, and particularly with his wives Joséphine and Marie-Louise, were often strained. In 1814 she and her husband conspired with Austria to retain their throne after Napoleon's defeat at Leipzig, but their intrigues were ultimately unsuccessful and in 1815 Murat was executed. Caroline married Francesco Macdonald in 1830 and spent her last years in Florence.

In both of the miniatures by Isabey and Aubry Caroline is shown wearing a superb blue velvet dress with a court collar called a *chérusque* (as worn by Joséphine at Napoleon's coronation; see no.44). Her magnificent jewels, a perfect match for the dress, comprise a tiara of diamonds radiating upwards from a large turquoise in the centre, with further turquoises set among diamond scrolls; earrings of turquoises and diamonds; and a necklace of alternate small and larger oval clusters of turquoises within diamond borders.[3] Isabey shows her wearing even more diamonds and turquoises under her bust. Aubry's miniature is painted throughout with his characteristic soft stippling. The frame is surmounted by a device comprising a ribbon and Napoleon's crown – not surprisingly, a design frequently to be found on miniatures of the Emperor and his family (see also no.44). SD

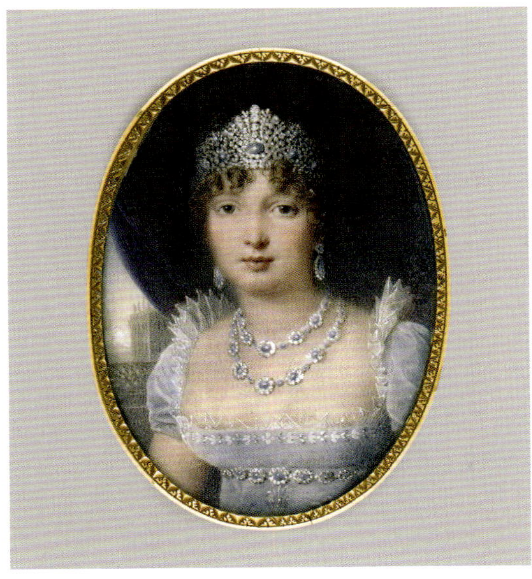

Fig.1 Jean-Baptiste Isabey, *Caroline Murat, Queen of Naples*, *c.*1808, ivory, 65 × 47 mm, Paris, Musée du Louvre (RF30753)

PROVENANCE: First recorded at Bethnal Green (1872–5), no.1611 (as *The Princess Pauline Bonaparte*)

M4

46 Daniel Saint (1778–1847)

Louis Bonaparte, King of Holland, *c.*1810

Ivory, 65 × 44 mm

Signed, along the left-hand edge: *Saint*

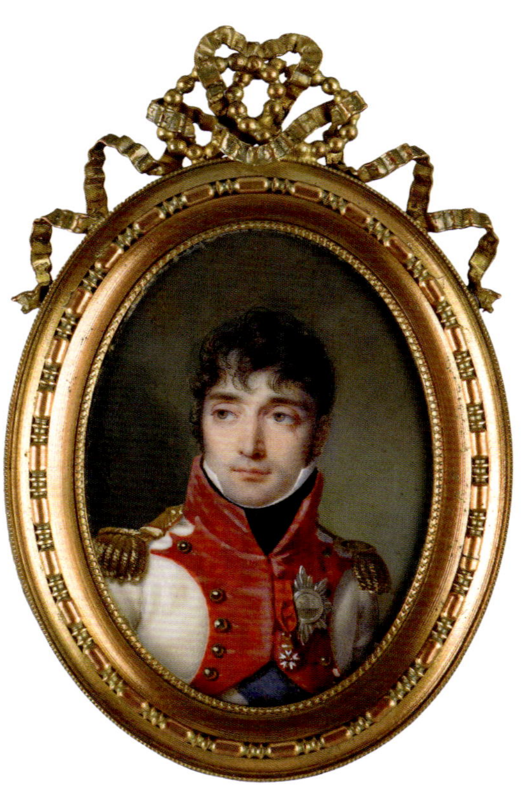

Daniel Saint was one of the many pupils of Augustin (see nos.38, 42 and 56) and was also perhaps a pupil of Aubry (see nos.44–5). Although he drew some pastels at the beginning of his career, it is as a painter of miniatures, and also as an art collector, that he is best known. He exhibited at the Paris Salon from 1804 to 1847, receiving a gold medal in 1806. After the fall of Napoleon he continued to enjoy much official success, being made Painter to the King (Louis XVIII) in 1818 and appointed a Chevalier of the Legion of Honour in 1836. His sitters included Charles X, Louis-Philippe and Queen Victoria's uncle, Ernest I, Duke of Saxe-Coburg-Gotha. In 1846 he sold his art collection at auction in Paris. It included a fine array of paintings by Watteau, Fragonard and Prud'hon as well as miniatures by Hall, acquired at a time when the work of many eighteenth-century French artists was unfashionable.

Saint assisted Isabey with his commissions for official portraits, and the gold medal he won at the 1806 Salon, where he exhibited a frame of miniatures of unnamed sitters, seems to have instigated the extensive patronage that he received thereafter from the imperial family. As well as Napoleon himself, he painted miniatures of, among others, the Empress Joséphine, Eugène de Beauharnais and Joseph Bonaparte's children Zénaïde and Charlotte. In 1810 he was entrusted with the highly important task of painting the portrait of Napoleon that the Emperor sent to his future Empress, Marie-Louise, in Vienna.

Saint's contemporary Louis Bonaparte (1778–1846) was born in Ajaccio, Corsica. A younger brother of Napoleon, he was the fifth surviving child of Carlo Buonaparte and Letizia Ramolino. He married Napoleon's step-daughter Hortense de Beauharnais in

1802. Four years later he was made King of Holland by Napoleon, but his reign was cut short when in 1810 Napoleon forced him to abdicate because of his pro-Dutch policies. After staying in the Netherlands for a further three years he returned to France, where he died more than thirty years later. His third legitimate son (though there are some doubts about his paternity) was the future Napoleon III.

Saint's miniature shows Louis wearing the white uniform of a colonel of the Dutch cavalry as well as the cross of the Legion of Honour and the ribbon and badge of the Dutch Order of the Union (which he himself founded). The composition recalls the full-length portrait of Louis by the English-born painter Charles Howard Hodges (1764–1837) painted in 1809 (fig.1). Besides showing only Louis's head and shoulders, it differs mainly in his head being turned more towards the viewer.[1] There are other versions of the Rijksmuseum's painting, including a bust-length oval by Hodges in the Frans Hals Museum, Haarlem. The present miniature has the appearance of an official portrait of the kind that Saint may well have produced in large numbers, and Leo Schidlof stated that the artist "did numerous copies", although none is known to the present author.[2] SD

PROVENANCE: Perhaps first recorded at Bethnal Green (1872–5), no.1620 (as *Jerome Bonaparte, King of Wurtemberg*); first catalogued in the Wallace Collection 1904

M294

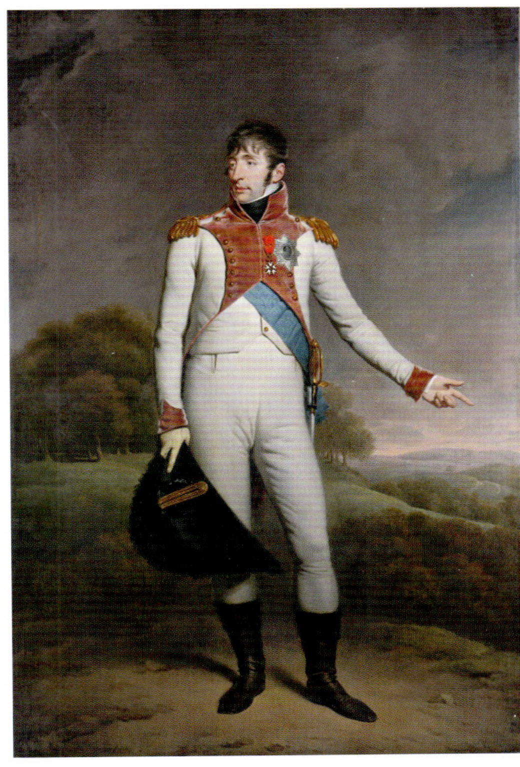

Fig.1 Charles Edward Hodges, *Louis Bonaparte, King of Holland*, 1809, oil on canvas, 223 × 147 cm, Amsterdam, Rijksmuseum (SKA-A-653)

47 Jean-Baptiste Isabey (1767–1855)

Mme Dugazon, 1813

Paper, 125 × 95 mm

Signed and dated, left centre: *Isabey/ 1813*

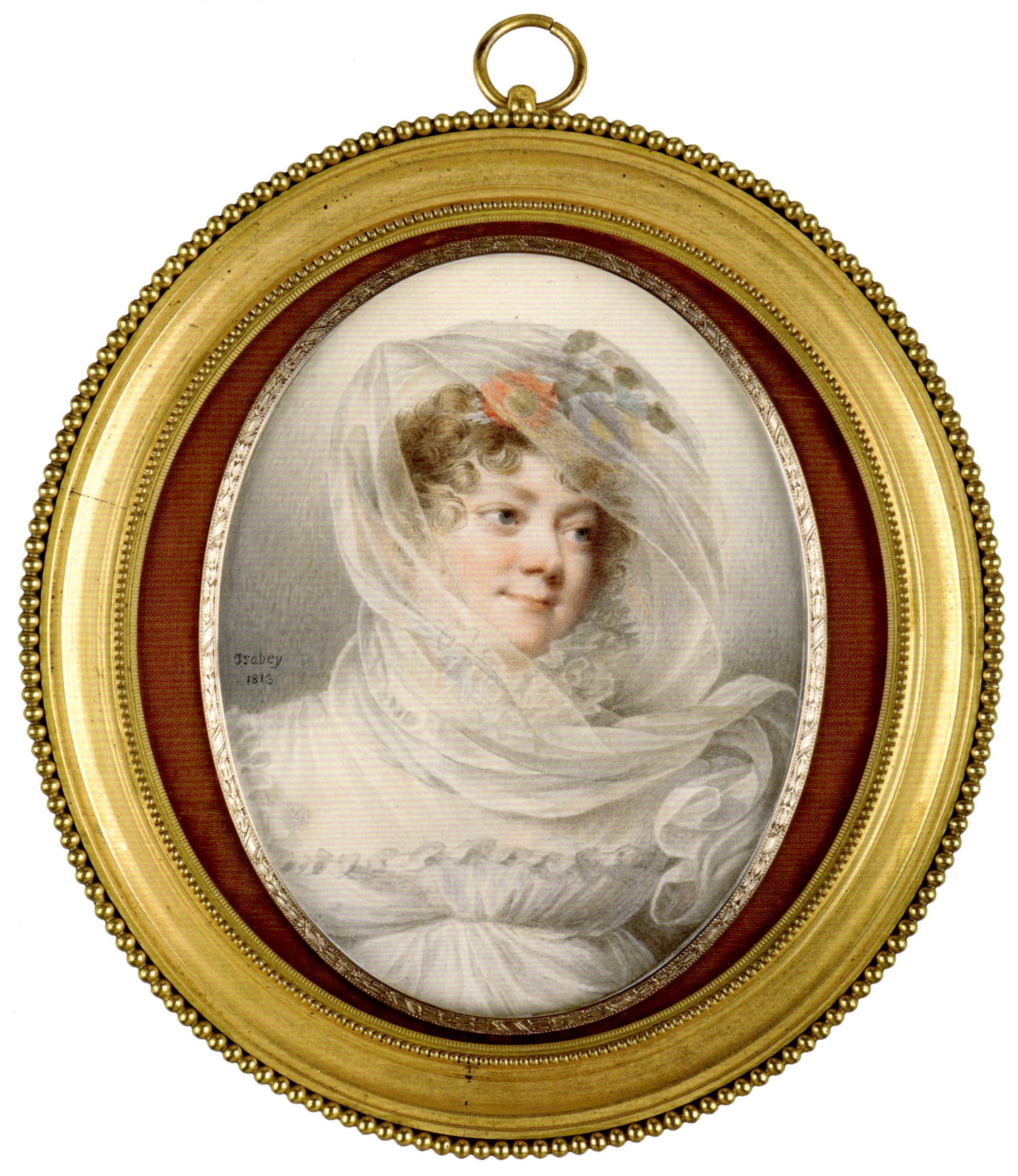

Isabey had many long-standing connections with the theatre. From his early years in Nancy he had been a theatrical designer, and under the Empire he became decorator in chief of the imperial theatres – that is the Opéra, the imperial academy of music and the court theatre at the Tuileries, Fontainebleau or wherever the court was temporarily based. From this time there are records of about thirty performances (operas and ballets as well as plays) for which he provided designs of the sets and costumes. His wide circle of friends included actors, writers and musicians as well as fellow artists, and his son-in-law Pierre-Luc-Charles Ciceri (1782–1862) was the most important French stage designer and scene painter of his generation. The two men often collaborated with one another on productions.[1]

Mme Dugazon, née Louise-Rosalie Lefèbvre (1755–1821), was a friend of Isabey and one of the leading French actresses of her time. She sometimes sang at the soirées which Isabey held for his friends.[2] Born in Berlin, the daughter of a dancing master at the court of Frederick II of Prussia, she moved to Paris with her family in 1765. Shortly afterwards she made her stage debut as a dancer, but it was as an actress and singer that she became famous, playing over sixty roles at the Comédie Italienne (later Opéra-Comique). Her marriage to Jean-Henri Gourgaud, known under his stage name Dugazon, was brief, but they continued to perform together for more than twenty years. Two types of character for which she was particularly regarded, young women in light romantic roles and mothers of a more mature age, are still known in the French theatre as '*jeunes dugazons*' and '*mères dugazons*'.

Isabey exhibited a portrait of Mme Dugazon (location unknown) at the Paris Salon in 1804. It has been suggested that it is not the actress who is depicted in this miniature because she would have been fifty-eight years old in 1813,[3] but comparison with other portraits of her, including another 'aerial' portrait by Isabey of similar date (fig.1), suggests that she is almost certainly the sitter. The Wallace Collection's miniature is a fine demonstration of how, by using gauzes to mask some less attractive features, such as a double chin, Isabey could gently flatter a sitter. The cult of celebrity, which dates from the eighteenth century, was as familiar to actresses in early nineteenth-century France as it is to their successors today,

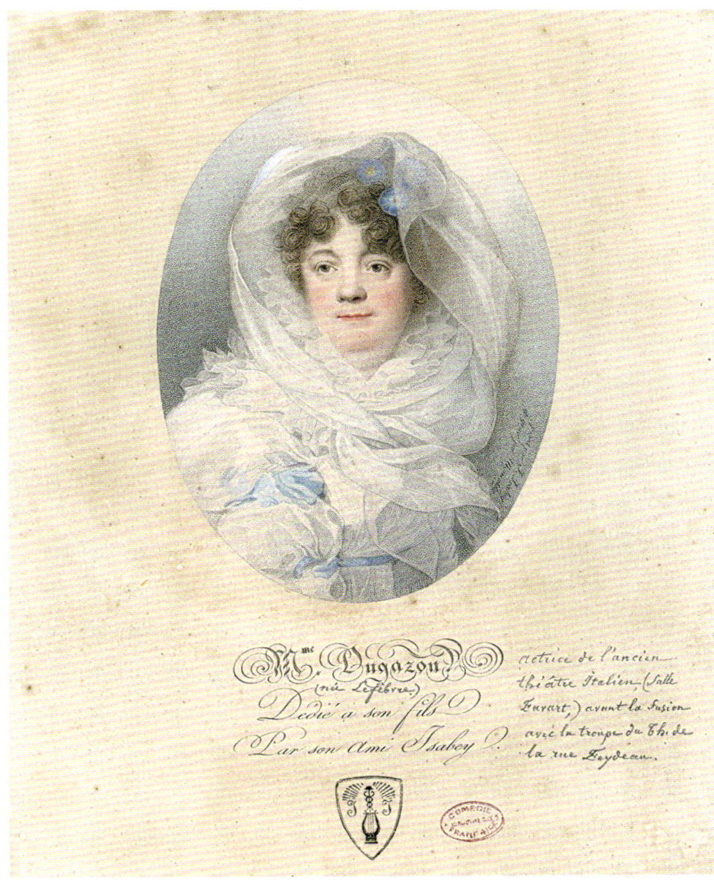

Fig.1 Antoine Monsaldy after Isabey, *Madame Dugazon*, engraving, *c.*1810–20

and the potentially lucrative role for artists in promoting their fame (as well as their own) was one that Isabey and his colleagues well understood.[4] By 1813 Mme Dugazon had retired, but the Wallace Collection owns another portrait miniature by Isabey of a famous French actress, Mademoiselle Mars (M224), painted in 1819 while she was still a star of the Paris stage. Like Mme Dugazon, she was also a friend of Isabey and often attended his soirées.[5] SD

PROVENANCE: First catalogued in the Wallace Collection 1904

M221

48 Jean-Baptiste Isabey (1767–1855)

The Empress Joséphine, *c.*1810–14

Paper, 135 × 94 mm

Signed, vertically, on the right-hand edge: *Isabey*

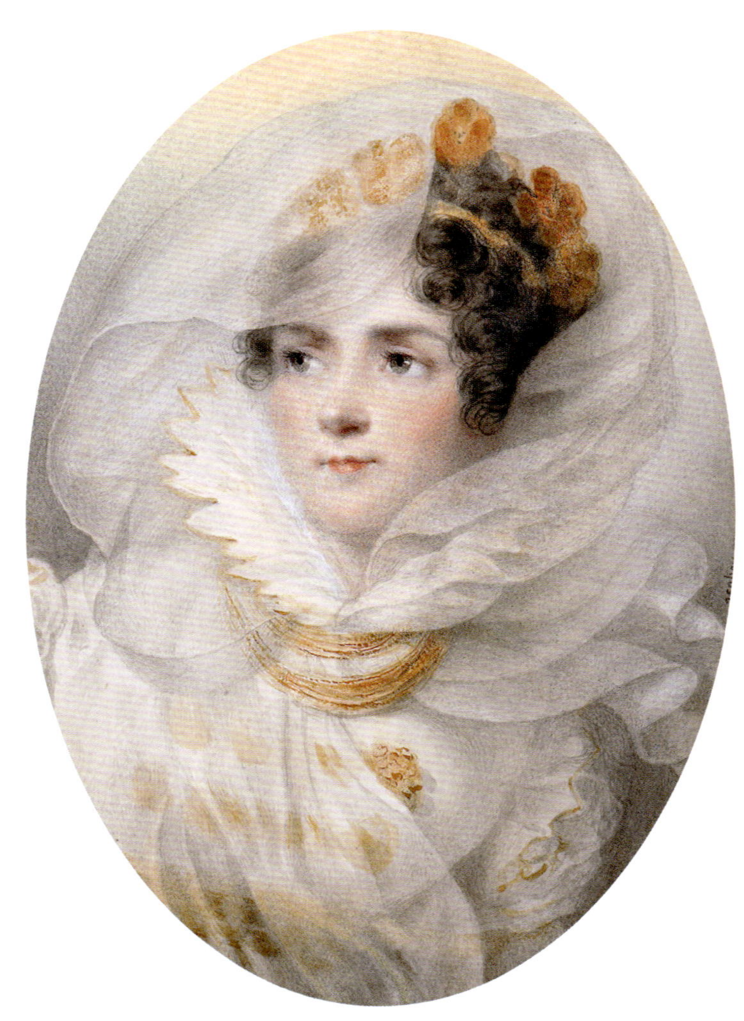

Isabey's duties for the imperial court were by no means confined to producing portraits of Napoleon. He also painted nearly every member of the Emperor's family, and included among his many duties the role of Joséphine's drawing master. The practice of veiling the heads of his female sitters in transparent gauzes which seem to be fluttering in a light breeze became widespread in Isabey's portraits in the second decade of the nineteenth century (*cf.* no.47). According to his biographer Mme Basily-Callimaki, it was Joséphine who had invented these veils, as a means of hiding the signs of ageing, but perhaps she only made them fashionable, as there were precedents in Isabey's art for figures caught in the wind, such as a drawing of 1795 of a mother and child which was subsequently engraved as *Le Coup de vent*.[1] Although clearly popular with many sitters, it was a practice which also attracted some harsh criticism. In 1817 *Le Constitutionnel* complained that the "never ending veils with which he envelopes the necks of women conceal essential features and become in time monotonous and mannered".[2]

Isabey's frequent use of gauzes for his female sitters, usually also with flowers in their hair, coincided with his adoption of a new support for his miniatures instead of ivory. This was a fine-grained paper, usually stretched over a sheet of metal (most often tin) to which a coat of paint had been applied to avoid rusting. (Since Isabey's time the tin has often been replaced by card.) The technique might be compared with Ingres's contemporaneous use of paper stretched over cardboard for many of his pencil portrait drawings.[3] Working on paper was cheaper and involved less labour than painting on ivory. The English miniaturist John Smart was another artist who began to paint on paper in the first decade of the century.[4] Isabey had made his reputation in the 1790s with portraits in black chalk (*en manière noire*) as well as miniatures, and occasionally he used other media, such as sepia on card (see no.43). This new method, applying gouache and watercolour to paper, therefore combined techniques of which he was already a long-established master. However, as this portrait of Joséphine

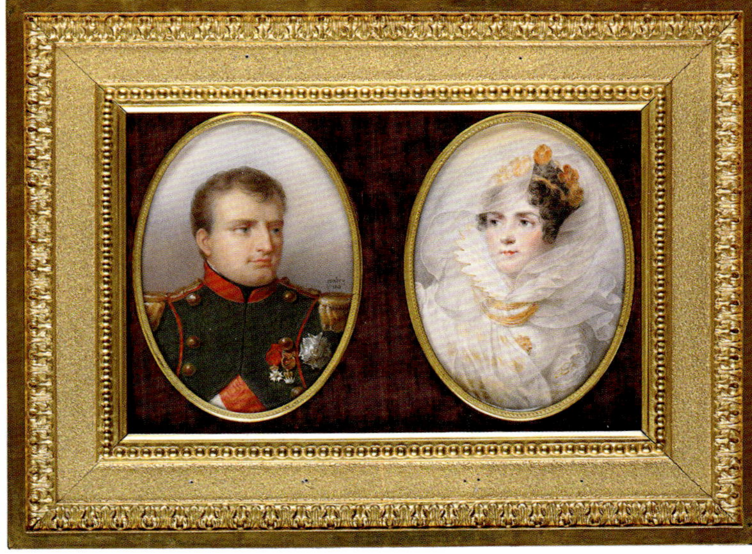

Fig.1 Jean-Baptiste Isabey, *Portraits of Napoleon I and the Empress Joséphine*, London, The Wallace Collection (M215 and M216)

demonstrates, a significant disadvantage of the new technique for later generations is that the paper often browns over time, distorting the original balance of the colours, particularly when some of the more unstable tones have also faded.

In the Wallace Collection this miniature is framed with an Isabey portrait of Napoleon, dated 1812 (fig.1). In the Louvre two similar portraits of Napoleon and Joséphine are also framed together. It seems unlikely, however, that these pairings were intended by Isabey – not because the couple were divorced by 1812 but because Joséphine is shown larger than her former husband.[5] Antoine Monsaldy (1768–1816) produced an undated stipple engraving after Isabey's portrait of Joséphine.[6] SD

PROVENANCE: First recorded at Bethnal Green (1872–5), no.1602

M216

49 Paolo-Ferdinando Quaglia (1780–1853)

The Empress Joséphine, 1814

Ivory, 112 × 88 mm

Signed and dated, on the right: *Quaglia/ 1814*

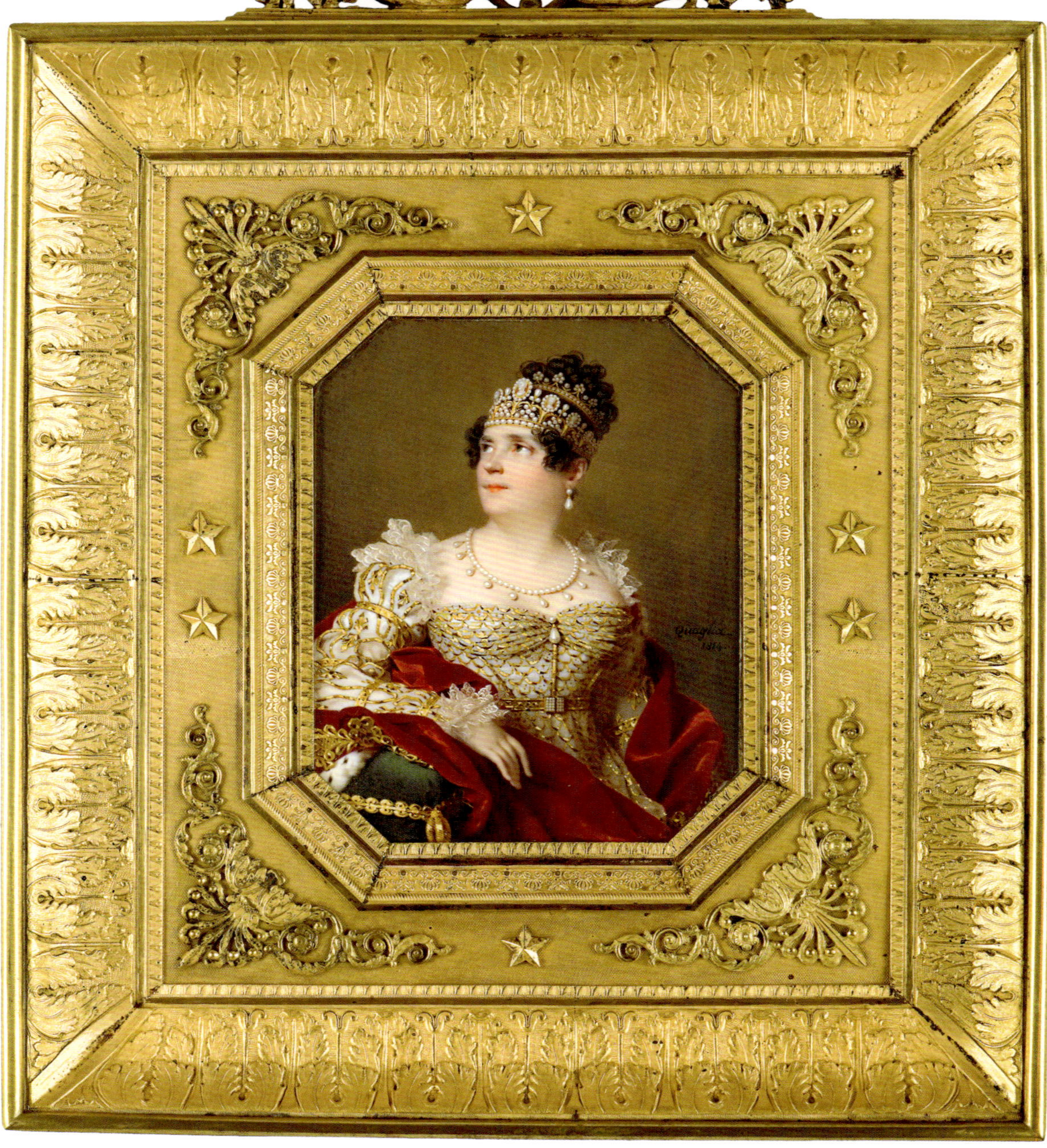

× 0.7

Quaglia was an Italian painter and lithographer, born in Piacenza, who established himself in Paris in 1805. One of many artists patronized by the Empress Joséphine, he produced innumerable portraits of the imperial family and its entourage, particularly the duchesse d'Abrantès, the wife of General Junot, and her family. Leo Schidlof gave high praise to Quaglia in his dictionary of miniature painters, describing him as "one of the greatest miniaturists of his period", and adding, "In his best works he reached or surpassed his contemporaries Isabey and Augustin …. His min[iatures] are amazing in expression and life, his drawing is faultless, as well as his sense of colour."[1] But, despite Quaglia's great abilities, little seems to be known about his later life. According to Schidlof, he obtained a pension from the King of Sweden, presumably Karl XIV Johan (Napoleon's former marshal, Bernadotte), but there are only two works by him in the Swedish Royal Collection and one in the Nationalmuseum, Stockholm.[2]

Dated 1814, this miniature was painted in the year of Joséphine's death and shows her four years after she had been divorced by Napoleon. Nevertheless, she is shown wearing a sumptuous court dress in white and gold, while the rich red cloak and ermine just visible beside it further proclaim her exalted status, as do her magnificent jewels.[3] These comprise a tiara in pearl and gold featuring onyx cameos of classical heads – Joséphine introduced cameos and intaglios into jewellery instead of reserving them for the cabinets of collectors – a comb, also in pearl and gold, allowing her to keep her hair piled high into a chignon; a superb pendant brooch with a large pear-shaped drop pearl; a necklace of pearls also with pear-shaped drop pearls; and a belt of gold openwork with a double plaque set with pearls. As pearls of this size and quality were even rarer than diamonds, Joséphine has been painted with a fortune displayed on her imposing person.[4] Her pose, more characteristic of an artist than a sitter of her social eminence, suggests thought or inspiration, perhaps in reference to her devotion to the arts.[5]

This miniature, which is painted with extraordinary proficiency, must be one of Quaglia's finest works. Every detail has been meticulously defined, but the harmony of the whole has been scrupulously maintained. Large in scale and housed in an elaborate Neoclassical frame which includes five pointed stars and anthemion devices, this is one of the grandest, as well as one of the most accomplished, miniatures in the Wallace Collection. At least two other portraits of Joséphine by Quaglia are known.[6] SD

PROVENANCE: Soret sale, Paris, 8 May 1863, lot 430, 950 fr.; first recorded in Hertford/Wallace ownership at Bethnal Green (1872–5), no.1606

M288

50 Jean-Baptiste Isabey (1767–1855)

Eugène de Beauharnais, *c.*1814–15

Paper stretched over metal, 143 × 106 mm

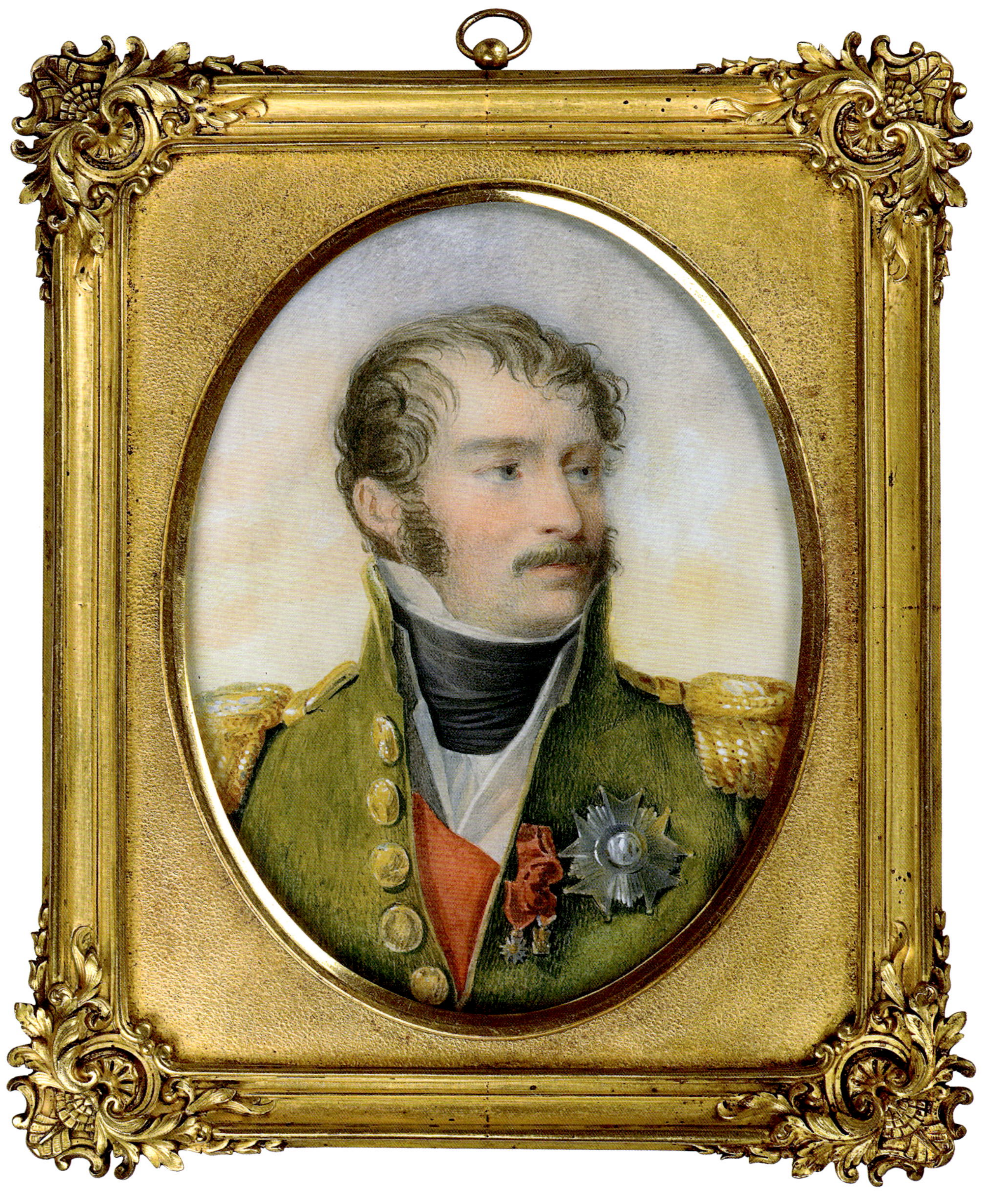

Eugène de Beauharnais (1781–1824), son of the Empress Joséphine by her first marriage to the vicomte de Beauharnais, was an able soldier and administrator who was much involved in many of Napoleon's campaigns between 1800 and 1814. During the retreat from Russia he showed commendable loyalty and concern for his troops, and for the rest of his life maintained a close interest in their welfare. After Napoleon's abdication in 1814 he conformed to the request of his father-in-law, Maximilian I of Bavaria, to refrain from taking up arms again. His last years were spent in Munich, where he died. His titles included Viceroy of Italy (1805–14), Duke of Leuchtenberg (1817–24) and Prince of Eichstätt (1817–24).

Isabey taught drawing to Eugène de Beauharnais and his sister when they were both children. When Isabey attended the Congress of Vienna in 1814–15 Eugène was his guide, introducing him to many of the most important dignitaries. Such was the artist's renown that during the six months he spent there even the King of Prussia and the Tsar of Russia came to his studio next to the Café Jüngling on the Prater. The studio also provided a useful place for some of the delegates to hold private discussions: Isabey himself said that his house formed a sort of "behind the scenes at the Congress".[1] The only sitters who were visited by Isabey to have their portraits painted were the Emperor and Empress of Austria.

There are several versions of the Wallace Collection's miniature, at least four of which are dated 1814 and one 1815. The last, now in Cincinnati, bears the additional inscription *à Vienne*, and a lithograph by Isabey and S.J. Le Gros indicates that the original was *peint à Vienne en 1814*.[2] Of these versions, the Wallace Collection's is not the finest, but it is a good example of Isabey's work without any obvious signs of intervention by his studio. Unfortunately, it has suffered from fading and also some discolouration in the sky. Eugène is wearing the ribbon, cross and Grand Eagle of the Legion of Honour with the star of the Iron Crown (see also no.42). His splendid costume, carefully groomed hair and piercing blue eyes perfectly convey the impression of a dashing military man of the Napoleonic era, although, as the portrait of Prince August demonstrates (no.54), this was not an interpretation that Isabey confined to French officers. SD

PROVENANCE: Probably first recorded at Bethnal Green (1872–5), no.1667

M247

51 Jean-Baptiste Isabey (1767–1855)

The Empress Marie-Louise and her Son, the King of Rome, 1815

Paper, 170 × 130 mm

Signed and dated, vertically, centre left: *J. Isabey 1815*

Marie-Louise (1791–1847), daughter of Francis I of Austria, married Napoleon in 1810 as his second wife after his divorce from Joséphine. By marrying a member of the house of Habsburg Napoleon sought to enhance the prestige of his regime and France's influence in eastern Europe. He also hoped that Marie-Louise would bear him the son that Joséphine had been unable to provide. This she duly did in March 1811, with the birth of Napoléon François Joseph Charles Bonaparte (1811–1832), who was immediately given the title King of Rome. In 1814, after Napoleon's first abdication, Marie-Louise left France with her son, never to return. She became Duchess of Parma, and in 1821, shortly after Napoleon's death, married her lover Count Neipperg. Her son was brought up at the Habsburg court in Vienna with the title Duke of Reichstadt, but died of tuberculosis at the age of twenty-one.

As Marie-Louise left Paris in March 1814, this miniature was painted when the Empress and her son were in exile from France. Presumably it was painted in Vienna or derived from studies made there by Isabey. The artist's relationship with Marie-Louise was friendly, as it had been with Joséphine, and dated from the time of her marriage to the Emperor. When General Berthier asked for Marie-Louise's hand on behalf of Napoleon at Vienna in 1810 he presented her with a portrait of Napoleon by Isabey which was surrounded by diamonds worth 175,000 francs. She wore it at all the ceremonies on her journey to Paris and also at her wedding.[1] Isabey and his studio produced many portraits of Marie-Louise, and he first drew the King of Rome when the child was only a few days old.[2] In 1814 Isabey organized parties for Marie-Louise in Vienna, and when he visited Italy in 1822 it was partly with the intention of calling on the ex-Empress at Parma.

The image of Marie-Louise and her son that Isabey presents in this miniature is remarkably informal, perhaps reflecting the reduced (though by no means humbled) circumstances of the sitters in 1815. With no jewellery or regalia visible and the clothes expensive but not luxurious, this could almost be any bourgeois mother with her son. The technique is very largely Isabey's characteristic soft-focus stippling, with only a few broader brushstrokes, particularly in the hair. He had occasionally made use of sky as a background since at least the 1790s.[3] SD

PROVENANCE: First recorded at Bethnal Green (1872–5), no.1817

M210

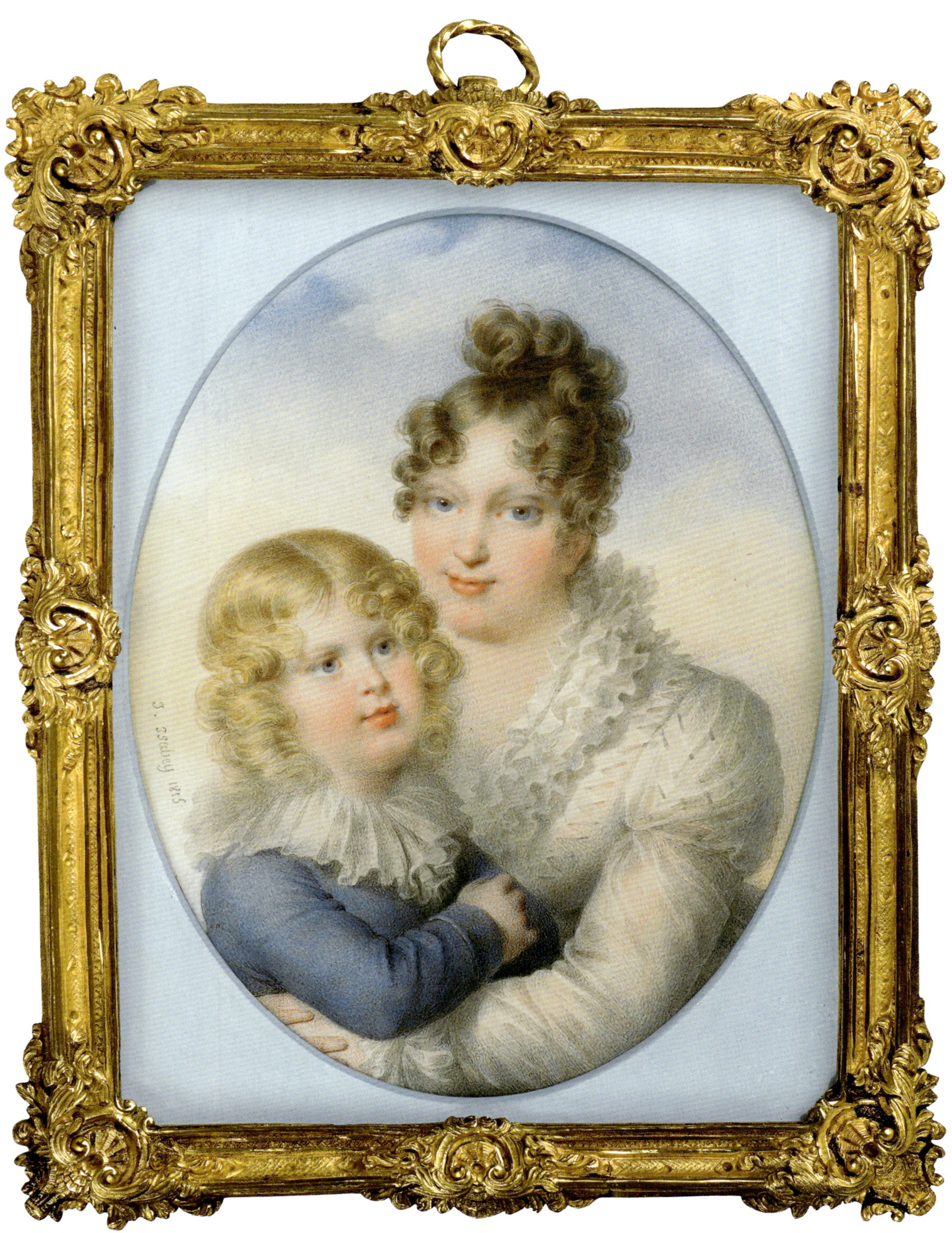
J. Isabey 1815

52 Daniel Saint (1778–1847)

An Unknown Lady, *c.*1815

Ivory, 97 × 75 mm

Signed, along the right-hand edge: *Saint*

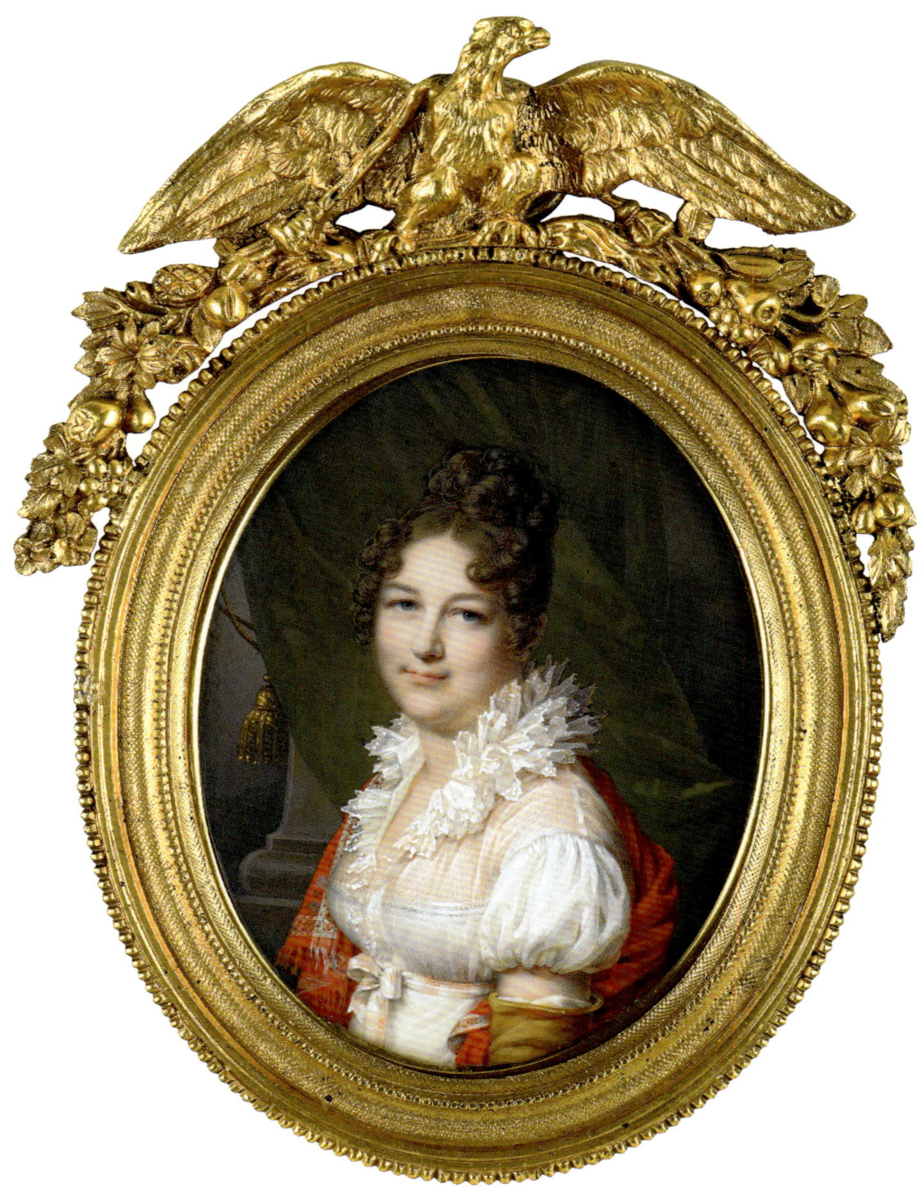

The sitter in this miniature has not been identified. She wears a white muslin dress and yellow gloves with a red shawl and is shown in a conventional composition with a column, drapery and gold tassel. She bears some resemblance to the actress Rose Dupuis (1791–1878), but the date of the costume, *c.*1815, makes it highly unlikely that she is represented here, as she would have been only twenty-four years old in this year.[1] The over-gown and the ruffled collar which frames the face are important parts of a costume which is particularly suited to a woman who is no longer in her first flush of youth.[2]

This is an attractive, though not outstanding, example of Saint's work, revealing a broader style than that shown in his earlier miniatures, when he was much influenced by Isabey. The use of stippling, particularly in the flesh tones, is very apparent, and the gauze and ruff of the lady's dress have been captured with great skill, minute dots of paint perfectly defining the highlights on the ruff. In the Victoria and Albert Museum there is a miniature by Saint of another unknown sitter with a similar composition. The frame of the Wallace Collection's miniature, surmounted by an eagle, an image with rather militaristic connotations, may not be the original. SD

PROVENANCE: First catalogued in the Wallace Collection 1904

M293

53 Henry Bone (1755–1834), after Reynolds
Lady Gertrude Fitzpatrick ('Collina'), 1810

Enamel on copper, 215 × 173 mm

Signed, bottom left: *H Bone* (the *H B* in monogram)

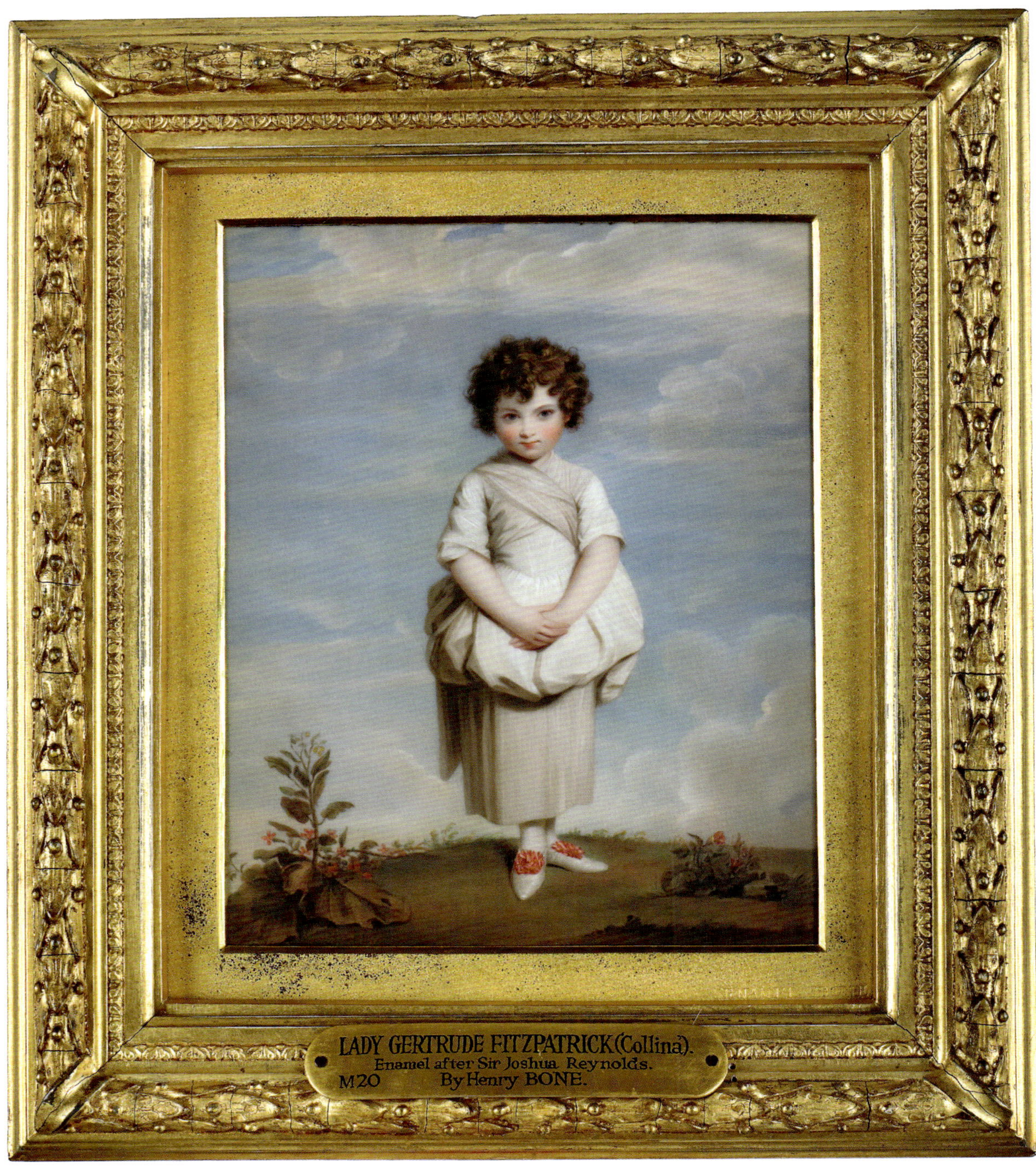

× 0.5

Henry Bone (see also nos.39, 57 and 63), a Cornishman, moved to London after an apprenticeship as a painter on porcelain in Plymouth and Bristol. He first exhibited at the Royal Academy in 1781, and thereafter showed enamels there almost every year until 1832. Although he produced works of his own design, his great contemporary renown rested on his enamel copies of oil paintings by other artists. Many of these were after religious and mythological pictures by Italian and Dutch masters such as Titian, Raphael and Rembrandt, but he also painted a considerable number after the great English portraitists of his own time.

This miniature is after a portrait by Sir Joshua Reynolds of Lady Gertrude Fitzpatrick (1774–1841), painted in 1779–80, for her father John, 2nd Earl of Upper Ossory, which is now in the Museum of Art, Columbus, Ohio. The popular title, *Collina*, referring to the little hill on which she stands, derives from J. Jones's reproductive engraving of Reynolds's painting published in 1792.[1] Lady Gertrude was the younger sister of Lady Anne Fitzpatrick, who was painted by Reynolds *c.*1775;[2] a miniature copy in enamel by Bone of this portrait, made in 1811 and clearly a pendant to the present work, is also in the Wallace Collection (fig.1). Both miniatures were first inventoried in the Hertfords' possession in 1842, when they were in the 3rd Marquess's bedroom at Dorchester House. They may have been acquired simply for their qualities as works of art, but perhaps a friendship between the two families explains their presence in the 3rd Marquess's collection.

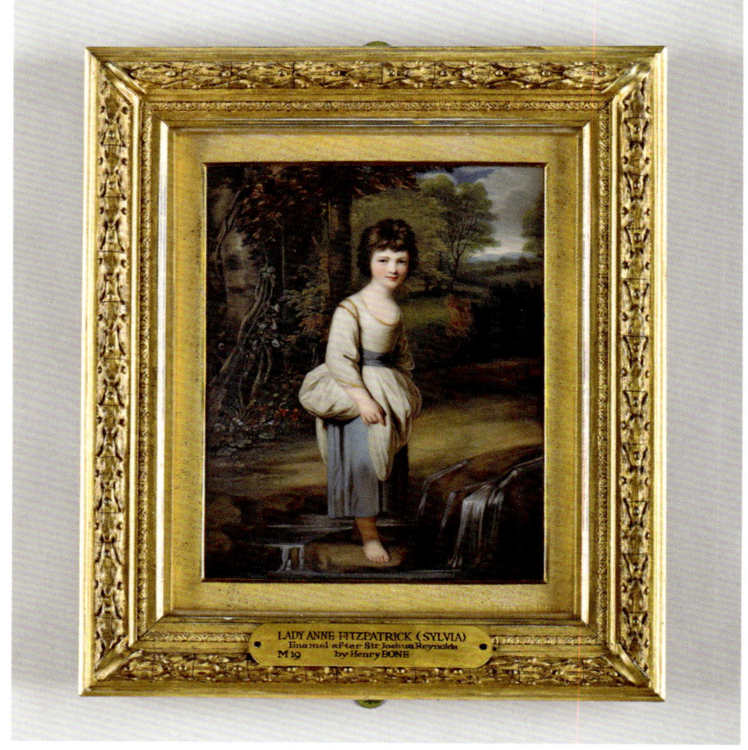

Fig.1 Henry Bone, *Lady Anne Fitzpatrick*, 1811, enamel, 211 × 172 mm, London, The Wallace Collection (M19)

This miniature was exhibited by Bone with four others, all in the same frame, at the Royal Academy in 1810 (no.653). As was his usual practice, he added a lengthy inscription on the counter-enamel: *Lady Gertrude Fitz Patrick/ second daughter of John Earl of Upper Ossory and Anne Liddell his Wife./ London March 1810 –/ Painted by Henry Bone A.R.A./ Enamel painter in Ordinary to His Majesty and Enamel painter to His R.H. the Prince/ of Wales after the Original by Sr Joshua Reynolds.–* Although characteristically effusive, it does not indicate for whom the miniature was made. If it was a commissioned work, the most likely patron would have been the sitter's father, who still owned the Reynolds original (as well as the portrait of Lady Anne) when Bone's miniatures were made. They may, however, have been an independent venture by Bone, or a commission from someone else, perhaps one of the Hertfords.

It was Bone's usual practice to make a carefully scaled pencil drawing of his chosen painting as the first stage in the preparation of his enamel copy. The drawing for *Collina*, like those for nos.39, 57 and 63, is bound in one of the albums of Bone's preparatory drawings now in the National Portrait Gallery (fig.2).[3] It would have been laid over another sheet covered with chalk and then traced through to the ground of the enamel plate, which was then fired to establish the compositional outlines. As many as twelve or more later firings would be required to complete the finished work – an undertaking of great complexity which could sometimes take up to three years to complete. It was a disadvantage of this process that some panels warped to varying degrees during the course of the firings, a defect which could to some extent be masked (as in this instance) by setting the miniature within a deep frame. On the other hand, one of the great advantages of enamels, that their colours remain unaltered by exposure to light and moisture, was particularly valuable in the case of Bone's miniatures after paintings by Reynolds, because even in the nineteenth century many of the originals were in a poor state of preservation. J.T. Smith, biographer of the sculptor Nollekens, wrote: "As much of the interest of many of Sir Joshua's pictures is annually lessened by the fading of his colours, I am sure that the reader will join me in congratulating the public upon the surest method of handing down to posterity that great Artist's fascinating style of colouring, by the correct copies which Mr Bone … has made of them in enamel".[4] Both artists, Reynolds and Bone, experimented with their techniques, as if seeking to enhance their almost magical status as artists, as well as gain a practical or financial advantage over their rivals. In a competitive market it could be beneficial for artists to have a unique style or technique which set them apart from rivals. SD

PROVENANCE: First recorded in the bedroom of the 3rd Marquess of Hertford, Dorchester House, posthumous inventory, 1842

M20

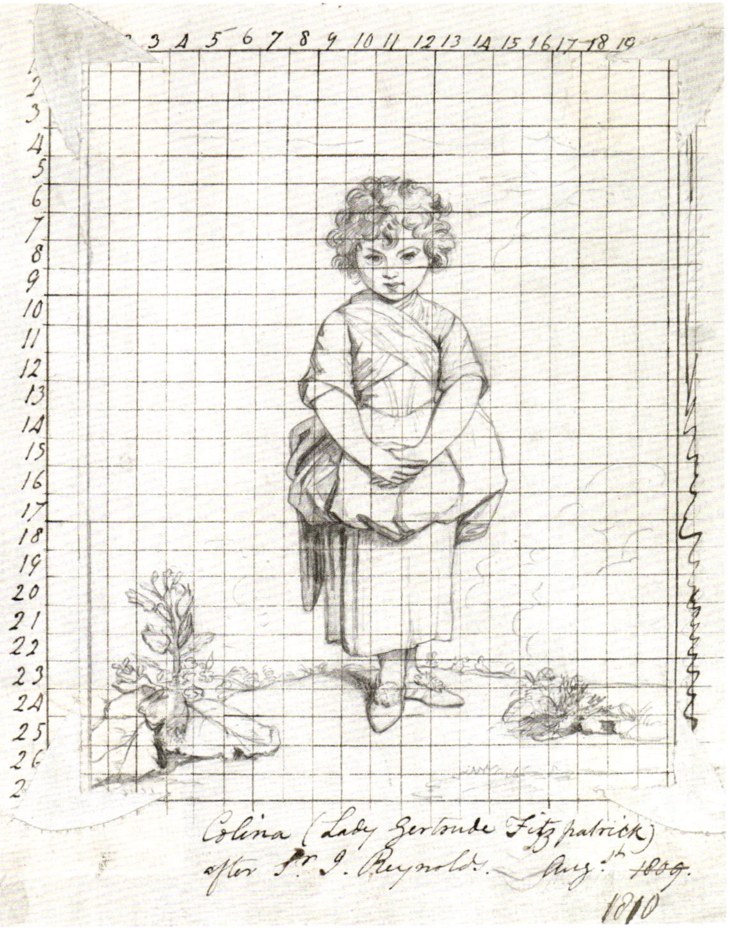

Fig.2 Henry Bone, Preparatory drawing for no.53, pencil, 265 × 202 mm, London, National Portrait Gallery (D17523)

54 Jean-Baptiste Isabey (1767–1855)

Prince August of Prussia, 1814

Paper, 113 × 98 mm

Signed and dated, centre left: *Isabey/ 1814*

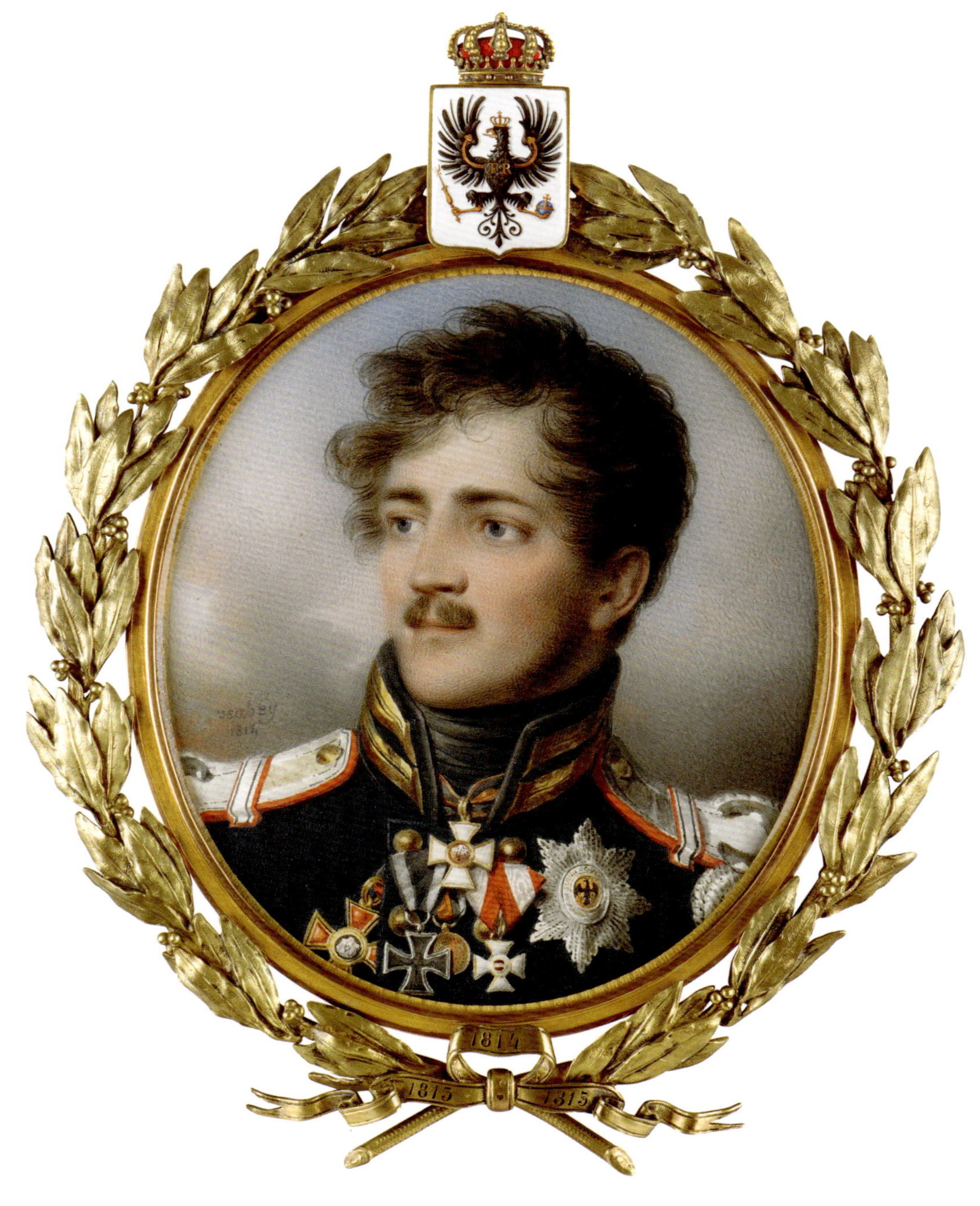

Prince August of Prussia (1779–1843) was the youngest son of Prince Ferdinand, brother of King Frederick II ('the Great') of Prussia.[1] Like many younger members of the Prussian royal family, he spent much of his life in the army. During the Napoleonic Wars he took part in some of the most significant battles, first in 1806, when Prussia was defeated by France. After the battle of Saalfeld on 28 October he was captured and brought to Paris, where he remained until the following summer. On his way back to Berlin, he spent some time at Coppet on Lake Geneva as a guest of Mme de Staël (see no.40). There he fell in love with the famous beauty Julie Récamier, the wife of a rich banker: the two stayed in touch for the rest of their lives. The Prince returned to Prussia and next came to Paris with the now victorious Prussian army in the spring of 1814. Over the following winter he attended the Congress of Vienna as part of the Prussian legation. It must have been at this time that he sat to Isabey for this portrait. The frame, since it bears the stamp of the Parisian maker Wiese, must have been made considerably later, in the mid nineteenth century. The laurel wreath and the Prussian eagle refer to August's contribution to the Prussian victory against Napoleon. The miniature may still have been with Isabey, or the Prince carried it with him when he returned to Paris in 1815 and had it framed.

One can only speculate about the original recipient of the miniature. Some locks of hair on the back suggest a romantic gift. In 1815 Prince August still had a strong attachment to Mme Récamier. Earlier, in 1808, after Récamier had withdrawn her promise to marry the Prince, she had given him her portrait by François Gérard (Paris, Musée Carnavalet). Although it is possible that the miniature was intended as a similar present for her, this does not seem likely. In 1828, August sent a portrait of himself by Franz Krüger to Récamier (Berlin, Staatliche Museen, Nationalgalerie), showing him in his Berlin palace standing in front of Gérard's portrait of her.[2] The Prince's face is obviously modelled on Isabey's miniature, though his appearance has been adjusted to take account of his more advanced age. Unless derived from a print, Isabey's miniature or another version of it must have been available to Krüger in 1828. Récamier is not the only candidate for the recipient of the Wallace Collection's miniature. August's emotional life had become increasingly complex. Even before he met Récamier, he had a mistress, Karoline Friederike Wichmann (after 1810, von Waldenburg), with whom he had had four children. She was with him in Paris in 1815. Their relationship ceased in 1817 and the following year he took up with Auguste Arend (after 1825, von Prillwitz), with whom he had seven children and whom he later married. August's portrait by Krüger was in the collection of the Waldenburg family in the late nineteenth century. Given that Karoline Friederike was in Paris with the Prince in 1815, it seems likely that the miniature was also at one point owned by her.[3]

August wears the uniform of the Prussian Guards, with the star of the Order of the Black Eagle, the badge of the Order of the Red Eagle, the Iron Cross of Prussia, the badge of the Order of Maria Theresa of Austria and the badge of the Order of Saint Vladimir of Russia. CMV

PROVENANCE: First catalogued in the Wallace Collection 1904

M219

55 Jean-Baptiste Isabey (1767–1855)

The 1st Duke of Wellington, 1818

Paper stretched over metal, 142 × 108 mm

Signed and dated, lower right: *Isabey./ 1818*

During the six months that Isabey spent in Vienna in 1814–15, mainly producing portraits of the most important representatives at the Congress, one of the delegates he was obliged to paint was the Duke of Wellington. Their first meeting in Paris a few months earlier after Napoleon's first abdication had not been a success. Isabey himself said that the Duke had come to see him with "an off-handedness that was typically British", obliging him to refuse "the honour of painting his august features", but, after realising that he had behaved badly, the Duke had returned with the Duchess of Santa Cruz and Isabey had consented to paint his portrait.[1] In Vienna, however, again according to Isabey himself, the Duke treated him with great consideration, though they must have spent little time together. Wellington arrived in Vienna on 3 February, and both men left the city soon after learning that Napoleon had landed on French soil on 1 March after fleeing exile on the island of Elba.[2] Wellington was subsequently included in profile in Isabey's great pen drawing of the meeting of the twenty-three delegates to the Congress which was bought by George IV and is still in the Royal Collection today.[3]

After Waterloo, Wellington returned to Paris as Commander in Chief of the allied army of occupation, and he was to remain there, apart from brief visits to England and elsewhere in France, until 1818. Presumably it was Wellington himself who commissioned the first version of the Wallace Collection's miniature, but several other versions are known, the earliest dated 1816. Indeed, it was inevitable that there would be much demand for portraits of such a revered figure as the Duke by an artist as celebrated as Isabey. François Gérard, probably the most fashionable portraitist in oil in Paris at the time, also painted a portrait of the Duke in 1814–15 (present location unknown).[4] When Isabey visited London in 1820 – he held a one-man exhibition of his own works in Pall Mall – he wrote to the dealer Dominic Colnaghi asking him to let his servant carry away three portraits of Wellington which were on deposit with him, these being in addition to six others that Isabey himself had already taken that morning. These may well have been prints, but it is not impossible that they were miniatures.[5] In most versions of the miniature Wellington wears the scarlet undress coatee of a British Field Marshal, but this version in the Wallace Collection is unusual (and perhaps unique) in showing him dressed in another uniform. Here he is wearing the undress coatee of a Spanish general officer. As he was a Captain General in the Spanish army, it is probably the uniform appropriate to that rank, though it would be necessary to see the cuffs of the coatee to be certain. His decorations are the badge of the Order of the Golden Fleece, the Army Gold Cross, the badge of a Knight Grand Cross of the Order of the Bath, Military Division (probably of the type unique to Knights Grand Cross of the Bath who were also Knights of the Garter), and the star of the Spanish Order of Charles III. The elaborate frame is particularly fine. Its decoration comprises the Collar of the Order of the Garter round the central oval surmounted by a trophy consisting of a General Officer's sword, a Field Marshal's baton, two crossed Colours probably intended to represent the King's and Regimental Colour of a British infantry regiment and a ducal coronet on a cushion; at the bottom is the letter *W* on a drapery.[6] The miniature is not recorded before 1852, when it appeared at the 'd'Hijar' sale in Paris and was bought by the 4th Marquess of Hertford. No collector called d'Hijar has yet been identified, but it may be significant, in view of the uniform that Wellington is wearing, that Hijar is in Spain.

The 4th Marquess of Hertford knew the Duke of Wellington, and owned several other images of him.[7] The 4th Marquess served in the 10th Hussars 1820–3, and one of his closest friends was John Gurwood, Wellington's private secretary 1837–44. When the Marquess was only fifteen Wellington helped him get out of a gambling scrape in Paris, and later in England the two men would have met on social occasions, partly through the 3rd Marquess (see no.63), who was an important figure in the Tory party (Wellington, a Tory, was Prime Minister in 1828–30 and again briefly in 1834). The Duke is said to have described the 4th Marquess as "a man of extra-ordinary talents", adding, "he deserves to be classed among those men who possess transcendent gifts. What a pity it is that he does not live more in England, and occupy his place in the House of Lords."[8]

Although often a generous patron, the Duke was notorious for the brusque manner with which he would sometimes treat others of an inferior social rank, including artists. Even if Isabey's later experience was happier, the low point of view he has adopted here, effectively conveying Wellington's *hauteur*, surely reflects something

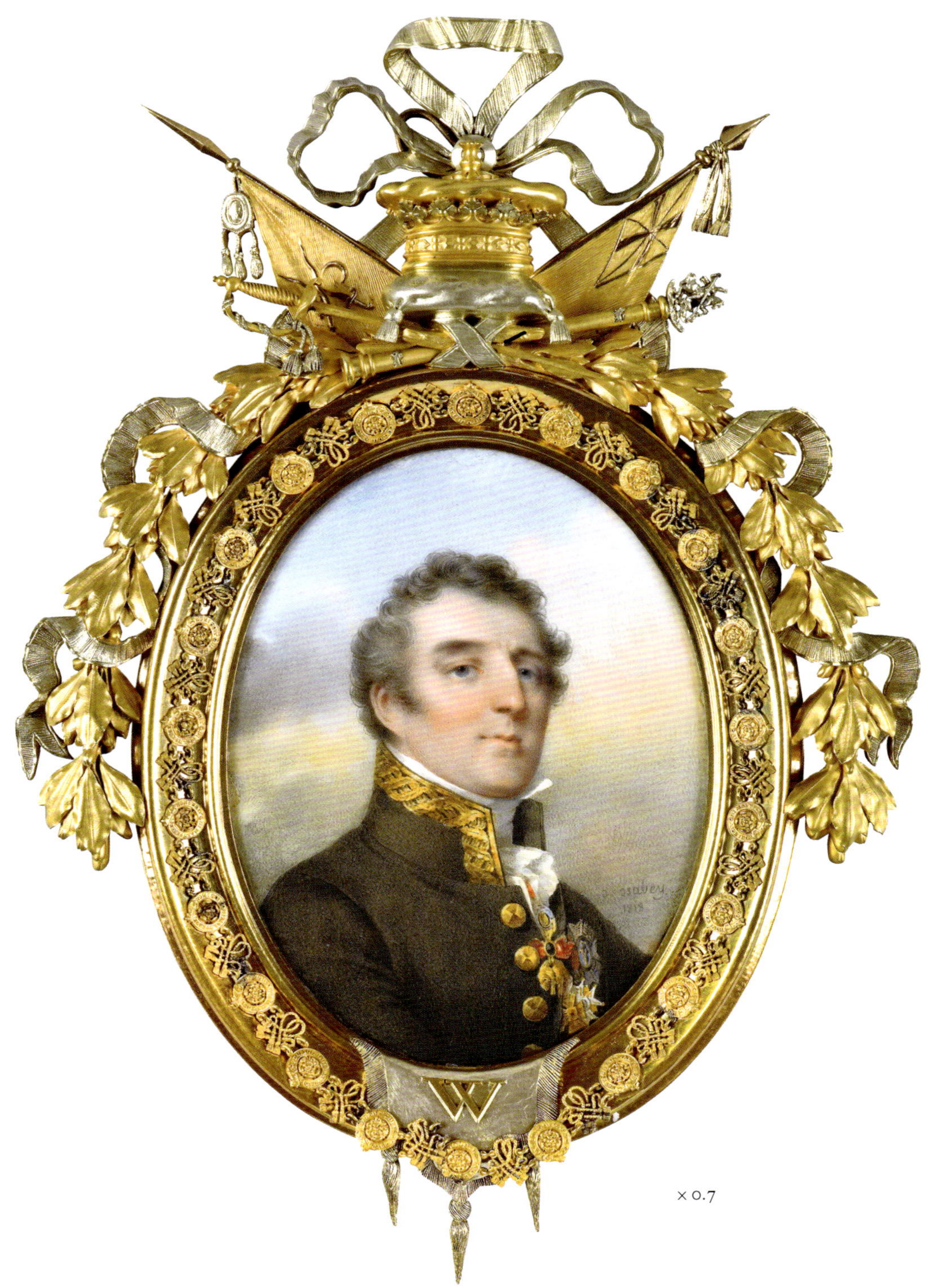

× 0.7

of the artist's dissatisfaction with their first meeting. Nevertheless, when Isabey came to England two years after this miniature was painted, the Duke is said to have recommended Isabey to possible patrons, including three members of the Seymour family who were also related to Lord Hertford and whose portraits he painted.[9] SD

PROVENANCE: D'Hijar sale, Paris, 5 November 1852 [not in Lugt], lot 262, bought for the 4th Marquess of Hertford, with a letter from Isabey (now unlocated), dated 4 November 1852, for 10,601 fr.[10]

M281

56 Jean-Baptiste-Jacques Augustin (1759–1832)

Prince Willem of Orange, later King Willem II of the Netherlands,

*c.*1818–20

Ivory, 76 × 59 mm

Signed, lower left: *Augustin*

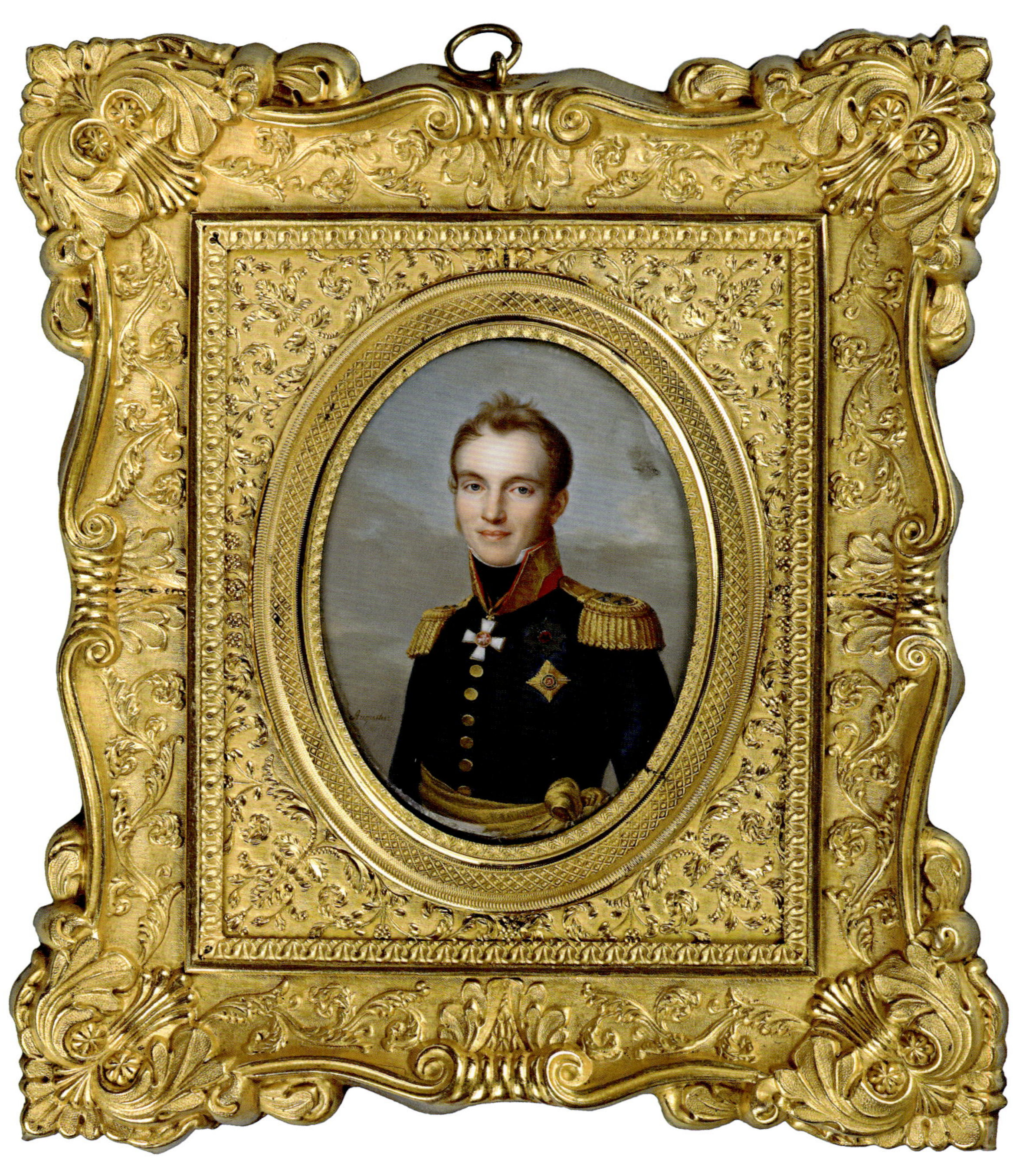

After the final defeat of Napoleon in 1815 Augustin enjoyed generous patronage not only from the restored Bourbons but from some of the many foreign visitors who flocked to Paris. The English were prominent among those he painted, but there were also sitters from Holland, Switzerland, Portugal and other countries.

The subject of this miniature, Prince Willem of Orange (1792–1849), who ascended the Dutch throne in 1840, is particularly interesting in the context of the Wallace Collection because, at the posthumous sale of the King's magnificent art collection in 1850, the 4th Marquess of Hertford was one of the principal purchasers. It was there that he acquired such masterpieces as Rembrandt's *Titus* and Van Dyck's portraits of Philippe le Roy and Marie de Raet.[1] The inclusion of this portrait of the Prince in his collection may be explained, however, less by Willem's eminence as an art collector than by his military career in the British army during the Napoleonic era. In 1795 the Netherlands became the Batavian Republic and the royal family was forced to flee the country. Willem, after studies at Oxford University, entered the British army, and in 1811 became aide-de-camp to the Duke of Wellington. He fought in the Peninsular War and at the Battle of Waterloo, where he was praised for his bravery but much criticized for the calamitous results of some of his decisions. Lord Hertford may well have known the Prince, and certainly this miniature would have fitted well in his collection with several others depicting the great royal and aristocratic enemies of Napoleon (see nos.54–5).

Willem is shown wearing the cross and star of the Russian Order of St George and the star of the Prussian Order of the Black Eagle. A miniature portrait of the prince by Augustin's former pupil Alexandre Delatour, painted in 1819, also shows him wearing these orders.[2] Augustin's miniature demonstrates that, thirty years after he had first exhibited in Paris, his outstanding draughtsmanship remained unimpaired and that he was still painting in the clear and vivid colours for which he was also much admired. SD

PROVENANCE: Perhaps W. William Hope sale, Christie's, London, 15 June 1849, lot 5, £7 10s.; probably first recorded in Hertford/Wallace ownership at Bethnal Green (1872–5), no.1812

M10

57 Henry Bone (1755–1834), after Newton
Mrs Paddon, 1817

Enamel on copper, 86 × 70 mm

Signed, bottom right: *H B* (in monogram) *1817*

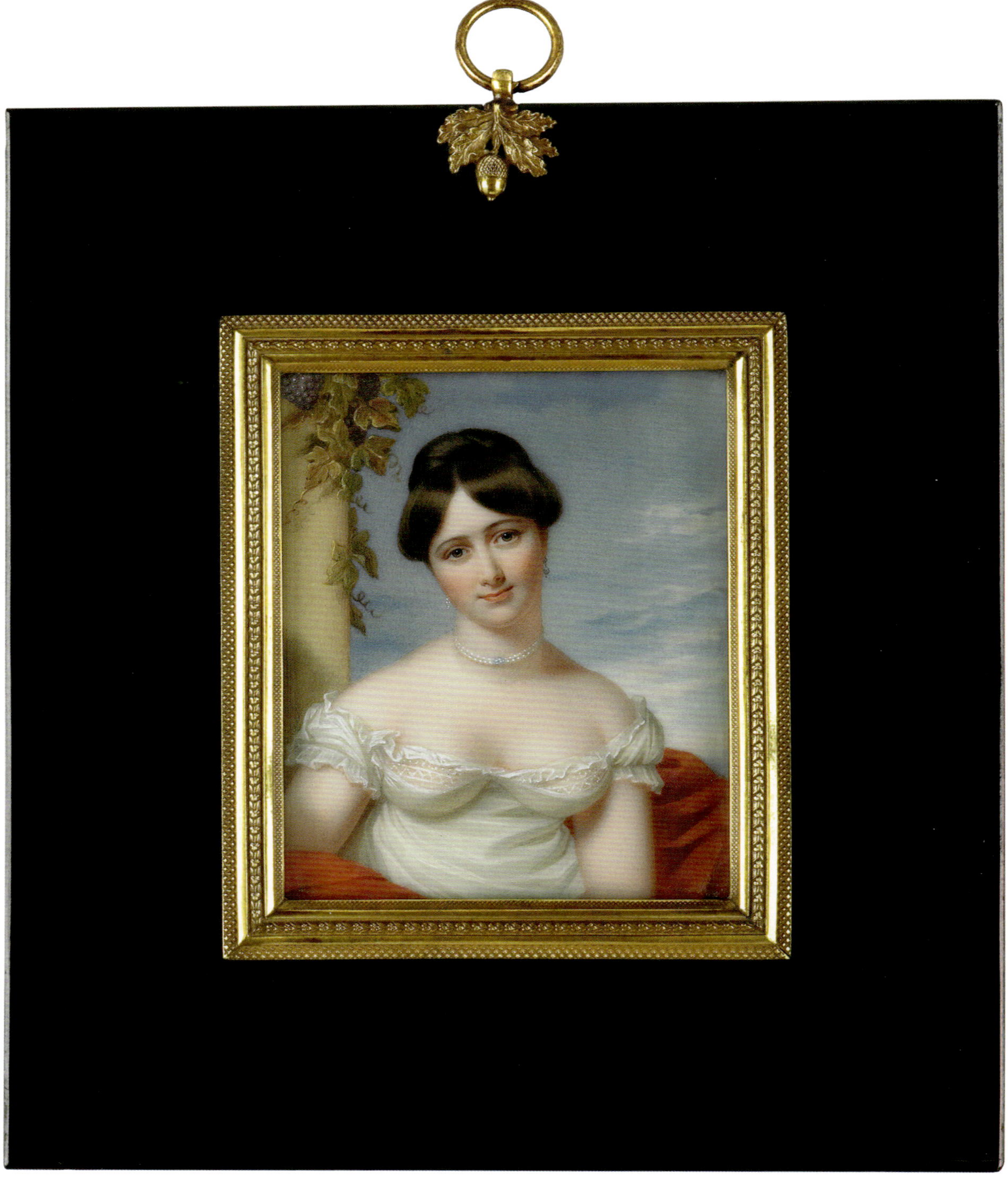

The counter-enamels of miniatures in enamel are not aesthetically appealing, but in the case of those by members of the Bone family they are usually very informative. That on the back of this enamel bears the inscription: *M*^{rs} *Paddon/ London/ April 1817/ Painted by Henry Bone R.A./ Enamel painter in Ordinary/ to His Majesty, and enamel/ painter to His R.H. the /Prince Regent, after a/ Miniature by – Newton./ 3/ P.* The identity of the sitter is confirmed by an inscription on Bone's preparatory drawing in the National Portrait Gallery, London, with the additional information that the miniature was painted for Lord Yarmouth – the future 3rd Marquess of Hertford (see no.63).[1]

Nothing is now known of Mrs Paddon or of her relations with the 3rd Marquess. The miniature, however, was perhaps among those "by the most celebrated artists, of at least half a hundred lovely women, black, brown, fair, and even carrotty for the amateur's sympathetic *bonne bouche*" that were noted by the courtesan Harriette Wilson at the Marquess's Hyde Park home, Dorchester House.[2] The inventory of this house compiled on his death in 1842 listed it as hanging in his library, next to an enamel by "Bone" of "Mrs Robinson", perhaps after one of the portraits of 'Perdita' Robinson by Reynolds, Romney and Gainsborough which were then in his possession (see no.36).[3]

The miniature on which Bone's enamel was based was presumably an early work of William John Newton (1785–1869), who became one of the most fashionable miniature painters of his day. He exhibited every year at the Royal Academy from 1818 to 1863, and was knighted in 1837 in Queen Victoria's first honours list. There are no miniatures by him in the Wallace Collection. During Victoria's reign he would be a rival to Sir William Ross (no.69), but it has been remarked that "His more mechanical handling does not approach Ross's suggestion of breadth and animation, and often his portraits of women are weakly drawn".[4]

His earlier works may have been freer, but Newton's problems with anatomy, if the original for Bone's enamel was indeed by him, are suggested here by the clumsy form of Mrs Paddon's arms and shoulders, though Bone himself was criticized for the heaviness of some of his female nudes.[5] The miniature demonstrates clearly Bone's ability to balance strong colours harmoniously, a talent which was assisted by his technical innovations. He discovered several enamel painting pigments which could be combined on his palette to give precisely the tones and colours he required. He said that he had reduced the number of colours traditionally used by enamel painters while also making them with similar properties of fusion, expansion and contraction so as to enable them in combination to be fired successfully.[6] By this means he was able to "combine the simple elementary colours so as to produce the harmony, richness and power attained by the most eminent painters in oil".[7] The desire to compete with the prestige of oil painting was strongly felt by many miniature (and watercolour) painters in the early nineteenth century. SD

PROVENANCE: Commissioned by the 3rd Marquess of Hertford at an unknown date

M18

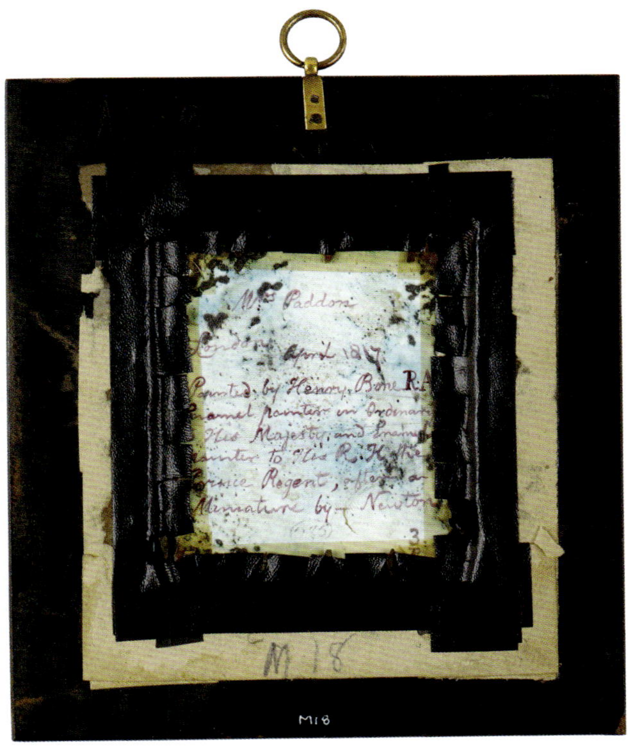

Fig.1 Reverse of no.57

58 Mme Lizinka-Aimée-Zoé de Mirbel (1796–1849)
Louis XVIII, 1819

Ivory, 151 × 121 mm

Signed and dated, lower right: *Mll. Lizinka/ 1819*

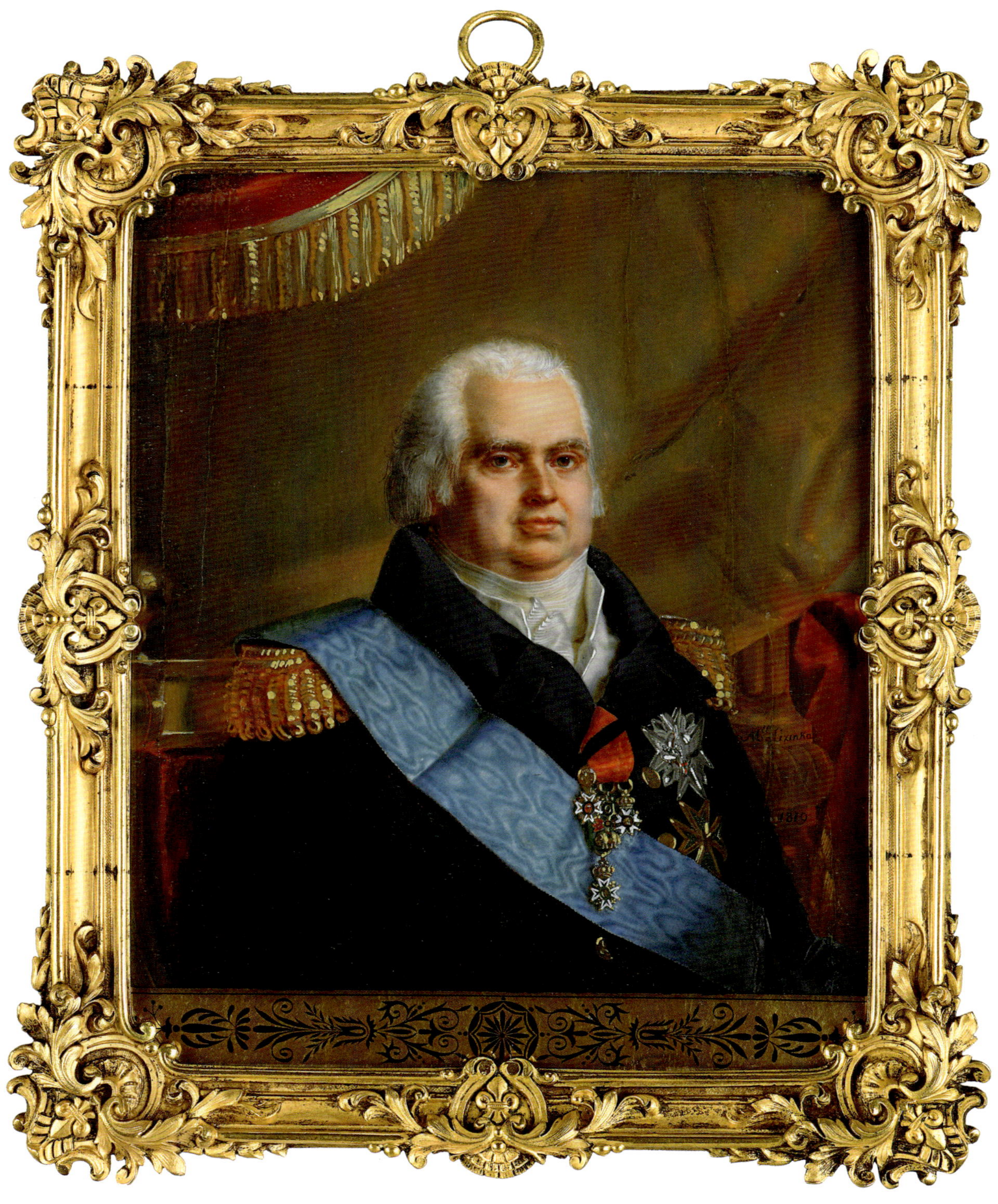

Lizinka-Aimée-Zoé de Mirbel, née Rue, born in Cherbourg, was a pupil of Augustin (nos.38, 42 and 56). In 1818 she painted a much admired portrait of Louis XVIII which led to her appointment as Peintre en miniature de la Chambre du Roi. In 1824 she married the eminent botanist Charles-François Brisseau de Mirbel, twenty years her senior, from which time she signed her miniatures with her married name. Intelligent and charming as well as talented, she was one of several women who attempted to revive the tradition of female salons in early nineteenth-century Paris. Under Charles X and his successor Louis-Philippe she retained her position as the principal miniature painter at court, and opened a studio in 1831 which attracted many pupils. She exhibited frequently at the Paris Salon between 1819 and 1849, winning first-class medals in 1828 and 1848. Her death in 1849 was due to cholera.[1] In addition to three miniatures by her (see also no.60), the Wallace Collection owns two watercolour portraits of Sir Walter Scott and James Fenimore Cooper, which she painted while the authors were visiting Paris in 1826 and 1827.[2]

Louis XVIII (1755–1824) was a younger brother of the executed Louis XVI. With the exception of the Hundred Days in 1815, he reigned as King of France from 1814 to 1824. After fleeing the country in 1791 during the Revolution he spent twenty-three years in exile. During the last six of those years he lived in England.

The Wallace Collection's miniature is a second version of Mlle Rue's portrait of Louis XVIII, painted (unlike the first version) with the aid of sittings from the King (at St-Cloud), and exhibited at the Paris Salon of 1819.[3] Louis wears the plaque and *cordon bleu* ribbon of the Order of the Holy Spirit, the jewel and ribbon of the Golden Fleece, the crosses of the Orders of St Louis and of the Legion of Honour, and the cross and plaque of the Order of St Lazarus. By wearing orders associated with the old aristocracy next to the Legion of Honour, which was founded by Napoleon, Louis symbolized his willingness to accept some of the changes in France brought about by the Revolution. His acceptance of a modified Legion of Honour was also motivated by the fear of antagonizing many of those, numbering at least thirty thousand, who had been awarded the order during the Empire.

Mlle Rue's composition recalls several earlier portraits of the King, including bust-lengths painted by Isabey and Jean-Antoine Gros in 1814. Isabey's miniature was produced in many versions, including one now in the Wallace Collection (M241).[4] Mlle Rue's composition is not exactly the same as Gros's or Isabey's, but it is unlikely that she was unaware of these precedents.

In an article published in the *Revue de Paris* in 1829 Mme de Mirbel would proclaim that portraiture should be regarded as the equal of history painting because of its ability to inspire intense emotions. "The first imperative of the portrait," she wrote, "is to capture not only the physical traits of the sitter, but also a faithful rendition of his or her physiognomy." However, "the artist navigates between two perilous reefs, betraying truth in an effort to correct the faults of nature and … exaggerating these faults, making nature ugly, and denying it nobility".[5] Here she has only lightly improved the less attractive features of the plump and florid King, choosing even to include the grey hairs protruding through his dark and bushy eyebrows. The tone is high-keyed, with some individual details (particularly the hair and the jewel of the Golden Fleece) treated with great precision, while many other parts are painted in a broad, more generalized manner.

The miniature has a strip in *verre eglomisé* decorated with classical motifs at the bottom of the glass. The frame, which may be the original, has *fleurs-de-lis* at its corners and centres. SD

PROVENANCE: first recorded at Bethnal Green (1872–5), no.1688

M282

59 Jean-Baptiste Singry (1782–1824)

Mademoiselle Adèle, 1823

Ivory, 150 × 114 mm

Signed and dated, on the left: *Singry 1823*

Singry was the son of a minor portrait painter, Nicolas Singry. As a pupil of François-André Vincent he presumably intended to paint in oils, but under the tutelage of Jean-Baptiste Isabey he became instead a painter of miniatures. Like Isabey himself, he was born in Nancy but pursued his career in Paris, exhibiting at the Salon from 1806 to 1824, the year of his early death. His first exhibit was a self-portrait. At his last Salon three works, including portraits of the duc d'Orléans and his daughter, were shown posthumously. His subjects and patrons included many people associated with the theatre.[1]

The identification of the sitter in this miniature as Mademoiselle Adèle derives from the catalogue of the sale in 1870 at which it was bought by the 4th Marquess of Hertford. The sitter was almost certainly an actress – this is suggested by her semi-classical dress and the omission of her surname in the catalogue entry – but in the present state of knowledge it is not possible to identify her. Lyonnet's *Dictionnaire des Comédiens Français* says that Mademoiselle Adèle is "a name carried by a great number of actresses", and provides a no doubt incomplete list of performances (eleven in all) by women with this name at Paris theatres between 1803 and 1825.[2] The salacious *Petite biographie dramatique* of 1826 includes only one Mademoiselle Adèle, of the Porte-St-Martin theatre: "… her voluptuous dance promises pleasure, and we are assured that Mlle Adèle fulfils all that her dance promises".[3] She may be the Adèle who is described by the *Dictionnaire des Comédiens Français* as "*ex-danseuse au Panorama dramatique*": "… she debuted with some success as an actress in *The Grey Man*, at the Porte-St-Martin on 15 March 1824."[4] Although one cannot be sure who is the subject of Singry's miniature, it is a fine example of the artist's technique – delicate, carefully drawn brushwork and a subtle range of colours employed to present an attractive personality who engages directly with the viewer.

The owner of the miniature before Lord Hertford was the flamboyant Russian collector Anatole Demidoff, Prince of San Donato (1813–1870). He always ensured that his paintings and miniatures were given fine-quality frames, some with motifs relevant to their subject. He may have provided the impressive frame seen here, with its laurel wreath and ribbon, though in view of the miniature's date and the possibility that ownership indicates some personal association, he perhaps inherited it from his father Nicholas (1773–1828), who was also a notable collector. Anatole lived most of his life either in Paris or at his magnificent villa at San Donato near Florence. In his youth he had an unbounded enthusiasm for luxury and display, but in his last decade, oppressed by illness and ennui, he sold much of his art in a series of spectacular sales in Paris at which the 4th Marquess of Hertford was one of the main buyers.[5] There were twenty-five miniatures in his March 1870 sale, of which Lord Hertford bought eight, only two of which are now in the Wallace Collection (see also no.66).[6] Among Demidoff's miniatures were several of actors and actresses, including portraits of Talma and Mlle Mars.[61] The seven by Singry included portraits of the actor Pierre Marie Nicolas Michelot and the actresses Mlles Delâtre and Vigneron. At San Donato Nicholas Demidoff had built an 'Odeon' for the performance of music and plays, and in his youth Anatole was an ardent theatregoer, doubtless making the acquaintance of many actors and (with particular enthusiasm) many actresses. SD

PROVENANCE: Bought by the 4th Marquess of Hertford at the San Donato (Anatole Demidoff), sale, Paris, 8–10 March 1870, lot 420, 105 fr.

M305

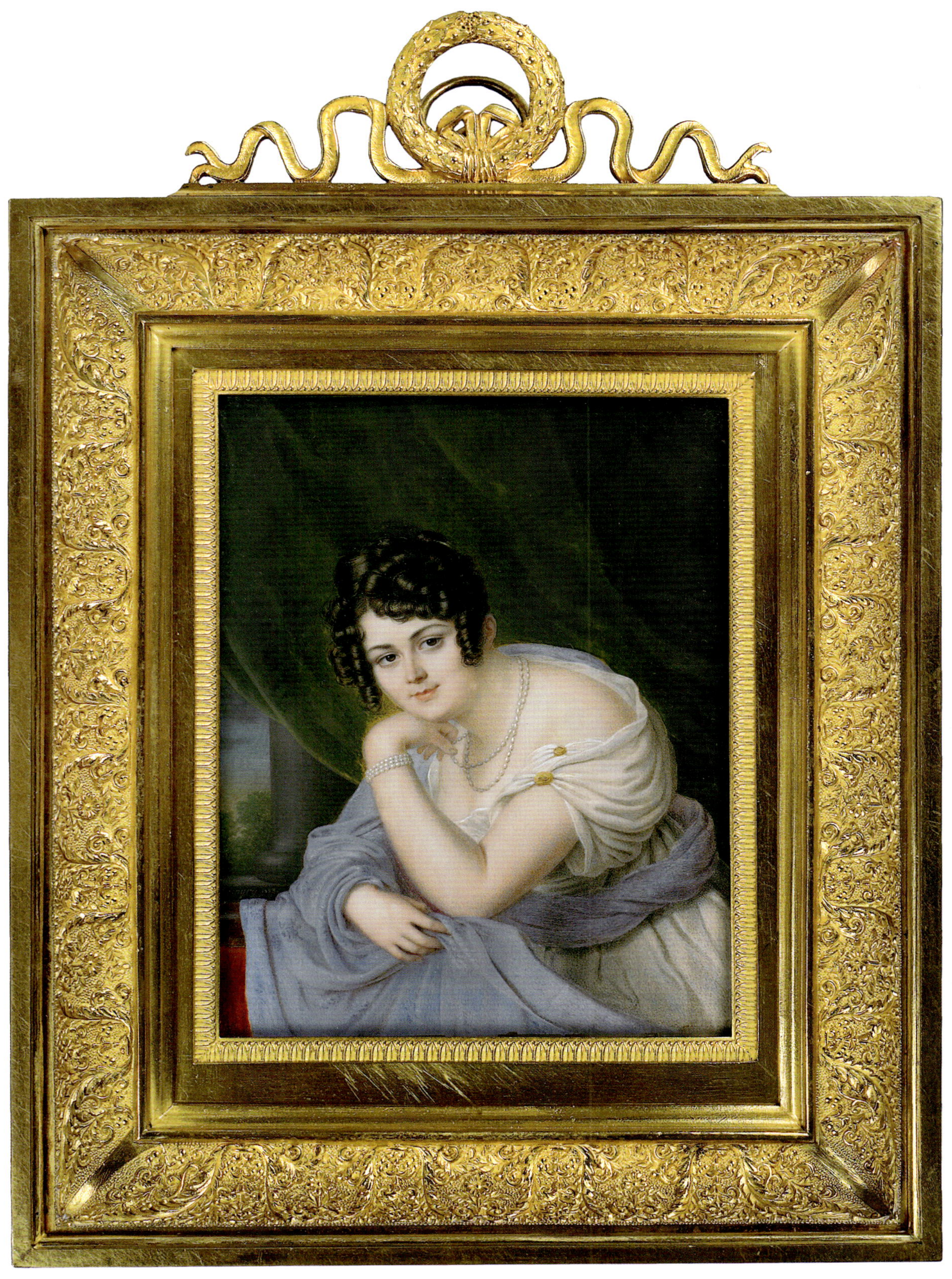

x 0.7

60 Mme Lizinka-Aimée-Zoé de Mirbel (1796–1849)

*Caroline, duchesse de Berry, c.*1828

Ivory, 111 × 87 mm

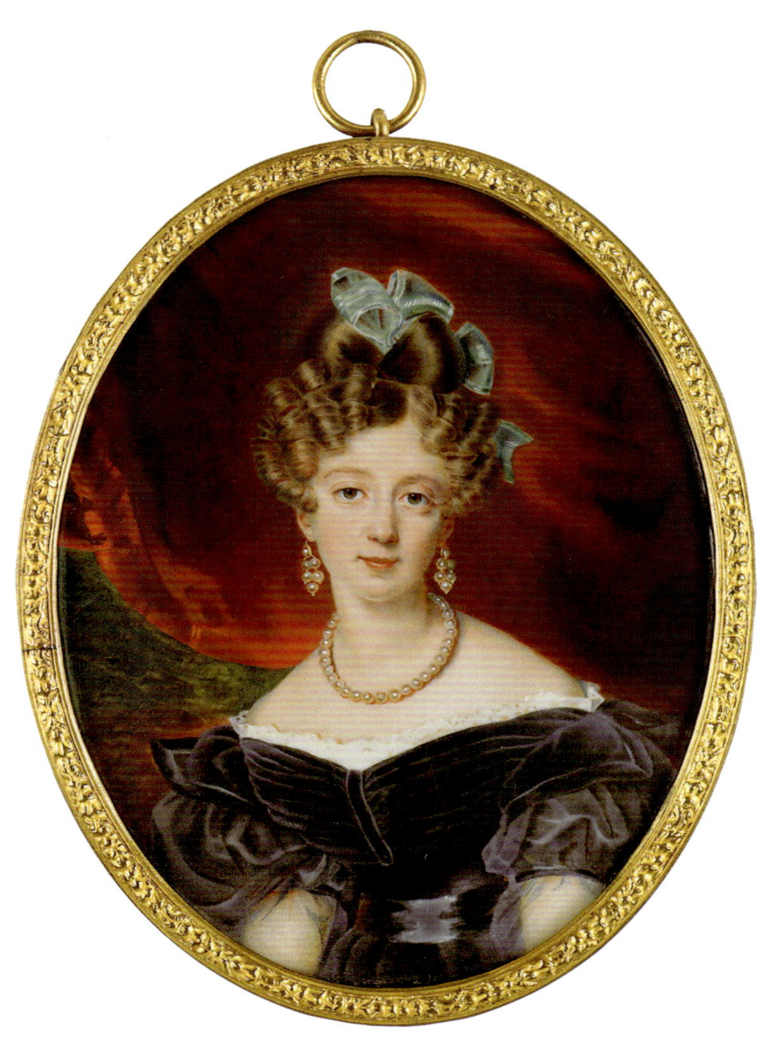

Marie Caroline Ferdinande de Bourbon (1798–1870), daughter of Francis I of the Two Sicilies, married Louis XVIII's nephew Charles Ferdinand, duc de Berry, in 1816. After the assassination of her husband in 1820 her status at the Bourbon court was enhanced enormously when her son, the *enfant de miracle* Prince Henri, was born soon after his father's murder, because he was the sole hope for the continuation of the Bourbon line. After the July Revolution of 1830 which overthrew Louis's successor Charles X and installed Louis-Philippe as King of the French she fled France, but returned in 1832 at the head of a rebellion in the Vendée which she hoped would secure the succession for her son. After its failure she was imprisoned for a short time and spent the rest of her life in Austria and Italy.[1]

The duchesse de Berry brought an enthusiastic and impulsive personality to what was often a dull and stuffy Bourbon court. During her fourteen years in France before the July Revolution she was also renowned, despite her fondness for hunting, for bringing a feminine elegance and refinement to what was essentially a masculine environment. Like her predecessor the Empress Joséphine, she took a particular interest in botany, in furnishing the interiors of her apartments and in collecting contemporary paintings. In Paris she lived in the Tuileries Palace after her husband's death, but her favourite residence was the château of Rosny in Yvelines, near the road from Paris to Rouen, which she restored and refurbished.

Portraits of the duchesse de Berry were painted by such major artists as Baron Gérard, Mme Vigée Le Brun and Sir Thomas Lawrence (when he visited Paris in 1825). Among those who painted miniature portraits of her were Garneray and Duchesne de Gisors.[2] All these painters, like Mme de Mirbel herself, could be classified in varying degrees as court artists, but she also commissioned subjects from Scott's novel *Quentin Durward* from Bonington and Delacroix and ordered a *Saint Vincent de Paul Preaching* (shown at the 1824 Paris Salon) from another up-and-coming young painter, Paul Delaroche. In 1829, she held a famous fancy-dress ball intended to evoke Mary Stuart's brief time at the French court as the wife of Francis II.[3] The Anglo-French aspects of her taste therefore anticipated those of the 4th Marquess of Hertford's own collecting, which began in earnest twenty years later.

In September 1823 the *Moniteur universel* reported that Mlle Rue (Mme de Mirbel before her marriage) had painted a portrait of the duchesse de Berry.[4] This cannot now be located, and the resemblance of the sitter in the Wallace Collection's miniature to a dated portrait of the Duchess by Alexandre-Jean Dubois-Drahonnet suggests a later date, *c.*1828.[5] De Mirbel shows the Duchess dressed in a characteristically elegant but restrained style, wearing a dress which emphasizes her slim waist. Although she owned an important collection of jewellery, here she wears a comparatively simple (though undoubtedly magnificent) pair of earrings of gold with round pearls close together like bunches of grapes and a necklace of impressively large pearls.[6] Painted in a smooth manner with dense stippling in the flesh tones, the miniature presents an unusually direct and engaging impression of one of the senior members of the Bourbon family. De Mirbel wrote that "… men should be painted as they are; women as they want or could be",[7] but this is a less idealized image than many royal portraits of the 1820s. SD

PROVENANCE: First recorded at Bethnal Green (1872–5), no.1689

M281

61 André-Léon Larue, called Mansion (1785–1831 or after?)

An Unknown Lady, 1823

Ivory, 142 × 105 mm

Signed and dated, on the left: *mansion./ 1823.*

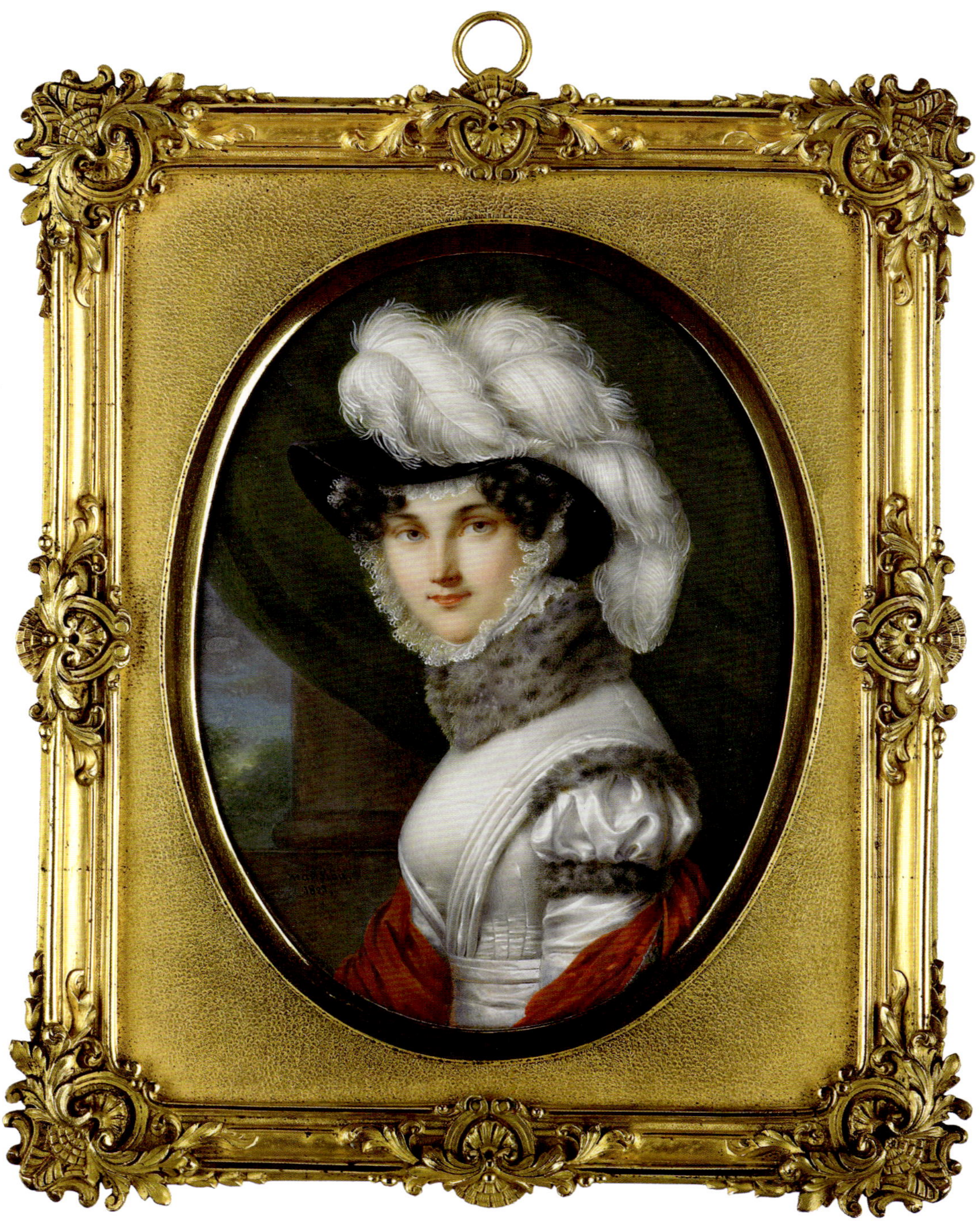

× 0.8

An Unknown Lady, *c*.1825

Ivory, 143 × 103 mm

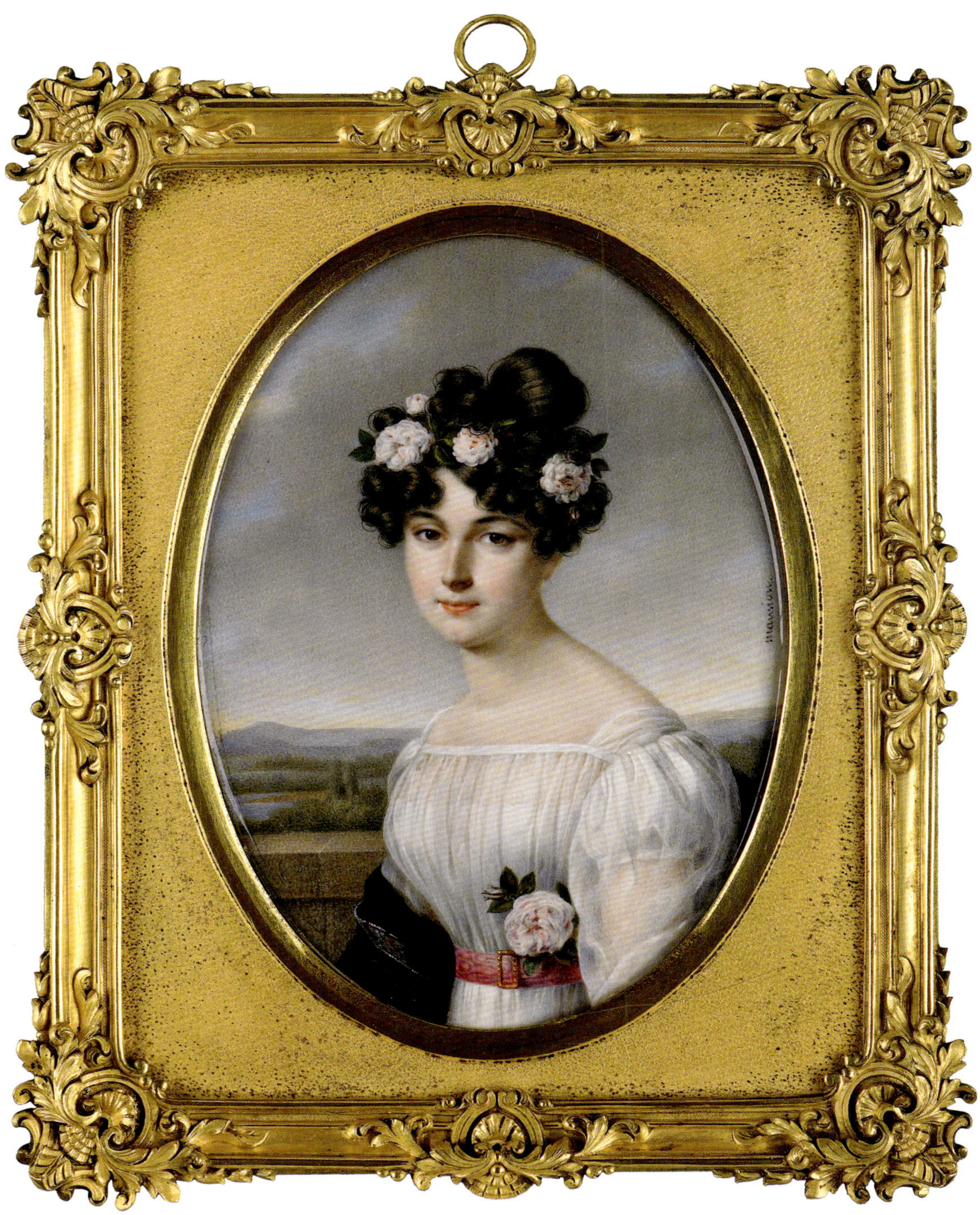

× 0.8

Mansion, born in Nancy, was a pupil of his father Jacques Larue, a portrait painter, and of Jean-Baptiste Isabey (*q.v.*). Miniatures by him were shown at the Paris Salon in 1808, 1819, 1822 and 1824 (when his exhibits included portraits of his wife and the painter Horace Vernet).[1] He was an able artist, but little is known about him. He developed close ties to Britain: his *Letters upon the Art of Miniature Painting* was published in London in 1822 (with a French edition, *Lettres sur la Miniature*, published in Paris the following year), and he is presumably the "L. Mansion" who exhibited three miniatures at the Royal Academy in 1829 and 1831 (from "Trebenshum" – *i.e.* Trebinshun House, Brecon, South Wales). His book takes the form of a series of letters between a French miniature painter, M. Deville, and his young English pupil, Miss Fanny, in which Deville provides practical advice while also commenting occasionally on the qualities of other miniature painters.

Mansion's clients were mostly French and English but also included some Russian and Hungarian sitters. The ladies in these two miniatures in the Wallace Collection, both painted in the mid 1820s, are unidentified, though their costumes suggest that they were French. The existence of at least three other versions of the first miniature may indicate that the sitter had some contemporary renown.[2] A version in oils (though with the composition in reverse) was recorded in the early twentieth century as bearing an inscription identifying it as a portrait of Mrs Mills, née Martyn, by Lawrence exhibited at the Royal Academy in 1823, but no 'Mrs Mills' is recorded among Lawrence's sitters.[3] The flowers worn by the lady in the second miniature imply that she was married. Both miniatures, like four others by the artist in the Wallace Collection, are fine demonstrations of Mansion's considerable abilities as an artist. His technique is meticulous, employing tight stippling and clear colours to produce a remarkably crisp and vivid image. SD

PROVENANCE: Both first catalogued in the Wallace Collection 1904

M272 and M276

62 Pietro de Rossi (1761-1831)

Grand Duke Nikolai Pavlovich, later Nicholas I, Emperor of Russia, c.1822–5

Ivory, 36 × 30 mm

Signed, along the right-hand edge: *P. de Rossi f.*

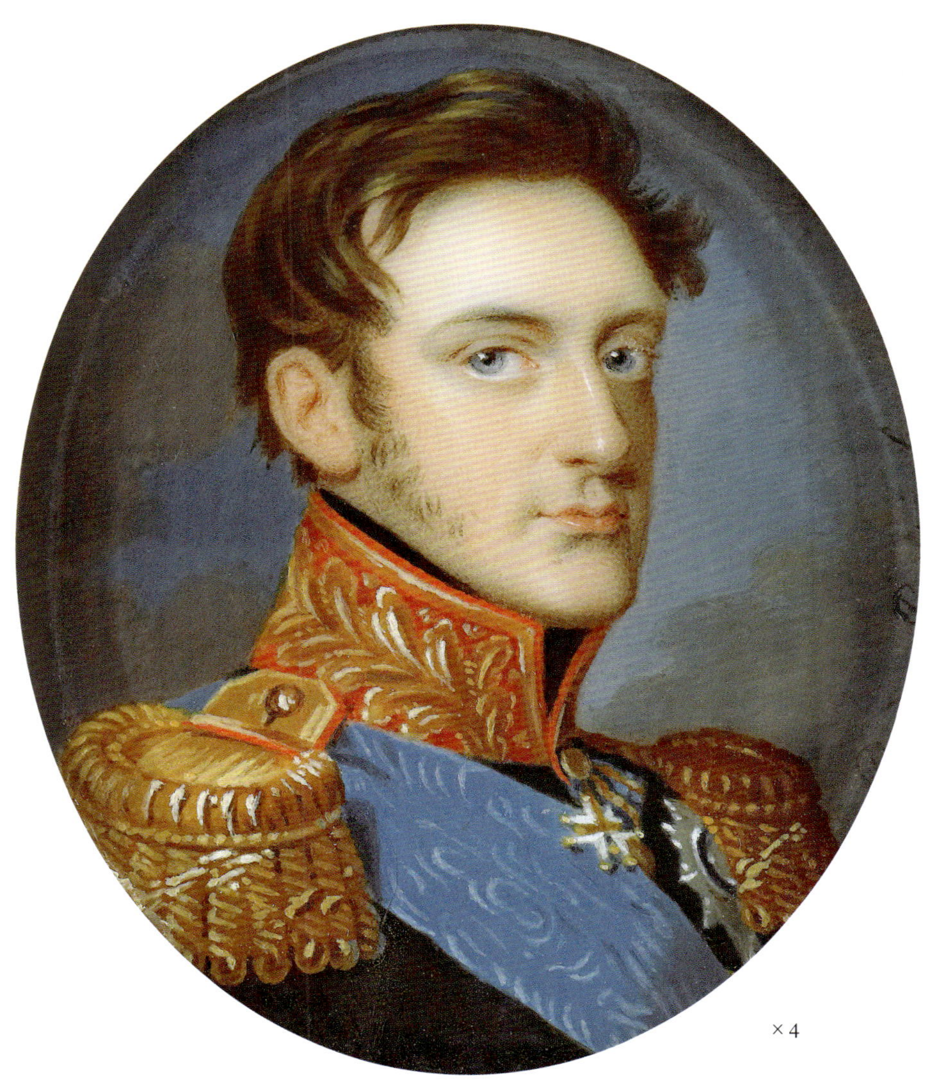

× 4

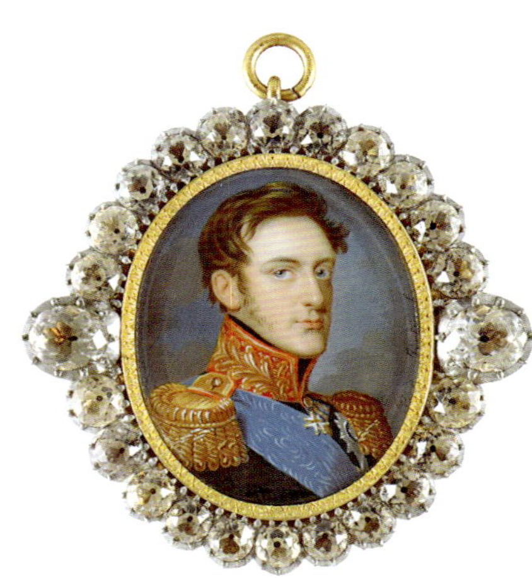

Nikolai Pavlovich (1796–1855) was a younger brother of Tsar Alexander I, on whose death in 1825 he succeeded to the throne, because Alexander's eldest surviving brother Constantine was unwilling to become Tsar. Although he disliked serfdom, he firmly believed in autocracy, and his reign would be characterized by increasingly repressive policies. He was a considerable collector and patron of the arts, acquiring many major paintings by historic and contemporary artists and playing a leading role in the establishment of the 'New Hermitage' as Russia's first public museum.[1]

Nicholas wears the ribbon and badge of the Order of Saint Andrew, the highest Russian order of chivalry, and perhaps the cross of the Polish Order of the White Eagle. Rossi's miniature is apparently based on a whole-length portrait of Nicholas painted by the English artist George Dawe in 1821, when Nicholas was still Grand Duke (fig.1). It was presumably painted shortly after Dawe's portrait, before Nicholas became Tsar. Rossi shows him wearing a different uniform to that in Dawe's portrait, but the head (including his carefully coiffed hair) is almost identical.[2]

In April 1825, six months before the accession of Nicholas, the future 4th Marquess of Hertford (at that time Earl of Yarmouth) was in Moscow. The evidence for this is the presence in the Wallace Collection's library of two books inscribed *Yarmouth/ Moscou/ Avril/ 1825*, but unfortunately nothing more is currently known of this visit. The books are a Russian-French-German dictionary and Charles-Philippe's Reiff's *Grammaire russe à l'usage des étrangers*. The future 4th Marquess's interest in Russia at this time is also suggested by his ownership of another book now in the Wallace Collection's library – an official report relating to the Decembrist revolt by Liberal and revolutionary elements within the army against Nicholas – *Conspiration de Russie: Rapport de la Commission d'Enquête de St-Petersbourg, à S.M. l'Empereur Nicolas Ier sur les Sociétés secrètes découvertes en Russie*, published in 1826, shortly after the revolt had been suppressed.

Only two years after this visit, in 1827, the future 4th Marquess's father, the 3rd Marquess, went to Russia on behalf of George IV to present Nicholas with the Order of the Garter. Six years earlier the 3rd Marquess had been appointed a member of the Russian Order of Saint Anna. It is therefore clear that there

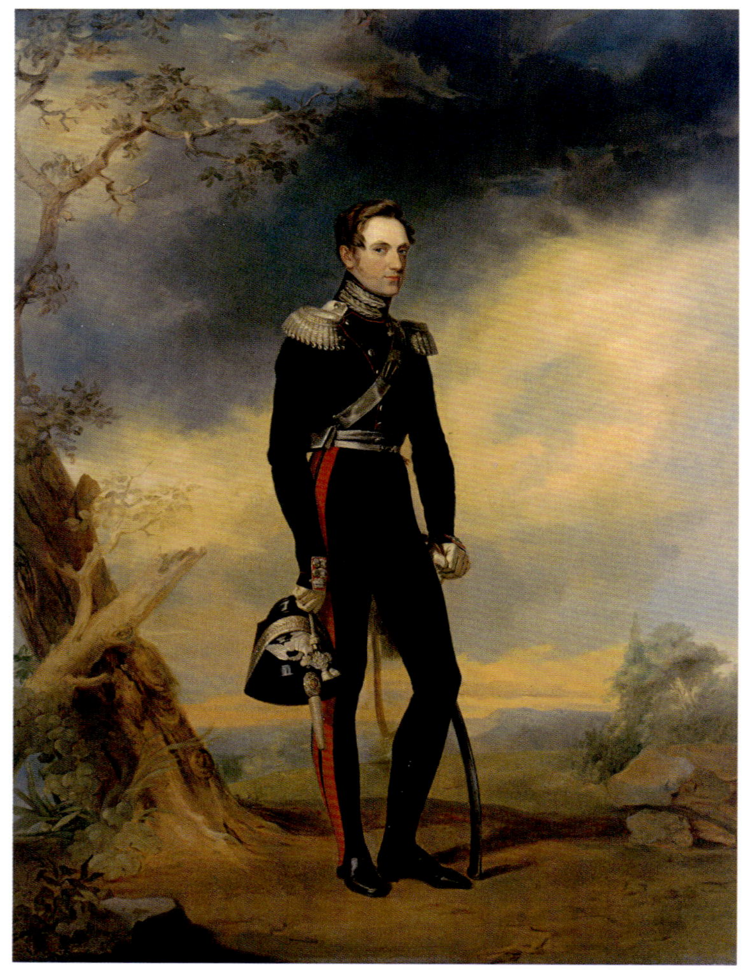

Fig.1 George Dawe, *Grand Duke Nikolai Pavlovich* (later Tsar Nicholas I, Emperor of Russia), 1821, oil on canvas, 277 × 187 cm, St Petersburg, Hermitage (GE5851)

were close associations between the Hertfords and Russia, but unfortunately very little more is known about them at present. Nicholas had visited Britain in 1816, when he is alleged to have had an affair with the much older Lady Conyngham, who became the mistress of the 3rd Marquess's friend George IV in 1820.[3] During his visit to Russia the 3rd Marquess was troubled by gout, but his splendid appearance and lavish expenditure are said to have made a deep impression on Nicholas and his court.[4] Alexander I had been the first foreign monarch to be appointed a 'Stranger Knight of the Garter', in 1813, and the 3rd Marquess himself had become a member of the order in 1822 (see no.63).[5]

It is not known when Rossi's miniature entered the Hertfords' collections. But, because it depicts Nicholas before he became Tsar, it seems more likely that it was given to the future 4th Marquess by the sitter in 1825 than to the 3rd Marquess two years later, although the latter is not impossible. The frame is decorated with fine-quality rock crystals rather than diamonds, which perhaps supports the hypothesis that it was given by the Grand Duke to an English Earl than by the Tsar to an English Marquess acting for his King.[6]

Although of Italian descent, Pietro de Rossi was born and died in St Petersburg. He produced many miniatures of members of the Russian court, usually on ivory or card but occasionally in enamel. This is a fine example of his work, meticulously painted in clear, fresh colours. SD

PROVENANCE: First catalogued in the Wallace Collection 1904

M291

63 Henry Bone (1755–1834), after Lawrence

Francis, 3rd Marquess of Hertford, 1824

Enamel on copper, 97 × 75 mm

This miniature was acquired in 1956 for the Hertford House Historic Collection (see also no.33).

The counter-enamel is inscribed: *Francis Charles/ Marq^s. & Earl of Hertford/ &c &c London/ Augt 1824/ Painted by Henry Bone R.A./ Enamel Painter to His/ Majesty & En^l Painter to/ H.R.H. the Duke of York &c/ after the Original by Sir/ Thos Lawrence P R A.* It copies the head and shoulders of a three-quarter-length portrait of the 3rd Marquess of Hertford (1777–1842) which had been painted by Sir Thomas Lawrence no more than two years earlier – the Marquess wears the star of the Order of the Garter to which he was appointed on his accession to the marquisate in 1822.[1] This painting is now owned by the National Gallery of Art in Washington, but has been on long-term loan to the Wallace Collection since 1993. It was clearly intended by Lawrence or his patron as a modest response to the splendid full-length portrait of George IV in a black frock coat (now in the Wallace Collection)[2] which Lawrence had painted in the same year. The 3rd Marquess, as Earl of Yarmouth, had been a close friend of the Prince Regent, acting on occasions as his agent for the purchase of works of art, and when the Prince became King he remained on respectful, though more distant, terms with his sovereign.[3]

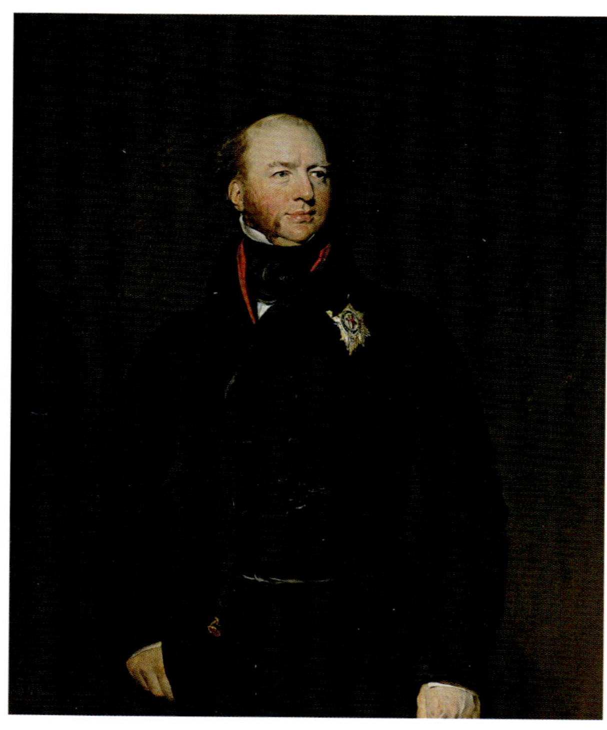

Fig.1 Thomas Lawrence, *Francis, 3rd Marquess of Hertford*, c.1822–3, oil on canvas, 127 × 100.3 cm, Washington, D.C., National Gallery of Art (inv.1968.6.2)

Bone's preparatory drawing is in the National Portrait Gallery.[4] It does not carry an inscription which would tell us whether the enamel was painted on speculation or as a commission. There is at least one other version of the miniature. A larger example is in the National Gallery of Ireland, Dublin, and there was one in the (posthumous) Henry Bone sale at Christie's, 7 June 1836, lot 23, which may be the Wallace Collection's – it was described in the sale catalogue as "imperfect", and the Wallace's Collection's miniature has a crack in the bottom left-hand corner – but was perhaps a third version. Bone's technique of using squared preparatory drawings enabled him to vary the size of his enamel copies.

Bone and other members of his family occasionally had recourse to the auction rooms as a means of selling their miniatures. Bone himself had a sale in 1832, and there were three further sales in 1836 and 1849, presumably from the family's collection.[5] This suggests that he may have found it difficult to sell his works individually later in life. An offer to sell his collection to the nation *en bloc* for £4,000 was declined, and most of the miniatures in his two posthumous sales in 1836 sold for less than 30 guineas. By then his great days, when in 1811 over four thousand people had paid to see his enamel copy of Titian's *Bacchus and Ariadne* in his Berners Street studio and it had sold later to George Bowles for 2,200 guineas, were long gone. SD

PROVENANCE: Count Berchthold of Budapest; Dr Emil Delmar, New York; Sotheby's, London, 21 June 1956, lot 73, £60, bought National Art-Collections Fund; presented in 1956 to the Library of the Wallace Collection (now Hertford House Historic Collection) by the National Art-Collections Fund

HHHC2007.4

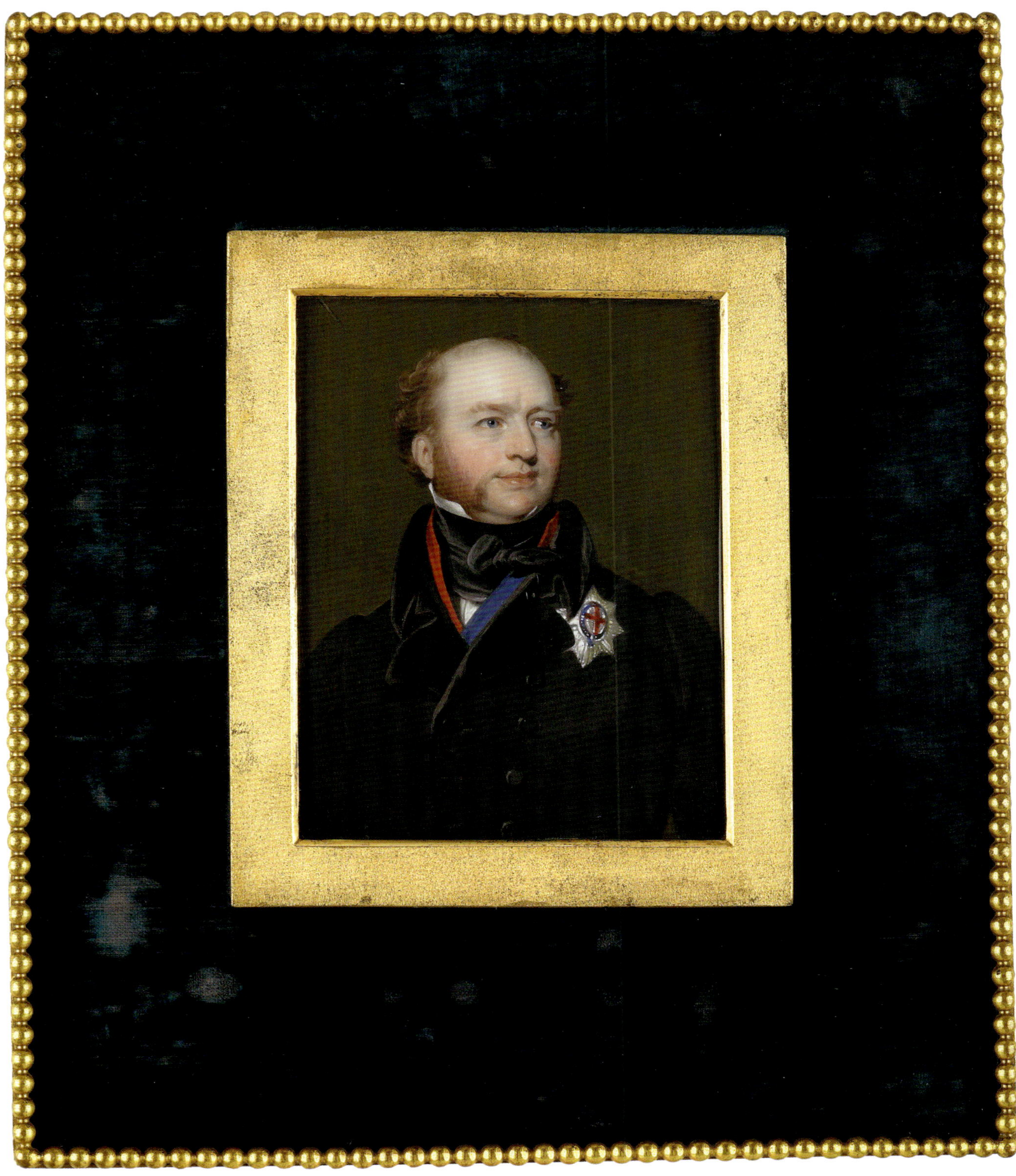

64 Jean-Baptiste Isabey (1767–1855)

Rose Maistre, Second Wife of the Artist, 1831

Paper, 138 × 104 mm

Signed and dated, centre left: *Isabey/ 1831*

This, one of the the last dated miniatures by Isabey in the Wallace Collection, shows the artist's second wife, Marie-Rose Maistre, whom he married in 1829, only six months after the death of his first wife, when he was sixty-two years old. Two children would be born of the marriage, a son and a daughter. Rose, who had been one of Isabey's many pupils, was less gregarious than Isabey's first wife, Jeanne Laurisse de Salienne, and did not usually accompany him on the many social visits that played an important part in his life. According to Leo Schidlof she was born in 1814 and died in 1861, but there must be some uncertainty over her year of birth, as it is difficult to accept the woman in the present miniature as only seventeen years old.[1] That she is Rose Maistre is supported by her resemblance to the sitter in another portrait by Isabey which is also said to show Rose (present location unknown).[2]

State patronage did not end for Isabey with the fall of Napoleon. Although he drew at least one private caricature attacking Louis XVIII as a puppet of the English and his Bonapartist sympathies attracted the attention of the police in 1817, he had already produced his first portrait of the new Bourbon king as early as 1814 (see no.58) and soon won further royal commissions from Louis and his family. In 1823, in an echo of his activities under the Empire, he was appointed Inspecteur dessinateur, chargé de l'ordonnance des fêtes et spectacles de la Cour, and in 1825 assisted at the coronation of Charles X. Nevertheless, by then the great days of patronage, under the Empire and then in Vienna, were past for Isabey. Although he was given some commissions by the Orléans dynasty which came to power in 1830, it is clear that the last decades of his career were a pale reflection of his glory under Napoleon.

Some of Isabey's later portraits reveal a weakening of his hand with increasing age, but this miniature shows that even at the age of sixty-four he was still on occasions capable of painting with the controlled precision of his earlier works. The more saturated colours, particularly in the sky and hair, are the result not only of a change in Isabey's technique but of the better preservation of this miniature, which has suffered some discolouration around the edges from dampness but has been less marred by fading than some of his other works in the Wallace Collection. The gilded frame, in a mid-eighteenth-century French style, has on the back a leather sheet stamped with the framer's name *A. JEANNE,/ 68, PASSAGE CHOISEUL.* The Paris framer Alexandre Jeanne supplied the frames for two other miniatures now in the Collection.[3] SD

PROVENANCE: First catalogued in the Wallace Collection 1904

M217

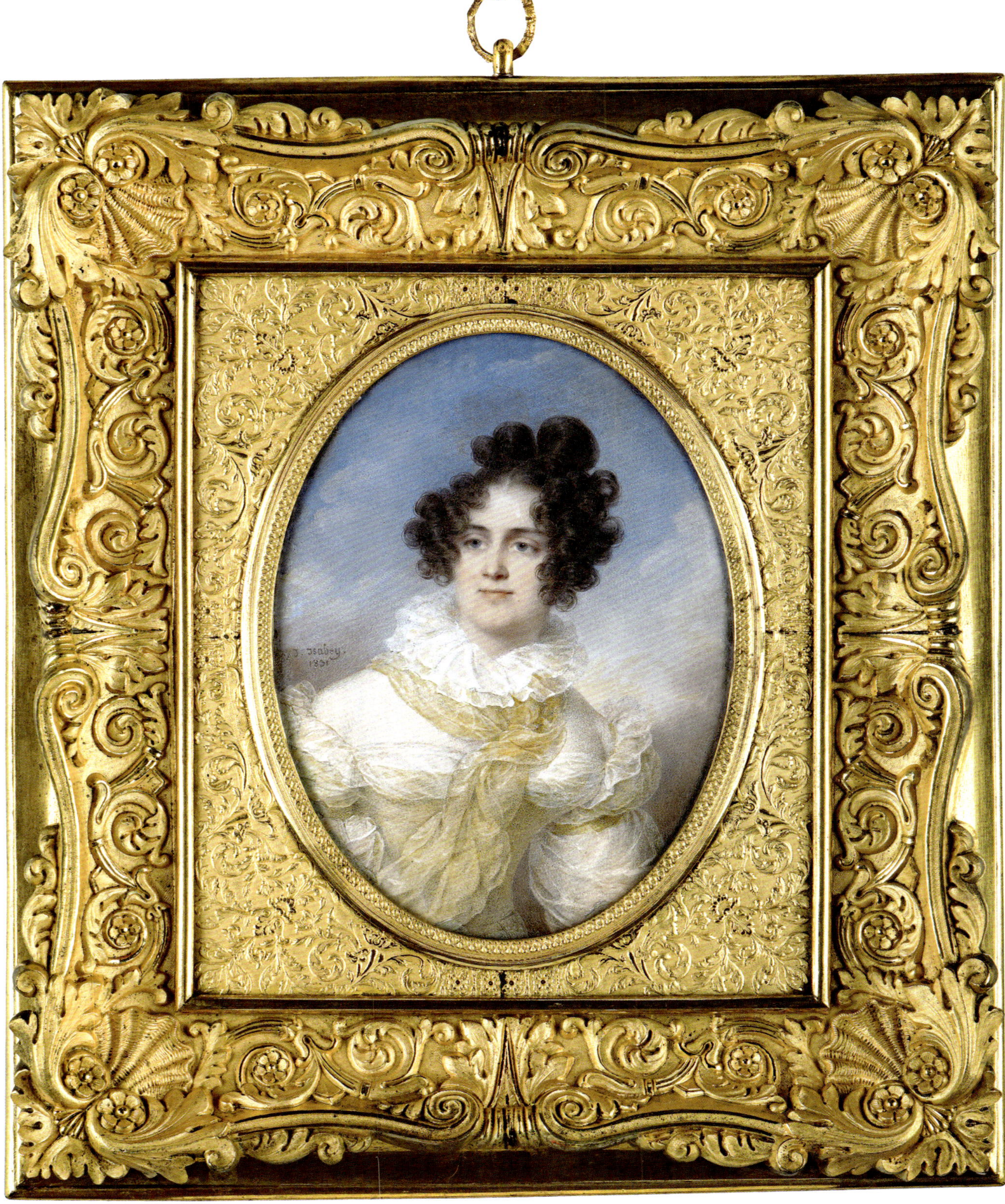

x 0.8

65 Henry Pierce Bone (1779–1855), after Reynolds

Lady Cockburn and her Three Eldest Sons, 1842

Enamel on copper, 333 × 250 mm

Signed and dated, centre right: *H P Bone/ 1842*
Inscribed on the hem of Lady Cockburn's cloak (as in Reynolds's original): *1773./ J.Reynolds.pinx.*

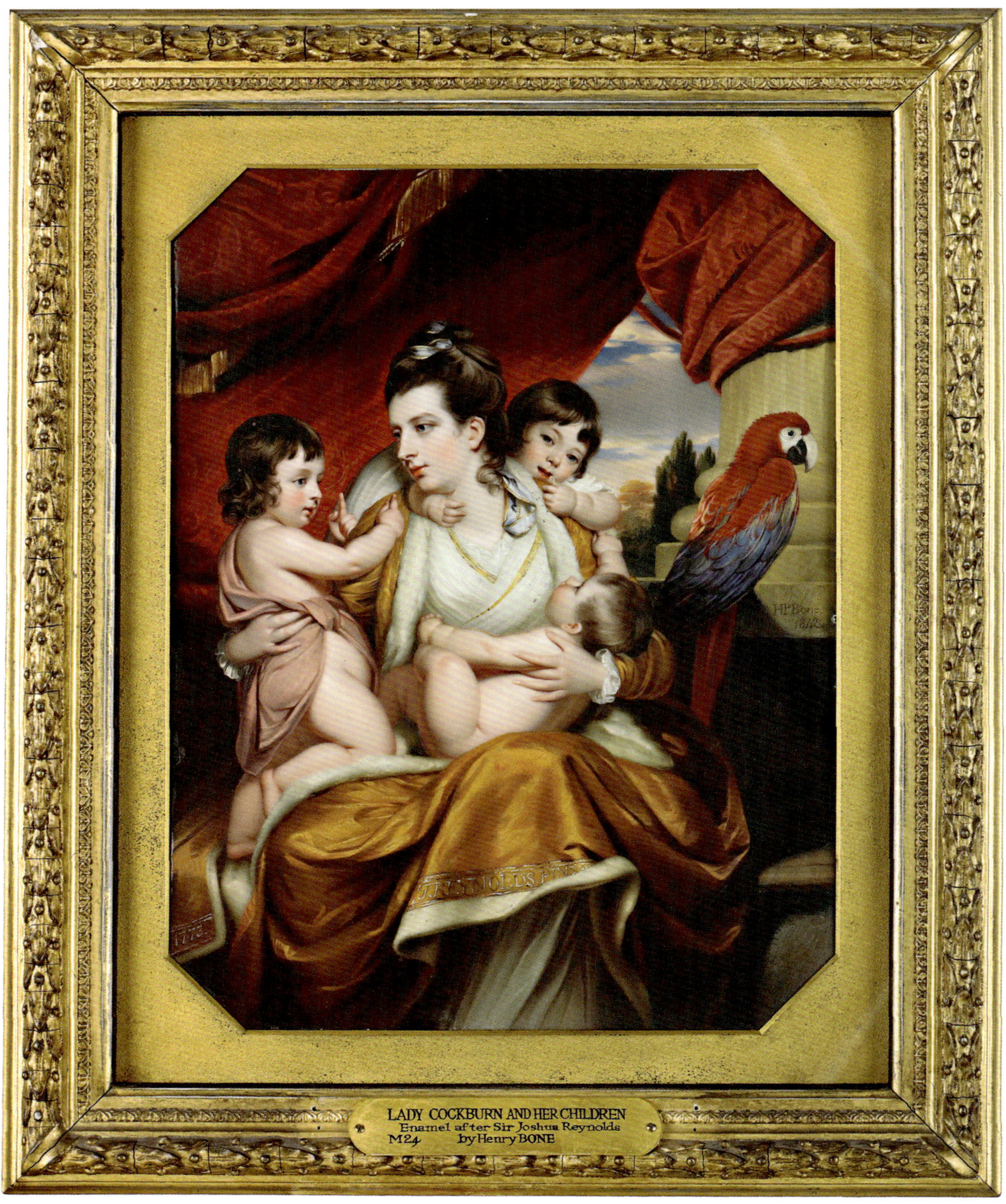

× 0.4

Some of the enamels of Henry Pierce Bone, the eldest son and pupil of Henry Bone (*q.v.*), would be difficult to distinguish from those of his father were it not for his signature and the family practice of adding informative inscriptions to their counter-enamels. The back of this miniature is inscribed by Bone (in a much neater hand than that of his father): *Augusta Anne Lady Cockburn & her Sons/ M. General Sir James Cockburn Bar$^{t.}$ G.C.H./ Admiral the R$^{t.}$ Hon$^{ble.}$ Sir George Cockburn, G.C.B./ The very Rev$^{d.}$ William Cockburn D.D. Dean of York./ London, Sept$^{r.}$ 1842. Painted by Henry Pierce Bone. Enamel/ Painter to her Majesty & H.R.H. Prince Albert, the Queen/ Dowager & H.R.H. the Duchess of Kent. From the/ original by Sir Joshua Reynolds in the possession of Sir James Cockburn Bar^{t}.* Reynolds's original painting is now in the National Gallery, London.[1] It is not known who, if anyone, commissioned Bone's enamel, or who acquired it subsequently, until it was first recorded when Sir Richard Wallace lent it with much of his collection to Bethnal Green in 1872–5.

Augusta Anne, Lady Cockburn (1749–1837) was the wife of Sir James Cockburn, 8th Baronet of Langton, Berwickshire. In all, she had six children and three stepchildren. Remarkably, her sons in the present portrait became, as the counter-enamel records, a Major-General, an Admiral and the Dean of York. Reynolds's composition recalls earlier allegorical representations of Charity, particularly two paintings by Van Dyck, one of which is also now in the National Gallery.[2]

Henry Pierce Bone, the most important of several children and grandchildren of Henry Bone to become professional artists, first exhibited portraits and then subject pictures at the Royal Academy.[3] These were in oil, but after Henry Bone became ill in 1833 his son took advantage of his father's training to make enamels, many of which (like the present miniature) were rather larger than those produced by his father. Between 1833 and 1855 he showed 115 works at the Royal Academy, mainly portraits in enamel after historical figures. Although, as the counter-enamel of this miniature proclaims, he received much royal patronage – there is a large group of his works in the Royal Collection – he did not enjoy institutional success. He did not become an Associate of the Royal Academy, let alone a full member, as his father had done. This must be explained at least as much by the decline in the standing of miniature painting as by any limitations in Bone's talent.[4]

Although it has been said that his enamels are "a little coarser" and "the quality of his work may not have the delicate finish of his father's",[5] this is a fine miniature entirely comparable to the work of Henry Bone. It has similarly deep, but clear, colours combined with delicacy in the flesh tones – a characteristic which Henry Bone had achieved through using large quantities of clear flux with his pigments and then firing at unusually low temperatures.[6] The clipped corners of the present work may be explained by a need to remove evidence of the cracks which could develop in the corners during firings – a frequent fault with large rectangular plaques. SD

PROVENANCE: First recorded at Bethnal Green (1872–5), no.614

M24

66 Johann Baptist Göstl (1813–1895), after Lampi

Catherine II, Empress of Russia, 1850

Ivory, 190 × 143 mm

Signed and dated, left (on the cushion): *Göstl/ 850*

Göstl was a Viennese artist who was employed at the Vienna porcelain factory painting ceramic plaques but occasionally worked in other media. The German-born Catherine II (1729–1796) was Empress of Russia from 1762. Although only half-length, and different in some of the details of dress and composition, this miniature apparently derives from a full-length portrait in oils of Catherine by Johann Baptist Lampi the Elder (1751–1830), the first version of which, painted in 1793, is now in the Hermitage, St Petersburg (fig.1).[1] Catherine wears a white dress with a blue-grey jacket and ermine mantle. She also wears the ribbon and badge of the Order of Saint Andrew, the first and highest Russian order of chivalry, instituted by Peter the Great. It is an imposing image of Catherine which, for all her Enlightenment sympathies, makes clear her status as an autocratic ruler. With its bright colours and smooth finish, the Wallace Collection's miniature demonstrates the continuing influence of Göstl's training as a porcelain painter.

The miniature was owned, and perhaps commissioned, by the Russian collector Anatole Demidoff, Prince of San Donato (1813–1870). It was at one of his sales in 1870 that it was bought, with seven other miniatures, by the 4th Marquess of Hertford. Only two, this and a portrait of Mlle Adèle by Singry (no.59), were part of Lady Wallace's bequest to the nation. Demidoff also owned two oil versions of Lampi's portrait in the Hermitage, one a whole-length and the other an oval, bust-length version with slight variations from the original.[2] He had an extraordinary fondness for images of royalty, which he indulged to the full at his villa of San Donato, near Florence. At his various sales there were scores of royal portraits, particularly Russian, Italian and French Imperial, and his marriage to Princess Mathilde, a niece of Napoleon, owed more to his devotion to the Napoleonic legend and the opportunity to marry into royalty than to love for Mathilde.

The frame of the Wallace Collection's miniature, with its Russian Imperial Crown decorating the top, is almost certainly Demidoff's original. With an acute sense of the decorative and historical potential of works of art, he was always keen to ensure that his frames were splendid objects which, where possible, made reference to the pictures they contained. SD

PROVENANCE: Bought by the 4th Marquess of Hertford at the San Donato (Anatole Demidoff), sale, Paris, 8–10 March, lot 427, 395 fr.

M175

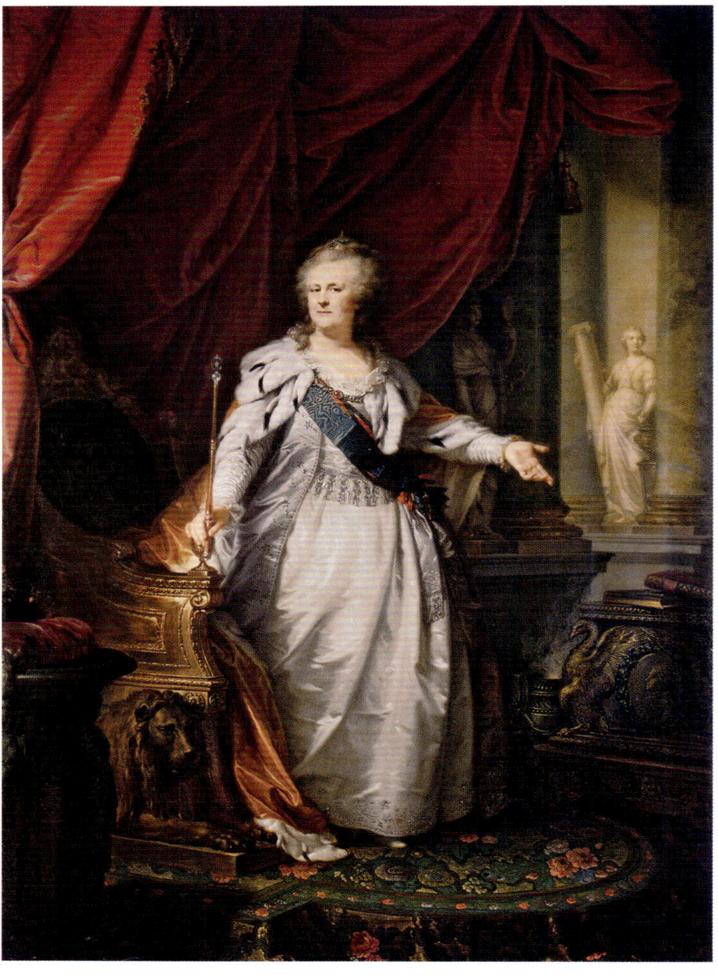

Fig.1 Johann Baptist Lampi the Elder, *Catherine II, Empress of Russia*, 1793, oil on canvas, 230 × 132 cm, St Petersburg, Hermitage (GE4451)

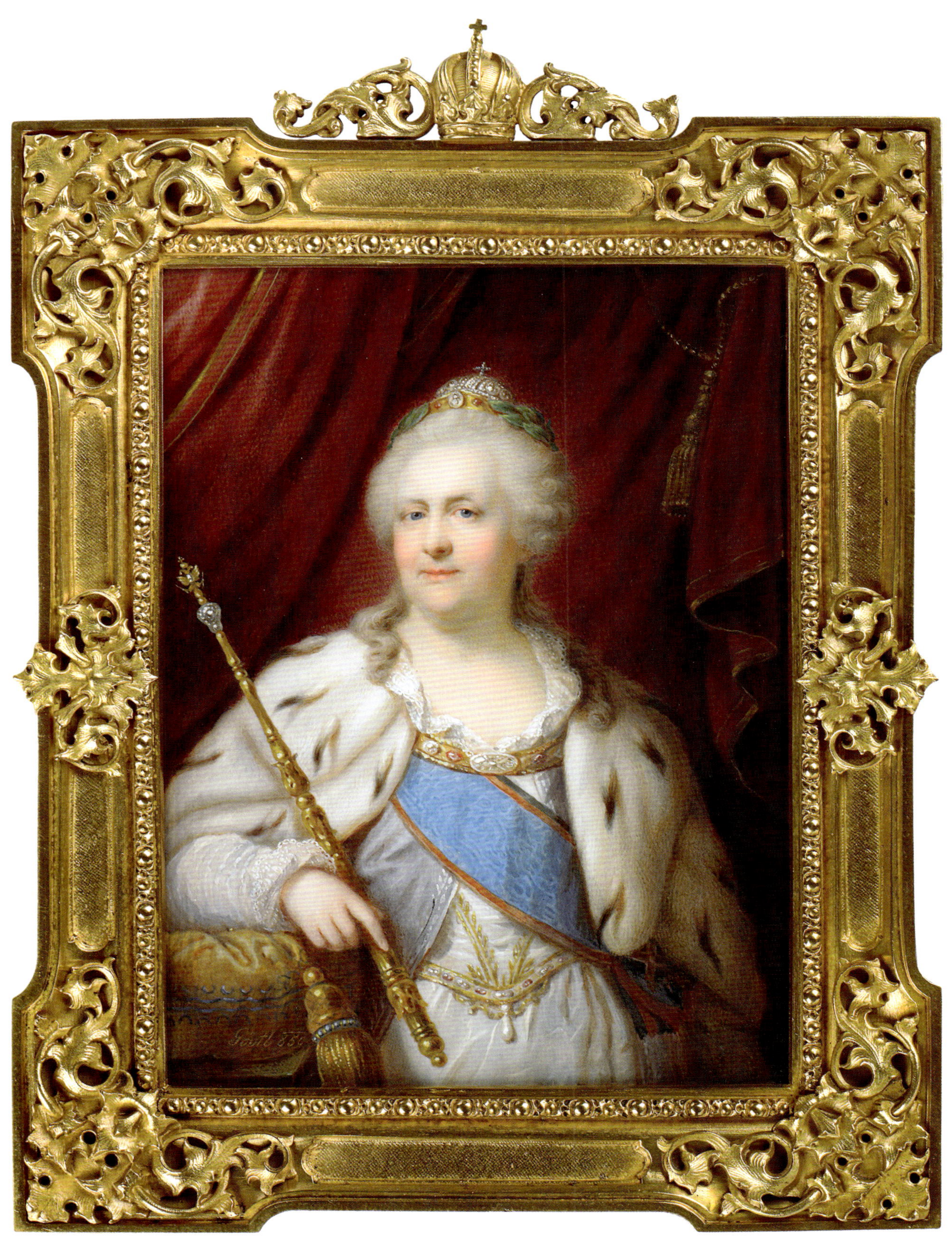

× 0.8

67 Ernest-Joseph-Angelon Girard (1813–1898)

Laura Bell, Mrs Thistlethwayte (called), *c.*1850?

Ivory, 212 × 167 mm

Signed, along the right edge: *Ernest Girard*

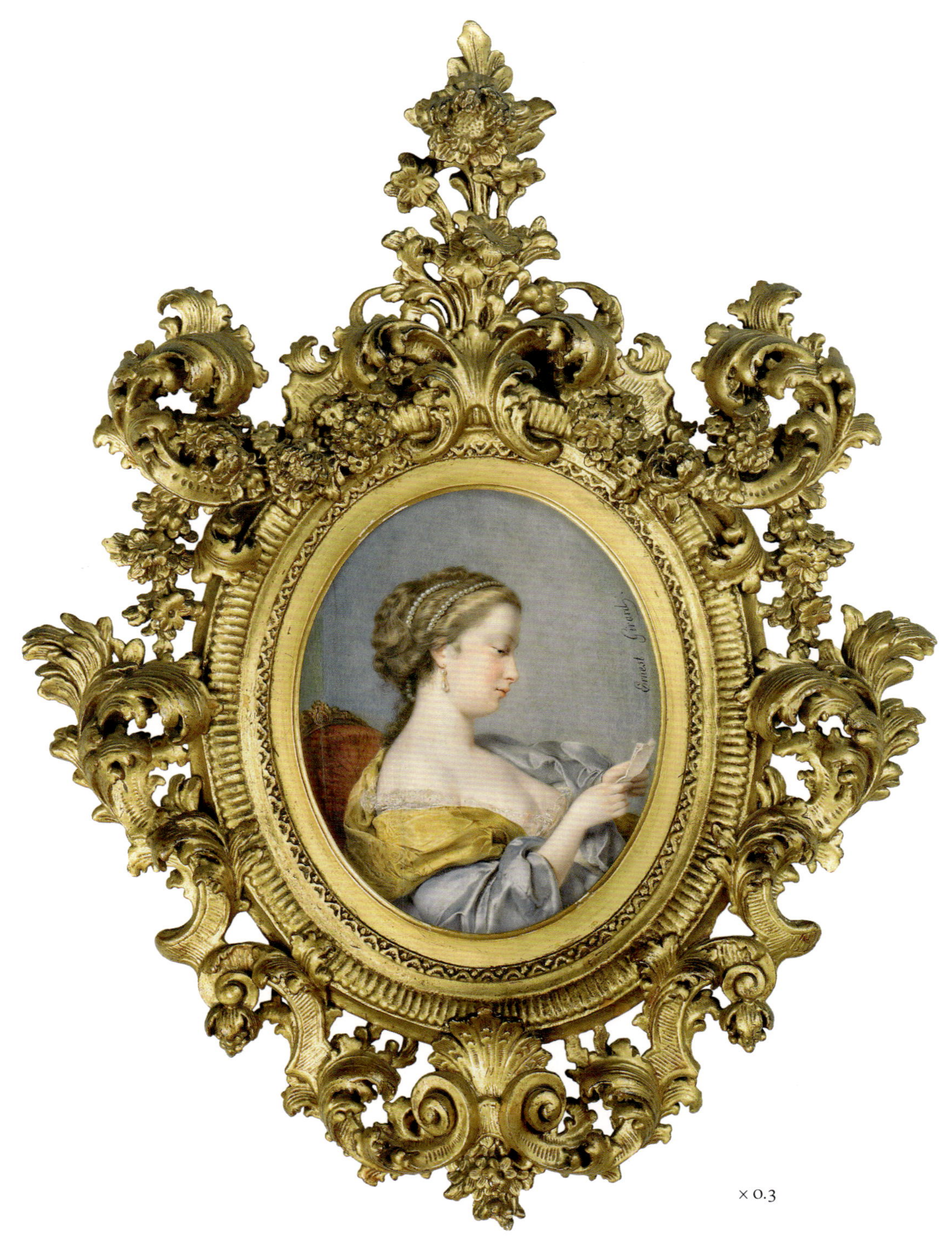

× 0.3

Because of its proposed sitter, this miniature has one of the largest archive files of any work of art now in the Wallace Collection. Laura Eliza Jane Seymour Thistlethwayte, née Bell (1831?–1894), led a remarkable life. The daughter of Captain R.H. Bell and his wife Laura Jane Seymour, an illegitimate daughter of the 3rd Marquess of Hertford, she was probably born in County Antrim or Dublin in 1831. Before moving to London in about 1849 she pursued a career as a prostitute in Belfast and then Dublin, where she flaunted her success by being driven in Phoenix Park in her own carriage. In London her several lovers included the Nepalese envoy Prince Jang Bahadur, before she abandoned her profession and married Frederick Thistlethwayte, a rich Army subaltern, in 1852. The marriage was unhappy, owing partly to Laura's extravagance with money. To the surprise of everyone, however, she underwent a religious conversion and became a lay preacher, praised for the eloquence with which she addressed congregations in London and Scotland. Although shunned by much of society, her dinner parties attracted public figures such as the Duke of Devonshire and Sir William Harcourt, and in 1864 she began a correspondence with William Gladstone which continued until her death. Very intense by the time Gladstone was Prime Minister in 1869, their relationship spawned much salacious gossip, though any improper conduct was denied by Gladstone's sons just before his death. When she died in 1894 her estate was valued at the not inconsiderable sum of over £41,000.[1]

Laura was renowned for her fine shoulders and golden hair. One contemporary, Sir Francis Burnand, recalled her "pretty, doll-like face, her big eyes, not ignorant of an artistic touch that added lustre to their natural brilliance, and her quick vivacious glances ... as she sat in an open phaeton, vivaciously talking with a variety of men, all 'swells' of the period ...".[2] The identification of this miniature as a portrait of her was first proposed by Lord Redesdale in the early years of the Wallace Collection as a museum.[3] It is now impossible to confirm, and a substantial measure of scepticism must remain, but it is not implausible on comparison with several portraits of Laura by the English artist Richard Buckner (1812–1883). One, in a private collection, shows her with similar earrings to those worn by the sitter in Girard's miniature.[4]

Laura Bell's association with the Hertford family went beyond her mother's parentage. Her father Captain Bell was the bailiff of the Irish estates of the 3rd Marquess of Hertford, and her name appears twice in the 4th Marquess's address book, noting her move from Westbourne Terrace to Grosvenor Square.[5] Whether she was ever a mistress of the 4th Marquess is unknown, but he owned a full-length portrait of her in riding habit by Buckner, which argues for at least an affectionate relationship. Inventoried at Hertford House in 1870, it passed to Sir Richard Wallace, who displayed it in his Billiard Room – a male preserve where it was doubtless the subject of ribald comment – but it was not part of Lady Wallace's bequest. (Its current location is unknown.) The present miniature was also displayed in a prominent central position among the miniatures in the Oval Drawing Room at the time of Lady Wallace's bequest (see p.13), but this may perhaps be explained by the need to accommodate its flamboyant nineteenth-century Rococo-style frame. Lord Hertford also owned a *Portrait of a Lady* by Buckner, now lost, which may also have been an image of Laura Bell.[6]

Ernest Girard was a pupil of Isabey and the miniaturist Jean-François Hollier. He exhibited miniatures at the Paris Salon from 1835 to 1864, later specializing in watercolour landscapes. He is not known to have worked in London, but Laura Bell was in Paris in September 1850, probably with Prince Jang Bahadur, and she almost certainly visited the city on other occasions.[7] SD

PROVENANCE: First recorded at Bethnal Green (1872–5), no.720 (as Ernest Girard, *Female Portrait*)

P779

68 Alessandro (Alexandre) Fiocchi (1803–1896), after Winterhalter
Mademoiselle Sontag, 1852

Ivory, 165 × 134 mm

Signed, lower left: *Fiocchi/ 1852*

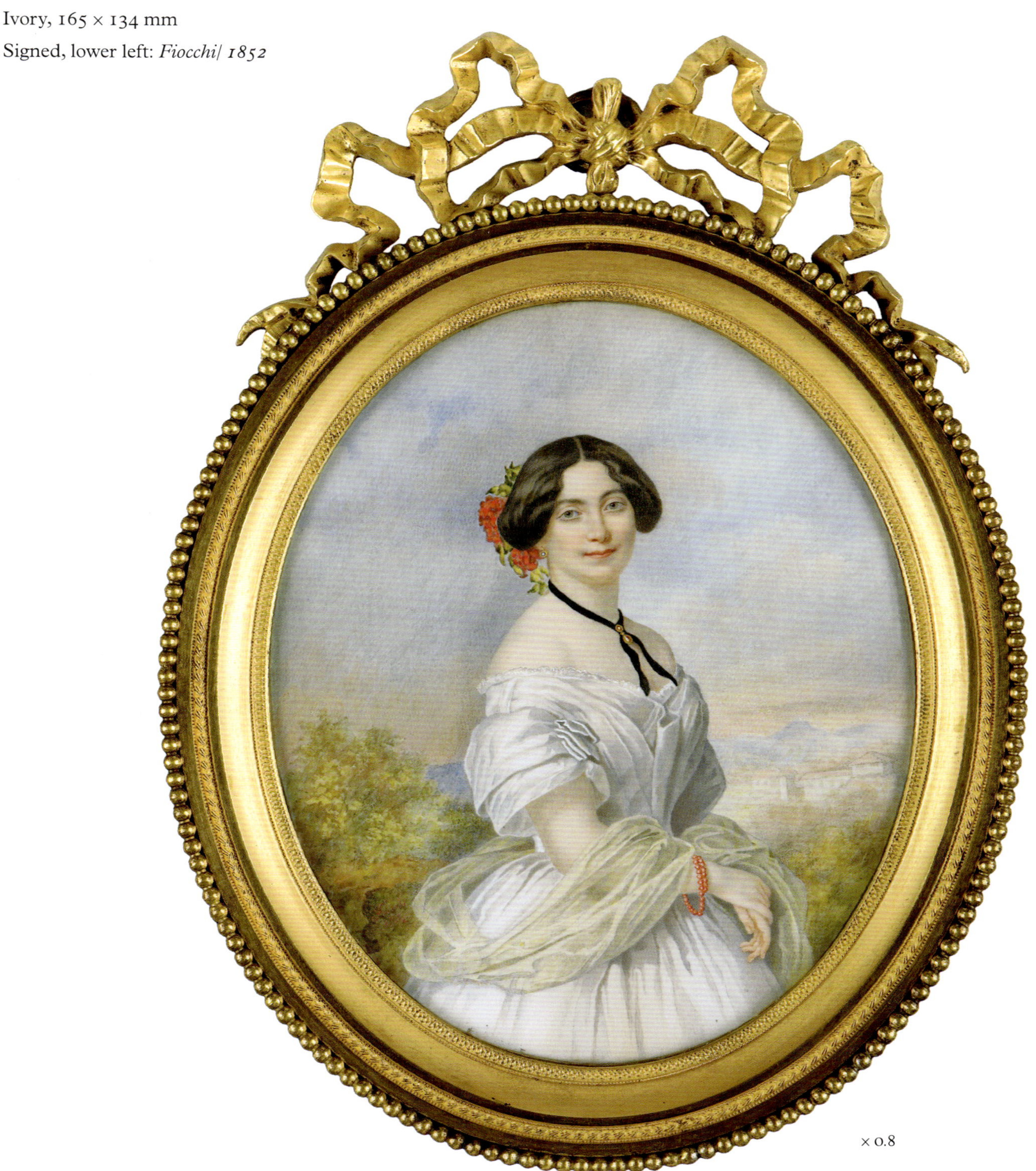

× 0.8

Henriette Sontag (1806–1854), born Gertrude Walpurgis Sonntag in Koblenz, was one of the leading operatic and concert sopranos of her time. Much fêted from an early age – her admirers included Goethe and Beethoven – she was only eighteen when she sang the solo soprano parts in the first performances of Beethoven's Ninth Symphony and *Missa Solemnis*. In 1828 she married in secret the Sardinian ambassador to The Hague, Count Carlo Rossi, and two years later, after their marriage had been publicly acknowledged, withdrew from professional life in deference to her husband's wishes. She then made only a few select private and concert appearances until in 1849 she returned to the public stage, performing in Donizetti's *Linda di Chamonix* in London. She died of cholera in Mexico City at the age of forty-eight.

Alessandro Fiocchi, who was born in Paris, the son of an Italian *artiste musicien*, is recorded as a pupil of Ingres and "Isabey" (presumably Jean-Baptiste). He never exhibited at the Paris Salon, but achieved sufficient renown to be commissioned by the state in 1855 to produce a copy in miniature of Franz Xaver Winterhalter's full-length portrait of the Empress Eugénie.[1] In 1859 he was appointed to the position of curator of the museum at the town of Rochefort, between Nantes and Bordeaux, a post he held until 1866. His own collection of paintings and drawings (which, though modest, included works by Rubens, Michallon and Decamps), acquired by the town on Fiocchi's appointment, was then the most important part of the museum's collections. He died at Angoulême, though it is likely that he spent most of his final years near Paris.[2]

According to an obituary of Fiocchi in a regional journal, he was on friendly terms with many artists, including Rosa Bonheur.[3] His miniatures are rare, and it is perhaps surprising that there are as many as four in the Wallace Collection – suggesting that he may have been known personally to Lord Hertford or Richard Wallace.[4]

The Wallace Collection's miniature has two labels on the back of its mount inscribed, probably in Fiocchi's hand, *Portrait de/ Mlle Sontag, Com^{sse} Rossi*, and *Winterhalter 8^{br}.1842*. The latter presumably refers to Franz Xaver Winterhalter (1805–1873), painter of the portrait of the Empress Eugénie and the most renowned court portraitist of the mid nineteenth century. No such painting by Winterhalter can currently be traced, but the existence of one painted in 1850 was recorded in 1913,[5] and the style and composition of Fiocchi's miniature are evocative of Winterhalter's works of the late 1840s and early 1850s. The reference in the inscription to October 1842 is therefore mysterious. It is possible that the medium of the original was watercolour rather than oil. Watercolours are more likely to be lost or unrecorded than oils, and the technique of Fiocchi's miniature, painted thinly in predominantly pale colours except the blacks and reds, is close to pure watercolour. A lithograph version (omitting the landscape shown in Fiocchi's miniature) was published by Alphonse-Léon Noël, an artist who frequently reproduced Winterhalter's works, in May 1851, and the engraved frontispiece of a biography of Mlle Sontag, published in New York in 1852, is clearly also based on the same original.[6] SD

PROVENANCE: First recorded at Bethnal Green (1872–5), no.1819

M105

69 Sir William Charles Ross (1794–1860)

The Empress Eugénie, *c.*1853–7

Ivory, 124 × 98 mm

Sir William Ross was the most prestigious painter of miniatures in Britain during the early years of Queen Victoria's reign. He came from an artistic family – both his parents exhibited portraits at the Royal Academy – and showed a precocious talent for drawing, winning several prizes in his youth. After a brief apprenticeship to the miniature painter Andrew Robertson as his painter of backgrounds, he gradually established his reputation as an independent artist in the 1820s and 1830s, rising to the position of Miniature Painter to Queen Victoria and, in 1842, the year he was knighted, Royal Academician. He exhibited at the Royal Academy for fifty years (from 1809 to 1859), and is said to have painted more than 2,200 miniatures. A natural courtier, he received many commissions from Queen Victoria and painted other European royal families, including those of Belgium and Portugal. He was the last great miniature painter in Britain before the rise of photography deprived miniature painting of its place among the most significant expressions of visual culture.[1]

Maria Eugenia Ignacia Augustina de Montijo (1826–1920), a Spanish countess, married Napoleon III in 1853. Her intelligence, grace and beauty added much needed lustre to Napoleon's regime, though her extreme conservatism may well have been a political hindrance to her husband. Her state visit to England with Napoleon in 1855, while Britain and France were allies during the Crimean War, was a great success for both the British and French royal families. Victoria was much taken by the Empress: "… she is very pleasing," she wrote to her uncle, "very graceful and unaffected, but very delicate. She is certainly very pretty and very uncommon-looking."[2]

This miniature, bought by Lord Hertford at a Christie's auction in 1860, was presumably painted during Eugénie's state visit to England or on one of Ross's frequent trips to Paris. It cannot be dated more than two years after the Empress came to England, as in 1857 Ross suffered a stroke and was no longer able to paint. Perhaps it was the anonymous seller of the miniature at Christie's in 1860 who had commissioned it shortly before. There is another version in the Royal Collection which is close in quality to the Wallace Collection's but it is a little harder in execution, and is probably a copy by Ross himself. Ross's receipt for the Royal Collection's version indicates that it was bought by Queen Victoria on 18 January 1859.[3]

Eugénie's dress in the Wallace Collection's miniature is now brown, but this is probably the result of fading from an original red, the colour of the dress in the better preserved version in the Royal Collection. She also wears a lace collar and bodice, and a gold-braided mantle or jacket which is probably Spanish.[4] Although it would be several years before she would begin to patronize her most celebrated couturier, Charles Worth, she was already by this time renowned for the sumptuousness of her costumes. The splendid necklace may be the collar of thirty-eight round and nine pear-shaped pearls which had been mounted by the firm of Bapst for the duchesse d'Angoulême at the Restoration and would be sold at the great sale of the French crown jewels in 1887.[5] There are also loops of pearls among the lace trimmings of her bodice.

The miniature shows well Ross's colourful, carefully detailed style. It also displays the naturalism which was acceptable from a society portraitist at this time, though it contrasts with the polished ostentation particularly associated with Eugénie's favourite portrait painter, Franz Xaver Winterhalter (see no.68). Ross captures Eugénie's beautifully applied make-up, and he conscientiously depicts her auburn hair (whereas Winterhalter darkened it). The elaborate gilt frame, with rays of light streaming from the Empress, festoons of laurel, an imperial eagle and an *E* in a cartouche surmounted by a crown, is far more grandiloquent than the miniature it holds.[6] The crown is a representation of the one created for Eugénie by Gabriel Lemonnier in 1855, and now in the Louvre.[7] According to the sale catalogue, the Wallace Collection's miniature was in a case when it was bought by Lord Hertford, but this is now missing. SD

PROVENANCE: Bought by the 4th Marquess of Hertford at an anonymous sale, Christie's, London, 12 May 1860, lot 91, £53 11s.

M162

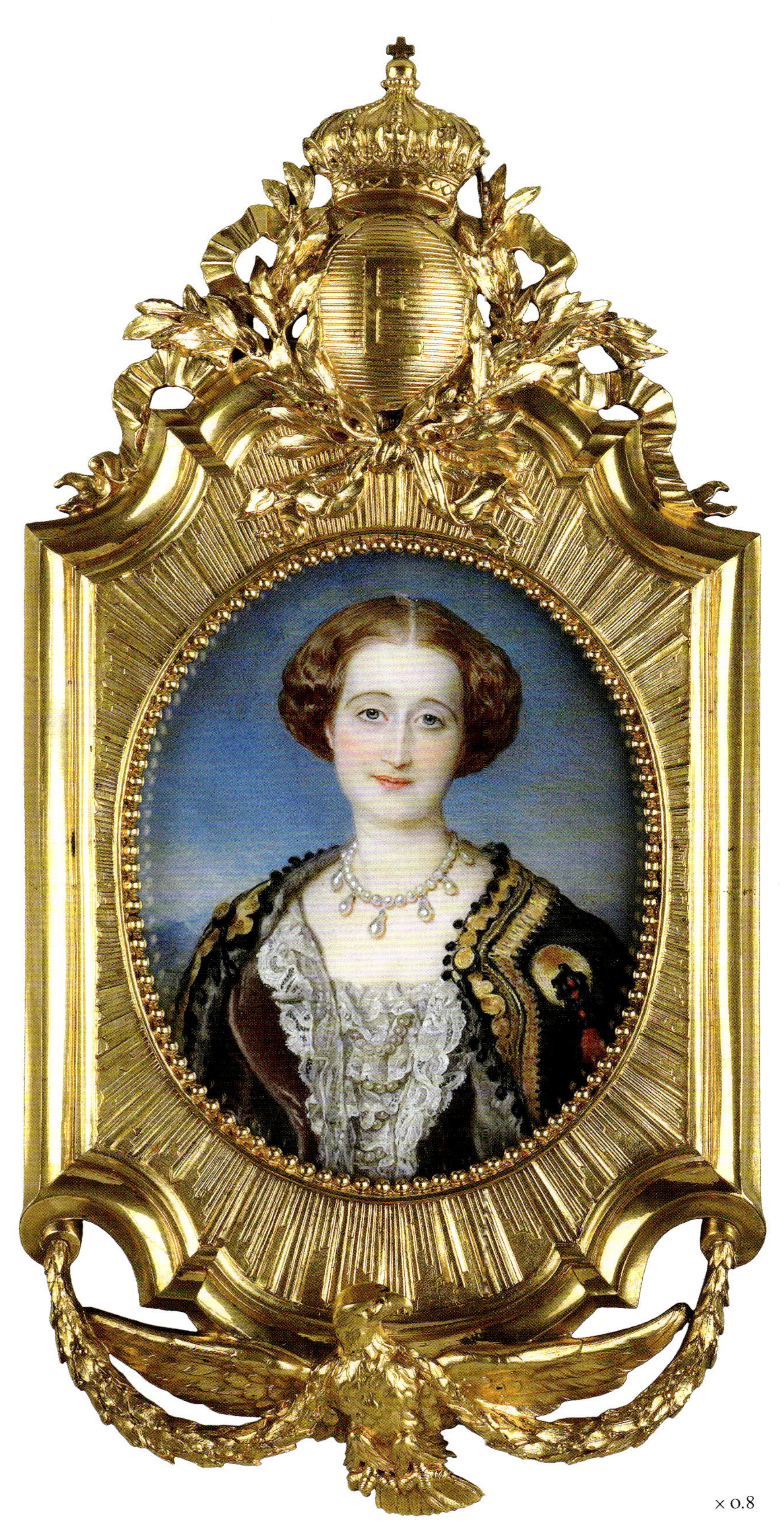

× 0.8

Literature and Notes

1.

LITERATURE: Dimier, vol.2, p.169, no.707 (the female portrait no.708, both as Anonyme Lécurieux); Reynolds 1980, no.1 (the pendant, M262, no.2)

NOTES

1 On the back of the male portrait: *iean de thou/ seigneur de/ Bonneuil fils/ aisnè* [an e added and later crossed out] *du premier/ president de thou* [in later hand:] *vivait en 1642 sous/ le regne de Louis XIII.* On the back of the female portrait: *Renee baillet/ dame de cloux/ fame de jean/ de thou seigneur/ de bonneuil.*

2 Tumulus; Durand, pp.3–7, 56–7.

3 On François Clouet: Dimier, vol.1, pp.32–61; Adhémar 1980; Jollet 1997; Zvereva, p.23.

4 Shelf mark Na22. On the Album Lécurieux: Dimier, vol.2, pp.150–69; Adhémar 1973, pp.142–8. The drawing of the same sitter (black and red chalk): Dimier, vol.2, p.162, no.670 (as a portrait of Jean de Thou by the Anonyme Lécurieux), copies p.167, nos.699–700; Adhémar 1973, p.143, no.130 (as possible portrait of Albert de Gondi, duc de Retz).

2.

LITERATURE: Ganz; Winter; Colding, p.79; Reynolds 1980, no.3; Hughes, p.39, pl.IV; Murdoch 1982, p.450; Strong, p.190, no.23; Rowlands, pp.239–40, fig.259; Lloyd 1996, p.70, no.7; Coombs, p.23; Foister 2004, p.14, fig.8

NOTES

1 Rowlands, p.235, no.R.31, pl.241.

2 Engravings by Lucas Vorsterman and by Hollar were made in the seventeenth century after one of the versions: see Ganz.

3 On Lucas Horenbout and the possible association of works with him: Strong 1983, pp.12–44, 189–93; Campbell and Foister 1986; Coombs, pp.13–24; ODNB, *s.v.* 'Horenbout, Lucas' (Susan Foister, 2004); Evans 2005, pp.240–7.

4 A group of more than twenty English portrait miniatures, most of them of royal sitters, have been identified as his work because they can be dated to about the time when Horenbout arrived in England and have a strong Flemish character. These miniatures reveal an obvious relationship with the royal court, which, according to the documents, Horenbout evidently had. While this identification is not unlikely, it has recently been examined much more critically. The most puzzling factor is that Horenbout is never mentioned as a manuscript illuminator or a miniature painter, even in sources where this title is used for other artists.

5 He was only proposed as the author of portrait miniatures because the Dutch art critic Karel van Mander relates in his *Schilder-Boeck* that Holbein learned the art of illumination in England from a Master Lucas, whom he soon surpassed in that art. It was an obvious assumption to identify Van Mander's Master Lucas with the Lucas Horenbout mentioned in the sources. The weak link in the argument is the conjectural identification of miniatures as Lucas Horenbout's work. Also, Van Mander's account is obviously modelled on Vasari's life of the young Giotto, who learned from and soon outshone his teacher Cimabue, and the entire story might have been taken too literally. The Holbein portrait in the Wallace Collection has been attributed to Lucas Horenbout because of its date, its obvious relationship with Holbein and because of parallels to the 'Horenbout group'. If one accepts that the Wallace Collection miniature depends directly on works by Holbein, most of these observations can be explained without bringing Horenbout into play. Within the 'Horenbout group' the Wallace Collection miniature is stylistically isolated. The existence of a sixteenth-century miniature portrait of Holbein was probably too suggestive for the attribution to Horenbout to be resisted, in spite of the obvious contradictions.

3.

LITERATURE: Reynolds 1980, no.5; Finsten, vol.2, pp.42–4 (replica of no.24); Edmond 1983, p.121, pl.34; ODNB, *s.v.* 'Leveson, Sir Richard' (Richard Wisker, 2004)

NOTES

1 On Isaac Oliver: Edmond 1983; Strong 1983, pp.142–85; Coombs 1998, pp.34–54; Reynolds 1999, pp.84–101; Edmond 2004.

2 On Leveson: ODNB, *s.v.* (Richard Wisker, 2004).

3 Reynolds 1947, p.41, no.153. The third version is in the Lucy collection, Charlecote Park, The National Trust.

4.

LITERATURE: Reynolds 1980, no.17

NOTES

1 On Samuel Cooper: Foskett 1974; Murdoch 1997, pp.115–72; Coombs, pp.61–76; Reynolds 1999, pp.127–46; Murdoch 2004.

2 For example two works in the Royal Collection: *Portrait of a Man, perhaps Edward Montagu, 2nd Earl of Sandwich* (RCIN420069), or the *Portrait of James Scott, Duke of Monmouth and Buccleuch* (RCIN420087).

5.

LITERATURE: Reynolds 1980, nos.6–7; Warren, p.546; Truman, forthcoming

NOTES

1 On Petitot: Strœhlin; Lightbown; Reynolds 1999, pp.234–54.

2 Enamel, 25 × 22 mm (RCIN 421380); Reynolds 1999, no.289.

3 Vellum, 26 × 23 mm (sight) (J542): Lemoine-Bouchard 2002, pp.128–9, no.51. Lemoine-Bouchard hesitates about both the attribution and the identification of the sitter as Louis XIV, probably because the work is, very unusually, painted on vellum. The relationship between the works in Paris and in the Wallace Collection will have to be clarified but there is no need to doubt the identification with Louis XIV.

4 Bimbenet-Privat; Thépaut-Cabasset.

5 OA12280, probably by Laurent Le Tessier de Montarsy, *c.*1670.

6 Bologna, Santa Maria della Vita, Museo della Sanità e dell'Assistenza, by Pierre Le Tessier de Montarsy, 1681, given by Louis XIV to Count Malvasia.

7 Gemeente Museum (O-Div.1–1929, 1683), by Pierre Le Tessier de Montarsy, given by Louis XIV to Anthonie Hensius. The precious stones have been taken out.

6.

LITERATURE: Reynolds 1980, no.36; Sani, p.114, no.99

NOTES

1 On Carriera most recently: Falconi 2008; Falconi 2009.

2 On Carriera's technical contribution to miniature painting: Colding; Bruijn Kops.

3 Sani, p.114, no.99.

4 Information given by Aileen Ribeiro.

7.

LITERATURE: Reynolds 1980, no.27 (as France, early 18th century)

NOTES

1 Dacier 1911; Vogtherr 2001.

8.

LITERATURE: Reynolds 1980, no.46

NOTES

1 On Zincke: Walker 1992, pp.26–72.
2 On Henry Seymour Conway: Towse.
3 Lord Waldegrave sale, London, Christie's, 10 February 1900, lot 34. It is mentioned in a letter from Henry Seymour Conway to Horace Walpole of 6 April 1746 as being still with Eccardt: Walpole, pp.233–7.
4 Victoria and Albert Museum, Gilbert Collection (Loan: Gilbert.282:1–2008).

9.

LITERATURE: Vuaflart and Bourin 1909, pp.7–8, pl.7 (as German school); Reynolds 1980, no.41 (as Austrian School. Artist Unknown)

NOTES

1 Lisholm, pp.104–5, nos.111–14, 116, pl.II, on Meytens's paintings and the engraving by Johann Christoph Winkler.
2 Ö.K. Meytens, f. 12,11.
3 Keil, nos.21, 22, 75, 126, 132, 140, 142, 144, 148.

10.

LITERATURE: Reynolds 1980, no.158 (as possibly Dutch or German, *c.*1750)

NOTES

1 Vogtherr 2001.
2 Lisholm, p.110, no.184, pl.26, and *passim.*

11.

LITERATURE: Reynolds 1980, no.71 (as manner of Charlier)

NOTES

1 There is no monograph on Charlier. For first reference: Maze-Sencier, pp.499–500; Lespinasse 1929, pp.44–9; *Gold Boxes and Miniatures at Waddeson*, pp.332–3.
2 For a brief discussion of the artist's later career, see no.14.
3 London, Christie's, 8 July 2005, lot 45.

12.

LITERATURE: Reynolds 1980, no.63

NOTES

1 Paris, Hôtel Drouot, 19 June 1992.

13.

LITERATURE: Reynolds 1980, no.83 (as imitator of Charlier)

NOTES

1 Paris, Palais Galliera, 5 December 1975.

14.

LITERATURE: For references to Charlier's biography: see no.11; Reynolds 1980, no.59

15.

LITERATURE: Reynolds 1980, no.87; Maillet-Chassagne, pp.175–6, pls.I, II; Maillet-Chassagne and Château-Thierry, pp.248–9, no.2–705–11 to 20, colour plates after p.294; Warren, pp.545–6; Truman, forthcoming

NOTES

1 Important literature on the Van Blarenberghes: *Gold Boxes and Miniatures at Waddesdon*, pp.232–318 (largely superseded by the following titles); Maillet-Chasagne; Maillet-Chassagne and Château-Thierry; Salmon; Méjanès.
2 Maillet-Chassagne, p.59.
3 Maillet-Chassagne, pp.51–2.
4 Maillet-Chassagne and Château-Thierry, pp.239–65.
5 Letter of 3 May 1822 to his mother.

16.

LITERATURE: Reynolds 1980, no.85; Maillet-Chassagne, p.160–1; Maillet-Chassagne and Château-Thierry, pp.211–22, no.2–541–1; Lemoine-Bouchard 2008, pp.506, 510, fig.i

NOTES

1 On the history of the fair: Fromageot 1902, esp. pp.65–112.
2 Maillet-Chassagne and Château-Thierry, pp.211–12, 230, 304–9.

17.

LITERATURE: Reynolds 1980, no.86; Maillet-Chassagne, pp.154–5, fig.66; Maillet-Chassagne and Château-Thierry, pp.270–1, no.2–781–8 to 13, colour plates after p.294; Truman, forthcoming

NOTES

1 Maillet-Chassagne and Château-Thierry 2004, pp.268–73.

18.

LITERATURE: Marie; Savill, no.14; Reynolds 1980, no.88; Maillet-Chassagne and Château-Thierry, no.4–613; Maillet-Chassagne, p.57

NOTES

1 For the dating of the Van Blarenberghes' work, and the chronology, see Maillet-Chassagne, pp.51–2.
2 See Everdell.

19.

LITERATURE: Wennberg, pp.45, 52, pl.9; Lundberg, fig.3; Reynolds 1980, no.97 (and 96)

NOTES

1 Washington, D.C., National Gallery of Art (inv.1983.100.1).
2 Ivory, 64 mm diameter, Paris, Musée du Louvre, Département des arts graphiques (RF5062).
3 E.g. Hodgkins collection, London (Paris, Galerie Georges Petit, 30 April 1914, lot 39).

20.

LITERATURE: Wennberg, fig.32; Reynolds 1980, no.95 (and 94)

NOTES

1 Bordeaux, pp.88–9, no.38; Ingamells 1989, pp.366–70; , *Watteau, Chardin and Fragonard* 2003, pp.162–3, no.22.
2 Wine, pp.268–71; Delaplanche, p.202, no.P62.
3 Wildenstein, pp.99–100, nos.443–9.
4 Sahut 1977, p.42, no.49; Fahy, pp.172–5.

21.

LITERATURE: Reynolds 1980, no.107; Plinval de Guillebon 2000, pp.34, 78–80, 105, no.5, p.159

NOTES

1 Quoted Plinval de Guillebon 2008, p.85.

22.

LITERATURE: Reynolds 1980, no.108; Fort 1999, p.308; Plinval de Guillebon 2008, p.86

NOTES

1 Salon of 1785, letter of 22 September 1785: Fort 1999, p.308: "Celui-ci [Hall] a la légèreté de la touche, la vigueur du coloris, la hardiesse du pointillé, l'esprit adapté à ses différents caractères de tête et surtout la variété et la grâce des ajustements".
2 Villot sale, Paris, 22 January 1864, lot 76.

23.

LITERATURE: Reynolds 1980, no.112; Plinval de Guillebon 2000, pp.61–2, 124, no.138, pp.147, 158

NOTES

1 Plinval de Guillebon 2000, p.158, as "*copie*", which might indicate a replica of an earlier work.

24.

LITERATURE: Reynolds 1980, no.111; Plinval de Guillebon 2000, p.120, no.107

NOTES

1 The self-portrait: Paris, Musée des Arts Décoratifs (inv. 39714).

25.

LITERATURE: Reynolds 1980, no.91 (as Jean-Honoré or Marie-Anne Fragonard); Rosenberg, p.68; Hyde, pp.84–5; La Nouëne, p.71

NOTES

1 Ivory, 70 × 53 mm (M111).

26.

LITERATURE: Reynolds 1980, no.134 (as portrait of Vigée-Le Brun); Hofstetter 1994, pp.268–9, no.166; Ribeiro, pp.138–9, fig.146 (as portrait of Vigée-Le Brun); Hyde, p.86, fig.15; *Le Cardinal Fesch* 2007, p.100, fig.35; *Marguerite Gérard* 2009, pp.16 (fig.1), 144

NOTES

1 Hofstetter 1994; Hofstetter 1995; Lemoine-Bouchard 2008, pp.211–25.
2 Hofstetter 1994, p.269.
3 Correspondence in the object file, The Wallace Collection.
4 One of these was sold in Paris in 1935: ivory, diameter 82 mm: Paris, Galerie Charpentier, 27 June 1935, lot 61; previously sold Georges Petit, 1 June 1928, lot 55. See Lemoine-Bouchard 2008, p.214.

27.

LITERATURE: Reynolds 1980, no.135; Hofstetter 1994, p.480; Lemoine-Bouchard 2008, p.214, fig.c

NOTES

1 Hofstetter 1995, pp.192–4.
2 A bust-length portrait of 1790, ivory, 36 × 29 mm, signed, private collection: Hofstetter 1995, p.192, fig.8. The portrait with his mother and sister: ivory, 195 × 143 mm, signed, Paris, Musée du Louvre, Département des arts graphiques (RF28719).
3 Gilt brass (front) and brass (back), 103 × 89 mm.
4 Pointed out by Aileen Ribeiro.

28.

LITERATURE: Jeannerat, pp.360–1, no.4; Kenworthy-Browne, pp.8–9, fig.9; Reynolds 1980, no.137; Lemoine-Bouchard 2008, p.273, fig.a

NOTES

1 On Guérin: Lemoine-Bouchard 2008, pp.272–5.
2 Information provided 2007 by Charles Noble.
3 On Lady Elizabeth: ODNB, *s.v.* 'Cavendish, Elizabeth Christiana' (Amanda Foreman, 2010).
4 On Georgiana: ODNB, *s.v.* 'Cavendish, Georgiana, duchess of Devonshire' (Amanda Foreman, 2008).
5 Jeannerat.
6 A drawing in the collection of the Ecole Nationale Supérieure des Beaux-Arts in Paris is an example of the studies produced by Guérin during sittings: female portrait, pencil on vellum, 13.1 cm diameter (E.B.A. 1058), probably of one of the Mesdemoiselles de la Vaupalière.
7 Reynolds 1980, no.140; the original: Jeannerat, pp.361–2, no.6.
8 Ivory, 70 × 57 mm, signed and dated 1790 on the back: London, Sotheby's, 14 July 2010, lot 109.
9 Enamel on copper, framed in gold with diamonds, 62 × 46 mm, inscribed on the back: *Georgiana/ Duchess of Devonshire/ Born June 9. 1757/ Horace Hone ARA/ Pintx. 1812 / London*, London, Victoria and Albert Museum (Loan: Gilbert.264:1, 2–2008).

29.

LITERATURE: Reynolds 1980, no.125; Lauraine, p.136, no.180, and p.170, no.318 (mentioned twice under different numbers)

NOTES

1 http://european-miniatures.blogspot.com/2006/ 04/sicard-louis-unknown-girl-in-scottish-costume.

30.

LITERATURE: Reynolds 1980, nos.28 and 29 (as attributed to Hubert Drouais); Lemoine-Bouchard 2008, p.201, fig.a (as by Hubert Drouais); Truman, forthcoming

NOTES

1 Oil on canvas, 118 × 96 cm, Bordeaux, Musée des Beaux-Arts (BxM5848). See Le Coat and Eggimann-Besançon 1986.
2 *Madame Du Châtelet* 2006, p.114, no.192; Loir's portrait: pp.18–19, no.3; further portraits mentioned and illustrated.
3 Apgar.

31.

LITERATURE: Reynolds 1980, no.332 (as by an unknown artist)

NOTES

1 Layton Elwes.
2 Walker 1992, pp.232–48, nos.484–707.
3 S419–422.
4 *Gli Uffizi*, nos.A874 ('Carracci'), A973 (Van Dyck), probably A23 (del Sarto), A863 (Titian), A792 (Rubens).

32.

LITERATURE: Reynolds 1980, no.149 (as portrait of Mrs Fitzherbert); Lloyd 1998, pp.46–7 (as portrait of Mrs Fitzherbert); Lloyd 1998, pp.46–7 (as portrait of Mrs Fitzherbert); Lloyd 2005, p.64–5, no.16

NOTES

1 On Cosway: Lloyd 1995; Lloyd 1998; Lloyd 2005.
2 Ivory, height 32 mm, private collection: Lloyd 1995, no.60.
3 Even closer is a drawing of Maria illustrated by Lloyd, 1995, no.33.
4 Dating suggested by Aileen Ribeiro.

33.

LITERATURE: Reynolds 1980, no.MA1; Hughes, pp.11–13, fig.7; Warren, p.544.

NOTES

1 See Lloyd 1998.
2 Hofstetter 2008, pp.154–5, nos.37–8.

34.

LITERATURE: Reynolds 1980, no.151

35.

LITERATURE: Reynolds 1980, no.161; Lemoine-Bouchard 2002, p.23

NOTES

1 The Wallace Collection owns a miniature of an unknown man (M1) by Benjamin Arlaud.
2 See Foskett, p.481, and Lemoine-Bouchard 2008, pp.49–50.
3 See Ribeiro, pp.13 and 109.
4 Royal Academy, 1796 (no.611); Walker 1992, pp.257–8, no.724.

36.

LITERATURE: Reynolds 1980, no.317; Ingamells 1978, p.9

NOTES

1 I am very grateful to to Fiona Woolley of the Maidstone Museum and Bentlif Art Gallery for information on the Bentlif's version. Like the Wallace Collection's miniature, it does not have a signature or any inscriptions.
2 On Robinson see Byrne.
3 See Ingamells 1978 and Ingamells 1985, pp.93–7, 155–7 and 171–2.
4 Mannings, vol.I, pp.393–4, no.1529.
5 *Ibid.* The Rubens is in the Gulbenkian Museum, Lisbon.

37.

LITERATURE: Reynolds 1980, no.178

NOTES

1 On Isabey see Basily-Callimaki, *Isabey* 2005 and Lemoine-Bouchard 2008, pp.295–301.
2 Halliday, pp.31, 106, 133 and 160.
3 *Isabey* 2005, pp.42 and 124–5, no.37.
4 Lemoine-Bouchard 2008, p.295; *Isabey* 2005, pp.40, 42, 124–5, 156 and 163.
5 *Isabey* 2005, pp.40 and 124, no.35.
6 *Isabey* 2005, pp.41 and 124, no.36; Siegfried, pp.96–101.
7 Ribeiro, p.95.
8 *Isabey* 2005, p.61. There is a version of the Wallace Collection's miniature by another of Isabey's pupils, Henriette Rath, in the Musée de l'Horlogerie, Geneva (1966–4).

38.

LITERATURE: Reynolds 1980, no.168; Pappe, p.54

NOTES

1 On Augustin see Lemoine-Bouchard 2008, pp.57–66, and Pappe. On his pupils: Bernd Pappe, 'Jean-Baptiste Jacques Augustin et son atelier à Paris', in Chantilly 2008, pp.100–5.
2 See Maison, pp.50–1.
3 *Cf.* Duffy and Hedley, p.178 (Greuze, P407).

4 Mansion, p.43; see Pappe in Chantilly, p.102. On the 1795 miniature see Pappe, p.26, note 51.
5 Mansion, p.84.
6 Pappe, p.54, no.33.

39.

LITERATURE: Reynolds 1980, no.306

NOTES
1 See Baillio, no.31, pp.87–90.
2 See Ittershagen.
3 Vigée Le Brun, vol.II, pp.90–1.
4 Ittershagen.
5 Ward and Roberts, vol.II, p.183, no.15; Ingamells 1985, p.442, no.74.
6 See ODNB, *s.v.* 'Bone, Henry' (R.J.B. Walker, 2004); Speel, pp.106–15; Walker 1999, pp.305–67. Bone's preparatory drawing for M21 is Walker's no.246.

40.

LITERATURE: Reynolds 1980, no.163

NOTES
1 See Goodden, p.235.
2 As first pointed out by Joseph Baillio in a letter of 9 March 1981 on file in the Wallace Collection's archives.
3 Nimmergut and Wager, p.230, no.F57; Reynolds 163.

41.

LITERATURE: Reynolds 1980, no.181

NOTES
1 See the table of production in Cyril Lécosse, 'La miniature au service de l'Empire: un éclairage sur la politique des présents diplomatiques', in Chantilly 2008, p.35.
2 On these and other Napoleonic symbols see Nouvel-Kammerer.
3 Basily-Callimaki, p.50; *Isabey* 2005, pp.128–9, nos.59–60.
4 *Isabey* 2005, p.56.
5 Basily-Callimaki, p.66.
6 "*S.M.* […] *a été fort mécontente des portraits de M. Isabey et elle désirerait ou qu'il fît mieux ou que l'on employât un autre peintre*": quoted Lécosse in Chantilly, p.31.
7 Lécosse, *ibid.*

42.

LITERATURE: Reynolds 1980, no.169

NOTES
1 Cyril Lécosse in Chantilly, p.31.
2 "*… de s'attacher moins à la parfaite resemblance, qu'à donner le beau idéal, en conservant quelques traits*": quoted Lécosse, *ibid.*, p.32.

43.

LITERATURE: Reynolds 1980, no.184; Bassily-Callimaki, p.105

NOTES
1 See Ingres 1999, pp.65–72.
2 *Isabey* 2005, pp.51, 55 and 133–5. On the invention of imperial iconography see Laveissière; Porterfield and Siegfried; and Nouvel-Kammerer.

44.

LITERATURE: Reynolds 1980, no.187

NOTES
1 On Joséphine and the visual arts see *France in Russia* 2007.
2 See Ribeiro, pp.160 and 173.
3 My thanks to Aileen Ribeiro and Diana Scarisbrick for their invaluable comments on the dress and jewellery in this miniature.

45.

LITERATURE: Reynolds 1980, no.226

NOTES
1 Jean-Richard, no.370; Isabey 2005, p.131, no.73. Another version, signed *I.A.*, is at Malmaison (M.M.71.11.4).
2 The Wallace Collection owns three miniatures of Murat by Isabey (M208 and M248) and the Monogrammist Co (M243).
3 My thanks again to Aileen Ribeiro and Diana Scarisbrick for comments on dress and jewellery.

46.

LITERATURE: Reynolds 1980, no.230; Schidlof 1964, II, p.711

NOTES
1 *Napoléon* 1969, pp.126–7, no.354.
2 Schidlof 1964, vol.II, p.711.

47.

LITERATURE: Reynolds 1980, no.192

NOTES
1 See Basily-Callimaki, pp.199–232, and *Isabey* 2005, pp.64–7.
2 Basily-Callimaki, p.324.
3 *Isabey* 2005, p.111.
4 On art, the theatre and the cult of celebrity see, for example, Postle.
5 Basily-Callimaki, pp.306 and 324.

48.

LITERATURE: Reynolds 1980, no.187

NOTES
1 Basily-Callimaki, pp.289 and 400, no.200; Halliday, p.130, note 8.
2 "*Ses éternels voiles dont il enveloppe le cou des femmes dérobent des accessoires nécessaires et accusent enfin une routine et une manière*": quoted Basily-Callimaki, p.274.
3 See Ingres 1967, pp.240–9.
4 Coombs, p.106.
5 Paris, Musée du Louvre (FR3840 and 3849). For the latter see *Isabey* 2005, p 136, no.96.
6 An impression is in the National Portrait Gallery, London.

49.

LITERATURE: Reynolds 1980, no.235; Lemoine-Bouchard 2002, p.133

NOTES
1 Schidlof 1964, II, p.657.
2 Thanks are due to Dr Lars Ljungström, Curator of the Swedish Royal Collections, and Dr Magnus Olausson, Director of the Swedish National Portrait Gallery and Royal Castles Collections, for information on works by Quaglia in these colletions.
3 The dress may be compared with one now at Malmaison (*France in Russia* 2007, p.109, no.58).
4 I am extremely grateful to Aileen Ribeiro and Diana Scarisbrick for their invaluable comments on the costume and jewellery.
5 *Cf.* Schidlof 1964, vol.IV, pl.468.
6 Lemoine-Bouchard 2002, p.133.

50.

LITERATURE: Reynolds 1980, no.195

NOTES
1 "*Ma maison fut, en quelque sorte, les coulisses du congrès*": quoted Basily-Callimaki, p.164.
2 On the various versions see Aronson and Wieseman, p.219, no.107, and *Isabey* 2005, pp.78 and 146, nos.147–8.

51.

LITERATURE: Reynolds 1980, no.188; Bassily-Callimaki, p.124

NOTES
1 Basily-Callimaki, pp.113–14.
2 *Ibid.*, p.127.
3 See, for example, *Isabey* 2005, pp.108 and 126, no.45.

52.

LITERATURE: Reynolds 1980, no.232

NOTES
1 *Cf.* an unpublished portrait in the Comédie Française, Paris, of Rose Dupuis by Henri Nicolas van Gorp. I am very grateful to Olivia Voisin and Aileen Ribeiro for their comments on the sitter in the Wallace Collection's miniature.
2 *Cf.* Ribeiro, pp.118–19.

53.

LITERATURE: Reynolds 1980, no.308

LITERATURE
1 Mannings, vol.I, p.193, no.632.
2 *Ibid.*, vol.I, pp.192–3, no.630.
3 See Walker 1999, pp.305–67. The drawing for M20 is no.200; that for M19 no.199.
4 Smith, vol.II, pp.292–3.

54.

LITERATURE: Reynolds 1980, no.193

NOTES
1 On Prince August see Ernst Graf zur Lippe-Biesterfeld, 'August (Prinz von Preußen)', *Allgemeine Deutsche Biographie*, vol. I, Leipzig 1875, pp.671–4.
2 Udo Felbiger, 'Das Interieurporträt als Geschenk. Julie Récamier und Prinz August von Preußen', in Dickel and Vogtherr, pp.251–60. It is

54 (cont.).

interesting to note that it is known from an undated letter from the 4th Marquess of Hertford to an unknown correspondent in the Wallace Collection's archives (HHHC2007.377) that he knew Mme Récamier. A miniature version in the Wallace Collection by François Soiron of Gérard's famous portrait (M309) was presumably owned by him.

3 Another possibility has been suggested by Udo Felbiger in an email of 11 August 2009. When he attended the Congress of Vienna in late 1815, the Prince had a relationship with Lady Emily Rumbold who might have received the miniature as a gift from the Prince and then brought it to England. While this may be feasible, it is not necessary to assume that the miniature came to England directly and during August's lifetime. Another work of art from Prince August's collection, Nicolas Lancret's portrait of Mlle Camargo (P393), reached the collection of the Hertford family later in the nineteenth century via France.

55.

LITERATURE: Reynolds 1980, no.198; Wellesley and Steegman, p.23, no.1: *Isabey* 2005, p.151 (no.171)

NOTES

1 Basily-Callimaki, p.164 ("*Il était venu me trouver avec un sans-façon tout britannique, qui m'avait obligé à lui refuser net l'honneur de peindre ses augustes traits*"). No portrait of Wellington by Isabey dated 1814 appears to be otherwise recorded.
2 Longford, p.384; *Isabey* 2005, pp.XXIII and 81.
3 *Isabey* 2005, pp.80 and 147, no.151.
4 Wellesley and Steegmann, pp.12 and 62.
5 For other versions see Reynolds 1980, nos.198 and 217 (M238, a very poor example of the scarlet uniform type) and *Isabey* 2005, pp.87 and 151, no.171. It should be noted that there are minor variations of detail among the various versions of Wellington in a scarlet uniform (one of which was copied by Joseph Mécou for a stipple engraving published in 1817).
6 I am very grateful to René Chartrand, Paul Wood and, above all, Stephen Wood for their invaluable assistance with the identification of Wellington's uniform and orders.
7 Including Andrew Morton, *The Duke of Wellington with Colonel Gurwood at Apsley House* (P632) and a watercolour portrait by William Derby after Lawrence and Evans, (P709). See Ingamells, 1985, pp.78–9 and 132–4.
8 Gronow, vol.II, p.323.
9 Bassily-Callimaki, pp.290 and 303; *Isabey* 2005, pp.87 and 151, nos.172–3.
10 The receipt for the transaction is in the Wallace Collection's archives.

56.

LITERATURE: Reynolds 1980, no.172: Pappe, p.24

NOTES

1 On Willem's collection see Hinterding and Horsch.
2 See Schaffers-Bodenhausen and Tiethoff-Spliethoff, p.133, no.81.

57.

LITERATURE: Reynolds 1980, no.310

NOTES

1 Walker 1999, p.339, no.394.
2 Blanch, p.177.
3 Dorchester House Inventory, 1842, f.176 (Wallace Collection Library). For the portraits of Mrs Robinson by Gainsborough, Romney and Reynolds see Ingamells 1985, pp.93–7, 171–2 and 441. There is no preparatory drawing for a miniature of Mrs Robinson among the Bone drawings at the National Portrait Gallery.
4 Murdoch, p.202. On Newton see also Foskett 1987, pp.426–7.
5 Speel 2008, p.108.
6 *The Annual Biography and Obituary: 1836* (vol.XX), p.41; Speel 1988, p.13.
7 *The Annual Biography and Obituary: 1836* (vol.XX), p.42.

58.

LITERATURE: Reynolds 1980, 237

NOTES

1 On Mme de Mirbel see Jean; Lambertson; Lemoine-Bouchard 2008, pp.385–7.
2 Ingamells 1986, pp.183–5 (P764 and P763).
3 Schidlof 1911, p.83; supplement to the 1819 Salon, no.1675. The original version is now unlocated. Either the same or another portrait of the King by Mlle Rue was exhibited at the 1822 Salon, no.1146.
4 The version in the Louvre, signed and dated 1814 (see Jean-Richard, pp.206–8, no.377), includes drapery and architecture omitted in the Wallace Collection's miniature. In 1816 Isabey drew a similar portrait of the King. It has been suggested that this was based on a sculpture by Valois shown at the Paris Salon of 1814 (see *Isabey* 2005, p.149, no.159). A version of Gros's bust-length portrait, based on his 1814 sketch, was sold Sotheby's, New York, 30 January 1998, lot 144.
5 Quoted Lambertson, p.19 (Lizinka Mirbel, 'De la Peinture. Du Portrait', *La Revue de Paris*, vol.VIII (1829), pp.91–2).

59.

LITERATURE: Reynolds 1980, no.248: Haskell, p.83, no.43

NOTES

1 On Singry see Lemoine-Bouchard, pp.470–1.
2 Lyonnet, vol.I, pp.4–5.
3 Anon., *Petite biographie dramatique, faite avec adresse par un moucheur de chandelle*, Paris, 1826.
4 Lyonnet, p.5.
5 On Demidoff see Haskell, and Tonini.
6 At a Demidoff sale in 1863 Lord Hertford acquired two gold boxes with miniatures (see also no.18).
7 Sale, Collections de San Donato, Pillet and Petit, Paris, 8–10 March 1870, lots 413–37.

60.

LITERATURE: Reynolds 1980, no.239

NOTES

1 On Marie Caroline, see *Marie Caroline* and Dupont-Logié.
2 See *Marie Caroline* pp.138–59, and Dupont-Logié, pp.141, 172 and 196; pp.102 and 123.
3 Bann and Whiteley, pp.60 and 88.
4 Jean, p.135.
5 In the Musée des Arts Décoratifs, Paris; illustrated and discussed in Dupont-Logié, pp.22, 128–9 and 180–1. The doubts on the identification of the sitter in the Wallace Collection's miniature expressed by Bodo Hofstetter, *Marie Caroline*, p.158, note 24, are unjustified. Another portrait of the Duchess by Mme de Mirbel was sold at Christie's, London, 14 October 1998.
6 I am very grateful to Diana Scarisbrick for her comments on the jewellery.
7 Quoted Lambertson, p.19 (Lizinka Mirbel, 'De la Peinture. Du Portrait', *La Revue de Paris*, vol.VIII (1829), pp.91–2).

61.

LITERATURE: Reynolds 1980, no.240 and 245; Schidlof 1911, p.138

NOTES

1 Not 1834, as stated by Schidlof 1964, vol.II, p.528, and some later historians.
2 Among them a replica in the Louvre, Paris (Jean-Richard, p.241, no.440), and a version (in reverse) inscribed *Augustin 1814*, sold Sotheby's, London, 14 May 1959, lot 106. I am very grateful to Aileen Ribeiro for her comments on the costume in the Wallace Collection's two miniatures.
3 On Lawrence's sitters see Garlick.

62.

LITERATURE: Reynolds 1980, no.333

NOTES

1 See Rebecchini.
2 See Dukelskaya and Renne, pp.48 and 76, nos.16 and 40. There is an

anonymous version of the Wallace Collection's miniature in the Hermitage, St Petersburg (see www.arthermitage.org/Miniatures/Portrait-of-Grand-Prince-Nikolai-Pavlovich.html).
3 Parissien, p.87.
4 Falk, p.131.
5 The posthumous valuation of the 3rd Marquess's jewellery in 1842 (Wallace Collection archives) was £1,876, of which by far the most valuable item (£1,000) was the Marquess's Diamond Star of the Order of St Anna. His Garter Stars were valued at £280 and £90.
6 Identification of the rock crystals was made by Christopher Cavey and Nigel Israel at the Wallace Collection, 21 April 2010.

63.

LITERATURE: Reynolds 1980, pp.343–4, no.MA3

NOTES
1 Garlick, p.208, no.404; Hayes, pp.158–60. Both authors date Lawrence's painting *c.*1825, but the inscription on the counter-enamel of Bone's miniature proves that this is too late.
2 For this painting see Ingamells 1985, pp.125–8, and Duffy and Hedley, pp.238–9. It was bought by Sir Richard Wallace in 1883.
3 See Hughes, and Duffy and Hedley, *op. cit.*, p.xx.
4 Walker 1999, p.330, no.264.
5 See Lugt, II, 1826–1860, The Hague, 1953.

64.

LITERATURE: Reynolds 1980, no.206; Bassily-Callimaki, p.337

NOTES
1 Schidlof 1964, I, p.391.
2 The other portrait of Rose is illustrated in Basily-Callimaki, p.339; a watercolour portrait by Isabey, dated 1831 like the Wallace Collection's miniature, in the Musée Carnavalet, Paris, however, shows a sitter who appears younger (Isabey 2005, p.155, no.197). Rose Maistre's dates of birth and death are omitted in Lemoine-Bouchard 2008.
3 Isabey, *An Unknown Lady* (M222) and Horace Vernet and E.E. Viollet-le-Duc, *Napoleon on Horseback* (M313).

65.

LITERATURE: Reynolds 1980, no.311

NOTES
1 Egerton, pp.210–17; Mannings, vol.I, pp.137, no.382.
2 See Egerton, *ibid.*
3 There is a miniature (on ivory) of Mary Queen of Scots, by William Bone, Henry Pierce Bone's brother, in the Wallace Collection (M25; Reynolds 1980, 314).
4 See Coffin and Hofstetter, pp.42–3.
5 Bayne-Powell, p.12; ODNB, *s.v.* 'Bone, Henry Pierce' (R.J.B. Walker, 2004).
6 Speel 2008, p.106.

66.

LITERATURE: Reynolds 1980, no.327; Haskell, p.83, no.44

NOTES
1 Reynolds catalogued the miniature as after Dmitry Levitsky's portrait of 1783 (Moscow, Tretyakov Gallery), but Lampi's portrait is closer. For another miniature after Lampi's portrait (by Ferdinand de Meys) see Aronson and Wieseman, pp.238–9, no.121.
2 Sale, Collections de San Donato, Pillet and Petit, Paris, 21–2 February 1870, lots 58–9.

67.

LITERATURE: Reynolds 1980, no.254; Drennan, p.39, pl.5

NOTES
1 On Laura Bell see Galliland; Matthew Harrison, 54, pp.256–7, and Drennan.
2 Francis Burnand, *Records and Reminiscences*, quoted Galliland, p.7.
3 Note on file in the Wallace Collection archives, P779, by D.S. MacColl, Keeper of the Wallace Collection, 1911–24.
4 Illustrated Drennan, front cover. In his account book Buckner recorded nineteen entries concerning Mrs Thistlethwayte, 1853–70 (letter in Wallace Collection archives, P779, from Brian Stewart, 1997).
5 Wallace Collection archives.
6 For both these pictures see Ingamells 1985, p.439. The whole-length can be seen in a photograph of the Billiard Room, taken *c.*1888.
7 Galliland, p.7; Drennan, p.29.

68.

LITERATURE: Reynolds 1980, no.256

NOTES
1 Lemoine-Bouchard 2008, p.236. Winterhalter's portrait was painted (with a companion portrait of Napoleon III) in 1853; it is now unlocated (see Ormond and Blackett-Ord, p.47). Fiocchi's copy is in the Musée d'Art et d'Histoire, Rochefort.
2 I am very grateful to Bénédicte Lafarge of the Musées Municipaux, Rochefort, for biographical and other information about Fiocchi.
3 *La Gazette des Bains de Mer et de Royan sur l'Océan*, November 1893 (information from Bénédicte Lafarge).
4 The other miniatures are M106 (*The Three Graces, after Raphael*), M107 (*A Lady going to Bed, after J. Van Loo*) and M108 (*An Unknown Girl, after Chaplin*).
5 Stümcke, p.307. No portrait of Mlle Sontag is included in the list of the artist's works drawn up by his nephew Franz Wild in 1894 (reprinted with notes in Ormond and Blackett-Ord, pp.226–37), but the list is incomplete. It is not impossible that the original was by Franz Xaver's brother Hermann Winterhalter (1808–1891), but the more celebrated Franz Xaver is more likely.
6 Scudo *et al.*, *Life of Henriette Sontag, Countess de Rossi*, New York, 1852 (signed A.W. Orr, NY). My thanks are due to Eugene Barilo von Reisberg for this and other references and for his assistance with questions relating to Winterhalter's authorship of the original portrait.

69.

LITERATURE: Reynolds 1980, no.305

NOTES
1 On Ross's life see ODNB, *s.v.* 'Ross, Sir William Charles' (V. Remington, 2008).
2 Benson and Esher, III, p.148.
3 Royal Archives PP/VIC/2/33/9706 (the price was 50 guineas for this miniature and another by Ross of Charles, Prince of Leiningen). I am very grateful to Vanessa Remington of the Royal Collection for this information and reference and also for the opportunity to discuss (with her and Alan Donnithorne) the two versions of Ross's miniature in the Royal and Wallace Collections and to compare them side by side.
4 I am very grateful to Aileen Ribeiro for her comments on Eugénie's costume and appearance in this miniature.
5 See Morel, p.380. My grateful thanks to Diana Scarisbrick for this reference and for her comments on the jewellery.
6 The Royal Collection's miniature has a comparatively simple 'Hatfield' frame. (On these frames see Lloyd and Remington, p.23.)
7 See Morel, pp.335–9. I owe this observation also to Diana Scarisbrick.

Bibliography

Adhémar 1973: Jean Adhémar, 'Les portraits dessinés du XVIe siècle au cabinet des estampes', *Gazette des Beaux-Arts*, 115 (6/82), 1973, pp.121–98, 327–50

Adhémar 1980: Jean Adhémar, 'Documents and Hypotheses Concerning François Clouet', *Master Drawings*, 18, 1980, pp.155–68

Apgar: Garry Apgar, '"Sage comme une image": trois siècles d'iconographie voltairienne', *Nouvelles de l'estampe*, 135, July 1994, pp.4–44

Aronson and Wieseman: Julie Aronson and Marjorie E. Wieseman, *Perfect Likeness. European and American Portrait Miniatures from the Cincinnati Art Museum*, New Haven, London and Cincinnati, 2006

Backhouse: Janet Backhouse, 'Illuminated Manuscripts and the Development of the Portrait Miniature', in *Henry VIII. A European Court in England*, ed. David Starkey, exh. cat., National Maritime Museum, Greenwich, London, 1991, pp.88–92

Baillio: Joseph Baillio, *Elisabeth Louise Vigée Lebrun 1755–1842*, exh. cat., Kimbell Art Museum, Fort Worth, 1982

Bann and Whiteley: Stephen Bann and Linda Whiteley, *Painting History. Delaroche and Lady Jane Grey*, National Gallery, London, 2010

Basily-Callimaki: Mme de Basily-Callimaki, *J.-B. Isabey, sa vie, son temps, 1767–1855*, Paris, 1909

Bayne-Powell: Robert Bayne-Powell, *Catalogue of Portrait Miniatures in the Fitzwilliam Museum, Cambridge*, Cambridge, 1985

Benson and Esher: Arthur Christopher Benson and Viscount Esher, *The Letters of Queen Victoria*, 3 vols., London, 1907

Bimbenet-Privat: Michèle Bimbenet-Privat, 'Les pierreries de Louis XIV. Objets de collection et instruments politiques', *Etudes sur l'ancienne France offertes en homage à Michel Antoine*, ed. Bernard Barbiche and Yves-Marie Bercé, Paris, 2003 (Mémoires et documents de l'Ecole des chartes, 69), pp.81–96

Blanch: Lesley Blanch (ed.), *Harriette Wilson's Memoirs*, London, 1964

Bordeaux: Jean-Luc Bordeaux, *François Lemoyne (1688–1737) and his Generation*, Neuilly-sur-Seine, 1984

Brainne, Debarboullier and Lapierre: C. Brainne, C.J. Debarboullier, Ch.-F. Lapierre, *Les hommes illustres de l'Orléanais, biographie générale des trois départements du Loiret, d'Eure-et-Loir & de Loir-et-Cher*, 2 vols., Orléans, 1852

Bruijn Kops: C.J. de Bruijn Kops, 'Een portretminiatuur door Rosalba Carriera (1675–1757) en de oorsprong van haar schilderkusnt op ivoor', *Bulletin van het Rijksmuseum*, 36, 1988

Byrne: Paula Byrne, *Perdita. The Life of Mary Robinson*, London, 2004

Campbell and Foister: Lorne Campbell and Susan Foister, 'Gerard, Lucas and Susanna Horenbout', *The Burlington Magazine*, 128, July 1986, pp.719–27

Chantilly: *La Miniature en Europe. Actes du Colloque, Chantilly, musee Condé. Maison de Sylvie, 10 et 11 octobre 2007*, Chantilly, 2008

Coffin and Hofstetter: Sarah Coffin and Bodo Hofstetter, *The Gilbert Collection. Portrait Miniatures in Enamel*, London, 2000

Colding: Thorben Holck Colding, *Aspects of Miniature Painting. Its Origins and Development*, Copenhagen, Edinburgh and London, 1953

Coombs: Katherine Coombs, *The Portrait Miniature in England*, London, 1998

Dacier: Emile Dacier, 'Les portraits gravés de la Camargo au XVIIIe siècle', *La revue de l'art ancien et moderne*, 30, 1911, pp.143–8

Delaplanche: Jérôme Delaplanche, *Joseph Parrocel, 1646–1704: la nostalgie de l'héroïsme*, Paris, 2006

Dickel and Vogtherr: Hans Dickel and Christoph Martin Vogtherr (eds.), *Preußen. Die Kunst und das Individuum. Beiträge gewidmet Helmut Börsch-Supan*, Berlin, 2003

Dimier: Louis Dimier, *Histoire de la peinture de portrait en France au XVIe siècle accompagnée d'un catalogue de tous les ouvrages subsistant en ce genre, de crayon, de peinture à l'huile, de miniature, d'émail, de tapisserie et de cire en médaillons*, 3 vols., Paris and Brussels, 1924–6

Drennan: Anthony S. Drennan, *Laura Bell. Courtesan and Lay Preacher*, Belfast, 2008

Duffy and Hedley: Stephen Duffy and Jo Hedley, *The Wallace Collection's Pictures. A Complete Catalogue*, London, 2004

Dukelskaya and Renne: Larissa A. Dukelskaya and Elizaveta P. Renne, *The Hermitage. Catalogue of Western European Painting. British Painting. Sixteenth to Nineteenth Centuries*, Moscow and Florence, 1990

Dupont-Logié: Cécile Dupont-Logié *et al.*, *Entre Cour et Jardin. Marie-Caroline, duchesse de Berry*, Musée de l'Ile de France, Sceaux, 2007

Durand: David Durand, *Continuation de l'histoire du XVI. siècle, septième partie; Qui contient, la vie de M. de Thou, Extraite de ses propres Mémoires jusqu'en 1601, & continuée jusqu'à sa mort en 1617. & Les Commencemens du Règne de François II.*, London, 1732

Edmond 1983: Mary Edmond, *Hilliard and Oliver. The Lives and Works of Two Great Miniaturists*, London, 1983

Edmond 2004: Mary Edmond, 'Oliver, Isaac (c.1565–1617)', *Oxford Dictionary of National Biography*, Oxford, 2004 (http://www.oxforddnb.com/view/article/20723)

Egerton: Judy Egerton, *National Gallery Catalogues. The British School*, London, 1998

Evans: Mark Evans, 'The Pedigree of the Portrait Miniature. European Sources of an English genre', in Bodo Brinkmann and Wolfgang Schmid (eds.), *Holbein und der Wandel in der Kunst des frühen 16. Jahrhunderts. Johann David Passavant-Colloquium, Städelsches Kunstinstitut, 22–23 November 2003*, Turnhout, 2005, pp.229–52

Everdell: William R. Everdell, 'The Rosieres Movement, 1766–1789: A Clerical Precursor of the Revolutionary Cults', *French Historical Studies*, 9, Spring 1975, no. 1, pp.23–36

FAHY: Everett Fahy (ed.), *Metropolitan Museum of Art: The Wrightsman Pictures*, New Haven, 2005

FALCONI 2008: Bernardo Falconi, 'Rosalba Carriera (1673–1757) et la miniature sur ivoire', in Nicole Garnier (ed.), *La miniature en Europe. Actes du colloque. Chantilly, musee Condé. Maison de Sylvie, 10 et 11 octobre 2007*, Chantilly, 2008, pp.80–3

FALCONI 2009: Bernardo Falconi in Giuseppe Pavanello (ed.), *Rosalba Carriera 1673–1757. Atti del Convegno Internazionale di Studi 26–28 aprile 2007. Venezia, Fondazione Giorgio Cini. Chioggia, Auditorium San Niccolò*, Venice, 2009, pp.215–36

FALK: Bernard Falk, *"Old Q's" Daughter*, London, 1937

FINSTEN: Jill Finsten, *Isaac Oliver. Art at the Courts of Elisabeth I and James I*, 2 vols., PhD Harvard 1979, London, 1981 (Outstanding Dissertations in the Fine Arts. A Garland Series)

FOISTER 2004: Susan Foister, *Holbein and England*, New Haven and London, 2004

FORT: Bernadette Fort (ed.), *Les Salons des « Mémoires secrets » 1767–1787*, Paris, 1999 (Collection Beaux-Arts histoire)

FOSKETT 1974: Daphne Foskett, *Samuel Cooper 1609–1672*, London, 1974

FOSKETT 1987: Daphne Foskett, *Miniatures. Dictionary and Guide*, Woodbridge, 1987

FRANCE IN RUSSIA 2007: *France in Russia. Empress Josephine's Malmaison Collection*, exh. cat., The Hermitage Rooms, London, 2007

FROMAGEOT: Paul Fromageot, 'La foire Saint-Germain des Près', *Extrait du Bulletin de la Société Historique du VIe arrondissement de Paris (Etudes historiques sur le VIe arrondissement de Paris)*, Paris, 1902

GALLILAND: Jean Galliland, *Gladstone's "Dear Spirit" Laura Thistlethwayte*, privately printed, 1994

GANZ: Paul Ganz, 'Holbein's Last Self-Portrait', *The Burlington Magazine*, 71, August 1937, pp.62–8

GARLICK: Kenneth Garlick, *Sir Thomas Lawrence. A Complete Catalogue of the Oil Paintings*, Oxford, 1989

GIBSON: Gibson, William Pettigrew, *Wallace Collection Catalogues. Miniatures and Illuminations*, The Wallace Collection, London, 1935

GLI UFFIZI: *Gli Uffizi. Catalogo Generale*, Florence, 1979

GOLD BOXES AND MINIATURES AT WADDESDON: *Gold Boxes and Miniatures of the Eighteenth Century. The James A de Rothschild Collection at Waddesdon Manor*, by Serge Grandjean, Kirsten Aschengreen Piacenti, Charles Truman and Anthony Blunt, London and Fribourg, 1975

GOODDEN: Angelica Goodden, *Madame de Staël. The Dangerous Exile*, Oxford, 2008

GRONOW: *The Reminiscences and Recollections of Captain Gronow*, 2 vols., London, 1892

HALLIDAY: Tony Halliday, *Facing the Public. Portraiture in the Aftermath of the French Revolution*, Manchester and New York, 2000

HASKELL: Francis Haskell *et al.*, *Anatole Demidoff, Prince of San Donato (1812–70)*, The Wallace Collection, London, 1994

HAYES: John Hayes, *The Collections of the National Gallery of Art. British Paintings of the Sixteenth through Nineteenth Centuries*, Washington, D.C., 1992

HINTERDING AND HORSCH: Erik Hinterding and Femy Horsch, '"A small but choice collection": the art gallery of King Willem II of the Netherlands (1792–1849)', *Simiolus*, 19, 1989, pp.4–122

HOFSTETTER 1994: Bodo Hofstetter, *Le miniaturiste François Dumont (1751–1831) – Catalogue raisonné*, unpublished PhD, Lille, 1994

HOFSTETTER 1995: Bodo Hofstetter, 'François Dumont, peintre de la Cour', *Le Pays Lorrain*, 76, 1995, pp.189–96

HOFSTETTER 2008: Bodo Hofstetter, *Die Welt der Bildnisminiatur. Meisterwerke aus der Sammlung Emil S. Kern. Museum Briner und Kern, Rathaus Winterthur*, Berne and Sulgen, 2008

HUGHES: Peter Hughes, *The Founders of the Wallace Collection*, 3rd edition, London, 2006

HYDE: Melissa Hyde, 'Women and the Visual Arts in the Age of Marie-Antoinette', in *Anne Vallayer-Coster. Painter at the Court of Marie-Antoinette*, exh. cat., National Gallery of Art, Washington, D.C.; Dallas Museum of Art; The Frick Collection, New York, 2002, pp.74–93

INGAMELLS 1978: John Ingamells, *Mrs Robinson and her Portraits*, The Wallace Collection, London, 1978

INGAMELLS 1981: John Ingamells, *The Hertford Mawson Letters*, The Wallace Collection, London, 1981

INGAMELLS 1985: John Ingamells, *The Wallace Collection. Catalogue of Pictures, I. British, German, Italian, Spanish*, London, 1985

INGAMELLS 1986: John Ingamells, *The Wallace Collection. Catalogue of Pictures, II. French Nineteenth Century*, London, 1986

INGAMELLS 1989: John Ingamells, *The Wallace Collection: Catalogue of Pictures III. French before 1815*, London, 1989

INGRES 1967: *Ingres Centennial Exhibition 1867–1967*, exh. cat., Fogg Art Museum, Cambridge, Mass., 1967

INGRES 1999: *Portraits by Ingres. Image of an Epoch*, Gary Tinterow and Philip Conisbee (eds.), exh. cat., National Gallery, London; National Gallery of Art, Washington, D.C.; Metropolitan Museum of Art, New York, 1999

ISABEY: *Jean-Baptiste Isabey (1767–1855), portraitiste de l'Europe*, exh. cat., Musée national des Châteaux, Malmaison, and Musée des Beaux-Arts, Nancy, 2005

ITTERSHAGEN: Ulrike Ittershagen, *Lady Hamiltons Attitüden*, Mainz, 1999

JEAN: René Jean, 'Madame de Mirbel', *Gazette des Beaux-Arts*, February 1906, pp.131–46

JEANNERAT: Carlo Jeannerat, 'Les petits portraits dans le goût pompéien de Jean-Urbain Guérin, *Gazette des Beaux-Arts*, 62 (5/6), 1922, pp.353–64

JEAN-RICHARD: Pierrette Jean-Richard, *Inventaire des miniatures sur ivoire conservées au cabinet des dessins – Musée du Louvre et musée d'Orsay*, Paris, 1994

JOLLET: Etienne Jollet, *Jean et François Clouet*, Paris, 1997

KEIL: Robert Keil, *Die Porträtminiaturen des Hauses Habsburg. Die Sammlung von 584 Porträtminiaturen aus der ehemaligen von Kaiser Franz I. von Österreich gegründeten Primogenitur-Fideikommißbibliothek in der Hofburg zu Wien*, Vienna, 1999

KENWORTHY BROWNE: John Kenworthy-Browne, 'A Marble Bust by Nollekens', *North Carolina Museum of Art Bulletin*, 14, 1977, no.1, pp.1–13

LA NOUËNE: Patrick La Nouëne, 'A propos des miniatures de la collection Pierre-Louis Eveillard de Livois conservées au musée des Beaux-Arts d'Angers', *La revue du Louvre et des Musées de France*, 53, 2003, no.5, pp.68–74

LAMBERTSON: John P. Lambertson, 'Lizinka de Mirbel and French Romanticism', *Woman's Art Journal*, 18, no.2, Fall 1997/Winter 1998, pp.17–21

LAURAINE: Michel Lauraine, *Louis Michel Sicard, dit Sicardi (1743–1825). Peintre miniaturiste. Biographie*, [no place indicated] 2005

LAVEISSIÈRE: Sylvain Laveissière (ed.), *Le Sacre de Napoléon peint par David*, exh. cat., Musée du Louvre, Paris, 2004–5

LAYTON ELWES: Rachael Layton Elwes, 'Giuseppe Macpherson 1726–c.1780. Self-portraits in miniature', *The British Art Journal*, no.2, Winter 2000/1, pp.53–7

LE CARDINAL FESCH 2007: *Le Cardinal Fesch et l'art de son temps*, Philippe Costamagna and Carole Blumenfeld (eds.), exh. cat., Musée Fesch, Ajaccio, 2007

LE COAT AND EGGIMANN-BESANÇON: Gérard Le Coat and Anne Eggimann-Besançon, 'Le portrait de Madame du Châtelet par Marie-Anne Loir. Emblématique et emancipation féminine au XVIIIe siècle', *Colóqio artes*, 68, March 1986, pp.30–9

LEMOINE-BOUCHARD 2002: Nathalie Lemoine-Bouchard, *Les Miniatures*, Paris, 2002 (Musée Cognacq-Jay. Musée du XVIIIe siècle de la Ville de Paris. Les Collections)

LEMOINE-BOUCHARD 2008: Nathalie Lemoine-Bouchard, *Les peintres en miniature actifs en France 1650–1850*, Paris, 2008

LES PEINTRES DU ROI 2000: *Les peintres du roi 1648–1793*, exh. cat., Musée des Beaux-Arts de Tours, and Musée des Augustins, Toulouse, 2000

LESPINASSE: Pierre Lespinasse, *La miniature en France au XVIIIe siècle*, Paris, 1929

LIGHTBOWN: Ronald W. Lightbown, 'Jean Petitot. Etude pour une biographie et catalogue de son œuvre', *Genava*, N.S. 18, 1970, pp.81–103

LISHOLM: Birgitta Lisholm, *Martin van Meytens d.y. Hans liv och hans verk*, Malmö, 1974

LLOYD 1995: Stephen Lloyd, *Richard and Maria Cosway. Regency Artists of Taste and Fashion*, exh. cat., Scottish National Portrait Gallery, Edinburgh, 1995

LLOYD 1996: Stephen Lloyd, *Portrait Miniatures from the Collection of the Duke of Buccleuch*, exh. cat., Scottish National Portrait Gallery, Edinburgh 1996

LLOYD 1998: Stephen Lloyd, 'Richard Cosway: *primarius pictor*, virtuoso e collezionista', in Tino Gippone (ed.): *Maria e Richard Cosway*, Turin, 1998, pp.45–60

LLOYD 2005: Stephen Lloyd, *Richard Cosway*, London, 2005

LLOYD AND REMINGTON: Christopher Lloyd and Vanessa Remington, *Masterpieces in Little. Portrait Miniatures from the Collection of Her Majesty Queen Elizabeth II*, London, 1996

LONGFORD: Elizabeth Longford, *Wellington. The Years of the Sword*, London, 1969

LUGT: Frits Lugt, *Répertoire des Catalogues de Ventes Publiques*, 2 vols., 1826–60, The Hague, 1953

LYONNET: Henry Lyonnet, *Dictionnaire des Comédiens Français*, 2 vols., Paris [1908]

MADAME DU CHÂTELET 2006: *Madame Du Châtelet. La femme des Lumières*, Elisabeth Badinter and Danielle Muzerelle (eds.), exh. cat., Bibliothèque nationale de France, Paris, 2006

MAILLET-CHASSAGNE: Monique Maillet-Chassagne, *Une dynastie de peintres lillois, les Van Blarenberghe*, Paris, 2001

MAILLET-CHASSAGNE AND CHÂTEAU-THIERRY: Monique Maillet-Chassagne and Irène de Château-Thierry, *Catalogue raisonné des œuvres des Van Blarenberghes 1680–1826*, Lille, 2004

MAISON: K.E. Maison, 'Unrecorded French Pictures in Scotland', *The Burlington Magazine*, 79, 1941, pp.44–51

MANNINGS: David Mannings, *Sir Joshua Reynolds. A Complete Catalogue of his Paintings*, 2 vols., New Haven and London, 2000

MANSION: [André-Léon Larue] Mansion, *Lettres sur la Miniature*, Paris, 1823

MARGUERITE GÉRARD 2009 : *Marguerite Gérard. Artiste en 1789, dans l'atelier de Fragonard*, exh. cat., Musée Cognacq-Jay, Paris, 2009

MARIE: Alfred Marie, 'The Château de Romainville and a Snuffbox in the Wallace Collection', *The Connoisseur*, 1951, pp. 18–23

MARIE CAROLINE: *Marie Caroline de Berry. Naples, Paris, Graz, Itinéraire d'une Princesse Romantique*, Paris, 2002

MAZE-SENCIER: Alphonse Maze-Sencier, *Le livre des collectionneurs*, Paris, 1885

MÉJANÈS: Jean-François Méjanès (ed.), *Les Van Blarenberghe: des reporters du XVIIIe siècle*, exh. cat., Musée du Louvre, Paris 2006

MOREL: Bernard Morel, *The French Crown Jewels*, Antwerp, 1988

MURDOCH 1981: John Murdoch *et al.*, *The English Miniature*, New Haven and London, 1981

MURDOCH 1982: John Murdoch, 'Review: The Wallace Collection: Catalogue of Miniatures. By Graham Reynolds', *The Burlington Magazine*, 124, July 1982, pp.450–51

MURDOCH 1997: John Murdoch, *Seventeenth-century English Miniatures in the Collection of the Victoria and Albert Museum*, London, 1997

MURDOCH 2004: John Murdoch, 'Cooper, Samuel (1607/8–1672)', *Oxford Dictionary of National Biography*, Oxford, 2004 (http://www.oxforddnb.com/view/article/6226)

NAPOLÉON 1969: *Napoléon*, exh. cat., Grand Palais, Paris, 1969

NIMMERGUT AND WAGER: Jörg Nimmergut and Anna-Maria Wager, *Miniaturen. Dosen*, Battenberg Antiquitäten-Kataloge, Munich, 1982

NOUVEL-KAMMERER: Odile Nouvel-Kammerer *et al.*, *Symbols of Power. Napoleon and the Art of the Empire Style 1800–1815*, New York and Paris, 2007

ODNB: *Oxford Dictionary of National Biography*, http://www.oxforddnb.com

ORMOND AND BLACKETT-ORD: Richard Ormond and Carol Blackett-Ord, *Franz Xaver Winterhalter and the Courts of Europe 1830–70*, National Portrait Gallery, London, 1988

PAPPE: Bernd Pappe, *Jean-Baptiste Augustin. Peintre en miniature*, exh. cat., Musée Pierre-Noël, St-Dié-des-Vosges, 2010

PARIS GUIDE: *Paris Guide par les Principaux Écrivains et Artistes de la France*, 2 vols., Paris, 1867

PARISSIEN: Steven Parissien, *George IV. The Grand Entertainment*, London, 2001

PLINVAL DE GUILLEBON 2000: Régine de Plinval de Guillebon, *Pierre Adolphe Hall 1739–1793. Miniaturiste suédois*, Paris, 2000

PLINVAL DE GUILLEBON 2008: Régine de Plinval de Guillebon, 'Pierre Adolphe Hall (1739–1793), miniaturiste suédois, peintre du Roi et des enfants de France', in Nicole Garnier (ed.), *La Miniature en Europe. Actes du colloque. Chantilly, musée Conde. Maison de Sylvie, 10 et 11 octobre 2007*, Chantilly, 2008, pp.84–9

PORTERFIELD AND SIEGFRIED: Todd Porterfield and Susan L. Siegfried, *Staging Empire. Napoleon, Ingres and David*, University Park, Pennsylvania, 2006

POSTLE: Martin Postle, *Joshua Reynolds: the Cult of Celebrity*, exh. cat., Tate, London, 2005

REBECCHINI: Damiano Rebecchini, 'An influential collector. Tsar Nicholas I of Russia', *Journal of the History of Collections*, 2009 (see www.jhc.xfordjournals.org/cgi/content/abstract/fhp030)

REYNOLDS 1947: Graham Reynolds, *Nicholas Hilliard and Isaac Oliver. An Exhibition to Commemorate the 400th Anniversary of the Birth of Nicholas Hilliard*, London, 1947 (Victoria and Albert Museum Handbooks)

REYNOLDS 1980: Graham Reynolds, *Wallace Collection. Catalogue of Miniatures*, London, 1980

REYNOLDS 1999: Graham Reynolds, *The Sixteenth and Seventeenth Century Miniatures in the Collection of Her Majesty the Queen*, London 1999

RIBEIRO: Aileen Ribeiro, *The Art of Dress. Fashion in England and France 1750 to 1820*, New Haven and London, 1995

ROSENBERG: Pierre Rosenberg, 'De qui sont les miniatures de Fragonard?', *Revue de l'art*, III, 1996, pp.66–76

ROWLANDS: John Rowlands, *Holbein. The Paintings of Hans Holbein the Younger. Complete Edition*, Oxford, 1985

SAHUT 1977: Marie Catherine Sahut, *Carle Vanloo, Premier Peintre du roi*, exh. cat., Musée Chéret, Nice; Musée Bargoin, Clermont-Ferrand; Musée des Beaux-Arts, Nancy, 1977

SALMON: Xavier Salmon, *Louis-Nicolas van Blarenberghe à Versailles : les gouaches commandées par Louis XVI*, Paris, 2005

SANI: Bernardina Sani, *Rosalba Carriera 1673–1757. Maestra del pastello nell'Europa ancien régime*, Turin, London, Venice and New York, 2007

SAVILL: Rosalind Savill, *The Wallace Collection: French Gold Boxes*, London, 1991

SCHAFFERS-BODENHAUSEN AND TIETHOFF-SPLIETHOFF: Karen Schaffers-Bodenhausen and Marieke Tiethoff-Spliethoff, *The Portrait Miniatures in the Collections of the House of Orange-Nassau*, Zwolle, 1993

SCHIDLOF 1911: Leo Schidlof, *Die Bildnisminiatur in Frankreich im XVII., XVIII., und XIX Jahrhundert*, Vienna and Leipzig, 1911

SCHIDLOF 1964: Leo Schidlof, *The Miniature in Europe*, 4 vols., Graz, 1964

SIEGFRIED: Susan L. Siegfried, *The Art of Louis-Léopold Boilly. Modern Life in Napoleonic France*, New Haven and London, 1995

SMITH: John Thomas Smith, *Nollekens and his Times*, 2 vols., London, 1829

SPEEL 1988: Erika Speel, 'The Enamel Painters – Henry Bone and his Workshop', *Glass on Metal*, 7, no.1, February 1988, pp.12–16

SPEEL 2008: Erika Speel, *Painted Enamels. An Illustrated Survey 1500–1920*, Aldershot and Burlington, 2008

STRŒHLIN: Ernest Strœhlin, *Jean Petitot et Jacques Bordier. Deux artistes Huguenots du XVIIe siècle*, Geneva, 1905

STRONG: Roy Strong, *The English Renaissance Miniature*, New York, 1983

STÜMCKE: Heinrich Stümcke, *Henriette Sontag. Ein Lebens- und Zeitbild*, Gesellschaft für Theatergeschichte, 1913

THÉPAUT-CABASSET: Corinne Thépaut-Cabasset, '*Présents du Roi*: An Archive at the Ministry of Foreign Affairs in Paris', *Studies in the Decorative Arts*, 15, no.1, Fall–Winter 2007–8, pp.4–18

TONINI: Lucia Tonini (ed.), *I Demidoff a Firenze e in Toscana*, Florence, 1996

TOWSE: Clive Towse, 'Conway, Henry Seymour (1719–1795)', *Oxford Dictionary of National Biography*, Oxford, 2004 (http://www.oxforddnb.com/view/article/6122)

TRUMAN: Charles Truman, forthcoming catalogue of the gold boxes in the Wallace Collection

TUMULUS: V.C., *Ioannis Thuani, Regis Consiliarij & libellorum supplicum in Regia Magistri*, Paris, 1580

VIGÉE-LE BRUN: Elisabeth Vigée-Le Brun, *Souvenirs*, Paris, 1835–7

VOGTHERR: Christoph Martin Vogtherr, *Nicolas Lancret. Porträt der Tänzerin Maria Sallé*, Berlin and Potsdam, 2001 (*Patrimonia 217*)

VUAFLART AND BOUDIN: Albert Vuaflart and Henri Bourin, 'Les portraits de Marie-Antoinette', in *Etude d'iconographie critique*, I: *L'Archiduchesse. 1755–1770*, Paris, 1909

WALKER 1992: Richard Walker, *The Eighteenth and Early Nineteenth Century Miniatures in the Collection of Her Majesty the Queen*, Cambridge, 1992

WALKER 1999: Richard Walker, 'Henry Bone's Pencil Drawings in the National Portrait Gallery', *The Walpole Society*, 61, 1999, pp.305–67

WALLACE 1902: *Provisional Catalogue of the Furniture, Marbles, Bronzes, Clocks, Candelabra, Majolica, Porcelain, Jewellery, Goldsmith's and Silversmith's Work, Ivories, Medals, Illuminations, and Objects of Art Generally, in the Wallace Collection, The Wallace Collection*, London, 1902 (second edition, including miniatures, 1904)

WALPOLE: Horace Walpole, *Horace Walpole's Correspondence with Henry Seymour Conway, Lady Ailesbury, Lord and Lady Hertford, Mrs Harris, vol. 1*, London, 1974 (The Yale Edition of Horace Walpole's Correspondence, ed. W.S. Lewis, 37)

WARD AND ROBERTS: Humphrey Ward and W. Roberts, *Romney*, London, Manchester, Liverpool and New York, 1904

WARREN: Jeremy Warren, 'The 4th Marquess of Hertford's early years as a collector', *The Burlington Magazine*, 150, August 2008, no.1265, pp.544–7

WATTEAU, CHARDIN AND FRAGONARD 2003: *The Age of Watteau, Chardin and Fragonard*, Colin B. Bailey *et al.* (eds.), exh. cat., National Gallery of Canada, Ottawa; National Gallery of Art, Washington, D.C.; Staatliche Museen zu Berlin, Gemäldegalerie, 2003

WELLESLEY AND STEEGMANN: Lord Gerald Wellesley and John Steegmann, *The Iconography of the First Duke of Wellington*, London, 1935

WILDENSTEIN: Georges Wildenstein, *Lancret*, Paris, 1924

WINE: Humphrey Wine, *National Gallery Catalogues: The Seventeenth-Century French Paintings*, London, 2001

WINTER: Carl Winter, 'Holbein's Miniatures', *The Burlington Magazine*, 83, November 1943, pp.266–9

ZVEREVA: Alexandra Zvereva, *Les Clouets de Catherine de Médicis. Chefs-d'œuvre graphiques du Musée Condé*, exh. cat., Musée Condé, Chantilly, 2002

CONCORDANCE OF NUMBERS

Inventory no.	Duffy and Vogtherr	Reynolds 1980	Inventory no.	Duffy and Vogtherr	Reynolds 1980
G36	15	87	M186	21	107
G42	17	86	M187	23	112
G62	18	88	M189	22	108
G67	5	6	M193	24	111
G80	30	28	M203	2	3
HHHC2007.2	33	MA1	M205	4	17
HHHC2007.4	63	MA3	M210	51	188
M3	35	161	M211	41	181
M4	45	226	M216	48	187
M5	44	227	M217	64	206
M8	42	169	M219	54	193
M10	56	172	M221	47	192
M14	38	168	M223	55	198
M17	16	85	M226	37	178
M18	57	310	M232	43	184
M20	53	308	M247	50	195
M21	39	306	M251	31	332
M24	65	311	M258	20	95
M40	36	317	M259	19	97
M56	14	59	M263	1	1
M61	12	63	M272	61	240
M62	13	62	M276	61	245
M67	11	71	M281	60	239
M69	10	158	M282	58	237
M87	32	149	M287	3	5
M88	34	151	M288	49	235
M100	27	135	M291	62	333
M101	26	134	M293	52	232
M105	68	256	M294	46	46
M110	25	91	M303	29	125
M130	7	27	M305	59	248
M162	69	305	M310	6	36
M175	66	327	M314	8	46
M177	28	137	P758	9	41
M180	40	163	P779	67	254

INDEX OF ARTISTS AND SITTERS

PHOTOGRAPHIC CREDITS

No.1, fig. 1: The Trustees of the 9th Duke of Buccleuch's Chattels Fund; no.2, fig.1: Collection of the Duke of Buccleuch and Queensberry; no.3: Private Collection; no.4: figs.1 and 2: Wallace Collection; no.5, fig.1: © RMN / Jean-Gilles Berizzi, figs 2 and 3: Wallace Collection; no.6: detail from Wallace Collection; no.7, fig.1: Wallace Collection, fig.2: © RMN / Droits réservés; no.8, fig 1: Wallace Collection; no.9: Albertina, Vienna; no.10, fig.1: Wallace Collection, fig.2: Private collection; no.11, fig.1: Wallace Collection; no.12, fig.1: © RMN / Jean-Gilles Berizzi; fig.2: The J. Paul Getty Museum, Los Angeles; no.13, fig.1: Madrid, Museo Nacional del Prado; fig.2: Wallace Collection; no.14, fig.1: Wallace Collection; no.15, fig.1: bpk/ Staatliche Kunstsammlungen Dresden/ Elke Estel/ Hans-Peter Klut; fig.2: Photo Les Arts Décoratifs/ Jean Tholance; no.16, fig.1: Wallace Collection; no.17, fig.1: © RMN / Jean-Gilles Berizzi; no.19, fig.1: Nationalmuseum, Stockholm, fig 2: Wallace Collection; no.20, fig.1: Wallace Collection, fig.2: © RMN / Hervé Lewandowski, fig.3 Wallace Collection; no.21, fig.1: 'Nationalmuseum, Stockholm', fig.2: © Musée Cognacq-Jay / Roger-Viollet; no.22, fig.1: Wallace Collection, fig.2: With permission of the Royal Ontario Museum © ROM; no.25, fig.1: Wallace Collection; fig.2: © RMN / Droits réservés, fig.3 © RMN / Droits réservés; no.28, fig.1: Wallace Collection; no.29, fig.1: Wallace Collection; no.30, fig.1: Wallace Collection; no.31, fig.1: The Royal Collection © Her Majesty Queen Elizabeth II; no.32, fig.1: Fondazione Cosway, Lodi; no.36, fig.1: Photo by A.C. Cooper, © The National Trust, Waddesdon Manor; no.38, fig.1: Wallace Collection; no.40, fig.1: Coppet, musée de Coppet; no.42, fig.1: Wallace Collection; no.44, fig.1: Wallace Collection; no.45, fig.1: © RMN / Droits réservés; no.46, fig.1: Collection Rijksmuseum, Amsterdam; no.47, fig.1: © Collections de la Comédie-Française; no.48, fig.1: Wallace Collection; no.53, fig.1: © National Portrait Gallery, London, fig.2: Wallace Collection; no.57, fig.1: Wallace Collection; no.62, fig.1: Photograph © The State Hermitage Museum / Photo by Vladimir Terebenin, Leonard Kheifets, Yuri Molodkovets; no.62, fig.1: © Board of Trustees, National Gallery of Art, Washington; no.66, fig.1: Photograph © The State Hermitage Museum / Photo by Vladimir Terebenin, Leonard Kheifets, Yuri Molodkovets